JEREMIAH

ABINGDON OLD TESTAMENT COMMENTARIES

JEREMIAH

LOUIS STULMAN

Abingdon Press
Nashville

ABINGDON OLD TESTAMENT COMMENTARIES
JEREMIAH

Copyright © 2005 by Abingdon Press

This book is printed on acid-free paper.

Library of Congress Cataloging-in-Publication Data

Stulman, Louis, 1953-
  Jeremiah / Louis Stulman.
      p. cm. — (Abingdon Old Testament commentaries)
  Includes bibliographical references (pp. 395-400).
  ISBN 0-687-05796-5 (pbk. : alk. paper)
  1. Bible. O.T. Jeremiah—Commentaries I. Title. II. Series.

  BS1525.53.S78 2005
  224'.207—dc22

                                                                    2004011463

All scripture quotations, unless otherwise noted, are taken from *The New Revised Standard Version of the Bible,* copyright © 1989, Division of Christian Education of the National Council of the Churches of Christ in the United States of America. Used by permission. All rights reserved.

Editor's note: Brackets are used to indicate the author's translation of the Hebrew text.

When quoting from the NRSV, we have followed the NRSV spelling of "Nebuchadrezzar," but the author has sometimes used the other spelling, "Nebuchadnezzar," in the text. Both spellings are correct.

05 06 07 08 09 10 11 12 13 14—10 9 8 7 6 5 4 3 2 1

MANUFACTURED IN THE UNITED STATES OF AMERICA

*To my beloved wife Kate
with deepest gratitude.*

CONTENTS

Commentary Book One: Jeremiah 1–25
Dismantling Judah's Social and Symbolic Worlds

FOREWORD

The *Abingdon Old Testament Commentaries* are offered to the reader in hopes that they will aid in the study of Scripture and provoke a deeper understanding of the Bible in all its many facets. The texts of the Old Testament come out of a time, a language, and socio-historical and religious circumstances far different from the present. Yet Jewish and Christian communities have held to them as a sacred canon, significant for faith and life in each new time. Only as one engages these books in depth and with all the critical and intellectual faculties available to us, can the contemporary communities of faith and other interested readers continue to find them meaningful and instructive.

These volumes are designed and written to provide compact, critical commentaries on the books of the Old Testament for the use of theological students and pastors. It is hoped that they may be of service also to upper-level college or university students and to those responsible for teaching in congregational settings. In addition to providing basic information and insights into the Old Testament writings, these commentaries exemplify the tasks and procedures of careful interpretation.

The writers of the commentaries in this series come from a broad range of ecclesiastical affiliations, confessional stances, and educational backgrounds. They have experience as teachers and, in some instances, as pastors and preachers. In most cases, the authors are persons who have done significant research on the book that is their assignment. They take full account of the most important current scholarship and secondary literature, while not attempting to summarize that literature or to engage in technical academic debate. The fundamental concern of each volume is analysis and discussion of the literary, socio-historical, theological, and ethical dimensions of the biblical texts themselves.

The New Revised Standard Version of the Bible is the principal translation of reference for the series, though authors may draw upon other interpretations in their discussion. Each writer is attentive to the original Hebrew text in preparing the commentary. But the authors do not presuppose any knowledge of the biblical languages on the part of the reader. When some awareness of a grammatical, syntactical, or philological issue is necessary for an adequate understanding of a particular text, the issue is explained simply and concisely.

Each volume consists of four parts. An *introduction* looks at the book as a whole to identify *key issues* in the book, its *literary genre* and *structure*, the *occasion and situational context* of the book (including both social and historical contexts), and the *theological and ethical* significance of the book.

The *commentary* proper organizes the text by literary units and, insofar as is possible, divides the comment into three parts. The *literary analysis* serves to introduce the passage with particular attention to identification of the genre of speech or literature and the structure or outline of the literary unit under discussion. Here also, the author takes up significant stylistic features to help the reader understand the mode of communication and its impact on comprehension and reception of the text. The largest part of the comment is usually found in the *exegetical analysis*, which considers the leading concepts of the unit, the language of expression, and problematical words, phrases, and ideas in order to get at the aim or intent of the literary unit, as far as that can be uncovered. Attention is given here to particular historical and social situations of the writer(s) and reader(s) where that is discernible and relevant as well as to wider cultural (including religious) contexts. The analysis does not proceed phrase by phrase or verse by verse but deals with the various particulars in a way that keeps in view the overall structure and central focus of the passage and its relationship to the general line of thought or rhetorical argument of the book as a whole. The final section, *theological and ethical analysis,* seeks to identify and clarify the theological and ethical matters with which the unit deals or to which it points. Though not aimed primarily at contemporary issues of faith and life, this section should provide readers a basis for reflection on them.

Each volume also contains a select bibliography of works cited in the commentary as well as major commentaries and other important works available in English.

The fundamental aim of this series will have been attained if readers are assisted not only to understand more about the origins, character, and meaning of the Old Testament writings, but also to enter into their own informed and critical engagement with the texts themselves.

Patrick D. Miller
General Editor

PREFACE

I am grateful to the editorial board of AOTC for the invitation to write the commentary on Jeremiah for the series. I am indebted to the editor of the present volume, Kathleen M. O'Connor, for giving generously of her time and attention to my work. Professor O'Connor has not only read numerous drafts and made countless suggestions, but she has also urged me on and encouraged me from start to finish. Special thanks are also due to the series editor, Patrick D. Miller, whose assistance has been invaluable. Three of my students have been kind enough to read sections of the manuscript. It is a pleasure to acknowledge the efforts of Megan Christy, Nannette Cropsey, and Sommer McClelland. With much gratitude, I also acknowledge the superb editorial work of Amy Stulman. My colleagues John Dasher, Robert Cecire, and Ron Tulley have taken time from their busy schedules to read parts of the commentary and offer suggestions from which I have benefited. A special debt of gratitude is due to my wife, Kate, and our children, Nate, Tim, Amy, and Michael, for their love and encouragement.

This commentary is a development of my earlier work, *Order Amid Chaos: Jeremiah as Symbolic Tapestry* (1998). In that relatively short book I made four arguments which inform my current reading of Jeremiah. First, the book of Jeremiah reflects a meaningful literary structure and final theological message, despite its chaotic character. While such a claim is consistent with more recent approaches to the Bible, it challenges one of the sure results of Jeremiah studies, which is that Jeremiah is a hodgepodge of sources, or traditions, thrown together without rhyme or reason. To make this case scholars have been quick to point to the book's

incoherent chronology, mishmash of topics and themes, bewildering history of composition, and intermingled prose and poetry.
When Sigmund Mowinckel argued in 1914 that Jeremiah not only
lacks any semblance of order, but also is completely haphazard, he
set the stage for modern Jeremiah scholarship (1914, 4). With this
assumption in place, few have even broached the book as a unified whole. When one does, however, Jeremiah's jumbled character "makes sense," not by standards of linear logic but as a rich
labyrinth of voices and countervoices which emerge out of the
wreckage of a national disaster that defies ordinary categories. Put
more modestly, although the prophetic writing is clearly a grueling read, it resonates with a marked propensity to bring order and
shape to its own dissonant symbolic world. Jewish readers will
recognize this tendency as "midrashic," although in the case of
Jeremiah the interpretive enterprise is inner-biblical.

Second, large composite units of Jeremiah provide salient clues
for negotiating the literary and theological terrain of the book.
While such collections have long been recognized, they are most
often read as arbitrarily located in the book rather than meaningfully arranged. These "macro-units" afford important interpretive
clues for understanding the over-all structure and final theological
claims of Jeremiah.

Third, and related to the previous point, the prose sections of
Jeremiah are extraordinarily important to the architecture of the
book. Since the work of Bernhard Duhm and Mowinckel at the
turn of the last century, there has been a clear predisposition in
commentaries and monographs to denigrate the prose materials
in Jeremiah. It is not unusual, for example, to find the prose literature—especially the prose sermons—described as haphazard,
late, dull, legalistic, stereotypical, secondary, and dogmatic, to
cite only a few disparaging remarks. In contrast to these negative
assessments, I propose that the prose material is actually the key
to understanding the final form of Jeremiah. This literature
appears at strategic locations in the book to give shape to the
whole, to produce symbolic and literary coherence, and to provide commentary on its immediate literary setting. Whether such
efforts are ultimately successful is debatable. In spite of the work

of the interpretive community of Jeremiah the book is admittedly still dangerous and discordant. It is still riddled with pain and ambiguity, and it is still one of the most undomesticated texts in the Jewish and Christian canons. Nonetheless, when the prose tradition attempts to bring order to its chaotic world, when it interprets its poetic subtext in light of its own focal concerns, the interpretive community of Jeremiah participates in the time-honored practice of reading the text as the living and dynamic word of God.

Finally, the book of Jeremiah presents a literary reenactment of the death and dismantling of one world (Jer 1–25) in preparation for the emergence of another (Jer 26–52). In the first act of the prophetic drama we witness the end of Judah's longstanding social and symbolic support systems. The text claims that the nation's most venerable institutions and theological understandings—its temple and systems of worship, covenant, land entitlement, election tradition, and kingship—will not avert imminent disaster. In fact, the first half of the book declares that Judah's most cherished traditions now testify against the nation. In the second act of the drama we learn that these losses do not signal the end. After Yahweh has "plucked up and pulled down" Judah's "first principles," Yahweh begins the work of "building and planting," enabling refugees to cope with and even thrive in their new marginalized setting. Once the text tells the truth about Judah's fissured world (Jer 1–25), it exploits almost every opportunity available to demonstrate that the community will survive its ordeal by the mercy and power of God (Jer 26–52). Accordingly, the book of Jeremiah is ultimately a survivor's guide for dispirited exiles living on the edge of despair. It is a map of hope for people whose lives have been utterly shattered.

In general Jeremiah has not been associated with hope. When reviewing the central teachings of the book, hope is usually last to be mentioned, if at all. More often, Jeremiah is read as a text of judgment that only rarely alludes to salvation. Notwithstanding the force of these arguments, there is much to point in the other direction. In the second part of the prophetic drama, for instance, individuals begin to emerge who are receptive to the message of

Jeremiah. These faithful few come to the prophet's aid when his life is on the line in the temple (26:16-19) and the royal court (36:9-19, 26), when he is thrown into a cistern (38:7-13), and during the siege of Jerusalem (39:11-18; 40:1-6). In each case, supporters not only rescue Jeremiah from harm's way, but they protect the nation from "bringing innocent blood upon itself" (26:15). The discourse on true and false prophecy in chapters 27–29, moreover, is essentially an ideological battle over the community's stance toward Babylon. Whether the nation will survive is not the issue. What is at stake is the developing character of the embattled nation. The most stunning display of hope is found in the "Book of Consolation" (Jer 30–33). Here Yahweh rescinds the judgments against Judah and introduces in their place a resilient script for the future. Even the so-called Baruch Narrative, which tells the story of the fall of Jerusalem and the suffering of Jeremiah, makes the case that the future of Israel lies with the exiles in Babylon and not with Judeans remaining in the land. That is to say, while the text is describing the end of one world, it is creating the symbolic space for the emergence of another, albeit in a faraway land. Finally, the three endings of Jeremiah, chapters 45, 46–51, 52, point to better times for the suffering people of God. The first is an oracle response to Baruch, in which Yahweh promises Jeremiah's scribe his "life as a prize of war" (45:5). This is clearly a modest promise, but it still carries the assurance of survival. The Oracles Against the Nations (Jer 46–51), another ending of the Hebrew text of Jeremiah, punctuate the book with implicit hope for exiled Judah. Specifically, the announcement of Babylon's defeat envisions an epoch of hope and salvation for captive peoples (Jer 50–51). And the concluding report in chapter 52 winds up with the kind treatment of King Jehoiachin in Babylon (52:31-34), apparently whispering that the future of Judah has not come to an irrevocable end. These overtures suggest that the symbolic logic of the book paves the way for survival, durable hope, and new life.

Hope was apparently a rare commodity for the first readers of the text. Indeed, despair may have been their most debilitating and palpable disease. The book of Jeremiah provides an alternative script to despair. It intends to inspire hope in those whose lives have been ransacked by loss. Not the kind of hope that imagines a return to the world as it was, but one that generates courage to live through massive upheaval. In this capacity Jeremiah is a map of hope for the vulnerable and disenfranchised. I would contend that it is also a map for our own troubled times.

INTRODUCTION

"Death has come up into our windows,
it has entered our palaces,
to cut off the children from the streets
and the young men from the squares."
(Jeremiah 9:21)

T he book of Jeremiah is the longest and most tumultuous prophetic writing in the Bible. It speaks of a nation under massive assault and a people whose lives are wracked with pain. With disturbing images and raw emotion, the book bears witness to a disaster that represents nothing less than the collapse of the world, cosmic crumbling, and the end of a culture: the tragedy in mind is the defeat of Judah by Babylon under King Nebuchadnezzar (605–562 B.C.E.). According to biblical narratives, three Babylonian offensives (597, 587, 582) shattered Judah's social and political order and left survivors beaten and disillusioned. The siege of Jerusalem in 587 was presumably the most costly. It resulted in death, displacement, and widespread destruction. The imposing Neo-Babylonian military machine burned to the ground the great temple of Jerusalem and the royal palace complex. With the infrastructure in disarray and many leading citizens already in exile, the remnant in the land faced a bleak future. Indeed, a world had fallen. Long-standing institutions associated with God's blessing, cherished belief systems, and social structures that appeared invincible had come to a cataclysmic end.

From survival literature, ancient and contemporary, we know that such upheaval not only causes physical and emotional devastation, but also evokes probing questions about ultimate reality. Where is God? How can such random and obscene acts of violence occur? Is it possible to live through the darkness and embrace life again? Jeremiah is a penetrating response to the multifaceted configurations of evil and the apparent silence of God. It

1

is a "survival manual" for people living on the brink of despair. First, the book faces the disaster head on and dares to speak of an experience that is too painful to utter. Against widespread opposition, Jeremiah embraces the devastation as a reality that the people of Judah would have to endure. This brutal honesty eventually leads to Judah's healing and restoration. Second, Jeremiah organizes the chaos in ways that provide avenues out of the abyss. Although Babylon looms larger than life, the text claims that God is the one who is "to pluck up and to pull down, to destroy and to overthrow" (Jer 1:10), in some measure as a consequence of Judah's unfaithfulness to God and mistreatment of its poor. In this way, the book testifies to Judah's responsibility in the ordeal and to God's involvement in it. Third, Jeremiah announces hope for newness after the nightmare. The hope that Jeremiah holds is not for a return to the old world, which is gone forever, but for a new start as survivors in a faraway place. Exile, thus, was not the end but the beginning of a new life and a new community.

HISTORICAL BACKGROUND

The series of devastating events happened swiftly. Only a few years earlier, life was altogether different. Under the leadership of King Josiah (640–609), national independence began to flourish once again after years of servitude to Assyria. With the weakening and eventual collapse of the Assyrian Empire in the last quarter of the seventh century, Josiah was able to reverse the pro-Assyrian policies of his father, Manasseh, and forge a new national identity. In 622 Judah witnessed one of the most sweeping religious and nationalistic reforms in its history. According to 2 Kgs 22–23 (see also 2 Chr 34–35), enormous efforts were made to repair a poorly maintained temple, centralize worship in Jerusalem, restore "the book of the law" to its former place of preeminence, and diminish foreign enculturation. During the final years of Josiah's reign (622–609), Judah enjoyed a season of stability and geopolitical autonomy. It was, however, only the calm before the storm.

This unprecedented period of renewal would be short-lived and have little lasting influence. Judah's hopes for a sustained period of independence ended when King Josiah died in battle at Megiddo in 609 while trying to prevent Pharaoh Neco II from assisting the Assyrians (see 2 Kgs 23:29-30; 2 Chr 35:20-24). Thereafter, the fragile nation found itself tossed to and fro by events over which it had little control. First, Egypt took control of Judah, deporting Jehoahaz, Josiah's successor, and appointing Eliakim, later named Jehoiakim, to the throne. Then, the Babylonians marched westward, routed the Egyptians and quickly advanced on Syria-Palestine. When Jehoiakim rebelled against Nebuchadnezzar (2 Kgs 24:1), the Babylonians converged on Judah, surrounded Jerusalem, and eventually conquered the city in 597. During the siege, Nebuchadnezzar looted the temple and carried off many of Judah's leading citizens to Babylon. Among those deported were King Jehoiachin (the successor of Jehoiakim), the queen mother, and others from the royal court. Nebuchadnezzar then installed Jehoiachin's uncle, Zedekiah, as Judah's last king.

The final years of Judah were no less turbulent. The country was now only a shell of what it once was. War, deportation, heavy tribute, and political domination had taken their toll. Responses to the situation were varied. National and international alliances were forged for the purpose of breaking free from Babylonian control (see Jer 28). A Jerusalem coalition held out hope that Babylonian control would be short-lived, that the exiles of 597 would soon return home, and that Judah would again enjoy national independence. This nationalist movement encouraged insurrection against foreign rule. At the same time, pro-Egyptian factions emerged that began to clash with pro-Babylonian blocs. The former held out hope that Egypt would come to Judah's aid if further conflict arose with Babylon. The latter, including the prophet Jeremiah, were convinced that the most prudent course of action was to ride out the period of Babylonian domination. Judah's plight, they believed, was a long-term geopolitical reality with which the state would have to come to terms. Indeed, its very survival depended on submission to Babylon; resistance would only lead to ruin.

Zedekiah found himself caught in the middle of this controversy. Conversations with Jeremiah represent him as an ambivalent ruler who was not up to the challenge of leading the nation. After repeated attempts to persuade Zedekiah to submit to Babylon, the king sided with Jeremiah's opponents and rebelled against Babylon. In 589 Zedekiah declared Judah's independence. Nebuchadnezzar responded quickly to the uprising. Although Egypt thwarted his assault for a short time, it could not hold off Babylon for long. After a brief respite, Babylon's armies entered Jerusalem, destroyed its fortresses, and punished their rebellious vassal Zedekiah. The account of the fall of Jerusalem is preserved in 2 Kgs 24:18–25:21, Jer 39:1-10, and Jer 52:4-30. The once flourishing capital of Judah was laid to ruins.

To care for those remaining in the land, King Nebuchadnezzar appointed Gedaliah governor of Judah. Gedaliah's family had played an important role in Josiah's reform (2 Kgs 22:3-13) and in Jeremiah's prophetic ministry (Jer 26:24). During his term, the Babylonian appointee encouraged loyalty to Babylon and offered amnesty to Judean nationalists who had fought in the war of 587. His overtures appeared to create a lull in the violence and even a period of prosperity. The calm, however, would not last. Ishmael, a member of the royal family and the leader of a small band of resistance fighters, assassinated Gedaliah at the provincial capital Mizpah (Jer 41:1-3). He continued his killing spree until Johanan and other loyalists to the slain governor pursued Ishmael and forced him out of the country. At that point Johanan and his troops fled to Egypt with Jeremiah and Baruch as their hostages. We last hear from Jeremiah addressing a community in Egypt that was more devoted to the queen of heaven than to Yahweh.

OCCASION AND CONTEXT

When considering setting and context, it is essential to make a distinction between Jeremiah the prophet and Jeremiah the book. Although the two are clearly interdependent, they represent separate stages in the history of the tradition. When Jeremiah's prophecies were preserved in written form, certain transformations occurred. For our purposes, the most germane of these was a shift in social setting and audience. According to the superscription (1:1-3), Jeremiah's "career" as God's spokesperson spanned forty years: from the thirteenth year of Josiah's reign (627) to the captivity of Jerusalem (587). Based on virtually all of the prose narratives in the book, it is safe to assume that his most active period extended from the inauguration of Jehoiakim (609) to the fall of Jerusalem (587). Jeremiah the book took shape in the aftermath of these events, and it specifically addressed the interests and concerns of the Jewish exiles in Babylon. One of the book's central claims is that the future of Israel lies with the Jewish community in Babylon, and not with those left behind in Judah or with Judeans who eventually settled in Egypt.

The Occasion and Context of Jeremiah the Prophet

As is true for the majority of prophetic books in the Bible, the spoken word defines the earliest stage of the Jeremiah tradition. Prophets in the ancient Near East were primarily speakers, not writers, and Jeremiah was no exception. While he appears in his book as one who dictates his own prophecies (e.g., Jer 29, 30, 36, 51:59-64), he was still, in the first place, a *spokesperson* for Yahweh. In the broadest terms, his work as a prophet encompassed the period described above in the historical overview. Nearly every prophetic utterance, symbolic act, and account of Jeremiah relates to the unstable social and political conditions in the years immediately before, during, and after the fall of Jerusalem. During these volatile years, the prophet addressed broad cross sections of Judean society experiencing enormous hardship. The nation was under massive assault and the ravaging effects of war, exile, economic ruin, and social disorder were palpable.

Nonetheless, this community maintained a staunch nationalism and religious confidence. It was confident, even smug, about its ability to fend off foreign armies, and therefore, it ardently opposed any attempt to subvert hopes for national autonomy. Judah rejected the mere inference that its cultural and formal structures would collapse. It viewed the temple as the center of the universe, the city of Jerusalem as invincible, and the national and religious traditions associated with David as enduring manifestations of God's faithfulness. After the initial deportation of Judeans to Babylon in 597, many still held the belief that the breakdown of institutional life was just a momentary disruption. Moreover, Judah's political posturing, its teeter-tottering between pro-Egyptian and pro-Babylonian policies, and its internal and external revolts, were primarily motivated by nationalistic zeal for the city and its shrine. Such religious and national fervor contributed to the mistreatment of Jeremiah whose prophecies were intended from the start to "destroy and overthrow" the nation's most venerated ideologies and institutions.

The Occasion and Context of Jeremiah the Book

Jeremiah the book reflects a very different social setting. It was written after the fall of Jerusalem with the Jewish exiles in Babylon in mind (Stulman 1998, 167-84). In contrast to the Judeans who first "heard" Jeremiah's prophecies and presumably had the opportunity to circumvent imminent disaster, the exiles in Babylon could only look back on worlds lost. They had lived through the disaster. Their beloved institutions had been destroyed. Foreign armies had leveled the seemingly impregnable Jerusalem and its grand temple. The wreckage had thrown into question ancient land claims as well as covenant and election traditions. Foreign armies had undermined God's sure and faithful promises to David. Cultural and religious categories, once well defined, now lacked clarity. And the process of power distribution, once precisely arranged in the hierarchical structures of a dynastic state, was in shambles. An array of perilous forces had divided the survivors' lives into stark categories of "before-and-after."

The disenfranchised refugees living in Babylon had to come to grips with a past that was gone and a future that was not yet inscribed. They found themselves living on the edge, eking out an existence and negotiating a new world after the old one had been dealt a deathblow. This frightful moment— this "already-not-yet" predicament, when honored images and practices and well-tested support systems had given way before new configurations of reality took shape—defined the dominant social location of the addressees of the book.

For this community, exile not only represented a real historical experience but also a code word, a metaphor, for its social location of vulnerability. Exile symbolized the end of the community's long-standing national identity, traditional state religion, political policies, social institutions, and intellectual traditions. However, it also created an avenue for promising beginnings. The metaphor of exile transformed scattered and isolated families into a community unified by the memory of communal pain and displacement. In lieu of the old geographic center (the land>> Jerusalem>> temple), a social location with power to give or withhold benefits, and a theological framework associated with a dynastic state, the dominant symbol and shared experience of exile provided meaning and identity for fragmented and disoriented people.

For this marginalized community in Babylon, the notion of "survivor" became all-important, and God's presence began to be associated more with personal and communal suffering than with the politics of brawny nationalism. The portrait of Jeremiah as suffering servant of God—and the so-called "Servant Psalms" in Isaiah 40–55—bears witness to this new way of thinking about the world. As a representative person, Jeremiah's faithful service involved hardship and conflict rather than reward and blessing. And apparently the exiles came to view his experiences as normative. How could they expect a lot different from that of Jeremiah, the righteous prophet? Furthermore, the exiles reached back to a complex of ancient teachings, untainted by the monarchy, as a basis for their theological framework, value system, and social organization. Traditional teachings associated with Moses authorized the community to reject hierarchical ideologies and adopt in their place a more human social order (e.g., Jer 34:8-22).

Two Editions of Jeremiah

The distinction between Jeremiah the prophet and Jeremiah the book is complicated by the fact that there are actually *two* "books" of Jeremiah. That is, Jeremiah is preserved in two authoritative versions: one in Greek (the Septuagint = LXX) and another in Hebrew (the Masoretic Text = MT). While there are Greek translations of every Hebrew book in the Bible, the Greek and Hebrew texts of Jeremiah represent two distinct *editions* of the book (Tov 1972, 189-99). The LXX of Jeremiah is a pristine translation of a substantially shorter Hebrew text (with about three thousand fewer words than the MT), and it reflects a different arrangement of some of its chapters.

The two witnesses of Jeremiah, the one underlying the LXX as well as the MT, ultimately derive from a common line. Only subsequently did this line diverge into two collateral branches. One of these branches—the one represented by the MT—underwent an extensive process of expansion, which is probably the reason the MT of Jeremiah is significantly longer than the LXX. The MT represents a relatively later form of the text that derives from the second temple period. Interestingly, fragments of both Hebrew traditions have been found in the vicinity of the Dead Sea, which suggests that a unified text of Jeremiah may not have existed until after the second century.

In light of these developments, one might think of the LXX and MT of Jeremiah as two textual performances of Jeremiah at different points in time and within separate communities of faith. Both editions reflect their own distinctive character and final theological message. For example, the location of the Oracles Against the Foreign Nations in the LXX (25:14–31:44) and MT (Jer 46–51) reveals conflicting theological agendas. Framing the Oracles Against the Nations in the LXX are two texts (25:1-13; 32:1-5) that highlight the defeat of Judah at the hands of the Babylonians. The initial prose sermon names Babylon and its king as Yahweh's instrument for punishing Judah and a concluding prose narrative describes Babylon's siege of Jerusalem. Following this description, Jeremiah insists that all nations, including Judah, drink from Yahweh's cup of wrath (32:15-29 in the LXX). This literary setting produces an ethos of judgment that diminishes the positive consequences of the Oracles Against the Nations for the people of Judah. The placement of the collection at the end of the book in the MT serves another set of structural and theological purposes. First, it creates a certain degree of literary symmetry by fleshing out Jeremiah's role as prophet to the nations (1:5, 10). Second, it heralds the sovereignty of God over all peoples, again a motif intimated in the first chapter. Third, it accentuates God's decisive victory over every oppressive human system and the establishment of a lasting reign of justice and peace. The prophecies against the nations in the MT bring the book to a close with a triumphant note celebrating the reign of God and the eventual cessation of Israel's sad times of trouble.

The two "books" or editions of Jeremiah attest to the dynamic nature of the canonical process (Stulman 1986, 49-118). Subsequent generations accepted the tradition as the vibrant and active word of God. It was never static or unchanging, until the emergence of a "standardized" text. The Jeremiah corpus would address the needs and concerns of later communities of faith as it was read and reinterpreted. This is why one should consider the book of Jeremiah to be a trajectory rather than a fixed point: it must have been continually changing and developing over a period of several centuries, albeit slowly. Although there is presently no consensus regarding the provenance of the developing texts, the origin of the MT of Jeremiah is often associated with communities in Babylon or Palestine and the text underlying the LXX of Jeremiah with the Jewish community residing in Egypt through the Persian and Hellenistic periods. Moreover, since the MT of Jeremiah tends to sympathize more with the exiles in Babylon than with those who remained in Judah, and the promises it elaborates often focus upon their return, the MT may reflect the viewpoint of those who returned to Judea during the Persian period and who saw themselves as the beneficiaries of God's promise (Stulman 1984, 18-23).

These social locations illustrate the point that the development of the book of Jeremiah involved a surplus of settings and audiences. This great cloud of witnesses ranged in time from the last quarter of the seventh century, when the preexilic community of Judeans first *heard* the message of the historical Jeremiah, to perhaps as late as the fourth or even third century when the scribal tradition associated with MT helped to shape the tradition in light of its own distinctive concerns.

Making Sense of the Multiple Settings of Jeremiah

How does one "make sense" of the multiple settings and audiences in Jeremiah? Does a particular setting or audience enjoy preeminence over others? It is not uncommon for one context or tradition to be pitted against another. And to some extent such tensions are present within the book itself, especially when various voices vie for ideological control. But a more rudimentary question must first be answered: is it at all helpful to speculate about settings and audiences, since we enjoy only indirect access to these networks of meanings? The answer is "yes and no."

Although we have more immediate access to the final form(s) of Jeremiah than to the workings "behind the text(s)," prophecy is never divorced from historical realities. For example, the threatened social world of the Jewish community in Babylon, for which Jeremiah was first *written*, is always in the purview of the reader. The anxiety bubbling beneath the surface of the text stems from a listening community that is caught between two worlds: a world that has fallen and one yet to be constructed. One cannot ignore these particularities when reading Jeremiah. The book grew out of concrete social realities: the realities of suffering, injustice, and religious systems gone awry. To "disincarnate" Jeremiah from them runs the risk of "spiritualizing" the book, which violates the prophetic genre itself. On the other hand, the text(s) of Jeremiah is no longer controlled by its original networks, but generates a wide range of values, emotions, understandings, and social possibilities. It resists being captive to historical constraints. Consequently, Jeremiah invites us to join the community of listeners who live *within* the world of the text. The book summons us to visit its quite particular world and participate in its dramatic representation of reality. It urges us to find ourselves disconcerted and ultimately changed by the story.

Therefore, as readers we immerse ourselves in three worlds:

(1) The world of the past, recognizing that the book of Jeremiah comes from a time and place that is different from our own. This world may at times resonate with our own construal of reality. At

other times, its social and cultural norms may be objectionable, but in either case, the text we encounter is an ancient one, composed and committed to writing long ago.

(2) The world of sacred literature, recognizing that Jeremiah in its final form(s) is accepted as word of God in Judaism and Christianity. That is to say, this book as it now appears—regardless of the workings behind it—has been treasured by the faithful for millennia. And finally

(3) the world of contemporary space and time, recognizing that we never read texts divorced from our own local context.

LITERARY GENRE, STRUCTURE, AND CHARACTER OF JEREMIAH

The Problem: Literary Chaos

Jeremiah's main themes and enduring images have earned it an honored place in the history of Judaism and Christianity. Yet rare is the person who is not baffled by this prophetic book. Its lack of form, literary coherence, and chronological order make Jeremiah a difficult read. Its plethora of genres, speakers, and competing theological claims present a formidable challenge to anyone. To compound the problems, Jeremiah is a mixture of prose and poetry. In the first half of the book, poetry is predominant, although it is interspersed with prose sermons. In the second half of the book, the literary landscape is governed by biographical prose, albeit spotted with collections of poems. The confluence of these various factors produces literary chaos. By conventional standards, the book of Jeremiah is arguably not readable. E. F. Campbell notes that Jeremiah is far "too bumpy" to be read as a coherent literary piece (1992, 812-15). John Bright put it more colorfully: the book of Jeremiah is a "hopeless hodgepodge thrown together without any discernible principle of arrangement at all" (1965, lvi). Robert Carroll says flatly: "the reader who is not confused by reading the book of Jeremiah has not understood it" (1989, 9).

Previous Attempts to Make Sense of Jeremiah

During a large part of the previous century, scholars looked to the compositional history of Jeremiah as a key to understanding the book's many enigmas. Consequently, an enormous amount of time and energy was spent trying to reconstruct the origins of the book. Perhaps the crowning achievement of these efforts was the realization that Jeremiah is the product of a long and complex literary history spanning as many as several hundred years. More specifically, scholars reached the conclusion that Jeremiah contains three primary literary strata: poetic oracles of Jeremiah, biographical prose materials (traditionally associated with Baruch), and prose sermons that are likely the product of later editors.

When attempting to identify more precisely the dynamics at work in the book's formation, the consensus crumbled under its own weight. The same could be said about nearly every historical issue related to Jeremiah. To this day there are deep and penetrating disagreements over dating, authorship, and the person of Jeremiah. Research into these questions, which is known as historical criticism, is presently at an impasse, and will probably not be resolved given our current state of knowledge. Nor has historical critical scholarship substantially eased the burden of interpretation. While it has solved some of the riddles as to why Jeremiah developed as an anthology of disparate literary pieces, the book still looks the way it does; the text before us is still plagued by incongruities, and it is still fraught with incoherence and instability. The dominant paradigm of historical criticism, which has assisted in identifying original sources and tracing the compositional history of Jeremiah, has failed to resolve the problems it has helped us to see.

Recent Attempts to Make Sense of Jeremiah

Aware of the need to seek new routes through the theoretical impasse, a number of scholars have recently suggested alternative approaches to the book of Jeremiah (Diamond, O'Connor, and Stulman 1999). While these interpretations of Jeremiah draw on a wide range of interdisciplinary models, including those informed by the social sciences, literary criticism, and modern and post-modern hermeneutics, they agree on three central points. First, they are skeptical that the quest for origins will help us solve the many problems of reading Jeremiah as a prophetic book. Thus they challenge the well-established assumption that understanding of the workings "behind the text" provides the key to its present form. Second, they show little interest in traditional historical questions, such as authorship and dating. Scant time, for example, is spent trying to figure out which material in the book derives from the prophet himself. Third, the newer approaches to Jeremiah proceed on the assumption that meaning is derived primarily from the text "in front of us." Consequently, Jeremiah is read holistically, whether as sacred canon or simply as a literary reality. While acknowledging the large number of originally independent traditions, these studies discern artful coherence or artful dissonance in the book as it now appears and therefore conclude that Jeremiah is amenable to final form readings.

The Methodological Approach of This Commentary

Following the direction of contemporary scholarship, this commentary proposes that the book of Jeremiah reflects an intentional literary organization and purposeful theological design. Despite its jumbled appearance, Jeremiah is far more than a random accumulation of miscellaneous materials. It is an artistically woven together literary work with unity and purpose that surpasses its individual parts. Put more modestly, despite the book's dense and chaotic character, it is readable, not by standards of linear logic, but as a symbolic tapestry with narrative seams. In other words, there is theological coherence amidst the chaos. Indications of this literary and theological structure are present throughout the book, but they are recognizable most clearly in (1) the strategic arrangement of large collections, (2) the prose sermons, which function as interpretive guides and structural markers, (3) the construction of the literary persona of the prophet, and in (4) prominent literary motifs. These four ingredients bring order and shape to a formless and incoherent text.

Collections in Jeremiah

Interpreters have long recognized large collections in the book of Jeremiah. The first twenty-five chapters, for example, represent a composite collection that comprises several smaller blocks with their own complex history of development. Jeremiah 1–25 is often described as "Judgment Oracles Against Judah and Jerusalem." The central theme of Jer 27–29 is less clear, although true and false prophets play leading roles in the prose cycle. The "Book of Consolation" in chapters 30–33 consists of prose and poetic materials that focus almost exclusively on hope and salvation. The so-called Baruch Narrative constitutes a literary unit that relates the story of Jerusalem's fall and Jeremiah's part in it (Jer 36–45). The Oracles Against the Nations is a collection of prophecies heralding the lordship of Yahweh in the world (Jer 46–51).

These collections have not merely been thrown together but are organized in a meaningful way. As can be seen in the following outline, their location in the book is significant:

Part One: Jer 1–25: Dismantling Judah's Idolatrous World

The Programmatic Introduction:
Judah's New Place Among the Nations (1:1-19)
> Unit One: Judah's Departure from Yahweh: The Basis for Guilt and Penalty of Death (2:1–6:30)
> Unit Two: Dismantling the Temple (7:1–10:25)
> Unit Three: Dismantling the Covenant (11:1–17:27)
> Unit Four: Dismantling Insider Privileges (18:1–20:18)
> Unit Five: Dismantling the Monarchy (21:1–24:10)
> The Conclusion: The Fulfillment of God's Plan for Judah Among the Nations (25:1-38)

Part Two: Jer 26–52: Rebuilding Out of the Ruins

The Programatic Introduction: A Sign of Hope (26:1-24)
> Unit One: Conflicting Theologies of Hope (27:1–29:32)
> Unit Two: The Book of Consolation (30:1–33:26)
> Unit Three: Moral Instruction for the New Community (34:1–35:19)
> Unit Four: The Baruch Narrative: Hope Lies with the

Babylonian Exiles (36:1–45:5)
Unit Five: God's Reign over the Nations (46:1–51:64)
Final Words: An Ending with Embryonic Beginnings
(52:1-34)

Far from being random and isolated blocks, these collections divide into two major parts, which form a two-part drama. Each part is composed of five units or acts held in place by an introduction and conclusion. The prophetic drama reenacts the death of Judah's preexilic world and the emergence of a new world order. Jeremiah 1–25, part one of the drama, predicts the dismantling of Judah's cherished beliefs and social structures—its temple, system of worship, covenant, election, land claims, and royal theology. All will go down to destruction, and Judah must, therefore, relinquish any hope that these old ideologies and institutions will survive and come to its aid. Jeremiah 26–52, part two of the drama, reveals that the devastation is not the final word. The ravages of war, exile, and the death of Judah's culture pave the way for fresh configurations of life. The second half of Jeremiah thus sculpts new beginnings out of the rubble of fallen worlds. It speaks of hope when none was expected. It fashions a silhouette of a community that will survive and even flourish despite the wreckage it has endured. As a whole, the final shaping of the book bears witness to a God who "destroys and overthrows" in order to "build and plant." Indeed, this is God's intention from start (1:10) to finish (45:4-5).

Prose Sermons

Prose sermons likewise play a significant role in the overall architecture of the book. Speeches or sermons in other biblical books are rarely present without good reason. They provide important rhetorical, literary, and theological clues for understanding the text. Prose speeches in the Deuteronomistic History (Deut–2 Kgs), for example, mark important structural transitions and highlight central themes. Second Kings 17:13-20 is a case in point. It reiterates the claim that the fall of Israel in 722 B.C.E. was a consequence of the nation's disobedience to the words of the prophets. Yahweh sent his "servants the prophets" to summon Israel to repent of its idolatry. Israel rejected this message and thereby brought disaster on itself.

Until recently, the prose sermons in the book of Jeremiah have been studied in isolation from their literary context. The near consensus of a generation of scholars is that these discourses are scattered haphazardly throughout the book, only adding to the book's disarray. However, when one reads the prose sermons *in context*, they are significant in the overall architecture of the book. They operate as structural devices that mark important transitions (Stulman 1998, 11-98). Prose sermons introduce four of the five major sections in the first book (Jer 1–25). They also serve as interpretive guides and theological commentaries. They echo, clarify, and accentuate themes as well as introduce new theological understandings (Wilson 1999, 413-427). In the case of Jer 1–25, prose discourses relativize every social and symbolic structure deemed idolatrous. In the case of Jer 26–52, they are equally zealous to speak of hope and salvation. We see this hopeful propensity at the start, when a few people finally heed Jeremiah's message (Jer 26:1-24), in prophecies of restoration (32:6-44), and in a word of encouragement to faithful Baruch, Jeremiah's scribe (45:1-5). In all, the prose sermons provide the theological grid and basic structure for the book of Jeremiah.

The Portrayal of Jeremiah

One of the most daring features of the book of Jeremiah is that the persona of the prophet looms as large as, or even larger than, the message itself. Ordinarily in the Old Testament, prophets are somewhat eclipsed by the oracles they announce. Consequently, it is difficult to construct a character sketch apart from the messages they proclaim. This is not the case with Jeremiah. Right from the outset, the reader confronts a prophet whose words and life experiences are inextricably interwoven. Throughout the book of Jeremiah, message and messenger share center stage. The marriage of the two—the prophetic word and prophetic persona—in many respects establishes Jeremiah's unique niche among the prophets in the Old Testament. It produces theological meanings that are greater than either by itself. One might even argue that the text transforms the person of the prophet into the message itself, so that the two become an authoritative witness to God.

The prophetic persona provides another clue for understanding the literary unity and theological message of the book. We see this most clearly in Jeremiah's solidarity with the people of Judah. The prophet's life is thoroughly connected to the people of Judah. Accordingly, he never addresses his countrymen in a detached and dispassionate manner, as if one could separate the message from the messenger. The prophet participates fully in the death of Judah's world. He suffers with, on behalf of, and because of his community. Jeremiah's very life and destiny are consociated with Judah's: God calls both prophet and people (Jer 1–2), both suffer the shattering and death of their world, and both survive the desolation. In this way, the persona of Jeremiah reflects the nation's descent into utter hopelessness in Jer 1–25 as well as its emergence as a wounded survivor in Jer 26–52. And so, the persona of Jeremiah corresponds to the book's overall literary structure and final message of dismantling and rebuilding.

Prominent Literary Motifs

In addition to carefully placed collections, prose sermons, and the prophetic persona, recurring literary motifs help locate major theological forces at work in the book. These major themes, especially when present at pivotal junctures, provide internal clues to salient features that transcend the part and unify the whole. The motif of the "nations," for instance, occurs twenty-six times in the book. Throughout Jeremiah, the nations are constantly in the sight of the reader. Jeremiah is called a "prophet to the nations" (1:5). He declares Yahweh as the "King of the nations" (10:7). The "nations" along with Judah must drink of Yahweh's "cup of wrath" (25:15-29). In Jer 27–28 God commands the "nations" to serve the king of Babylon "and his son and his grandson, until the time of his own land comes; then many nations and great kings shall make him their slave" (Jer 27:7). By the close of the book, Jeremiah appears as a full-fledged international figure, "a prophet to the nations" (Jer 46–51). In light of the density and distribution of this motif, the book implies that God's sovereign program transcends national boundaries and provincial interests. God's acts in history concern the entire world.

The "foe from the north" theme is another example of a literary motif that is a key to the literary architecture of the book. The term first appears in Jeremiah's call narrative and then again periodically in the early chapters of the book. The northern enemy is an unidentified military force that God enlists to bring judgment on Judah. Portrayals are thick and hauntingly vague. The very mention of the nebulous entity evokes fear. Eventually, the enemy from the north materializes in the person of Nebuchadnezzar and his fierce army. God chooses Babylon to usher in judgment on defiant Judah. However, once Babylon accomplishes its military and political objectives, and in fact oversteps this mission, it too becomes a recipient of divine judgment. In the Oracles Against the Nations, northern forces appear again, this time to rein in Babylon for its hubris and cruel treatment of others.

Results

These four maps of the literary terrain of Jeremiah—strategic collections, prose sermons, the prophetic persona, and recurring themes—suggest that there is order amidst the chaos. Editorial forces at work within the text have brought a measure of literary and theological coherence to a jumbled text throbbing with symbolic anxiety. The present shape of the text testifies to the uprooting and rebuilding of the Judean people. At almost every juncture, Jer 1–25 highlights the dangerous work of dismantling known symbol systems and social structures. The language of dismantling anticipates the end of human institutions and human possibilities; it refutes every claim that God is permanently committed to Judah's established religious and cultural systems. And it demands that Judah abandon its trusted support systems. In Jer 26–52 the siege and fall of Jerusalem still occupy the center of interest, but now the text begins to chart a new theological terrain beyond the collapse of its symbolic universe (that is, its cardinal beliefs, values, and assumptions about reality). The second half of Jeremiah risks speaking of hope and survival. It claims that the God who judges also transforms death into life by the power of love.

This final pattern of judgment and salvation is clearly overly simplistic. The book is far too complex to be placed under any single structural or theological rubric. Nonetheless, as it now appears, the interpretive community of Jeremiah contains the discordant voices of the text within a framework of judgment and deliverance. This superimposed structure of destruction and renewal, judgment and salvation, mirrors the pattern of the canonical corpus of prophetic literature. Thus, Jeremiah joins the chorus that proclaims "the message of the hope of coming salvation in relation to all of the forewarnings of doom which individual prophets made" (Clements 1996, 196).

THEOLOGY AND ETHICS

Jeremiah and Other Prophetic Books in the Bible

Jeremiah speaks squarely within ancient Israel's prophetic tradition. Like Isaiah, Jeremiah proclaims that the God of Israel is one who sustains, judges, and is thoroughly involved in human affairs. As sovereign ruler, no realm or power structure lies outside the sphere of God's control. In a world that is under siege by a myriad of forces, Jeremiah asserts that God is still ordering and governing with the intent to accomplish God's purposes. Sovereignty, however, does not nullify human responsibility and freedom. Like Amos, Jeremiah exposes the scandal of economic exploitation and indicts the powerful, whose self-interests have blinded them to the needs of the poor and marginalized. Acts of injustice, Jeremiah insists, are reprehensible to a God who demands justice and who defends the poor (see, e.g., Jer 7:5-7; 22:3, 13-17; 23:5-6; 34:8-22). Injustice is no mere misdemeanor but a disaster to God (Heschel 2001, 3-6, 64-65). Indeed, God's solidarity with those in need represents a core conviction of Jeremiah. Spirituality divorced from ethical behavior, particularly a commitment to economic/social justice, is a perverse departure from God's word and therefore lies at the heart of the nation's problems.

Like Hosea, Jeremiah warns his community that constraining human categories cannot pigeonhole the God of Israel. God is wild, undomesticated, and free to shatter all conventional categories and systems of control. However, this free and unrestrained God does not direct human affairs from above in an aloof and dispassionate manner. God is instead a wounded participant due to Judah's disloyalty and idolatry. And like Jonah, Jeremiah declares that God's moral sovereignty is in no way provincial and localized: God's domain extends beyond the diminutive boundaries of Israel to the far reaches of the earth. Consequently, there are few signs of xenophobia in Jeremiah.

Jeremiah's Distinctive Ethical-Religious Teaching: An Overview

Defining Jeremiah's *distinctive* ethico-religious world, however, is fraught with difficulties. The book's composite texture and multiple voices present the impression of a miscellaneous collection of theological claims rather than a unified perspective. Tensions and disparities in the poetry and prose literature provide an ample case in point. In the poetry, Jeremiah often speaks of imminent disaster by using military imagery; he poignantly describes the people's moral bankruptcy for which judgment is coming; and with richness of ideas and forms, he describes the painful involvement of God in the nation's demise. In contrast, the prose materials present Jeremiah as a member of an institutional succession of preachers, beginning with Moses, who reprove the people for violations of the Deuteronomic Law. Here the prophet accuses the ancient and contemporary people of God of disobeying God's commandments. The prose sections often lack the imagination, vitality, and perspicacity that are present in the poetry. Yet, they create order and contain the rich theological diversity of the poetry within a frame. All theological claims, as we have noted, are now an integral part of the text's two-part drama that enacts the dismantling of Judah's preexilic systems (Jer 1–25) and the rebuilding of a shattered and scattered community (Jer 26–52).

Within this broad structural framework, several theological motifs emerge: (1) God's judgment or "wrath of love"; (2) God's

INTRODUCTION

suffering love; (3) God's gratuitous love; (4) God's word; (5) God's sovereignty; (6) a defense of God's justice in light of immense suffering; and (7) Jeremiah as an archetype or model of faithful living. By the expression God's "wrath of love" or divine judgment, I mean the many expressions of unresolved anger that grow out of passionate affection for humanity and for Israel in particular. As such, divine judgment in Jeremiah is fundamentally instrumental and not vindictive. It is not an end in itself. Its intent is to pluck up and to pull down *in order to* build and plant. In Jeremiah God's anger breaks forth as a penultimate reality. God's "suffering love" takes shape as profound anguish occasioned by abject rejection. It is the forceful outburst of grief in the face of idolatry and scorned affection. God's "wrath of love" and God's "suffering love" are most clearly evident in the first part of the drama and as such serve to introduce the second and final act of the drama.

"God's gratuitous love" is the inexplicable gift of new life when none is expected. Such love is not only surprising, but seemingly absurd in light of rebellion and idolatry. It makes no sense at all! Nonetheless, it is an abiding expression of the core character of God who is "full of love." Although God's gratuitous love is present throughout the entire book, one can discern God's gracious and compassionate overtures towards Israel most visibly beyond the perimeters of Jer 1–25.

Although "the word of God" is a mainstay of every prophetic book in the Bible, it holds a special place in Jeremiah. The word of God, among other things, authorizes the dissolution of the old world order in Jerusalem as well as the development of a survival manual for a colonized community in Babylon. "God's sovereignty" is the claim that God is managing the world despite indications to the contrary. The affirmation that "God reigns" is one of Jeremiah's central assertions. It speaks to an underlying fear that life is spiraling out of control. Next, much of the book develops as a "defense of God's character" in light of events that put God in a bad light. Given the terrible suffering of the Judean people, God's justice came into disrepute. The interpretive community of Jeremiah responds to this problem with a compelling theodicy. Finally, the considerable attention to the prophetic persona suggests that Jeremiah's life had meaning beyond his own personal experiences. Jeremiah became a "model of faithful living" for the exiles in Judah.

Divine Judgment or the "Wrath of Love"

Throughout the book of Jeremiah, but especially in the first twenty-five chapters, we witness divine judgment at almost every juncture. God's judgment grows out of a passionate longing for a relationship with Israel as well as a savage intolerance for evil. The wrath of love is grounded in enormous pain and is expressed in acts of justice. This understanding of judgment is evident by the way that God treats wayward Judah. God extends to the nation repeated invitations to return to the One who has nurtured, protected, and liberated it from oppressive and abusive systems (e.g., Jer 3:12, 14, 22; 4:1; see also 24:7). But Judah insists on abandoning Yahweh, "the fountain of living water" (Jer 2:13), for a myriad of competing interests and loyalties. Judah does "not listen" (e.g., 3:13, 25; 7:27), "plays the harlot" (e.g., 2:20-25, 33-37), "trusts in lies" (7:4, 8; 13:25; cf. 27:16; 28:15), "forgets" or "forsakes" Yahweh (3:21; 5:7; 13:25), "is obstinate" (e.g., 7:24; 9:14; 11:8), "provokes Yahweh to anger" (e.g., 7:18; 11:17; 32:29), "burns incense to other gods" (e.g., 7:9; 11:12, 13; 19:4), and does "not incline the ear" (e.g., 7:24, 26; 17:23). Moreover, the nation fails to live up to its commitment to covenant justice; it shows little compassion towards the destitute (34:8-22). And it attempts to skirt God's judgment and pigeonhole God (e.g., 7:1-15). To gain a hold on God Judah exchanges the presence of the free and unfettered God for myopic and idolatrous categories, and thereby joins the nations in their stringent opposition to the Lord (25:15-26).

In response, Jeremiah announces that divine judgment is imminent. God will deliver the people of Judah to the sword before "their enemies" (15:9) and cause them to "fall by the sword of their foes" (19:7); God threatens to deliver Judah "into the hands of adversaries" (34:20; cf. 21:7) who will scatter the nation on the day of calamity (18:17). A holy convocation from the north will usher in disaster on account of Judah's unfaithfulness and idolatry

(1:13-16). This alien horde will descend upon Jerusalem and all the cities of Judah in a grand display of military might. Then Judah's trusted social and symbolic structures will be overthrown and its sacred pillars—including temple, covenant, land claims, election, and Davidic dynasty—will be toppled. Without land, king, shrine, and privileged position, Judah will lead the doomed nations to the fountain of Yahweh's cup of wrath (25:15-18).

Although divine judgment leaves its indelible imprint, it is not vindictive but purposeful and grounded in raw emotion. The intent of God's judgment is not to annihilate or get even but to bring Judah to its senses. As such, judgment dismantles the nation's inadequate categories to make possible new and profound expressions of faith. The architecture of the final form of text bears this out again. Whereas the first part of the prophetic drama is governed by the *preliminary* work of "plucking up and tearing down," the second part anticipates a time of "rebuilding and planting," albeit out of the rubble of a collapsed world. In Jer 1–25, Jeremiah announces the destruction of the nation without a well-defined script for the future. While the destruction of Jerusalem still occupies the center of interest in Jer 26–52, Jeremiah begins to construct arrangements of hope for a new-yet-old community. Part one is the inescapable prerequisite to part two. Together they juxtapose the rhetoric of dismantling with hope-filled configurations of new beginnings. The structure of the book thus indicates that God's judgment is not the final message for Judah but the dangerous condition for Judah's redemption. Or, to echo the refrain of the entire book, the One who "tears down and destroys" also "builds and plants" (Jer 1:10; 12:14-15, 17; 18:7; 24:6; 31:28; 42:10; 45:4). God exposes the nation's idolatrous pretensions and illusions of certainty so that Judah can embrace and be embraced by the love of God.

God's Suffering Love

God's suffering love in Jeremiah not only includes the wrath of love or divine judgment, but goes far beyond it. Suffering love grows out of divine vulnerability and weakness. As such, its language is jumbled and incongruous not only because of a long and complex history of development, but more important, because it reflects a situation of anguish occasioned by a broken relationship. This suffering is hinted at in the book's introduction (Jer 1), which anticipates the conflict and rejection that Jeremiah, God's messenger, will endure at the hands of Judah's leadership (Jer 1:17-19). It takes more definitive shape in the first two literary units (Jer 2–6 and Jer 7–10), both of which are rooted in the metaphor of Yahweh as a scorned lover. And it is most clearly evident in the prophet's laments or confessions (11:18-23; 12:1-6; 15:10-21; 17:14-18; 18:18-23; 20:7-18) where we encounter a God who enters fully into dialogue with Israel and who participates wholly in the divine-human interchange. This interaction creates for God enormous pain in the face of abject rejection and betrayal. One can therefore discern in suffering love a range of emotions from profound sadness, disappointment, and bitterness, to declarations of war, hope, yearning for reunion, tenderness mingled with harshness, and sympathy. Grief, especially over acts of betrayal and unrequited love, is rarely tidy and coherent. It is chaotic, utterly engaged, and tortured by the past.

Amid painful memories of lost love (Jer 2), Yahweh whirls at Israel a series of questions: "What wrong did your ancestors find in me that they went far from me, and went after worthless things, and became worthless themselves?" (2:5); "Has a nation changed its gods, even though they are no gods?" (2:11*a*); "Is Israel a slave? Is he a homeborn servant? Why then has he become plunder?" (2:14); "Why do you complain against me?" (2:29*a*); "Have I been a wilderness to Israel, or a land of thick darkness? Why then do my people say, 'We are free, we will come to you no more'? Can a girl forget her ornaments, or a bride her attire? Yet my people have forgotten me, days without number" (2:31*b*-32). In all, Yahweh is jilted lover and Israel is betrayer (2:20-25). These queries reveal bewilderment and disappointment.

The ensuing chapters do nothing but add to the portrait of divine grief and human infidelity. God offers defiant Israel/Judah repeated opportunities to "come home," but the nation is intent on going its own way. Yahweh responds to the rejection of the people as a distraught lover. Painfully, Yahweh longs for reunion

(Jer 3–4) and even imagines words of regret coming from the mouth of beloved Judah (3:24-25). However, imagined hope soon gives way to rage (Jer 5–6) as Yahweh sweeps away treasured systems and self-indulgent idolatries. Still this is nothing more than a response to unrequited love.

God's suffering love surfaces most forcefully in the anguish of Jeremiah. The rejection of the prophet is clearly a repudiation of the God he represents. The ostracism and ridicule of Jeremiah betray the community's renunciation of God. Moreover, the prophet's screams of pain reveal the pathos and suffering of God. We encounter the convergence of divine and human suffering in the confessions of Jeremiah to such a degree that it is difficult in places to discern whether God or Jeremiah is speaking. "My anguish, my anguish! I writhe in pain! Oh, the walls of my heart! My heart is beating wildly; I cannot keep silent; . . . For my people are foolish, they do not know me; they are stupid children, they have no understanding. They are skilled in doing evil, but do not know how to do good" (Jer 4:19, 22). "My joy is gone, grief is upon me, my heart is sick. Hark, the cry of my poor people from far and wide in the land" (Jer 8:18, 19a). With intentional ambiguity, the text unites the prophet's sorrow with God's sorrow. The two now merge. Jeremiah's final confession, his plunge into utter despair, his descent to hell (Jer 20:7-18), uncovers the utter darkness that eventually envelops both the prophet *and* God (H. Kremers 1953, 122-40). Alongside Jeremiah, God goes down to destruction with his beloved people. Thus, the sovereign God becomes "powerless" as a consequence of suffering love.

God's Gratuitous Love

In some respects, gratuitous love—that is, love that is an unguarded, open-handed gift and thus wholly independent of merit or virtue—begins where suffering love ends. God surprises Israel with new beginnings when none seem possible, when Judah's final chapter appears to have been etched in stone. However, gratuitous love and suffering love are never really divisible. The two are thoroughly interwoven. Such an understanding lies at the heart of Paul's understanding of the gospel: "while we were enemies, we were reconciled to God through the death of his Son" (Rom 5:10). The intersection of gratuitous and suffering love broaches the mystery of God's character which is defined in large measure by mercy, steadfast love, and forgiveness (see, e.g., Exod 34:6-7). Distinguishing the two—gratuitous love and suffering love—is therefore merely for convenience.

While God's gratuitous love for Israel is hidden in the shadows of Jer 1–25, it erupts for all to see in Jer 26–52. The second part of the drama accentuates God's gracious workings and maps out a new symbolic terrain for the people of God. And even though God's judgment permeates the literary terrain of Jer 26–52, God heralds renewal and restoration beyond national despair and humiliation. The message of comfort for a suffering nation is a strong expression of divine love. Overtures of unmerited grace are present in the framework of Jer 26–52; they are intimated in words of hope for individuals (e.g. 39:15-18; 45:5) and in the acts of kindness on behalf of Jeremiah (26:16-24; 36:19; 38:7-13; 40:1-6); and they appear in full bloom in the "Book of Consolation" (Jer 30–33) and in the Oracles Against the Nations (Jer 46–51).

The "Book of Consolation" (Jer 30–33), the centerpiece of God's gratuitous love in Jeremiah, delineates in extensive detail Jeremiah's hopeful script for beloved Israel/Judah. This block of poetic and prose materials presents a wonderful picture of God's gracious acts. God promises to "restore the fortunes" of Israel and Judah (30:3), "bring them back to the land" given to their ancestors (30:3), and liberate them from their oppressors (30:8). Rather than serving oppressive foreign rulers, the people will follow "the LORD their God and David their king" (30:9); God "restore[s] health" and heals the wounds of a wounded community (30:17). Because of the mercies of God, "the tents of Jacob" enjoy honor, safety, and well-being (30:18-24; 31:10-14). As survivors of the sword, the once overthrown nation will be rebuilt and will again delight in the harvest (31:4-6) and in a marvelous homecoming (31:7-14). Unlike the unjust arrangements of the former state religion, the new age wrought by God is inclusive, more egalitarian, and profoundly human. Israel's union with Yahweh includes "all the families" of the scattered community (31:1), especially its most vulnerable members (31:7-9); the knowledge of God is available to all persons, sometimes without mention of priestly mediation (31:34); and great joy and dignity is afforded to the entire people (30:18-19; 31:1-6, 7-9, 10-14; 32:36-41). All this takes place because God loves Judah/Israel "with an everlasting love" (31:3*b*).

The "new" relation of which Jeremiah speaks, described in one place as a "new covenant" (Jer 31:31, see esp. vv. 31-34) and in another place as an "everlasting covenant" (Jer 32:40, see esp. vv. 36-44), carries with it the assurance of full forgiveness (31:34; 33:6-8), divine favor and protection (30:10-11; 32:36-44; 33:1-9), deliverance from captivity (30:10-11, 18-21; 31:7-14, 23-25), joy (30:18-19; 31:3-6), and inner transformation (31:33; 32:39-40). Unlike the old piety, which stresses Israel's responsibility and subsequent history of failure, this new spirituality involves the extraordinary workings of God. The "if" of the divine–human relation is superseded, perhaps even eclipsed, by the gratuitous love of God and the declarative words, "I will." In other words, God, in sheer grace, resolves to create the "new Israel" and the wonderful conditions of the new world order.

The Word of God

One of the fundamental struggles in Jeremiah has to do with "words" or ideologies/ideas. Even though the book is presented from start to finish as the "words of Jeremiah"—Jer 1:1 introduces the book as "the words of Jeremiah son of Hilkiah" and 51:64 concludes the writing, "Thus far are the words of Jeremiah"—it actually contains many conflicting words from a variety of sources. One finds the utterances of prophets and priests, enemies and supporters, kings and officials, and Judah and Israel. Often these "words" render clashing interpretations of life and reality, and in particular of the geopolitical situation of the late-seventh and early-sixth centuries. Despite these many words, the fifty-two chapters of Jeremiah are unwavering in their conviction that God has authorized Jeremiah's "words" and his construal of social and symbolic reality. In contrast to some who supposedly speak the words of Yahweh (see, e.g., Jer 28:2-4, 11), Jeremiah stands in the council of Yahweh and faithfully disseminates the divine message. With few exceptions, the prophetic formula "thus says [Yahweh]" or "the word(s) of [Yahweh]" is, therefore, reserved for the oracles of Jeremiah.

Central to all prophetic writings in the Bible is the word of Yahweh. By virtue of their "office" prophets proclaim "the word" (e.g., Jer 18:18). In the book of Jeremiah, however, the high density and even distribution of the Hebrew term for word (*dābār*) elevate the concept of "the word of Yahweh" to one of central importance. *Dābār* occurs over ninety times in the book, which is far greater than its usage in any other book of the Bible. The clause "the word of [Yahweh]," "the word that came to Jeremiah," or "oracle of [Yahweh]" occurs in every chapter of the book except chapters 41 and 52. A word-theology clearly plays a prominent role throughout Jeremiah. Utterly trustworthy and sure (Jer 1:4-10, 11-16), the "word of Yahweh" authorizes, critiques, sanctions, warns, and empowers. It is the decisive voice that evaluates every social institution and every theological assertion. No assumption, no social structure, no ideology or value is exempt from its judgment. Yahweh's word wields the authority to decree disaster and generate hope. It legitimates the territorial expansion of Babylon of the Levantine to encroach into Syria-Palestine and then reduces the superpower to dust. The message spoken by the prophets surpasses all other ways of communicating God's will. Whereas the divine program is at times revealed through dreams, visions, and symbolic actions, in Jeremiah the word is the primary way of revealing God's will. The word towers over all other types of authority in Judean society including royal, wisdom, sacral, and military. "The word is king! The word is the true and only authority which determines the structures of society and all opposition to it is futile" (Carroll 1989, 99). Indeed, refusal to heed the prophetic word of Jeremiah is the primary cause of the fall of Jerusalem and the exile to Babylon.

When the *spoken* word is *written* (e.g., Jer 29; 30, 36; 45; 51:59-64), something startlingly new transpires. Written prophecy assumes an authoritative place that surpasses its oral counterpart.

Now the word of Yahweh has no geographical or temporal boundaries. As a scroll (Jer 30, 36) or letter (Jer 29), for instance, the written word communicates God's program to those who reside in Judah, Egypt, or Babylon. Geography is no barrier. When the written word is preserved in a sealed earthenware jar (Jer 32), it reveals Yahweh's message to future generations. Time is no barrier. In each case, the written word is freed from the person of Jeremiah to take on independent authority, which is not entirely unlike Jesus' assurances in the Gospel of John that he must leave (die) in order that the Holy Spirit might come. Consequently, a metamorphosis takes place: the authority of the written word displaces the oral proclamation of the prophet.

Written prophecy provides a sure foundation for a community whose social structures have fallen, whose authority figures have been confounded, and whose theological world has been shattered (Carroll 1989, 99). The written word fills the symbolic gap created by the loss of Judah's preexilic world. Unlike all other tangible signs of God's presence—including king, temple, land, *and even prophet*—the word cannot be readily thwarted. It is buoyant and resilient. And even when kings destroy scrolls, others can be made, showing Yahweh's determination not to be silenced. Clements says in regard to Jer 36: "far from destroying the word of God, Jehoiakim's attempt to burn the scroll of Jeremiah's prophecies led only to its acquiring new force and range" (1988, 214). Brueggemann also observes: "God will generate as many scrolls as necessary to override the king's zeal for autonomy" (1998, 353). Despite the destruction of the scroll by the king, God's word endures.

Jeremiah asserts that the written word (the scroll) is the living, enduring, and trustworthy word of God. This word, and the God whose unrestrained and intrusive identity it renders, not only nullifies self-serving structures but also gives birth to a countercommunity in a faraway country. It is no accident that the final words of Jeremiah are not the spoken words of Jeremiah; they are the "written words" of Jeremiah, which *Seraiah* is to read in Babylon (51:59-64). Henceforth, the Jewish exiles begin to be people of the scroll/book.

God's Sovereignty

The declaration that Yahweh reigns is one of the dominant faith claims in Jeremiah. While the book bears witness to a wide range of metaphorical constructions, the affirmation that "[Yahweh] reigns" functions as a core metaphor. To some degree, most other assertions about God are rooted in this metaphor. From beginning to end, the book of Jeremiah affirms God's sovereign rule in the world. In a geopolitical milieu in which nations resort to raw force, the text claims that no realm lies outside God's sphere of influence. Despite instability, moral uncertainty, and an assortment of dangerous forces, God is still ordering and governing the world with the intent to accomplish God's purposes. For Jeremiah God's dynamic sovereignty is administered primarily in acts of judgment and salvation in history. Overall, the present architecture of Jeremiah testifies to God's activity as judge (in chs. 1–25) and God's involvement as savior (in chs. 26–52). Put differently, Jeremiah as a whole envisages the "uncreation" and "recreation" of Judah as direct expressions of Yahweh's sovereign activity in the world.

The texts that surround part one of the prophetic drama, Jer 1 and Jer 25, set the stage for Yahweh's sovereign program. Yahweh's program will involve cosmic destruction from which the people of God will not escape. In fact, Judah is the target of divine judgment and therefore must brace itself to face a God who derides his adversaries and judges justly. In the intervening chapters, the first five acts of the drama, Yahweh does battle with Judah over its idolatrous loyalties and trusted support systems. The nation's core values and tenets, including its approaches to worship, are deemed "false" or "deceitful" because they usurp the role of one who expects undivided devotion. No belief system or alliance with worldly modes of power can provide sanctuary from a sovereign God who directs history and abolishes rival forces.

In Jer 26–52 we continue to see the dynamic sovereignty of God administered in the activity of judgment upon Judah and the nations. Jeremiah asserts that Babylonian rule is a facet of Yahweh's sovereign program in the world (Jer 27–29). Nebuchadnezzar is Yahweh's servant, his vassal, and his instrument of destruction. The siege of the "city and its shrine" by the Babylonian armies in Jer 37–41 fulfills God's plan. However, God's program also involves hope and mercy. "For surely I know the plans I have for you, says the LORD, plans for your welfare and not for harm, to give you a future with hope" (29:11). Yahweh offers beleaguered Judah a second chance. Even more, in a grand display of power, Yahweh will reverse Israel's bad fortunes and create something that transcends all previous theological and social arrangements. Yahweh will intervene to save and deliver (see 30:1–33:26). Thus, a new day will dawn for those who have had more than their share of disappointments.

The final section of Jeremiah (in the Masoretic Text) pulsates with conviction that Yahweh rules the world despite the raging nations (Jer 46–51). In the Oracles Against the Nations, several prominent images of dynamic sovereignty converge: Yahweh appears as judge, warrior, and deliverer. While Yahweh engages in a massive assault against Judah in the first scroll, now Yahweh declares war on the contemptuous and arrogant nations. Yahweh, the king (46:18; 48:15; 51:57) overturns every power that opposes his rule (see e.g., 46:17, 23; 48:7, 13, 14, 17, 18; 48:29; 49:4, 16, 31). As part of Judah's liturgical imagination, the Oracles Against the Nations announce that Yahweh puts down those who practice the politics of force and lifts up those who have suffered under its tyranny. As warrior-king Yahweh destabilizes raw military-political power and establishes a just moral order in its place.

This leveling of the field under the sovereign rule of God demands the overthrow of the Babylonian Empire (Jer 50–51). Yahweh's decisive action against Babylon concerns the punishment of a rebellious vassal. The king of Babylon is a belligerent, power-driven, and vicious ruler. Since Yahweh's just rule requires an assessment of all who would usurp Yahweh's role as king, Babylon's recalcitrance must be punished. Therefore, the same God who authorized Babylonian rule tames and subjugates it. The text is unequivocal: the Lord reigns! As Brueggemann observes, Yahweh is "the real king. The others, including Nebuchadnezzar, have been transitory pretenders. History in the empire is bent irresistibly toward the undiminished rule of Yahweh" (1998, 483).

Theodicy in Light of National Tragedy

Jeremiah is a book about suffering. Every claim that God rules and every construction of hope is somehow related to cosmic destruction. Much of the book's literary landscape anticipates and then depicts the terrible experience of a nation going down in ruins. The prophet, too, experiences unspeakable hardship. Even God is beset by pain in the book. All God's acts are entrenched in suffering. This harsh and perilous environment, in which Judah, Jeremiah, and Yahweh are partners in grief, evokes existential quandaries about life, death, and justice. Who is to blame for the mounds of rubble in Jerusalem? Does the defeat of Judah signal the impotence or injustice of Yahweh? Has God abandoned Israel or reneged on past promises? Is the loss of life, the devastation to families, and the widespread violence possible in a morally meaningful world? The book of Jeremiah is, in many respects, a rich and multifaceted response to these questions, and as such represents a thick theological interpretation of suffering.

The national disaster and social upheaval of the first decades of the sixth century raised the problem of theodicy. Deriving from the Greek words *theos* and *dike* ("God" and "justice" respectively), the word "theodicy" means to justify the ways of God in the face of suffering. Theodicy is an attempt to place suffering and evil within a framework of meaning. In addition to materials from ancient Egypt and Mesopotamia (e.g., "The Protests of the Eloquent Peasant," "Atrahasis," "I Will Praise the Lord of Wisdom," and "A Dialogue About Human Misery") there are numerous sections of the Bible devoted to theodicy. One thinks of Job, Psalm 73, Habakkuk, the Deuteronomistic History, and the Passion Narratives in the Gospels, to name only a few. In this literature one finds a surplus of responses to and understandings of moral chaos. Suffering is disciplinary and pedagogical; it reveals genuine faith and can be redemptive, and even vicarious, suffering is punishment, catharsis, or even a mystery. Unlike most other writings in the Bible which make great efforts in constructing *one* well-defined and carefully formulated theology of suffering (e.g., Deuteronomy), Jeremiah appears as a polyvalent theodicy. It comprises an array of voices and points of views, each attempting to come to terms with tragic events that defy ordinary understandings.

The conflicting responses to suffering in Jeremiah generally fall under one of two categories: the first maintains that the universe is orderly and congruent, moral and stable, and exacts punishment on wrongdoers; the second raises questions regarding the character of God and the morality of the universe. Influenced to a large measure by Deuteronomic theology, the prose sermons most clearly articulate the former perspective. These prose pieces, buttressed by their poetic context in Jer 1–25, assume that Judah's political and social devastation is a direct consequence of its own unjust actions. Yahweh warned Israel by "[his] servants the prophets" to turn from their evil ways and keep his commandments; but Israel rejected this message, and therefore Yahweh brought judgment upon his people (see, e.g., Jer 7:25-34; 25:4-11; 26:4-6; 29:17-19; 44:4-6; cf. 2 Kgs 17:13-18). Consequently, the destruction of Jerusalem and the exile to Babylon do not impugn the integrity of God. God is neither impotent nor unjust, but has only acted in accordance with God's revealed will. Next to these orderly arrangements, one finds a theodicy of protest that is far more comfortable with ambiguity and moral dissonance. Those engaged in this "anti-theodicy" are less inclined to exonerate God of responsibility for human suffering and are more open to the possibility of innocent suffering. Belonging to this category are the confessions of Jeremiah and also the portions of the book that depict the prophet's persecution at the hands of enemies.

The prayers of Jeremiah and the depiction of his suffering contribute to the construction of a theodicy of protest. In the laments (or confessions), Jeremiah lashes out over the injustice in the world and God's apparent silence (11:18–12:6; 15:10-21; 20:7-18). The narratives of the prophet's persecution (e.g., Jer 37–44) depict a world that is hostile and replete with innocent suffering. Jeremiah's mistreatment undermines a retributive view of life with clear-cut rewards and punishments. In fact, Jeremiah not only suffers innocently, but he suffers *because* of his obedience to God; that is, he suffers for God's sake. Instead of bringing peace and repose, the prophet's devotion to God wrecks havoc on his life.

From the time he was called to prophetic service until his exile in Egypt, Jeremiah's fidelity results in nothing but pain and hardship. Thus, the portrait of Jeremiah, as a suffering servant of God, affirms that the relationship between acts and consequences is not neat and predicable. Suffering is at times a consequence of obedience, rather than disobedience. In this manner, the beleaguered prophet becomes a symbol of hope for all oppressed and innocent (Jerusalemite) people whose affliction can now be perceived as evidence of their piety (see Matt 5:11-12; Luke 6:20-26).

Admittedly, there is a strong tendency in the present form of the book of Jeremiah to use his suffering and prayers of protest to reinforce symmetrical moral categories. The rejection and harsh treatment of Jeremiah serve to demonstrate the guilt of Judah. Judah deserves divine judgment because it rejects Yahweh and the words of Yahweh's messenger Jeremiah. Such an interpretive strategy, however, is only partially successful in that it does not totally blanket the cries of the prophet and those he represents. Thus, both theodicy and anti-theodicy strands in the book create a rich theological tension.

Jeremiah as a Model of Faithful Living

Jeremiah functions in his book as an archetypal or representative figure. In the Joban tradition, Jeremiah becomes a larger-than-life individual whose experiences and piety transcend his own solitary world. As such, he not only speaks for God, articulating the disappointment and vulnerability of Yahweh, but also embodies a new spirituality and ethic for future generations of readers/listeners. Jeremiah's obedience, his devotion to God, and his life of prayer all take on paradigmatic force. His suffering service and surrender to God in defeat and utter trust, as well as his solidarity with the community and with the oppressed in particular, become facets of faithful living.

Most important, the literature portrays Jeremiah as a servant of God and exemplary righteous sufferer. As a suffering servant whose very life embodies God's message, Jeremiah finds himself in a place of extreme vulnerability. His social environment is harsh and dangerous with few structures in place to protect him. He endures great hardship at the hands of his enemies; he is ridiculed and cries to Yahweh for help. He faces scorn, abject humiliation, and reproach. The opponents of the prophet threaten to kill him unless he abandons his prophetic mission (11:18-23). They conspire against him (18:18-23; cf. 11:9) and dig pits to trap him (18:22). Those who pursue Jeremiah attempt to "prevail" over him (20:7-13), they bar him from the temple precincts (36:5), and eventually arrest and imprison him (20:1-6; 37:11-16). This lack of protection and moral symmetry results in anxiety and sorrow, so much so that Jeremiah longs for death (20:14-18). Yet, like Job and the embattled psalmists, in the face of adversity and persecution Jeremiah declares his innocence, maintains his personal/ prophetic integrity, and takes an active stance against oppressors and evildoers (11:20; 12:3; 15:15; 17:18; 18:21-22; 20:12). His life is never easy, and is certainly never without conflict.

As one who suffers in solidarity with God and those deprived of justice, Jeremiah gives voice to a radically new understanding of suffering. Suffering is not a shameful consequence of wrongdoing or evidence of divine injustice. In the body of Jeremiah suffering becomes a witness of faithful service to God (von Rad 1983, 88-99). In the prophet's pleas for justice and in his cries of protests, Jeremiah aligns himself with the poor and oppressed. His scandalous confessions *speak for* the alien, the orphan, and the widow, as well as for women and men whose innocent blood has been shed (7:6). By doing so, Jeremiah becomes a symbol of hope for those whose suffering is inexplicable or borne in obedience to God.

COMMENTARY
BOOK ONE: JEREMIAH 1–25

DISMANTLING JUDAH'S SOCIAL
AND SYMBOLIC WORLDS

THE CALL OF JEREMIAH AS PROPHET
TO THE NATIONS (JEREMIAH 1)

The first chapter of Jeremiah does not appear in its present position by accident. Jeremiah 1 provides a literary overview and programmatic introduction to the entire book. Its three major parts—a superscription (1:1-3), the call of Jeremiah proper (1:4-10), and related vision reports (1:11-19)—operate as an interpretive guide that helps the reader negotiate the many difficult twists and turns in this untidy prophetic work.

Literary Analysis

Like almost every prophetic collection in the Bible, Jeremiah begins with an editorial heading that introduces the speaker or supposed writer, his family, and situational context (1:1-3). Modern readers often dismiss these beginnings as inconsequential. To do so, however, risks missing interpretive clues for understanding the present shape of the work and how the material functioned as a sacred text for historical Israel. Beyond introducing Jeremiah son of Hilkiah from the village of Anathoth, the superscription makes the astonishing claim that God authorizes the words that follow. The book of Jeremiah is thus no mere human artifact but a collage of oracles, stories, and prayers with transcendent claims.

At the same time, the editorial heading anchors this literature to ordinary human categories. The divine message bursts into space and time at a particular moment in history: "the word of the LORD came in the days of King Josiah . . . in the thirteenth year of his reign . . . until the captivity of Jerusalem in the fifth month." Yahweh's utterance is culture-specific; it is geographic and is not disengaged from history, the arena of God's redemptive activity. To universalize the particular is to read against the grain of the text. Local contexts and real-life situations are the playing fields of the divine-human drama and the proper context for interpretation. The paradox of this prophetic speech is that it is both beyond history and rooted in history. Specifically, "the words of Jeremiah," a phrase that opens and closes the collection in 1:1 and 51:63, are nothing less than "the word of Yahweh" or sacred scripture (1:2).

Jeremiah is one of only two prophetic books that opens with the genesis of the prophet's activity (see also Ezek 1–3; cf. more obliquely Hos 1–3). The beginning of Jeremiah's prophetic career appears in the form of an "autobiographical" account of his call. The dialogue between Jeremiah and Yahweh divides into two parts: the call of Jeremiah proper, mostly in poetry (1:4-10) and two supporting vision reports written in prose (1:11-19).

The call of Jeremiah follows a literary pattern (Exod 3; Isa 6; Ezek 1–3; Judg 6:11-18) involving a divine encounter (Jer 1:4), a word of identification (Jer 1:5*a*), the commission (Jer 1:5*b*), an objection (Jer 1:6) followed by divine reassurance (Jer 1:7-8) and a sign (Jer 1:9-10; see also vv. 11-13) (Habel 1965, 297-323). This conventional genre functions as *textual* validation of the *written* words of Jeremiah. From the outset, the call account represents Jeremiah as a genuine prophet sent by God to speak God's words to the nations. The source of Jeremiah's speech is, therefore, neither the Jerusalemite establishment nor antiestablishment structures, or any other human agency. God authorizes Jeremiah to present in word and deed a harsh critique of Judah and the nations. Given the plethora of competing ideologies in the book, an assertion regarding Jeremiah's authority is critical.

The prose section that follows contains two visionary reports supporting the call of Jeremiah (1:11-19). As is customary in the book, prose material clarifies and elaborates poetry that precedes it. In this instance, the vision experiences underscore Yahweh's resolve to fulfill the divine word amid cosmic shaking. In particular, the text prepares Jeremiah for fierce battles and assures him of God's faithfulness throughout the upheaval.

The call and supporting vision reports together introduce salient aspects of the book. In the most elementary way, we meet its main characters, Yahweh and Jeremiah, whose presence and interplay are essential for the accomplishment of the divine program on earth. We also encounter the text's dominant themes in cryptic form: a "prophet like Moses" proclaiming the word of Yahweh (1:4-10), the utter reliability of this word (1:11-13), its rejection and the resultant dismantling of Judean life by an enemy from the north (1:14-16), a war waged against Jeremiah by the upper-tiers of the social hierarchy (1:17-18), and the cryptic hope of salvation while social and symbolic supports collapse (1:19). Chapter 1 is thus a thematic microcosm of the entire collection.

Exegetical Analysis

"Historical" Introduction (1:1-3)

The superscription of Jeremiah introduces the book as a literary unity despite its complex origins and miscellaneous character (1:1-3). Its major divisions—chapters 1–25 and chapters 26–52—create a unified "scroll." The superscription ascribes this scroll to Jeremiah. The designation "the words of Jeremiah son of Hilkiah" is significant. It represents the book as the product of a single individual. Apparently the incongruities that beset modern readers do not trouble the early framers. They attribute the multiple voices of the text to the prophet Jeremiah. Later developments are thereby not secondary or inauthentic accretions but are part of a rich reservoir of interpretations and reinterpretations, subsumed under the heading "the words of Jeremiah son of Hilkiah."

Jeremiah's association with a small village several miles from Jerusalem suggests that the lead character of the book is an outsider to the Jerusalem establishment and its recognized clergy. The writer of 1 Kings records that when Solomon consolidated his reign in the tenth century, he banished the treasonous Abiathar to

Anathoth and authorized his rival Zadok as the legitimate family of priests in Jerusalem. Jeremiah's hometown thus implies a fringe and disenfranchised social location. The prophet is not a member of the guild. Nor is he a part of mainstream urban life. Jeremiah is simply an ordinary person with familial and social liabilities. This peripheral role, however, does not prevent Jeremiah from challenging the truth claims and repressive politics of the urban elite. Though uncredentialed, he confronts Judah's power brokers and shatters their entrenched assumptions. His insubordination to state rule creates anxiety and hostility in those well placed in the franchise. The prophet's refusal to knuckle under evokes bitter opposition and earns him the label of communal pariah.

The reference to the "thirteenth year of [King Josiah]" (627) and "the eleventh year of King Zedekiah . . . the captivity of Jerusalem in the fifth month" (587) constitutes the temporal boundaries of Jeremiah. These forty years were the final years of statehood. During Josiah's reign, Judah's well-established systems of governance and piety were still in place. The monarchy was strong, the temple was reformed, the monopoly of the Jerusalem establishment was intact, and foreign forces were held at bay. The nation was robust and stout. But this would soon change. Throughout the reigns of Josiah's successors, Jehoiakim (609–598) and Zedekiah (598–587), Judah would come under attack from within and without, its social and political worlds would unravel, its culture would falter, and its belief systems would come unglued. *Creation would return to chaos.* The massive breakdown culminates in the "captivity of Jerusalem," which symbolizes the nation's last stand. Although segments of the book come from a period later than 587 (Jer 42–44; 52:31-34), the dark cloud of exile leaves its shadow over every word and event. The exile's shocking, perplexing, and disorienting memory shrouds all reality. The "captivity of Jerusalem" represents the defining moment of the book.

The Call of Jeremiah (1:4-10)

This ominous background sets the stage for the call of Jeremiah. The call narrative presents itself as a conversation between

Yahweh and Jeremiah. Yahweh is the one who immediately takes the initiative. The Lord "chooses" Jeremiah before birth, "sets him apart," and "appoints" him "a prophet to the nations." This language of election is well-attested to in the Bible. For example, the "Servant of the Lord" in Isa 40–55 is "formed in the womb" (Isa 44:2, 24) and called before birth (Isa 49:1). Moses, whom God knows by name, is "made/appointed to be" like god to the pharaoh (Exod 7:1). The people of Israel are "known" or "chosen" by God (Hos 13:5; Amos 3:2). And priests are customarily "set apart" or "consecrated" for sacred tasks and sacred places. Using similar words, Paul defends his apostolic vocation by asserting that God had "set him apart" before he was born and called him through grace (Gal 1:15).

Like other great figures in the scriptures, Jeremiah shrinks at the prospect of divine service. "Ah Lord GOD! Truly I do not know how to speak, for I am only a boy" (1:6). Jeremiah's shortcomings and self-doubt haunt him. He insists that he is too young and inexperienced to address the nations. His hesitation is reminiscent of two heroic figures: Moses and Solomon. When confronted with the huge responsibility of governing Israel, Solomon acknowledges that he is only a "young man" who "does not know how to go out or come in" (1 Kgs 3:7). Described as a "child" himself (Exod 2:7), Moses maintains that he is not "eloquent . . . but slow of speech and slow of tongue" (Exod 4:10). Together with those who went before him, Jeremiah merely acknowledges his inability to fulfill the divine mandate, which is an appropriate response to God's beckoning.

God immediately quells Jeremiah's fears. Jeremiah need not be afraid because God promises to protect and go with him. "Do not be afraid of them, for I am with you to deliver you, says the LORD" (1:8). Although this exact construction occurs primarily in Jeremiah, these words of assurance are far from unusual. Yahweh promises to be near many who find themselves debilitated by fears and uncertainties (e.g., Gen 31:3; Exod 3:12; 19:9; 33:14; Josh 1:5, 9; Judg 6:12, 16). Accompanying God's promise to Jeremiah is the assurance of deliverance, which calls to mind God's liberation of Israel from Egyptian bondage (see Exod 3:8; 5:23; 6:6;

12:27; 18:4; 1 Sam 10:18). As God delivered an oppressed and dispirited people from slavery, so God will rescue a reluctant and conflicted prophet from his enemies.

The Lord then touches Jeremiah's timid mouth, consecrating and empowering him for the task at hand (1:9). When God calls, God empowers. When God demands, God provides the resources to accomplish the assignment. The language here is significant in several accounts. First, the word placed in Jeremiah's mouth by God serves as a sign demonstrating the divine authority of the book. Again, the text claims that God authorizes the words that follow. Second, it casts Jeremiah in a Mosaic mold. The pledge "now I have put my words in your mouth" (1:9b) harkens back to the promise made to the "prophet like Moses" (Deut 18:18). The new Moses will be a "prophet . . . from among [his] own kin" in whose mouth God "puts [God's] word" and "who shall speak to them everything that I command" (Deut 18:18). The text intimates that Jeremiah is this figure. Like the first Moses who led the people of Israel out of Egypt to the promised land, so Jeremiah, the second Moses, will straddle two worlds, a country behind him and a country ahead of him. The new Moses will pronounce the death of one world and the birth of another.

Commissioned and equipped for his prophetic task, Jeremiah is now privy to God's work on earth. God appoints Jeremiah as a prophet "over nations and over kingdoms, to pluck up and to pull down . . . and to build and to plant" (1:10). This mission not only summarizes the major themes of Jeremiah but it also shapes the major contours of the book. Jeremiah 1–25 highlights the dangerous work of dismantling Judah's civic, cultural, and religious life, while 26–52 moves toward "building and planting." The first part of Jeremiah is a script for demolition, whereas the second begins to map out a new world beyond the cessation of the old one. Jeremiah 1:10 is thus the motto of Jeremiah.

Supporting Vision Reports (1:11-19)

Two vision reports support and embellish the call of Jeremiah. In the first report Jeremiah sees a "branch of an almond [watching] tree" *(šāqēd)*. God assures Jeremiah that he will "watch over" *(šōqēd)* the word and eventually fulfill it (1:11-12). This "word" will perplex, disturb, and eventually transform the interior of Judah's social and religious life (cf. Heb 4:12-13). It will subvert political agendas, economic forces, and social conventions in order to accomplish its purposes. Yahweh will see to this. Next Jeremiah observes a boiling pot tipping over from the north, foreshadowing dangerous forces that will descend upon Jerusalem in a dreaded military assault (1:13-16). This alien horde will "set their thrones at the entrance of the gates of Jerusalem, against all its surrounding walls and against all the cities of Judah" (1:15). The identity of these forces is unspecified. Their attack, however, will be no mere geopolitical incursion but a divine offensive against a nation in revolt. Yahweh warns Jeremiah that he too must prepare for a formidable battle. However, unlike Judah, his enemies originate from inside the boundaries. The established social and religious hierarchy—the power brokers of the state— will wage combat against him (1:17-19). Though they rise up against Jeremiah, they will not prevail, for Yahweh will be with him and will deliver him.

Theological and Ethical Analysis

Chapter 1 introduces Jeremiah's inaugural encounter with Yahweh as the "[coming of the word of the Lord]" (1:4, 11, 13), a formula customarily reserved for prophetic oracles. The autobiographical call narrative apparently places the "personal" in the "public eye" and affords the prophetic persona a status comparable to that of prophetic speech. Henceforth Jeremiah's experience and mission will transcend his individual existence. His private life, his struggles, prayers, persecution and rejection, and his call— all that creates the prophetic persona—are brought into *public* scrutiny and in the purview of the listening community. Conventional distinctions between the prophetic word and the prophetic life collapse. In this prophetic drama, the synergy of message and messenger generates the dynamic word of Yahweh. As Abraham Heschel has argued, the prophet is no mere instrument or mouthpiece, no disengaged messenger of God (2001, 30). Jeremiah is a partner or an associate whose entire being embodies

God's work on earth (2001, 30-31). As such, the words of Jeremiah together with his screams of protest, rejection, and suffering body bear witness to the divine program for the nations.

Jeremiah appears as a larger-than-life figure in another way. In the opening chapter of the book, a symbiotic relationship between the life and destiny of Jeremiah and Judah begins to take shape. Jeremiah is on a course that corresponds to, contrasts with, and at times intersects that of the community. God calls the prophet and promises to save him; subsequently, God calls and promises to save the nation. The prophet is told that he will suffer the shattering of a world and yet come through the desolation as a wounded survivor. Likewise, the nation will experience the death of a world, which it will survive. In this way, Jeremiah mirrors and fully participates in the fate of his countrymen. The persona of Jeremiah, however, not only parallels Judah but also counters it. The prophet emerges as foil character whose conflicted obedience accentuates the nation's unambiguous disobedience. Whereas Judah and Jerusalem eventually decline God's many gracious invitations, Jeremiah reluctantly accepts God's call. Whereas Judah and Jerusalem cast their lot with other gods, Jeremiah casts his with Yahweh. In due course the obedient prophet will supplant the disobedient nation. God will transform a timid prophet into a "fortified city, an iron pillar, and a bronze wall" (1:18). In lieu of one "fortified city" (Jerusalem) going down in ruin, Jeremiah will develop into a "surrogate" city (Nasuti 1987, 258-62). Jeremiah represents one of the faithful who will form a new community of faith.

The call narrative is less concerned with actual personal experiences than theological construction. The text renders a quite particular theological world when it portrays the two major players: God and Jeremiah. As the divine-human drama opens, we encounter a God who is intimately involved in human affairs. God "forms from the womb," "knows," "consecrates," and "appoints" (1:5). In the face of fear and looming opposition, God promises to protect, defend, empower, and support (1:8, 11-13, 19). But God does not choose Jeremiah for Jeremiah's sake. God appoints Jeremiah for the sake of the world. Indeed, Jeremiah's mission as "prophet to the nations" signals God's profound concern for a wayward and rebellious world (see also Jer 46–51). Thus we meet in this first chapter a God whose interests reach far beyond the borders of any single nation (see esp. Jer 46–51).

The theological portrait of Jeremiah, God's messenger, is no less engaging. The text depicts Jeremiah as a conflicted character (Brueggemann 1986, 10-31). Though chosen for a global mission, he is uncertain about his abilities and standing in the community. Such ambivalence, however, does not disqualify him from service. On the contrary, the prophet's humanity becomes the arena for the power of God (cf. 2 Cor 12:10). In the company of Moses, Gideon, David, and others who recognize their inability to fulfill the divine charge, Jeremiah must rely on the sufficiency of God and the penetrating character of his call. Such a portrait inverts conventional categories of power. When the crossfire of the great empires on the Tigris-Euphrates and the Nile brings Judah to its knees, God sends *a weak and conflicted prophet* to help the people of Judah through their turbulent times. God does not choose a strong and self-confident person for the job, but one whose weakness and doubt to some degree paralyze him. And yet at the end of the day, this weak and conflicted prophet confounds the strong and proud. Human frailty leaves an indelible mark on the book.

DIVINE GRIEF TURNED TO RAGE (JEREMIAH 2–6)

The initial literary unit of Jeremiah (Jer 2–6) divides neatly into two sections: 2:1–4:4 and 4:5–6:30. The first describes the relationship between Yahweh and Israel as a marriage that gets off to a wonderful start but ends in bitter divorce. The second represents divine love turning to rage after repeated infidelities. Together the two sections establish the theological foundation for Jer 1–25, which is a prophetic drama of divine dismantling. By deploying a wide range of metaphors, literary motifs, and genres, these opening chapters attempt to make sense of Judah's national catastrophe. They contend that the events about to befall the nation are no accident or consequence of geopolitical power plays. Nor are they a result of divine impotence or capriciousness. The approaching dissolution of well-established institutions, belief systems, and social structures are the outcome of Judah's rebellion and idolatry. Judah, not Yahweh, is responsible for the unraveling.

ISRAEL AS PROMISCUOUS SPOUSE AND YAHWEH AS DEVASTATED LOVER (JEREMIAH 2:1–4:4)

Literary Analysis

Jeremiah 2:1–4:4 begins with memories of a good marriage that turns sour. Long ago Yahweh and Israel were deeply in love (2:1-3), but Israel rejected Yahweh's affection and ran off after other lovers. Such rejection sets in motion a wide range of impassioned responses. To begin, Yahweh brings a long list of charges against his wayward and unfaithful spouse. The wounded lover takes Israel to court on grounds of infidelity (2:4-13). Next Yahweh contends that Israel's current troubles are a direct consequence of persistent rebellion (2:14-19). Israel seeks help from Egypt and Assyria rather than Yahweh. An in-depth probe unearths even greater wrongdoing and culpability (2:20-28). Israel is like a stubborn beast, a wild vine, a restive young camel, a thief caught in the act, and a nymphomaniac. Despite protests of innocence, Yahweh's charges against Israel stick and judgment ensues. The warring parties find themselves estranged (2:29-37) and eventually in divorce court (3:1).

The rest of the section is difficult to read because of its jumbled character (Jer 3:1–4:4). The disjointed text reflects both a complex history of composition and the anguish of grief. The presence of prose and poetry, the plurality of voices, the intermingling of feminine and masculine imagery, and the sudden shifts in themes suggest a long and complicated literary development. Apparently, many hands were involved in the production of this text. Later writers comment on the text by filling in literary gaps and by clarifying and elaborating existing materials. They echo and enunciate ideas; they tame dissonant voices, as well as disturb safe and symmetrical subtexts. Kathleen O'Connor refers to the conversational quality of the text as a "colloquy of voices" (2001), Mark Biddle as a "symphony" (1996), and Robert Carroll as a "cacophony" (1986).

The chaotic character of the text is also rooted in the dominant metaphor of a spurned lover. Similar to the portrayal of God in Hosea, Yahweh is beside himself in sorrow and so responds to the nation's betrayal as a distraught lover. Pulsating with passion and throbbing with pain, God longs for reunion and embrace, extending to Judah multiple invitations to return. At the same time, God lashes out in anger and vengeance. Hope and disappointment, shame and punishment, and blame and forgiveness are all expressions of divine grief in the face of rejection. And expressions of grief are hardly ever well organized.

Scathing accusations fly in Jer 3:1–4:4. Divorce proceedings establish Israel's guilt beyond question (3:1-5). The nation has engaged in the worst sort of infractions of the religious order. Yahweh tells a sad story of two faithless sisters, Israel and Judah, who have broken their marriage vows and refused to return to their spouses (3:6-14). Judah's indifference to her sister's idolatry makes her guiltier than Israel. Interrupting this biting tone, Yahweh imagines a time when all will be right (3:15-18). One day the house of Judah and Israel will unite under faithful shepherds. For now, however, Yahweh is distraught over the ingratitude of his lover, both as a prodigal child and as an adulterous spouse (both metaphors are used in 3:19-21). They have perverted their way and forgotten their God. Still Yahweh holds out for reconciliation, puts words of repentance in Israel's mouth (3:22-25), and extends additional invitations to "return" home (4:1-4).

At the core of the broken marriage-rejected lover metaphor is the word "return" or "turn" *(šûb)*. This word appears fifteen times in Jer 3:1–4:4. The NRSV translates *šûb* and its related forms as "return," "faithless" (one who "turns" away), and "faithlessness" (the state of "turning away"). As a scorned lover who is tormented by the nation's fleeting affections and promiscuous lifestyle, Yahweh pleads with his wanton wife/children to come home (3:14, 22; 4:1). "Return, O faithless children, I will heal your faithlessness" (3:22; cf. Hos 14:4). Intoxicated with remorse and despite legal prohibitions (3:1), Yahweh invites wayward Israel to return to her first love and enjoy the blessings of the ancestral promises. "If you return, O Israel, says the LORD, if you return to me . . . then nations shall be blessed by him, and by him they shall boast" (4:1-2). The divine outbursts of anxiety and anger, appeal and accusation, and wrath and compassion all express the interior life of God, which is defined by passionate love and longing for reconciliation. By the end of the section, Israel's reply to Yahweh's many invitations remains indecisive.

Exegetical Analysis

The Prelude: A Happy Marriage (2:1-3)

In the opening scene, God remembers and revels in Israel's faithful beginnings. Long ago Israel was Yahweh's devoted bride. With simplicity of heart she showed unrestrained affection for her lover. Israel followed her covenant partner in the dangerous "wilderness, in a land not sown," and Yahweh protected his beloved from harm. In those early days Israel was "set apart" for Yahweh alone. Just as the firstfruits of harvest belonged to Yahweh (Exod 23:19; Lev 23:9-11), so Israel was Yahweh's special people. The two belonged together and nothing could weaken their relationship. This idyllic love-poem ends abruptly. It is only nostalgia. The fleeting memory of betrothal reveals what could have and should have been but was not. It is a story of lost love. The marriage is over. Distant memories of joy and intimacy arouse sorrow, for now Israel is unfaithful and rebellious. Only in the distant past does Israel love Yahweh. In the present, such devotion is altogether absent. Yahweh yearns for Israel's affection, but Israel refuses to render it. Instead, Israel "went after worthless things" (2:5), "things that do not profit" (2:8), "the Baals" (2:23), and "other gods" (e.g., 7:6, 9; 11:10; 16:11), but no longer Yahweh.

Yahweh Takes Israel to Court (2:4-13)

The bittersweet love-poem is the point of departure for a lawsuit oracle in which Yahweh takes Israel to court for infidelity. The proceedings begin with a declaration of innocence. Yahweh has been a faithful covenant partner. God's gracious acts on Israel's behalf dispel any hint of wrongdoing. Devoted without reserve, Yahweh delivered Israel from the land of Egypt, guided them through the wilderness, and brought them to place of bounty. Israel, on the other hand, shows nothing but disdain for Yahweh's kindness. The people turn away from Yahweh and pursue "worthless things" (2:5). Suffering from amnesia and callous indifference, Israel dismisses the story of divine love. Neither people nor priest cares enough to ask, "Where is the LORD?" (2:6, 8). The repositories of the faith—priest, prophet, and ruler or shepherd—all fail in their sacred duties. Priests who are charged with teaching the Torah (2:8; 18:18) "do not know" Yahweh; the political rulers or shepherds violate the covenant, and the prophets prophesy in the name of Baal rather than Yahweh. The nation's apostasy is systemic and so Yahweh indicts: "Once more I accuse you, says the LORD, and I accuse your children's children" (2:9).

So preposterous are Israel's offenses that they would even astonish foreign peoples from the West (Cyprus) and the East (Kedar). Outsiders know better than to betray their own god. But not Israel! Israel nonchalantly swaps gods. To witness this shocking conduct and to hear the closing statement of the plaintiff, Yahweh invokes the heavens: "Be appalled, O heavens, at this, be shocked, be utterly desolate, says the LORD" (2:12). Israel's unfaithfulness and betrayal leave the ill-treated party hurt and humiliated. The Hebrew word order accents Yahweh as object of Israel's scorn. With emphatic language, Yahweh exclaims, "[Me] they have [abandoned], the fountain of living water . . . for [broken] cisterns that [are unable to hold water]" (2:13).

Israel's Ills Brought On by Unlawful Political Alliances (2:14-19)

In this section, infidelity is still of central interest, although accusations no longer focus on Israel's love affair with other gods but with other nations. Jeremiah insists that Israel's preoccupation with Egypt and Assyria is tantamount to idolatry, a treacherous act of disloyalty against Yahweh. To drive home this point, Yahweh hurls at the nation a battery of disturbing questions.

Is Israel a slave? Is he a homeborn servant?
Why then has he become plunder? (2:14)
Have you not brought this upon yourself
by forsaking the LORD your God,
while he led you in the way? (2:17)
What then do you gain by going to Egypt,
to drink the waters of the Nile?
Or what do you gain by going to Assyria,
to drink the waters of the Euphrates? (2:18)

Each rhetorical question makes the point that Israel has brought on its own troubles by forsaking Yahweh for Egypt and Assyria. Political promiscuity leads to political servitude. Once free and unfettered, Israel now becomes a forlorn slave to the people of Memphis and Tahpanhes. When Israel drinks from "the waters of the Nile . . . [and] the Euphrates" (2:18), it sacrifices its freedom and independence for the sake of security. Like Isaiah of Jerusalem, Jeremiah contends that such alliances are disastrous. To collude with geopolitical power brokers is to sell one's soul.

Such alliances not only compromise Israel's integrity, but they also violate the kind of trust that Yahweh demands of a covenant people. In ancient Near Eastern treaties, suzerains or leaders of major states would demand unwavering trust of their vassals. The great lord in turn would guarantee protection from predatory nations. As is well known, the international treaty form helped to shape Israel's understanding of the Sinai covenant. Yahweh the great suzerain/king expected radical trust and loyalty of vassal Israel. One can hear echoes of this long-standing tradition in Jeremiah's insistence that reliance upon human strength and ingenuity, military and geopolitical coalitions, or any surrogate power structure is both futile and idolatrous. To rely on such forces is to reject the voice of the One for others that only *appear* more efficacious. To trust in Assyria and Egypt is to delude oneself into

believing that raw political power is trustworthy. While such delu-
sions of security may get Israel through the day, they eventually
lead to bondage and irrevocable harm.

Adulterous Israel's Illicit Relationships (2:20-28)

Yahweh tells Israel another story. Whereas the first (2:1-3)
recalls moments of intimacy between Yahweh and Israel, before
the radiant flame of love went out, this story has few good memories. It is a tale of infidelity and rebellion, guilt and ingratitude.
Yahweh's bride has become a harlot and so violates the relationship with her divine spouse. "For long ago you broke your yoke
and burst your bonds, and you said, 'I will not serve!'" (2:20a).
The rich use of metaphors—often erecting metaphor on top of
metaphor—depicts the nation's involvement in unauthorized
and anomalous practices. At the heart of the indictment is the
accusation that Israel has engaged in the worst sort of violations
of its symbolic code, deeds that are punishable by death/divorce
(see ch. 3). Whether Jeremiah is making a veiled condemnation
of Assyrian or Babylonian religious practices or is simply referring to indigenous Canaanite fertility rites is uncertain.
Regardless, native or imported practices that compromise the
people's undivided devotion for Yahweh are the worst kinds of
transgressions.

To portray Israel's apostasy, Jeremiah employs some of the most
provocative and colorful language of the entire book. With satirical wit, the prophet compares faithless Israel to a defiant ox that
insists on bolting away from its master (2:20), a wild and worthless vine that spurted unexpectedly "from the purest stock"
(2:21), and a thief caught in his tracks (2:26). In addition,
Jeremiah depicts Israel as a starved nymphomaniac (2:20, 25,
33-35), a frenzied camel in heat and a wild ass driven crazy with
passion (2:23-24). So deluded is Israel that she embraces inani-
mate stone and tree—the objects of her adoration—as father and
mother (2:27). Underlying the majority of these mocking images
is the metaphor of Israel as a promiscuous consort of God: Israel
has cast off all restraints in brazen harlotry. Not only does she
show contempt for the gracious acts of her divine lover but she

also exhibits no inclination to return home. Even worse, Israel is utterly callous to her folly (2:23, 25).

The metaphor of Israel as promiscuous spouse of Yahweh is an elaboration of the harlotry metaphor found in Hosea. In Hosea, Yahweh's many expressions of loyalty and devotion *(ḥesed)* eventually lead to reconciliation. The restoration of Hosea's adulteress wife symbolizes Israel's hard-earned redemption. In an act of gutsy love, Hosea redeems his unfaithful wife and brings her home to remain with him "for many days" (Hos 3:1-5). Unlike the portrait of Israel in Hosea, Yahweh's unfaithful spouse in Jeremiah remains defiant: "It is [no use], for I have loved strangers, and after them I will go. I am innocent; surely his anger has turned from me. I have not sinned" (2:25, 35). Hence, there is no resolution, no restoration, and no mercy for obdurate Israel this side of judgment. Her many denials and protests of innocence serve only to accentuate her guilt and rebellion.

Evidence to Implicate Israel (2:29-37)

Addressing Israel directly, Yahweh continues to mount a fiery case against Israel. The mistreated divine lover defends himself against false allegations, exposing Israel's charges as bogus. To bring a legal suit against Yahweh, as suggested by the question, "Why do you complain [*rîb*] against me?" (2:29), is nothing more than a smokescreen. To claim that Yahweh is a threat to her existence ("a wilderness . . . or a land of thick darkness," 2:31) is entirely without merit. Israel is the one guilty of sin, not Yahweh. One need only review the evidence. After painstaking efforts on the part of Yahweh to get Israel's attention, the people of God remain rebellious and adverse to correction. They kill the prophets and insist on going their own way. When Israel exclaims, "We are free, we will come to you no more" (2:31), they implicate themselves.

To marshal further evidence against rebellious Israel, Yahweh inquires whether a bride can forget her ornaments and wedding dress. The answer is obvious. Yet, Israel scandalously rejects her bridegroom. "My people have forgotten me, days without number" (2:32). So proficient is Israel in her sexual liaisons that she instructs others in the field (2:33). So deluded is faithless Israel that she declares, "I am innocent . . . I have not sinned" (2:35). Yahweh, however, can produce incontrovertible evidence to the contrary including the blood of the innocent on her skirts (2:34), a dubious confession in her mouth (2:35), and cunning duplicity that will soon lead to her undoing (2:36). The verdict is certain: the nation has violated the essence of the covenant relationship with Yahweh. Israel has lost its way and wandered off to a far-away place, leaving Yahweh rejected and humiliated.

Overall Jer 2:1-37 is a treatise on idolatry. It focuses almost entirely upon Israel's apostasy. The chapter asserts that Israel has violated the first commandment, "You shall have no other gods before me," and thereby placed its relationship with Yahweh in jeopardy. When Israel forsakes Yahweh for other gods and unlawful political alliances, it rejects the One whose voice of love and liberating power transformed an enslaved people into a people of hope. Such blatant infidelity betrays the nation's raison d'être, its very reason for existence. Perhaps the only thing worse than the act of betrayal is the audacity to *forget* the wrongdoing committed. Not to remember is sheer indifference; it trivializes what is forgotten. For Israel to erase Yahweh from its memory is a breach of the first obligation of the community: "Remember the LORD your God." This is why Yahweh cries out in anguish and disappointment: "my people have forgotten me, days without number" (2:32).

The placement of this chapter at the beginning of the book has a certain logic to it. Some argue that the logic is linear and chronological. The material appears in its present position because it embodies the earliest oracles of Jeremiah, perhaps delivered in the years preceding the reform of King Josiah. Whether or not such a historical claim has merit, one can discern a symbolic or thematic logic to the literary organization: Israel's infidelity serves as the compelling opening performance to the prophetic drama. It lays the groundwork for the terrible dismantling that Judah and its capital city Jerusalem would soon endure, especially as told in the first half of the book (Jer 1–25). This initial scene contends that Israel, and not God, is responsible for its dire circumstances. The nation's unabashed idolatry, which is depicted in relational terms as betrayal, is the cause of chaos and loss. In this way, the second chapter serves as an apology for God's justice and as a defense for the moral workings of the universe. Jeremiah 2:1-37 provides the underpinnings for all that follows.

Divorce as Seemingly Inevitable (3:1-5)

A familial law in Deut 24:1-4 is the basis for three rhetorical questions that Yahweh poses to his rebellious spouse Israel/Judah in Jeremiah. The complex statute forbids remarriage to a wife who subsequently marries another man. The ancient law code regards such behavior as reprehensible and destructive to the fabric of community life. To remarry under these types of circumstances is "abhorrent to the LORD . . . and bring(s) guilt on the land . . ." (Deut 24:4).

Jeremiah truncates the old civil law in Deuteronomy and uses it to expose Judah's wrongdoing. Unlike the *twice*-divorced woman in Deuteronomy, Judah has "played the whore with [a *multitude* of] lovers."

> If a man divorces his wife
>   and she goes from him
>   and becomes another man's wife,
>   will he return to her?
> Would not such a land be greatly polluted?
> You have played the whore with many lovers,
> and would you return to me? says the LORD. (Jer 3:1)

The nation's harlotry provides clear grounds for divorce. But it does far more. Judah's love affairs with other gods preclude her reconciliation to Yahweh, her first husband. Fickle Judah and faithful Yahweh must remain apart. Judah can neither return to Yahweh (as the LXX emphasizes) nor can Yahweh return to Judah (as the Hebrew stresses). The sacred code forbids it.

Jeremiah's commentary on the remarriage statute in Deuteronomy introduces a scene in which jealous Yahweh stigmatizes his consort in a court of law. The court scene opens with a statement of the Torah statute: the land would be "greatly polluted" if a twice-married woman returns to her first husband (Jer 3:1). Then Yahweh accuses Israel of breaking the law: "You have played the whore with many lovers. You have polluted the land with your whoring and wickedness" (3:1-2). Next the punishment for the infraction is elucidated: "the showers have been withheld, and the spring rain has not come . . ." (3:3). After this, the prosecutor reiterates Israel's lame defense: "Have you not just now called to me, 'My Father, you are the friend of my youth—will he be angry forever, will he be indignant to the end?'" (3:4-5a). The scene concludes with the prosecutor's rationale for refusing to grant a reprieve: ". . . you have done all the evil that you could [do]" (3:5b). Yahweh thus makes a definitive case against the nation. Israel has committed infractions of the Torah that must be punished. Defense pleas fail to convince the prosecution that Israel is innocent. There is no way out. However, as the drama unfolds, we discover that the dissolution of the covenant relationship is only a means to an end. The accusation against unfaithful Judah grows out of longing for reunion, not out of malice or retribution. This is apparent in the next discourse where Yahweh/husband risks "humiliation and defilement" (Brueggemann 1998, 43) and begs defiant Judah to come home.

Divorce Reconsidered (3:6-14)

Using Jer 3:1-5 and its underlying text Deut 24:1-4 as the point of departure, Jer 3:6-14 further develops the broken marriage metaphor. Instead of a public forum to call attention to Judah's illicit acts, Yahweh now confers in private with his confidant, Jeremiah (3:6). Yahweh tells Jeremiah the heartbreaking story of Israel's betrayal and infidelity. Israel, Judah's faithless sister, has "played the [harlot]" (3:6) "on every high hill and under every green tree." After she had engaged in such activities, the Lord had hoped for reconciliation but was sorely disappointed (3:7). Israel refused to "return" (šûb) to him. So Yahweh "sent her away with a decree of divorce" (3:8).

Then Yahweh informs the prophet that all along Judah has been aware of the divorce proceedings but has shown total disregard for the parabolic lesson. "Her [faithless] sister Judah did not fear, but she too went and played the whore. Because she took her whoredom so lightly, she [Judah] polluted the land, committing adultery with stone and tree" (3:8-9). Judah's callous indifference is paramount to collusion. Her halfhearted and duplicitous response (3:10; a return "in pretense") betrays a flagrant disregard for Yahweh's gracious pleas. Thus, she is guiltier than faithless Israel and her condition is more grave.

Jeremiah 3:6-14 exploits the broken-marriage metaphor in still one other way. Whereas Jer 3:1-5 stresses the absolute *prohibition of remarriage* of the first husband to his twice-divorced wife, Jer 3:6-14 emphasizes *the possibility of eventual reconciliation.* Unexpectedly Yahweh reconsiders his "decree of divorce" (see Deut 24:1-4) and commands Jeremiah to press fickle Israel to return home (3:11, 14). The invitation is motivated by pure mercy. If Israel returns home and acknowledges its wrongdoing, Yahweh will welcome and embrace with open arms (3:13; 4:1-2). "I will not look on you in anger, for I am merciful" (3:12). The radical change in mood and disposition, while indicative of multiple layers of literary activity, reveals intensity of desire. Israel's infidelity cannot extinguish the flame of God's passionate love.

A Vision of Reunion and Restoration (3:15-18)

Jeremiah 3:15-18, a prose voice in the dialogue which likely originates from the period of Babylonian captivity, seizes the opportunity to imagine a new epoch of hope. In place of rulers/shepherds who disregard the covenant, Yahweh will appoint faithful rulers/shepherds after his "own heart" who will govern "with knowledge and understanding" (3:15). The land parched with drought (3:3) will once again enjoy the ancestral promises of abundance. At that time, those who return to Jerusalem "from the land of the north" will neither mention nor miss "the ark of the covenant of the LORD." The text does not explain the absence of the traditional symbol of divine presence. It simply declares it. Perhaps Jerusalem is so resplendent with the presence of God that traditional forms of worship are rendered unnecessary. Judah/Israel is not alone in this grand celebration. All nations stream to the holy city where Yahweh reigns to bask in the divine presence.

Another Invitation Extended to Israel (3:19–4:4)

Although the tone and subject change abruptly, Jer 3:19–4:4 is still linked to its literary context. First, words form a bridge: "all the nations" (3:17 and 3:19), "children" (3:14 and 3:19), "My Father" (2:27; 3:4, 19), "faithless wife/one" (3:8, 11, 20), "land" (2:7, 31; 3:2, 19), and "return/turn" (3:1, 7, 10, 12, 14, 19; cf. 3:22; 4:1). Jeremiah 3:19-25 apparently draws upon and responds to the language of its immediate literary setting. Second, marital (and parental) metaphors continue to play a crucial role in depicting the divine-human relationship. Yahweh is a faithful husband and Israel is again a shameless spouse. Finally, the conversational character of Jer 3:19–4:4 anticipates the section to follow (4:5–6:30), which resounds with multiple voices.

Three voices emerge in the present dialogue: Yahweh, the narrator, and the children of Israel.

Yahweh laments the people's idolatry (3:19-20)
The Narrator develops Yahweh's accusation against
    Judah (3:21)
Yahweh once more invites his children to return home (3:22*a*)
The Prodigal Children of Israel confess their sin (3:22*b*-25)
Yahweh clarifies the conditions of repentance (4:1-4)

The dialogue begins with Yahweh brooding over his failure to restore Israel (3:19-20). The gift of a "pleasant land, the most beautiful heritage of all the nations," does not produce in Judah the desired results. Yahweh had expected a response of gratitude and devotion, but instead encountered another rejection of generosity. The repetition of the words, "I thought" (3:19) conveys Yahweh's bitter disappointment. Parent/Husband Yahweh suffers the disregard of his children/wife. Even the report of the weeping and pleading of the children of Israel on the bare heights is of little comfort to Yahweh since there is no evidence of true repentance (3:21). They have "perverted their way" and have "forgotten [Yahweh] their God" (3:21). Nonetheless, in sturdy resilience and sheer determination, Yahweh extends another invitation (3:22*a*). Inspired by a passionate longing for reunion,

Yahweh risks everything—abject rejection, indignity, and scandal—to restore the broken relationship.

The conversation then takes a strange turn (3:22b-25). Prodigal Israel unexpectedly heeds God's plea. Instead of continued recalcitrance and indifference, the people admit to the futility of their ways and return to Yahweh. Addressing Yahweh directly, as the expression "the LORD [*our*] God" (321) suggests, their liturgy of repentance includes the following elements:

1. A Recital of Faith (3:22b)
2. A Renunciation of False Loyalties (3:23a)
3. A Profession of Trust (3:23b)
4. An Admission of Sin and Guilt (3:24-25)

By acknowledging that they have sinned since their "youth" (3:25), the people of Israel finally accept Yahweh's position that rebellion and infidelity have soiled their entire history (2:2).

Israel's repentance *appears* to be all that Yahweh has longed for. However, the divine reply in 4:1-4 and Israel's persistent rebellion cast serious doubts on the sincerity of their words. How then should we interpret Israel's contrition? Several explanations are plausible: (1) The text may indicate Israel's actual, albeit momentary or fleeting, change of heart. (2) It may express Israel's duplicitous effort to appease God, an attempt that God flatly rejects when insisting that true repentance ("returning") involves more than words; it requires a radical reorientation of life (4:1-4). (3) The text may intend to taunt a people who have absolutely no inclination to "return" to Yahweh. With stinging satire it sets off and heightens Israel's propensity to go its own way without regard for Yahweh. (4) Israel's repentance may be literary fiction; that is, it may represent Yahweh's imagined words. Yahweh desires reunion with such force that he imagines words of sorrow spoken by his beloved. Still tormented by sadness and disappointment over betrayal, the divine lover retreats into a world of fantasy that replaces the unbearable world of reality. While the rich and generative poetry does not preclude any of these interpretations, the last perhaps produces the most coherent reading of the literature.

Jeremiah 2:1–4:4 ends with two exhortations: the first addresses "Israel" (4:1-2) and the second "the people of Judah and the inhabitants of Jerusalem" (4:3-4). It is telling that the final words of the unit are directed toward the southern kingdom since it has really been the target audience of Jeremiah's words all along. The two exhortations clarify the true conditions of repentance. By drawing on a legal reference (oath taking in 4:1-2), an agricultural image ("break up your fallow ground . . ." in 4:3), and a religious metaphor ("circumcise . . . the foreskin of your hearts" in 4:4), the prophet urges Judah to abandon its tough exterior and preoccupation with idols for an interior life of devotion and sincere obedience. Israel would then reestablish its covenant relationship with God.

English translations of the first exhortation differ significantly (4:1-2). Why do modern translations differ? Because they have (1) made different decisions about their source text (i.e., the Masoretic Text here), (2) arrived at different understandings of the passage, or (3) chosen different expressions to convey their understanding to the modern reader. In the case of Jer 4:1-2, the first reason comes into play most prominently. The Hebrew syntax of the text lends itself to multiple renderings. Specifically, it is difficult to determine where the "if" clauses end and where the "then" clauses begin. That is to say, the conditions and outcomes of repentance blur. The NRSV offers a plausible translation of the problematic text. Israel must meet four conditions, constructed as four consecutive "if" clauses, in order to live as God's people. Israel must return to Yahweh, abandon its worship of other gods, remain firm in its commitment (to Yahweh), and take solemn oaths in Yahweh's name alone. When it meets these conditions, the nations will enjoy divine blessings and exult/boast in God (e.g., Gen 12:1-3; 18:18; 22:18).

The prophet now directly addresses the people of Judah and the inhabitants of Jerusalem (4:3-4). The exhortation is stern and ends with a threat. The writer uses two metaphors in the address. Judah is first to "[plough up] the fallow ground and to not sow among thorns" (4:3). The admonition to "[plough up] your fallow ground" occurs only here and in Hos 10:12. It denotes the need for "break[ing] up" hard rocky soil so that seeds can grow and produce a good harvest. One can discern in this process echoes of Jeremiah's motto: "to pluck up and pull down, to destroy and to overthrow" (Jer 1:10). Yahweh's program of "pluck[ing] up and pull[ing] down" coincides with Judah's task of tilling its hard soil. Divine and human work is a prerequisite for the redemptive program of "build[ing] and plant[ing]." Judah's entrenched world must be torn down and its long-established social and symbolic structures destroyed before new life springs up. Tenderness of heart, docility of spirit, and a commitment to justice and generosity provide the turf for newness.

The second metaphor derives primarily from the realm of ritual. "Circumcise yourselves to the LORD, remove the foreskin of your hearts, O people of Judah and inhabitants of Jerusalem" (4:4). Circumcision was a sign/symbol of Israel's covenant relationship with God. "This is my covenant, which you shall keep, between me and you and your offspring after you: Every male among you shall be circumcised" (Gen 17:10). As such, it was a rite of initiation into the covenant community. Circumcision, moreover, separated insiders from outsiders. It also excluded women. Jeremiah subverts and reconfigures this well-established practice. With more attention placed on interiority than external observance, Jeremiah envisions a different kind of circumcision, one that involves a radical change in heart/action. The removal of the "foreskin of your heart" (see Deut 10:16; 30:6) suggests that true repentance demands sincere and faithful obedience to God (see also Jer 9:25-26). In addition, it makes the covenant community far more inclusive.

The consequence of not heeding this injunction is as grave as violating the physical rite of circumcision (4:4; Gen 17:14; Exod 4:24-26). Noncompliance carries the first explicit threat of divine wrath in the book: ". . . Or else my wrath will go forth like fire, and burn with no one to quench it, because of the evil of your [acts]" (4:4). Since passionate words of tenderness and love have not brought Judah to its senses, Yahweh resorts to explosive threats of judgment. In punctuating this literary unit (2:1–4:4) with the pathos of anger, the text takes up a major theme in the next section: the divine declaration of war against Judah and Jerusalem.

Theological and Ethical Analysis

Beginnings in the Bible are rarely insignificant. Elie Wiesel has well noted, "As with every genuine work of art, [the] opening statement contains all that is to follow" (1981, 101). The book of Jeremiah has several beginnings. The first is the *seemingly* inconsequential superscription (1:1-3) that presents the main characters of the book, family background, and situational context. This editorial heading, among other things, locates the prophetic activity of Jeremiah in a specific corner of the world. The call narrative of Jer 1 serves as another beginning. It authorizes the words of the prophet Jeremiah and presents the major motifs of the book in microcosm. Jeremiah 2:1–4:4 embodies a third beginning to Jeremiah. Unlike the superscription and the call narrative, this largely *poetic* unit organizes the first oracles of Jeremiah around a central metaphor: the marriage, or more accurately, the broken-marriage metaphor. This metaphor depicts Yahweh as a faithful and generous husband who is injured by betrayal and infidelity. Yahweh initiates a relationship with Israel, provides for his beloved, and more than anything else longs for intimacy and union. Israel, on the other hand, fractures the relationship by going after other partners and refusing to return to her first love. Such interaction causes Yahweh enormous pain and heartache, which evokes compassion for God and disdain for Israel.

By virtue of its position at the beginning of the book, this particular formulation enjoys a privileged place. To some degree, all subsequent God-talk is rooted in this initial metaphor. One might even argue that the theological discourse of Yahweh as scorned lover *generates* the rich tapestry of symbolic constructions in the following chapters. Just as grief gives rise to many discordant expressions, so Israel's rejection of Yahweh fuels a wide range of divine emotions, responses, musings, and strategies. Harsh interrogative questions, divine warfare, cosmic crumbling, and announcements of judgment are not primarily retributive or puni-

61

tive but rather are grounded in pain and exasperation as well as hope and pining for reconciliation.

The central metaphor of the broken marriage, and particularly the portrait of God as scorned lover, has far-reaching implications for theological construction in Jeremiah. First, it honors language of divine affection and love over divine rage and punishment. While expressions of anger and vindication are clearly present, they grow out of divine grief and disappointment. God's judgment is not to annihilate but ultimately to restore a broken relationship. God's love underlies the metaphorical construction. Second, the dominant metaphor of rejected lover suggests that God is terribly vulnerable to Israel's whims. This is dangerous business. The God of Israel is not safe and sheltered but engaged and involved. Divine pathos and vulnerability thus dominate the theological terrain of the book. To re-establish the broken relationship with the people of Judah, God will do just about anything. Third, the metaphor of a betrayed lover reveals a suffering God. Yahweh suffers because people have rejected him. In the fractured and tortured world of Jeremiah, there is enormous suffering: the prophet suffers, Israel/Judah suffers, and God suffers, especially in this early literature. For this reason, the poetic introduction to the book reminds the reader that no one suffers alone. God participates in the world of human pain and serves as an advocate for all those in need of healing.

Finally, the broken marriage/rejected spouse metaphor not only addresses facets of God's character, it also emphasizes the forlornness of Israel. God's people run off to faraway places in search of love. They show blatant disregard for their lover. They become deaf to gratuitous love and attentive to the seductive voices of others. This proclivity to leave home for a distant land is also present in Hosea's story of a promiscuous wife and in Luke's parable of the prodigal son. In each the beloved squanders God's good gifts for dissolute living. Luckily, the wayward wife and rebellious son eventually realize the folly of their ways. After suffering public humiliation and personal deprivation, Hosea's harlot Israel returns to Yahweh, her faithful husband. "Then she shall say, 'I will go and return to my first husband, for it was better with me then than now' " (Hos 2:7). After encountering a series of setbacks, Luke's prodigal son comes to his senses and remorsefully whispers: "Father, I have sinned against heaven and before you; I am no longer worthy to be called your son." In each situation, God embraces and restores without hesitation. In blind love, Luke envisions the father dashing out to greet his lost son and throwing him a lavish party. "He was lost and has been found" (Luke 15:32). No less obvious is God's unconditional love in Jeremiah. God desires to shower the wayward and rebellious with unrestrained affection.

COSMIC WAR AGAINST JUDAH (JEREMIAH 4:5–6:30)

The second half of the first literary unit, Jer 4:5–6:30, announces devastating judgment and cosmic desolation. Yahweh no longer invites Israel or Judah to return. The desire in Yahweh's voice gives way to rage. Whereas the previous section pulsated with divine tenderness, disappointment, and anguish, Jer 4:5–6:30 reflects little of this vulnerability. Instead, we witness a decisive display of divine resolve. Images of chaos, mourning, darkness, and military might give this collection its distinctive quality. Its ominous tone is in large measure the product of a new core metaphor: Yahweh as dreaded warrior engaged in battle against Judah. While vestiges of Yahweh as rejected spouse and Judah as promiscuous lover are still present (4:30; 5:7-8), they no longer control the literary landscape. Yahweh appears here as an untamed adversary about to turn Judah's world upside down. At the prompting of Yahweh, an enemy from the north will invade and devour. Despite the prospect of judgment, Judah remains stubborn, smug, and secure (e.g., 5:20-24; 6:10-12, 6:13-17).

Literary Analysis

Jeremiah 4:5–6:30 is an extended dialogue unified by a singular theme: the terrifying announcement of divine judgment. Yahweh and Jeremiah are the principal protagonists in the conversation. The voice of Yahweh controls the tenor of the exchange. It is bold, denunciatory, and speaks almost exclusively about cosmic war against Judah. God's prophet Jeremiah is involved all through the dialogue. He intercedes on behalf of the people of Judah, protests their plight, and empathizes with their suffering. Jeremiah's mediatorial role, however, subsides toward the end. Yahweh's case against Judah is so persuasive that the prophet must concede and accept Yahweh's judgment. Judah is another participant in the dialogue. Although the conversation is almost entirely about the fate of God's people, Judah speaks only occasionally, and then merely to express trepidation at the approaching foe from the north (4:13; 6:24-25). More often, it is Yahweh who puts words in the people's mouth (6:16-17; see also 4:8). Surprisingly, even enemy forces are part of the conversation. They interject their own concerns about war preparations (6:4-5).

The dialogue breaks down into a series of brief conversations. Because the individual poems run together, their boundaries are often blurred. The motif of the foe from the north holds together the first cycle of poems in chapter 4. Yahweh urges Judah to prepare for military aggression (4:5-10). From the north comes an army that will invade and lay to waste the cities of Judah. The people of Judah must immediately seek shelter. Jeremiah responds to the announcement by complaining that God's judgment is unfair. Yahweh, Jeremiah argues, has not adequately warned the people. The prophet, however, fails to persuade Yahweh, and so declarations of war resume (4:11-18). With chariots like a whirlwind and horses swifter than eagles, the dread invader advances from the northern region into the land of Judah. Yahweh begs Jerusalem to "wash [its] heart clean of wickedness so that [it] may be saved" (4:14).

In solidarity with the people of Judah, Jeremiah grieves over the destruction of the city, as if it had already occurred (4:19-22). The devastation, however, is not without cause. God's people have been proficient in "doing evil" and thus must assume some responsibility for its condition. Then Jeremiah dares to describe the wreckage. Creation reverts to chaos; death conquers life (4:23-28). Even with a mitigating clause—"yet I will not make a full end"—the prophet imagines the world on the brink of extinction.

An unidentified voice tracks Judah's response to imminent invasion (4:29-31). Fearful and desperate, daughter Zion seeks the comfort of her lovers, but to no avail. The metaphors of a rejected harlot and a woman dying in childbirth drive home the utter hopelessness of Judah's condition.

Chapter 5 continues the themes of coming judgment and cosmic war. It consists of several independent judgment oracles that retain a conversational texture. While the voices in dialogue are at times indistinct, the chapter breaks down into three main parts, each introduced by a plural imperative: 5:1-9, 10-19, and 20-31. In the first, Yahweh accuses Jerusalem of unmitigated guilt (5:1-9). A thorough examination reveals that all are corrupt. Jeremiah's own investigation cannot refute this claim. The second poem calls for divine punishment (5:10-19). Yahweh provides additional proof of Judah's sins, including those of pride and complacency. The nation is accountable for its actions. To bring Judah to its knees, "an enduring nation . . . an ancient nation . . . [with] mighty warriors" will fall upon the land and strip it clean. Yahweh's voice completely dominates the final speech of the chapter (5:20-31). Yahweh addresses Judah as a "foolish and senseless people" who have a "stubborn and rebellious heart." The lengthy inventory of offenses clearly justifies God's judgment. There is little doubt regarding the verdict. All three indictments assert that the community is on the way to destroying itself by its social malaise and infidelity to Torah. In enumerating the reasons for the coming disaster, the poems establish the responsibility of the nation, exonerate God of blame, and demonstrate that God's judgment is fully just and justified.

Chapter 6 is structured around five relatively short poems, several of which are introduced by the prophetic messenger formula "thus says the LORD (of hosts)." The first four develop the motif of the nation's guilt and the ensuing judgment against Judah's capital city Jerusalem. Various voices converge in 6:1-8 to describe the assault of Jerusalem by a northern enemy, an assault commissioned by God to punish the "[city of license]." Jeremiah 6:9-15 presents Yahweh and Jeremiah discussing the sweeping harvest of judgment. Jeremiah 6:16-21 recounts the nation's missed oppor-

tunities and the devastating consequences of obduracy and duplicity, and 6:22-26 reiterates the threat of imminent disaster from the
north, which now strikes fear in "daughter Zion." The final dialogue (6:27-30) brings closure to the larger unit, Jer 2–6, by clarifying Jeremiah's role in the wreckage. Whereas God had "made"
Jeremiah a "prophet to the nations" at the start of his prophetic
career (1:5), God now commissions ("made"; the same Hebrew
word) him to be a "tester" and "fortress" (cf. Jer 1:18) among the
people of Judah.

Exegetical Analysis

A Call to Arms (4:5-10)

After repeated attempts to coax the people of Judah to repent
(Jer 2:1–4:4), Yahweh now resolves to "pluck up and pull down,
destroy and overthrow." Consequently, disaster and death loom
ominously on the horizon, resulting in the inescapable and total
shattering of all conventional structures. Yahweh gives a command
to blow the trumpet signaling a state of emergency. The nation is
to prepare for an invasion from the north, an invasion that represents nothing less than Yahweh's full-fledged, frontal attack (Jer
4:6). The commands in preparation for war are basically defensive,
although nothing can truly protect the nation from the impending
assault. All the community can do is to brace itself for the coming
disaster. The people of Judah are urged to communicate the news
with due urgency, to take shelter in the fortified cities, and to "flee
for safety" immediately (4:5-6). The text describes the ominous
invader as a "lion" on the hunt and as "a destroyer of nations"
(4:7). The intent of the invasion is clear: to destroy the country.
The inhabitants of the land can only don the garb of mourners
(4:8). Judah's leaders, who have not heeded earlier signs and who
therefore must bear the brunt of responsibility, can only stagger
in shock and bewilderment at the impending invasion. "On that
day . . . courage shall fail the king and the officials; the priests
shall be appalled and the prophets astounded" (4:9).

An enemy from the north will inflict great harm on Judah. The
notion of a "northern foe" appeared in the first chapter of the

book. Yahweh revealed to Jeremiah that "all the tribes of the king-
doms of the north" will descend upon the land to wreak havoc on
Jerusalem (Jer 1:14-16). The text now elaborates the cryptic
motif. The term "north" is associated with peril and alarm.
In summarizing the nature and function of the northern foe,
B. S. Childs observes that it comes

> from a distant land (4:16, 5:15, 6:22). It is an "ancient" and
> "enduring" nation (5:15) speaking a foreign tongue (5:15). All
> of them are mighty men (5:16) and without mercy (6:23). The
> suddenness of the attack is emphasized (4:20, 6:26). The enemy
> rides upon swift horses (4:13, 4:29) with war chariots (4:13) and
> is armed with bow and spear (4:29, 6:23). He uses battle for-
> mations (6:23) and attacks a fortified city at noon (6:4, 5).
> (1959, 190)

While speakers use a rich array of metaphors to describe the
threat from the north, they most often draw on war imagery. The
"northern foe" is engaged in a military campaign that will result
in utter desolation.

The attack from the north is no mere military-political activity.
Yahweh arouses the northern forces with a particular plan in
mind: Yahweh "commissions" the formidable enemy to invade the
land of Judah (1:15). The alien horde sweeping down from the
north over Jerusalem and all the cities of Judah represents the
divine instrument of judgment against those who have forsaken
Yahweh for other gods. Whether this invading force is mythological or historical is incidental, for the real agent of impending disaster is Yahweh himself. That, observes W. Brueggemann, "makes
the danger massive, ominous, inescapable. Yahweh is now
engaged in a dread military exercise against God's own beloved
Jerusalem" (1998, 54).

In the turbulent world of Jeremiah, northern invaders are servants of Yahweh. The yet named, faraway forces are instrumental
in establishing Yahweh's just judgment upon a lawbreaking community. In other words, hostile forces are an integral part of the
text's symmetrical arrangements. Outsiders, therefore, do not
intrude upon this exacting moral universe. They do not place this

coherent world in danger, nor do they threaten to undermine the divine program regarding Israel. Foreign armies and kings, foes from the north, and all other enemies serve to uphold and reinforce the perilous workings of Yahweh. As such, the text renders these forces powerless. They merely serve the divine purposes. The terrible effects of invasion are, therefore, not gratuitous but a necessary part of a system of reciprocal justice which places full responsibility for shattered worlds on the shoulders of "us" rather than "them."

Jeremiah takes issue with God's judgment, insisting that it is too harsh and without cause. The prophet dares to accuse God of deception. "Ah, Lord GOD, [surely] you have deceived this people and Jerusalem by saying [that they will have peace when the sword threatens life]" (4:10). Instead of warning the people of Judah, God beguiles them into believing that all is well. In doing so, Yahweh intentionally dupes the people. No explanation is given as to how Yahweh tricks the nation, although many commentators suggest that Jeremiah is referring to the prophets' false words of hope. And Jeremiah's charge is not entirely without merit. According to the writer of 1 Kings, both true *and* false prophecies originate with God. Micaiah asserts that Yahweh is responsible for the "lying spirit in the mouth of all his prophets" (1 Kgs 22:22). If this understanding informs Jeremiah's protest, then Yahweh may indeed be responsible for the prophets' deceptive words of peace (see esp. Jer 6:14; 8:11; 23:17). This should not surprise us since divine sovereignty in the ancient world often implies that God is responsible for all things, including suffering and misfortune (e.g., Isa 45:7).

Whether or not Jeremiah's stance is justified, it nonetheless represents a stunning act of protest and solidarity with Judah. Jeremiah insists that God is in the wrong and the people are right. As such, he identifies with his suffering people. He gives voice to their outrage as well as their misgivings about God's justice. Not unlike Abraham who questions the justice of God in the wholesale destruction of Sodom and Gomorrah (Gen 18), Jeremiah intervenes on behalf of his country which is at the point of collapse. Ironically, this intercessory role validates his prophetic authority (Jer 27:18).

The Enemy on the Horizon (4:11-18)

Apparently unfazed by Jeremiah's attack, Yahweh resumes the invective against the nation (4:11-18). Using rich metaphorical language, the text describes Yahweh's impending judgment against Jerusalem in terms of cosmic war. The foe from the northern regions approaches with the force of a desert windstorm, "a hot wind" that scorches everything in its path (4:11-12). Dangerous, aggressive, and massive, the enemy comes by divine right to destroy the existing order of the world. "Look! He comes up like clouds, his chariots like the whirlwind, his horses are swifter than eagles" (4:13). Warning of the invader alone rouses a sense of alarm and despair. "Woe to us, for we are ruined!" In response to this cry, Yahweh offers Judah an opportunity to wash its "heart clean of wickedness . . . be saved" (4:14). The invitation, however, is not entertained for long before war imagery resumes. By the end of the poem, the case is made that the dreaded incursion is neither the act of a capricious god nor a consequence of realpolitik. It is the outcome of Judah's social and religious failure (4:18). The trumpet sounds and the destroyer approaches because of the "wickedness" of Jerusalem. Judah's ills are a consequence of its ethical ineptitude, which is described in sweeping terms: rebellion (4:17) and acts of wrongdoing (4:18). For the poet, therefore, the world is no neutral or morally ambiguous place but a morally exacting universe.

Jeremiah's Anguish Over the Coming Disaster (4:19-22)

The earlier inkling of Jeremiah's role as an advocate of Judah (4:10) is now explicit in 4:19-22. Jeremiah indeed functions as mediator. The prophet is no mere functionary whose sole purpose is technological. God's spokesperson is no outsider disengaged from the harsh realities of Judah's life. Nor does Jeremiah stand above or beyond the people he addresses. Like Yahweh, Jeremiah aches with compassion over the terrible fate reserved for the people of God. Deeply moved by Judah's plight, he identifies with the people's burden and their devastated condition. "Suddenly *my* tents are destroyed, *my* curtains in a moment" (4:20, emphasis added). When hearing the "sound of the trumpet, the alarm of war," Jeremiah "writhes in pain" and cries out to God on Judah's behalf. In doing so, *he becomes the people's voice and their strong ally*. Some see in this intercession the convergence of divine and human pain: the prophet's lament mirrors the community's pain as well as the pathos of God. In this way, the first person anonymous speech represents the anguish of Judah, Yahweh, and Jeremiah. Such anguish is evident in the structure of the language itself. By introducing the second line of 4:22 with a pronoun, "*Me* they do not know," the text once again calls attention to the intense disappointment of Yahweh. Both Yahweh and Jeremiah are distraught over the people's wound.

Creation Returns to Chaos (4:23-28)

Jeremiah 4:23-28 may be the most stunning piece in the entire book. With disturbing images of death and destruction shrouding his vision, Jeremiah describes the terrifying results of Yahweh's military assault on Judah, that is, the horrific effects of war and armed occupation. The order of creation collapses and reverts to its primeval state of chaos. The world comes unglued and is void of form, coherence, and beauty. Social arrangements no longer sustain meaningful existence. All is reduced to rubble. Ironically, this text of chaos is intricately structured. The fourfold parallel construction, "I looked . . . I looked . . . I looked . . . I looked" is followed in each case by the Hebrew particle of existence *(hinnê)*, "there was . . . there was . . . there was . . . there was," although no life signs can be found. The literary symmetry accentuates the dread.

This portrait of chaos and death draws heavily upon the imagery and theology of the creation account in the first chapter of Genesis. In this story God, the artisan king, creates out of chaos. By the power of poetry, by the power of the *word*, God speaks a world into being, a world that is "[formless and empty]," "[wild and] waste," "[without form and void]" (all translations of the Hebrew *to-hû vabo-hû* in Gen 1:2). The unformed world is not a state of nonexistence, but a chaotic place lacking order and meaning. From this undifferentiated and incoherent mass of water, God "sorts things out," "dividing" and "separating" so as to bring shape, structure, and definition. The divine work of creation thus involves the transformation of chaos into order. Beauty, symmetry, and form arise out of cosmic disorder and mess.

Jeremiah reverses this portrait. Rather than moving from chaos to order, the prophet imagines the disintegration and deconstruction of a coherent universe: that is, he envisions the erosion of an orderly world. The earth returns to primordial disarray, "wild and waste"; the heavens become dark, mountains and hills tremble, birds take flight, fertile land turns into an uninhabited desert, and cities are laid waste. The world collapses under the weight of "[Yahweh's] fierce anger." Not unlike the psalmist's imagery of cosmic upheaval (Ps 46:1-3), Jeremiah's vision of the uncreation of creation signals the end of life as it was known, the reduction of a world to tears. That which looked permanent and invincible crumbles before the reader's eyes. Judah's world is under siege and its principal antagonist is Yahweh.

Judah's Eleventh Hour Response (4:29-31)

An unidentified voice—perhaps the voice of Jeremiah, God, or the narrator—reports the reactions to the terrifying assault (4:29-31). At the sound of approaching soldiers people flee in panic. Leaving their towns deserted, they take flight to the supposedly safe places of the desert. In desperation, daughter Zion dons herself in the attire of a prostitute to entice her lovers (4:30). She seeks their help in her time of trouble. But she does so in vain, for her lovers come only to rape and murder. In an abrupt shift in metaphors, harlot Zion turns into a woman giving birth (4:31). An observer hears her crying, gasping for breath while in the throes of death. She "stretch[es] out her hands" in mourning, although the gesture may also indicate her protest. Hers are no ordinary birth pangs and her screams are no ordinary cries. For the cry of daughter Zion, ailing Jerusalem, is her last breath. The helpless harlot dies giving birth ["faints in exhaustion"]. In the presence of her murderers, who were once her lovers, she laments, "Woe is me! I am fainting before killers!" The end has come for the city of God.

"None Is Righteous, Not Even One" (5:1-9)

The first dialogue in chapter 5 (5:1-9) is reminiscent of Abraham's prayer of intercession for Sodom and Gomorrah (Gen 18). Both texts depict God as a "righteous judge" who is about to bring judgment. Both texts portray God in search of "righteous" people in order to mitigate looming judgment. And both reveal the futility of the inspection; God seeks for the righteous in vain, which demonstrates the wholesale corruption and the inevitability of destruction. In Jer 5:1-9, Yahweh challenges Jeremiah—though the imperative is plural—to comb the marketplace of the city in search of a just person, one who is faithful and lives with integrity. If he finds one honest and just person, Yahweh will pardon Jerusalem and presumably halt the coming disaster (5:1-3). Although God yearns for such a person, indeed craves for a community committed to the practice of economic justice, truth-telling, and authenticity, the command is likely a veiled provocation. By pointing out the absence of these Torah qualities among the people of Jerusalem, the inquiry serves to justify the threat of disaster.

As Israel's staunch advocate, Jeremiah challenges God's charge of wholesale corruption. The prophet assumes that only the "poor" are guilty, since they "do not know the way of the LORD, the law of their God" (5:4). The "great" among the people, the prophet believes, must surely "know the way of [Yahweh] and the law of their God." However, after a thorough scouring of Judah's leaders, the prophet must abandon his position. His investigation confirms Yahweh's initial insinuation of guilt. "All [have] broken the yoke [and] burst the bonds" (5:5). In wanton disregard for God's ways, all have moved beyond the perimeters of Torah obedience. Or, to use Paul's language, as he quotes the psalmist, "[None] is righteous, not even one" (Rom 3:10; Pss 12:1; 14:1, 3; 53:1). Jeremiah's findings demonstrate that judgment is inevitable (see 5:1 and 5:7). Despite Yahweh's desire to forgive, Judah's lack of integrity frustrates God's intent.

The Mockery of God and God's Response (5:10-19)

The next oracle intensifies the exposé on judgment (5:10-19). Yahweh enlists destroyers to prune Judah's vineyards (cf. 2:21; Isa

5). The unidentified forces are to climb up the terraces and tear down the branches that do not belong to Yahweh (5:10). However, they too must abide by Torah standards (Deut 24:19; Lev 19:9): like landowners in Israel, the gleaners of God's vineyard must not strip the land bare (5:10, 18). This qualifying clause is somewhat unexpected, but divine judgment is not: Judah's faithlessness and blithe contempt fully account for God's intent to punish. The nation not only rebels but also mocks Yahweh. "He will do nothing. No evil will come upon us, and we shall not see sword or famine" (5:12). Such hubris amounts to a total dismissal of God's person and power. It is a strong declaration of practical atheism and human autonomy. Jeremiah insists that the prophets encourage this insolence when they abdicate their responsibilities. They are "nothing but wind, for the word is not in them" (5:13). Judah's moral and religious malaise makes the need for pruning urgent.

To prove Judah wrong in its insistence that Yahweh is unable or unwilling to act, Yahweh, the God of hosts, presides over a pageantry of power and control (5:14-17). Yahweh commissions a faraway nation to topple Judah (5:15). This ancient nation, full of warriors, will devour Judah's children, agricultural systems, and military defenses. The fourfold use of the word "devour" or "eat" stresses the force of the attack (5:17). The enemy will destroy everything in its path. Despite the desolation, Judah will survive. Yahweh will "not make a full end of you" (5:18). Mercy will one day triumph over judgment. But in the meantime, when survivors of the wreckage seek to understand their harsh geopolitical realities, they must know that their plight is no mere accident of history but the consequence of moral and religious failure. They have forsaken Yahweh for foreign gods and therefore will serve strangers in an alien land (5:19).

A Catalog of Torah Infractions (5:20-31)

Jeremiah brings newfound charges against the people of Judah (5:20-31). Rather than a broad sweep of ritual transgressions, like apostasy and infidelity to God, the prophet delineates the community's ethical infractions of the Torah. His catalog of offenses is specific and detailed (see esp. 5:26-28): robbery, treachery, greed, exploitation, and mistreatment of the poor and vulnerable. Despite a shift from crimes against God to crimes against humanity, the two are not to be compartmentalized. Offenses against God, within the context of worship, influence the fabric of community life no less than offenses against people. Conversely, acts of social injustice are violations of divine law. Any real distinction between these two sides of the same coin is dangerous and misleading (cf. Matt 25:40).

With a full arsenal of wisdom language, Yahweh lectures an obstinate people (5:20-25). They are "foolish and senseless"; they have "eyes, but [cannot] see, [and] ears but [cannot] hear" (5:21). Whereas the sea, waves, and rains abide by the laws of nature, Judah is too rebellious to recognize God's moral boundaries and its own wickedness. Judah has gone its own way and lost its "fear of God," the starting point of wisdom. If the accusation were not so grave, it would be humorous. The people lack all good sense. They are totally insensitive and self-absorbed, which leads to intransigence and the deprivation of goodness (5:25).

Judah is not only ignorant of the acts of God but also is "deaf and blind" to the deterioration of its own culture. Contempt for Yahweh (5:20-25) has led to disdain for the poor (5:26-28). The trivialization of God has brought about a depreciation of human dignity and the commercialization of people. The wicked—which is a social designation often juxtaposed with the righteous in the Psalms—enjoy complete freedom among the people. They steal at will and set traps for humans. They deceive and defraud the defenseless. Their greed is insatiable; their self-indulgence knows no limits. They exploit the "nameless" people located at the bottom of the social hierarchy in order to improve their own positions in life. No one sees these "trivialities" except God who "executes justice for the orphan, widow, and sojourner" (Deut 10:18) and who is "father of orphans and protector of widows" (Ps 68:5). While other nations sometimes practice power politics and economics rooted in greed and self-interest, Israel cannot do so. To be true to its vocation as God's people, God's creation, Judah must embrace and embody the *politics of Torah*. The quintessential quality of Torah politics is the practice of justice and mercy.

Consequently, when Judah ignores the plight of the powerless and vulnerable, it abandons its own story. Its silence is collusion; its insensibility is complicity. The only thing more appalling (5:30) is the systemic support for these violations. And indeed the prophets and priests provide this for a compliant people (5:31).

As a whole, chapter 5 is an exposition on justice. The Hebrew word *mišpāṭ* [justice] occurs four times in the chapter. It is translated "act[ing] justly" (5:1 in conjunction with a verb), "law" (5:4, 5), and "justice" (5:28). In the first occurrence, Yahweh declares that the presence of one person who "acts justly and seeks truth" will save the city from destruction. It is far from incidental that the search for such a person takes place in "the streets of Jerusalem" and in "its squares." The public place of commerce and government is the arena for the practice of justice. It is there that the righteous practice their trade. Their gracious dealings grounded in Torah ethics provide the marketplace with an alternative language. It is the language of justice. Sadly, this language is foreign in the land of Judah (5:1-3). In 5:4-5, the "law" *(mišpāṭ)* of God is poetically parallel to the "way of the Lord," which suggests that the two are closely related. To know the "way of the Lord" is to know and practice the justice of God. The final usage of "justice" (5:28) relates the term to the ethics of generosity. Indeed justice in this context is a synonym for mercy rather than evenhanded retribution. The practice of justice in 5:28 precludes all forms of greed, exploitation, and brutality, as well as an indifference to and tolerance of judicial partiality. Put positively, the practice of justice, the essence of Torah economics, involves the movement "from hostility to hospitality" (Nouwen 1975), especially in relation to those located on the fringes of society.

Jerusalem Under Attack by the Northern Foe (6:1-8)

The initial section of chapter 6 appears at first only to reiterate earlier motifs of the book. As before, one encounters warnings that Jerusalem must prepare for military attack in light of evil looming out of the north. Earlier phrases also reappear in this section: the introductory imperative, "flee for safety" (6:1 and 4:6), "blow the trumpet" (6:1 and 4:5), "raise" a "standard/signal" (6:1 and 4:6), "evil from the north" (6:1 and in 4:6), "desolation" (6:8 and 4:27), and "woe to me/us" (6:4; 4:13, 31).

Notwithstanding these links, much is distinctive. First, it is significant that the warning to Jerusalem, albeit attested previously, is the *last* one in the first literary unit of the book (Jer 2–6). Second, the geopolitical and mythic assault on Judah intensifies. Yahweh, or Yahweh's spokesperson, declares "holy war" on the city (6:4). The NRSV translation of the first imperative in Jer 6:4 obscures the "holy war" motif. It translates the Hebrew verb *qādaš* as "prepare" (see also Joel 3:9), whereas a more literal rendering of the word is to "sanctify" or "consecrate." In other words, Yahweh formally declares war on Judah. Third, the text focuses specifically on its capital city Jerusalem. Jeremiah refers to Jerusalem or Zion by name four times in the passage (6:1, 2, 6, 8). He exhorts the "children of Benjamin" to flee "from the midst of Jerusalem" (6:1) as the invasion draws nigh. Using love language mingled with war rhetoric, he likens "Zion" to the "loveliest pasture" to which shepherds come with their flocks (6:2-3). This serene setting, however, suddenly becomes the turf for bloodshed. Addressing the enemy, Yahweh issues a command to "cut down" Jerusalem's trees and "throw up a siege [mound] against" the oppressive city (6:6). Jerusalem must reform its ways or be reduced to "a [desert, a land without people]" (6:8).

The direct speech of the enemy provides another distinguishing feature of the text. For the first time in the dialogue, the narrator allows the approaching "shepherds" (i.e., the kings with their military machine) to speak. We discover that Judah's northern foes are not only willing but eager to destroy Jerusalem. If 6:4*b* is the voice of the enemy camp and not a cry of anguish by inhabitants of Jerusalem—"Woe to us, for the day declines, [and] the shadows of evening lengthen!"—then there is sadness in the ranks that the assault must wait until daylight. Unconvinced of any need to delay, another presses hard for an attack by night (6:5). This latter voice apparently prevails as Yahweh agrees that the offensive must begin immediately (6:6). As the voices unite (6:6-7), the poet points out that Yahweh's invective against Judah is not without provocation; it is instead a justified attack upon the state's oppressive systems. Its "sickness and wounds" are the consequences of Judah's "oppression" and "wickedness," "violence and destruction."

Systemic Evil in Jerusalem (6:9-15)

Yahweh initiates another dialogue with the prophet (6:9-15). The Lord commissions Jeremiah (emending the text to read as a singular imperative) to "[glean what remains of Israel like a vine]"; like a grape-harvester, the prophet must pass his "[hand repeatedly over the tendrils]" (6:9). While some understand this metaphor as positive, the majority view it negatively. The image of "harvest" here and elsewhere in the Hebrew Bible suggests a time of divine punishment. The "gleaning" of vineyard Israel represents thoroughgoing judgment. The broad context and allegations against the entire community support this position. Jeremiah 6:13-15 asserts that everyone is culpable of wrongdoing and, therefore, is without excuse. "From the least to the greatest, [all] are greedy for gain; from prophet to priest, [all practice falsehood]" (6:13). Strategies for accumulation, systemic avarice, as well as callous indifference to the "wound" of God's people (6:14), and a shameful absence of remorse (6:15), all demonstrate collective guilt.

On this occasion Jeremiah does not object to Yahweh's critique but responds with his own denunciatory query: "To whom [can] I speak and give warning [so] that they may hear? See, their ears are closed, they cannot listen" (6:10). Like Isaiah of the exile, who contends that delivering the message is useless given the people's unfaithfulness—the "people are grass, [and] their constancy is like the flower of the field" (Isa 40:6-8)—Jeremiah is sure that any attempt to warn is utterly futile. According to him, the community is incapable of heeding Yahweh's word. For that reason, Jeremiah is "full of [Yahweh's wrath]" and is "weary of holding it in" (6:11). Indeed, Yahweh insists that he not suppress it. Unlike God's rejoinder to Isaiah of the exile, which encourages faith and reliance upon the word of God, Yahweh authorizes, even demands, that Jeremiah explode with wrath (6:11-12). No one will escape the dangerous work of demolition and dismantling.

The Earth Stands in Judgment Against Judah (6:16-21)

God recaps Judah's repeated refusals to "heed" divine warnings and then sets forth the consequences of their actions. As such, the text presents itself as a commentary on "not heeding." God exhorts the community to "ask for the ancient paths where the good way lies." But Judah declines to do so (6:16). Likewise, the nation scoffs at the counsel of the prophets to "*give heed* to the sound of the trumpet" (6:17, my emphasis). Afterward God assembles the nations to witness the consequences of Judah's intransigence or "not [heeding]" (6:19). Yahweh will bring disaster on this people, which is merely the "fruit of their schemes." The determination not to heed Yahweh's "words" and "teaching" is so appalling that conventional burnt offerings are unable to atone for it (6:20). Judgment must therefore be thorough and unqualified (6:21).

For a brief, albeit fleeting, moment, Yahweh offers a way out. Jeremiah places the people of Judah at the crossroads of their history (6:16). If they search for the "ancient paths," "where the good way lies," they will "find rest for [their] souls." The religious practices of the state religion had led to a host of economic obscenities (e.g., 6:13-15). So, the poet urges the nation to look, ask, and walk down a different path. Exactly what the ancient paths mean, however, is not clear. The text may refer to the way of the patriarchs/matriarchs, the way of Torah, the ways of Moses, the way of covenant, the way which God had instructed Israel, or simply an ancient way of life uncontaminated by the monarchy. There is no reason that any one of these options must exclude the others. Jeremiah merely invites the people of Judah to look to its rich heritage as a way out of the present impasse.

There is no illusion here that Israel could turn back the clock and recapture bygone days. Nor do we find a rejection of urban life or "modern" society for some earlier period of simplicity and innocence. The good old days are gone. Yet, amidst a period of enormous social disintegration and symbolic turmoil, Jeremiah reaches back to the past for an ethical compass. The prophet contends that returning to "the ancient paths" is a way to navigate through the present wreckage. In order that it not lose its way, Jeremiah urges the community to embrace the stories, teachings, and values that God had entrusted to them long ago. To do otherwise was to surrender everything.

The Hebrew word "way/crossroad" *(derek)*, which occurs twice in 6:16, and again in 6:25, 27, appears hundreds of times in the Bible and over fifty times in Jeremiah alone. Enjoying a wide semantic range, the word denotes far more than a route from one place to another. It denotes passage toward liberation, a journey of life, a defining approach to reality, a place of mystery (e.g., Ps 77:13, 19), and pivotal values. Throughout Jeremiah, Judah's evil "ways" stand in contradistinction to God's just "ways" (see 3:13, 21; 4:18; 6:27). Judah has "perverted [its ways]" (3:21), "scattered its ways/favors" (3:13), and indulged in the "way of Egypt" (2:18). It has taught its "[ways]" to "wicked women" (2:33) and waited for its lovers "by the way" (3:2). Judah's "ways" have brought disaster upon itself (4:18). Its "way" has been obstinate from youth (22:21). Therefore, God admonishes the nation to "amend [its] ways" (7:3, 5) and not follow the "way of the nations" (10:2). In contrast to Israel's "evil way" (18:11), God has graciously led Israel "in the way" (2:17). The "way of [Yahweh]" is the way of justice (5:4, 5). If Judah walks in this "way," then all will go well (7:23). God thus sets before Israel "the way of life and the way of death" (21:8), and promises to give Judah "one heart and one way" to fear God (32:39). And here in Jer 6:16, while standing at the "[cross-way]" of life, Jeremiah pleads with the community to review the paths of old as a means to discover "the good way."

Besides the tutelage of these "ancient paths/good ways," God posts sentinels to provide ample warning of impending doom (6:17). The metaphor of the watchman describes the role and function of the prophet in Israel (6:17; Ezek 3:17-21; 33:7; Hab 2:1; Hos 9:8). As sentinel, the prophet guards against the dangers that attend deliberate disregard to covenant obligations. When the community rejects the Torah teachings and the prophetic message of counsel, disaster becomes inevitable (6:19).

Acting as Judah's watchman, Jeremiah alerts the community to the futility of offering costly "frankincense from Sheba" and "sweet cane" as well as conventional "burnt offerings" and "sacrifices" to appease God (6:20). Such attempts to circumvent the way of justice with liturgical rites, no matter how extravagant and compelling, are doomed to fail; they can neither atone for willful transgressions nor masquerade for true obedience to God. In the spirit of the time-worn teaching that "obedience is better than sacrifice, heeding [God] than the fat of rams" (1 Sam 15:22), the iconoclastic prophet declares that religious observances or ritual purity cannot substitute for moral righteousness and Torah obedience (see also Ps 15; Isa 1:10-17; Amos 5:21-24; Mic 6:6-8; cf. also 1 John 4:16-21). In fact, worship divorced from obedience is especially dangerous since it deadens people to the weightier matters of justice, mercy, and faith (see Matt 23:23) and creates an illusion of certainty.

Daughter Zion Paralyzed by Fear (6:22-26)

The hostile invasion by the northern enemy again comes into full view in 6:22-26. A cruel and menacing nation armed with "bow and javelin" closes in on daughter Zion. Although she does not "hear" the words of Yahweh, she indeed "hears" the news of the encroaching invaders (6:24-25). And the news strikes fear into her heart. Panic-stricken Zion now joins the liturgical cacophony of voices. She recognizes and confesses, perhaps for the first time, that she is totally vulnerable to the onslaught of the enemy and therefore must brace herself for disaster. Yahweh responds to the cry of "the daughter of my people," but only to reiterate the inevitability of destruction (6:26).

Jeremiah as Tester and Refiner (6:27-30)

The first major literary unit, Jer 2–6, ends with Yahweh assigning Jeremiah the task of assayer of the people; God charges him with the work of testing the value and worth of their "ways"

(6:27). The prophet's findings are recorded in 6:28-30. Jeremiah discovers a paucity of precious metal and an abundance of dross. The people are "stubbornly rebellious . . . [and] all of them act corruptly" (6:28). "They shall be called [silver-reject], because [Yahweh] has rejected them" (6:30). These final verses again demonstrate the total failure of Judah's social and theological systems as well as the impossibility of reformation. They also absolve Yahweh of any wrongdoing. Before arriving at a verdict of guilt, Yahweh has tried everything. Yahweh has sought the "return" of the beloved (Jer 2-4), has scoured the city for "one person who acts justly and [practices] truth" (5:1), and now searches for "[precious metal]." All lead to the same conclusion.

The call of Jeremiah operates as subtext to the concluding words of chapter 6. In the call report Yahweh "[appoints]" Jeremiah to be "a prophet to the nations" (1:5). In the closing words, Yahweh "[appoints]" Jeremiah as an assayer (6:27), a function ordinarily reserved for Yahweh (9:7). When Yahweh commissions Jeremiah, Yahweh transforms the prophet into "a fortified city" (1:18). Once again Yahweh makes Jeremiah "a fortress" (cf., however, the NRSV translation of 6:27), apparently so that he is able to stand against the wiles of the nation. To highlight the intransigence of Judah, the rebellious nation is described as "bronze and iron" (6:28), terms used in the call report to describe Jeremiah's tenacity and force (1:18; cf. 15:20). Read together, Jer 1:4-19 and 6:27-30 create an envelope-structure or thematic *inclusio* that holds together the first literary unit. The opening and closing texts emphasize the mission of the prophet to a recalcitrant people. The concluding text, Jer 6:27-30, also anticipates the next major literary section of the book, Jer 7–10, where Judah's errant "ways" are further considered (Jer 7:3, 5 (cf. 7:23).

Theological and Ethical Analysis

Some moments in life are so devastating that they defy rational analysis. During such periods of crisis, we often yearn for neat and congruent answers, and yet we know, often intuitively, that they will not satisfy. Rarely do clear-cut, unambiguous explanations of life take seriously fractured human experience. The book of Jeremiah knows this and offers a rich labyrinth of political, social, and symbolic understandings that address the tragic events that afflicted Israel in the years immediately before and after 587. As such, the whole of Jeremiah reads as a complex theology of suffering. Immersed in chaotic times of exile and loss, Jer 4:5–6:30 uses symbolic language and thick descriptions of reality to speak of seismic shifts in the life of Israel. Specifically, Jer 4:5–6:30 employs the dominant metaphor of cosmic war to depict these defining moments. Battle imagery and war poems permeate the ethos of the entire text. An enemy from the northern regions ominously looms over the horizon ready to attack. The assault eventuates in total destruction (e.g., 4:23-28). The invaders turn Judah's world upside-down and leave it utterly desolate. What makes this language even more shocking is the claim that God inspires the invasion. That is, the text not only depicts a world under siege, but imagines Yahweh as Israel's principal assailant, a fierce catalyst of demolition.

That God should wage warfare on Israel and be the agent of Israel's ills is a disturbing assertion. We are far more at ease with a God "who [comforts] us in our afflictions" (2 Cor 1:3-4) than a God who causes trouble! However, such a notion is certainly not without precedent. Throughout the book, the text employs violent imagery, amidst violent times, to depict Yahweh as the one who "[plucks] up and [pulls] down, [destroys] and [overthrows] . . . " (Jer 1:10). Jeremiah envisions Yahweh as the "troubler of Israel" (cf. 1 Kgs 18:17). The Hebrew Bible in general acknowledges the divine role in prosperity and disaster, weal and woe.

While this claim may irk the sensitivities of modern readers, it apparently never scandalized the first readers of the book. This is, in part, because the "adversarial" role of God attends to a central theological conviction: in spite of the whims of aggressive nations, human power games, and the vicissitudes of life, *God ultimately controls the destiny of the world*. God rules, despite Babylonian imperialism. God rules despite a world in disarray (Jer 4:23-28; cf. Ps 46). The reign of God, however, does not exempt Judah from suffering. In the contrary, Yahweh intrudes into Judah's settled existence in unsettling ways—to afflict the comfortable, to hold all accountable, and to act on behalf of the oppressed (5:26-29), even if that means acting against Israel. God's assault and the resulting devastation is nothing less than a sure sign of God's sovereignty. Jeremiah 4:4–6:30, therefore, contends that the God who longs for Israel's embrace (Jer 2:1–4:4) is also the God who rules, and the God who rules is capable of shattering worlds and bringing judgment.

The text's rhetoric of war, its invective against Judah, may seem to contradict God's core character of compassion and love. However, whenever the poor are exploited and their rights are deprived and wherever the values of the kingdom of God are inverted, God's towering indignation comes to the fore. Tolerance for the deprivation of human rights is inherently anti-evangelical and anti-gracious. Genuine love cannot embrace scornful injustice without becoming malevolent indifference. Hence, "in disgust" and in violent love God "[turns away]" (6:8) from the oppressor and takes decisive action on behalf of Jerusalem's oppressed.

The text's disturbing rhetoric also serves to shape the community's understanding of the "other." When Jer 4:5–6:30 asserts that Yahweh incites the enemy from the north, it, in some measure, absolves Judah's northern foe of unilateral blame. By envisioning the invasion and deportation as a direct consequence of Judah's stubborn disobedience, moreover, the text urges insiders to take responsibility for their lives. We therefore do not find in Jer 4:5–6:30 an attempt to prevent incursions or banish outsiders from within the borders. Nor does Jeremiah divide the world sharply into categories of faithful and diabolical, insiders and outsiders. The text affords outsiders an ambivalent and yet sanctioned place in the world. In this way, Jeremiah directs the first readers, the refugees in Babylon, to view their foreign cultural setting in conciliatory rather than vengeful ways. Eventually the prophet will make it altogether clear that life in Babylon is part of the dangerous and yet sure work of God (e.g., 29:1-9). Judah's challenge is thus to embrace its disenfranchised place among the nations before imagining the possibility of homecoming and restoration (see, e.g., 24:1-10; 29:1-14).

The theological and ethical claims in Jer 4:5–6:30 emerge as a chorus of voices. The chorus includes Yahweh, Jeremiah, anonymous supplicants, and daughter Zion. It even allows Judah's assailants to speak as they plan their attack (6:4). The polyphonic text serves more than artistic purposes. First, the symphony or cacophony reflects the multiple audiences involved in the production of the text. The text is thick and complex, and many hands were involved in its production. Second, it represents a wide range of interests and interpretations of the national catastrophe. The terrible suffering inflicted upon the people of Judah was too massive for any monolithic reading. Multiple voices and claims must grapple with the emotional and physical toll of invasion and exile. Third, the plurality of voices, here and elsewhere in the book, suggest that the text was related to public worship. In recent years several scholars have made this case (e.g., Reventlow 1966, Biddle 1996, and to some extent Nicholson 1970). Jeremiah 4:4–6:30 performs in public worship experiences that would otherwise be too painful and unmanageable to utter. As liturgical drama, the text and its cast of characters dare speak of, reenact, and eventually embrace these painful realities. Thus we encounter a reperformance of the many scenes of chaos and death, the repeated failures of the community, God's unleashed fury as well as grief, the prophet's warnings and solidarity with the people—that is, the collage of voices and memories that surrounds the maelstrom of suffering exiles. The re-enactment of a fallen world together with the re-construal of reality through the prism of worship makes healing possible. But not before all feel the pain without analgesic.

Next, Yahweh is by far the dominant voice in the chorus, but Israel's God speaks from the midst of and not above the din. Yahweh is engaged in a dynamic exchange with the prophet and the people. This divine engagement holds serious implications for the character of God. Divine involvement with Israel involves a move from power to vulnerability, from transcendance to presence, from wholeness to brokenness. When entering this turbulent arena, God is no longer shielded from pain and rejection. Nor is God able to elude the world of human suffering. On the contrary, God becomes immersed in it, in anguish and anger, and in judgment and mercy. Thus, the image of God that emanates from these conversations is that of one who is accessible and vulnerable to Israel.

Notwithstanding such vulnerability, God is still unrestrained, dangerous, and not to be controlled or contained by either the prophet or the people. As an undomesticated participant in the dialogue, Yahweh is neither for nor against Israel—"Are you [for us or against us]?" . . . "Neither; [I am the captain of the LORD of Hosts"] (Josh 5:13-15, my translation)—but beyond safe and innocuous categories. Yahweh's presence and purposes indeed disturb and subvert the provincial boundaries of Israel's domesticated world as well as those of the prophet. Yahweh is capable of passionate love and fierce anger, giving and taking life, and upholding and shattering traditional systems. No wonder Yahweh's dangerous program eventually elicits from Judah a marked sense of dread and alarm (6:24-25).

Finally, the conversational texture of this literary unit presents Jeremiah as a full participant of God's work on earth, and not as a mere puppet. Jeremiah's part in the performance reflects a spirituality of protest. Unwilling to accept the divine point of view passively, the prophet embodies a piety that is bold, daring, and willing to push to the limits. "Ah, Lord GOD, how utterly you have deceived this people and Jerusalem, saying, 'It shall be well with you,' even while the sword is at the throat!" (4:10). The prophet's involvement represents an approach to God that is more active than deferential, more combative than submissive. The voice of the prophet, and the interpretive community behind it, speaks with remarkable authenticity and force. The voice is that of an Israel that is comfortable wrestling with Yahweh over the extremities of life and a future that appears destined for ruin (cf. Gen 32:22-32). Rooted in covenant as the axis of such an encounter, Jeremiah's theology of engagement leaves a lasting impression on the text's dialogical character. We shall eventually see an escalation of this daring speech and piety in the so-called Confessions.

DISMANTLING THE TEMPLE AND ITS CULTURE OF CERTITUDE (JEREMIAH 7–10)

Jeremiah 7–10 is a diverse body of literature that reflects a wide range of genres, concerns, and themes. Despite the miscellany, there are grounds for treating this material as a distinct literary unit. First, like other major divisions in the first half of the book, Jer 7–10 begins with a prose sermon (7:1-15) that introduces the unit and encapsulates its most important motifs. Among these is the claim that the temple, the traditional sanctuary from violence and travail, will not save Judah from imminent disaster. Second, the introductory prose sermon serves as a literary link to its broader context. Specifically, this prose passage clarifies ambiguous elements of the preceding block of poetry (Jer 2–6). Whereas Jer 2–6 depicts the coming judgment in thick, mythic terms, Jer 7:1-15 gives concrete shape to the coming destruction. Third, the prose sermon launches a campaign that will unmask and dismantle Judah's long-standing belief systems, institutions, pivotal values, and power structures. The community's "first principles," its fundamental understandings of reality, will soon come under the biting scrutiny of prophetic speech. And Yahweh's spokesperson, Jeremiah, begins the assault with a critique of the epicenter of Judean life, the Jerusalem temple. As a whole, Jer 7–10 denounces false worship, delineates its grave consequences, and gives voice to a huge outpouring of grief on the part of Yahweh, Jeremiah, and the people over the nation's bleak fate.

Literary Analysis

Jeremiah 7–10 consists of two main parts, 7:1–8:3 and 8:4–10:25. The first is a prose collection held together by its concern for abuses in corporate worship (7:1-15, 16-20, 21-28; 7:29–8:3). Though less defined, the second block is a complex of poems that hones in on the disaster about to befall Judah and the profound sadness it evokes (8:4-13; 8:14–9:3, 4-11, 12-16, 17-22, 23-26; 10:1-16, 17-25). The so-called "temple sermon" introduces the former, Jer 7:1–8:3, by taking aim at the practice of religion in the "house of the Lord" (7:1-15). Jeremiah chides the people of Judah for divorcing worship from the ethical demands of the Torah and for loving the temple more than the One whom the temple represents. Then Yahweh instructs the prophet to look beyond the temple area to outlying shrines in Judah where the queen of heaven is being worshiped (7:16-20). Apostasy is so deep-rooted and widespread that intercession on behalf of the people is now futile. Judah's infatuation with other gods, however, is nothing new (7:21-28). The entire history of the people of God—from the time that they left Egypt to the present crisis—testifies against them. This history of rebellion, in tandem with the heinous practice of sacrificing children on the altars of Topheth, leaves God no choice but to bring judgment (7:29–8:3).

Jeremiah 8:4–10:25, the second part of the larger unit, begins with an oracle in which Yahweh holds the nation responsible for refusing to return (8:4-13). Such an unthinkable act of defiance on top of unabashed greed will result in divine judgment. The announcement of divine judgment triggers a flood of tears (8:14–9:3). There is "no balm in Gilead" and thus all don the garb of mourners. Abruptly, mourning turns to accusation. Judah's corruption is endemic: all deceive, no one speaks truthfully, and cheating and oppression are rampant (9:4-11). Yahweh is entirely justified in bringing retribution, but justification does not prevent tears. Afterward a prose voice interjects a series of questions (9:12-16): Who can understand the events that have taken place in Judah? Who can explain them? Why has the land been laid waste? Yahweh responds without a trace of ambivalence: the disaster has occurred because Judah has forsaken the law, disobeyed Yahweh's voice, and insisted on going its own way. Professional mourners enter the arena not only to express palpable grief but also to demonstrate the inevitability of judgment. Indeed, the mourning women are an unequivocal sign that Judah's world is coming to an end (9:17-22). Once more a prose voice enters the fray, this time to expose the inadequacy of knowledge, power, and wealth. As by-products of the state and its systems of governance, each pales in light of knowing Yahweh, who acts with "steadfast love, justice, and righteousness in the earth" (9:23-26).

The conclusion of Jer 8:4–10:25 consists of two sections. The first is an antiphonal hymn of praise in which one voice celebrates the power and sovereignty of Yahweh while another disparages the gods of the nations (10:1-16). The closest analogy we have to this kind of structure in the Bible is Ps 115, which contrasts the power of Yahweh with the impotence of the nations' gods (see also Isa 44:9-20). The psalmist declares that "our God is in the heavens . . . " whereas "[their idols are silver and gold . . . with mouths that cannot speak, eyes that cannot see, ears that cannot hear, noses that cannot smell, hands that cannot feel, and feet that cannot walk]." Similarly, Jer 10:1-16 sets before the reader two ways (10:2), two diametrically opposite approaches to life, two contrasting ideological systems: the text claims that "way of the nations" is illusionary, but the way of Yahweh is real and trustworthy; the "customs of the peoples" are ineffectual and worthless while the worship of Yahweh is effective and true. Although this hymn is utterly confident about its claims, the implied readers— the exiles in Babylon—were probably not. Immersed in a foreign world as a subject people, they were faced with the pressing question as to which system to accept as their own ultimate reality.

The second part (10:17-25) is an assorted block of material composed of at least four distinct poems or fragments of poems. Resembling the unit as a whole, the material presents itself as a polyphonic text. *Yahweh* implores the people to depart from the land in light of impending devastation and forced deportation (10:17-18). Bereft of her children, the siege and deportation leave *mother Zion* forlorn and broken-hearted (10:19-21). A *piercing cry* warns of an encroaching foe from "land of the north" (10:22); and finally, *a prayer, perhaps uttered by the prophet*, entreats God to punish the nations for their cruel treatment of Judah (10:23-25). One encounters in these final words escalating anxiety, a marked sense of panic, and an urgency to evacuate the land before night falls.

In summary, Jer 7–10 is a daring assessment of Judah's systems of worship and the false sense of security they engender. The Jerusalem temple is the centerpiece of this critique. At the start of the literary unit, an extensive prose block denounces false worship within and outside of the temple precincts (7:1–8:3). It maintains that Judah has been involved in practices that represent a grave breach of the first commandment: "You shall have no other gods before me." Near the end of the literary unit, a hymn of praise exemplifies a true form of worship (Jer 10:1-16): foreign gods are exposed as false and Yahweh is exulted as the incomparable God. Although the intervening cycle of laments in Jer 8:4–9:26 lacks any direct reference to the temple, this collection is read in synagogues to commemorate the destruction of the temple in 587 B.C.E. and again in 70 C.E. For many years, Jewish scholars have understood the tears of God, Jeremiah, and the people of Judah to be signs of profound grief over Jerusalem's fallen sanctuaries.

Exegetical Analysis

Worship That God Abhors (7:1-15)

The temple sermon appears at first to disrupt its literary context. Without warning, the text moves from wild poetry in Jer 2–6 to prose that is markedly similar to Deuteronomy and the Deuteronomistic History. This juxtaposition of poetry and prose, however, is not coincidental; nor is it evidence of a disjointed and chaotic text. As elsewhere in the book, prose discourse is a response to and a commentary on poetry. Jeremiah 7:1-15, for instance, implies that the smugness exuded by Judah in the earlier poetry derives in part from its confidence in the temple. Indeed, the prose homily suggests that the people of Judah flee to the temple in order to escape the devastating indictments pronounced in chapters 2–6. Bizarrely, the community seeks sanctuary in the temple from a God who has become its dangerous adversary. With considerable force, the prose sermon reveals the absurdity of such efforts. Yahweh sees through Judah's efforts to circumvent the sovereign word and derail the divine program of "plucking up and pulling down." Even the great Jerusalem temple cannot save the people from the disaster to come. For Judah there is no mercy or sanctuary this side of judgment. Jeremiah 7:1-15 thus declares that there is nowhere for Judah to run, nowhere to hide, and no denying the coming desolation at the hands of northern foes.

In addition to responding to and providing commentary on its poetic context, the temple sermon also stabilizes the wild world of poetry. Univocal prose sublimates the multiple and dissonant voices of poetry in Jer 2–6 like a composer and an improvisational musician who controls the dissonance within a frame until resolution is found. The prose sermon tames the stormy voices of the poetry. This domestication involves clarifying earlier motifs and pronouncing them more forcefully. In the prose, it becomes crystal clear that false worship has social consequences that result in death. We discover that disobedience to the central principles of the Decalogue lies at the heart of the community's ills. Equally poignant is the presentation of Yahweh as an untamed and dangerous reality that will not let Judah get away with abuses in worship and social violence. Consequently, the prose spells out the reasons for the dismantling of Judah's social system and hierarchical power arrangements—especially those associated with the temple.

The temple sermon is a searing assault on worship at the holy shrine in Jerusalem. The text insists that Judah's liturgical life has masqueraded itself as true piety. In the process it has become callous to the cause of justice. Not the least fascinating aspect of this argument lies in the claim that God is on the verge of departing from the temple (and the land) if worshipers continue to behave inhumanely. In the homily, Jeremiah explains that God will not inhabit space Jerusalem has violated by mistreating its poor. Those who use worship to cheat and defraud will not find the God of Israel. True worship, the prophet contends, is manifest in obedience, wholehearted trust, and the practice of justice towards "the [refugee], orphan, and widow" (7:5-7). In this manner, the troubling prophet shatters the national myth of "Zion's invincibility" and its delusion of control and security. God is under absolutely no obligation to reside in the temple or to protect the people of Judah when they worship there.

Jeremiah stations himself at the center of the Jerusalem establishment—at the entrance of the temple grounds where the nation gathers for worship (7:2). He then assails the belief that the temple provides unqualified protection. Ritual is not intrinsically efficacious. Liturgy and ethics are inseparable. And spirituality divorced from right conduct is a dangerous distortion *(šeqer)* of the practice of faith. Worship without compassion represents an obscene caricature of true Yahwism. Jeremiah proclaims that only when worshipers amend their "ways and their doings" will God "dwell with them" (or "let them dwell") "in this place" (7:3). God's presence is dependent on Israel's repentance. Contrary to the official party line, it is not a state entitlement. The phrase "this place" is grammatically ambiguous. The expression may refer to the "temple" or to the "land." The ambiguity is likely intentional. The presence of God in the temple *and* in the land is integrally dependent on what worshipers do. Not even mantra-like liturgies, such as "The temple of Yahweh, the temple of Yahweh, the temple of Yahweh," can nullify this bond. Before Yahweh will show up Israel must act justly, care for the vulnerable and "untouchables" (see Exod 22:21-24 and Deut 24:17-22), and renounce other gods (Jer 7:5-7). When Israel ignores God's commandments, even pious prayers and sacred space cannot ensure God's presence and blessing. The God of the temple is a God who demands moral sensitivities and obedience.

The temple sermon turns bolder and more chilling when Jeremiah asks two rhetorical questions that are really damning assertions (7:8-11). How can worshipers break the commandments and then enter God's house for sanctuary! Using the temple to shirk responsibilities toward others transforms God's house into a "den of robbers." Israel's duplicity and religious games, however, will not dupe God; God is not blind! "You know, I too am watching, says the LORD" (7:11). The beloved temple will not insulate the nation from ruin. To emphasize this point, the prophet reminds his audience of the shrine at Shiloh which the Philistines, we presume, had destroyed in the days of Samuel (7:12-15; 1 Sam 4-6). The lesson is haunting: When worshipers desecrate sacred shrines with idolatry and injustice, when communities of faith become recalcitrant and inhuman, there is no place to hide (7:14).

This harsh critique of the temple piety subverts three crucial assumptions of the Jerusalem establishment. First, it challenges the belief in the temple as a place where God is ever present. God's presence there is dependent on Israel's Torah obedience and God is completely free to leave if Israel reneges on its obligations toward its neighbor. Second, the text disputes the claim that the house of God provides an unqualified refuge from danger. The temple is only a refuge for those deprived of justice, not for those who use its machinery to oppress and exploit. Third, the prose sermon attacks the notion that the temple is fundamental to the maintenance of social and cosmic order. The temple, the text insists, is not effectual in and of itself. Its ritual and theological underpinnings can neither manipulate God nor hold at bay the chaotic forces of the universe (see, e.g., Pss 46–47). The fundamental arrangements of society rest on the preservation of social justice and the practice of neighborly love, not upon the Jerusalem temple.

This frontal attack on the temple serves the interests of the first readers of the text, who were living in the aftermath of 587. By all indications most survivors of the Babylonian invasion were ill-prepared for collapse of traditional forms of worship. For centuries historical Israel had built sanctuaries as places where heaven and earth met and where God was especially near. And when God was near, victory was sure. By as early as the end of the tenth century, the Jerusalem temple had become God's principal residence on earth, and worshipers had come to understand God's residence as the most stable structure on earth and the abode of God's effective presence. At the dedication service, King Solomon established the house of the Lord as a sacred place that would ensure blessing, forgiveness, fertility, success, and well-being. Thereafter, the people of Judah looked to the temple as a sanctuary from danger and harm. After attempting to usurp the throne, Adonijah grasped the "horns of the altar" for protection from Solomon's wrath (1 Kgs 1:49-53). When under siege by the Assyrians, Hezekiah entered the temple for solace and safety. In the temple precincts, he met the prophet Isaiah who assured him that he would retain his throne and that Jerusalem would survive intact (Isa 36–37; 2 Kgs 18:17–19:37). After King Josiah's reform in 622 (2 Kgs 22–23), the state establishment asserted that Jerusalem was inviolable and its magnificent temple was the source of unconditional blessing. Following this lead, many citizens of Judah were convinced that no harm would befall them with God in their midst. With the Jerusalem temple as the center of national life, the axis of the universe, Judah's future could not have looked more promising, or so they thought!

To help the community in exile come to grips with unimaginable loss, the prose sermon testifies that the destruction of the temple was no arbitrary historical event, but a direct fulfillment of the prophetic word. Jeremiah had prophesied that the nation's waywardness, misplaced trust, and disdain for the poor would bring down the grand house of the Lord, and it surely did! Although this assertion may have done little to ease the emotional pain of survivors, it at least made the loss more rationally manageable. In addition, the sermon filled a huge symbolic void. Bereft of a spiritual center and a traditional ceremonial life, Judean refugees in Babylon would have to look elsewhere for its religious structures and life of worship. The prose sermon exhorts its readers to foster communal life that is rooted in justice, generosity, and concern for the weak and disenfranchised.

The Worship of the Queen of Heaven (7:16-20)

Although the prose sermon proper concludes with verse 15, the prose commentary continues to elaborate Judah's apostasy and Yahweh's displeasure. The prophet condemns a form of idolatry practiced *outside* of the temple environs. Devotion to the queen of heaven is widespread "in the towns of Judah and in the streets of Jerusalem." Indeed, Yahweh is astonished that family life in Judah revolves around the worship of this deity. Even children are involved in preparing offerings. Such worship, along with abuses at the temple, makes prophetic intercession impossible (7:16). Judah's devotion to the astral deity, the "queen of heaven," represents a late stage of community amnesia that precludes all forms of mitigation. This scathing rhetoric accentuates the gravity of people's predicament: the nation and its support systems are beyond help. The prohibition on interceding, in conjunction with the absence of the temple's protection, marks the end of "this place" (7:20; cf. 7:3, 6, 7). As we have seen, in the temple sermon proper this phrase is intentionally ambiguous, referring to the temple or the city. In the present context, however, "this place" more likely alludes only to the city of Jerusalem since the condemned activities take place beyond the temple precincts. Consequently, the text broadens the scope and intensity of Yahweh's judgment.

Obedience Is Better Than Sacrifice (7:21-28)

Worship continues to occupy center stage in the next prose section. The text echoes a prophetic critique of religious observances embedded in the scriptures (e.g., Jer 6:20, 7:1-15; Hos 6:6; Amos 5:21-24; Isa 1:10-20; Mic 6:6-8). "For in the day that I brought your ancestors out of the land of Egypt, I did not speak to them or command them concerning burnt offerings and sacrifices" (7:22). Some interpret the pronouncement that God did not demand sacrifices from Israel as a dismissal of ritual for ethical religion. More likely the text uses hyperbole to show that true piety requires ethical commitment, that "obedience is better than sacrifice" (see 1 Sam 15:22), and that religious practices can never circumvent social responsibility. As the temple sermon has already implied, religious ceremonies can create an illusion of certitude and well-being, even when one is engaged in inhumane activities. Jeremiah reminds the community that the crux of its covenant relationship is obedience: "obey my voice, and I will be your God, and you shall be my people . . . " (7:23). Obedience is the pivotal value that is to define Israelite faith.

God makes clear that the people of Israel have missed this mark. They have shown no inclination whatsoever of "[walking in the way]" that God commands. They do "not obey or incline their ear"; they insist on going their own way and paying no attention to the prophets whom God has sent. They "[stiffen] their necks" and resolve not to listen. More recent generations are even worse than earlier ones. In light of this history of recalcitrance, God warns Jeremiah that he must brace himself for an unreceptive audience. The people will be no more inclined to listen to him than they were the prophets who preceded him.

Such stubbornness clearly jeopardizes the favored status of God's people.

Descent into Hell: Human Sacrifice in Judah (7:29–8:3)

Jeremiah 7:29–8:3 is a composite piece that begins with a dirge lamenting the death of Israel (7:29). Feminine singular imperatives suggest that Yahweh is addressing daughter Zion. Since Yahweh has rejected and forsaken "the generation that provoked his wrath," daughter Zion is to cut off her hair as a sign of mourning. The balance of the passage explains the "evil" committed by the people of Judah and the outcome of their deeds. God's people desecrate the temple with idols (7:30) and build "the high place of Topheth" in the valley of Hinnom (Gehenna) where they "burn their sons and their daughters in the fire" (7:31-32). The reference to the heinous offenses at "the high place of Topheth" is particularly alarming. As part of his 622 reform, Josiah had destroyed the Topheth—a term that likely derives from the Aramaic word *tēp̄aṭ*, "fireplace"—in order to eradicate the sacrifice of children to the Canaanite deity Molech (2 Kgs 23:10; cf. 2 Kgs 21:6). Verse 31 claims that Jeremiah's contemporaries continue to carry out this ritual. Though it is possible that worshipers may have understood their offerings as a means of fulfilling the law demanding the consecration of the firstborn (Exod 13:1-2, 11-16; 22:29-30), human sacrifice was still strictly forbidden (Lev 18:21; 20:2-5). To engage in such brutality was to choose death over life and thus to incur the harshest penalties. Indeed, the sacrifice of children was nothing less than a total abrogation of Judah's own story and status as Yahweh's people. Whether this taboo was actually practiced in the years immediately prior to 587 or is merely employed here hyperbolically is unclear. Regardless, it represents in the text the most gruesome act imaginable and the epitome of false worship.

With wild imagination, indeed horrifying imagination, the phrase exploits the grotesque images of death in yet another way (7:32–8:3): Jeremiah imagines Judah's sacrificial shrine as its own mass grave. The sheer number of dead—both innocent children along with the perpetrators of the heinous act—justifies a name change from Topheth, their place of worship, to "valley of

Slaughter." In this valley, the dead cover the ground and vultures and wild animals pick apart the corpses. Drawn in part from the inventory of covenant curses in Deuteronomy, these metaphors drive home the finality of judgment (cf. 7:33 with Deut 28:26). In the end Jerusalem will become an eerie place of silence, death, and shame. Nothing will remain except the bodies of its leaders exhumed, desecrated, and spread "like dung on the surface of the ground" (Jer 8:2). Violence and horror dominate the entire landscape of this text. All that supports civility and the order of creation is now gone. One might ask whether such dark voices of torment, construed here as divine judgment, implicate or exonerate God of injustice.

The Deep-Seated Nature of Judah's Transgression (8:4-13)

Jeremiah 8:4-13 opens a collection of oracles that is perhaps the most cacophonous in the book (8:4–10:25). For this reason, there is much debate over its central theme, or if one even exists. R. E. Clements recognizes thematic coherence in the unit's "sharply threatening and admonitory character, interspersed with brief comments upon the nature of divine wisdom and the depth of insight and wonder that belongs to God's action" (1988, 52). L. Boadt sees chapters 8–10 held together loosely by a "wisdom" motif (1982, 71). W. Brueggemann contends that their underlying intent is to depict the nation "as a community on its way to death because of its refusal to be faithful to Yahweh" (1998, 86). J. A. Thompson discerns "twin themes" in this heterogeneous collection: "Israel's stubborn and incurable rebellion, and the inevitable doom which will befall her" (1980, 297). Both P. D. Miller and T. E. Fretheim call attention to the many laments that punctuate the unit (Miller 2001, 642-43; Fretheim 2002, 147). As darkness descends upon the nation, an explosion of voices erupts. And many of these voices, including Jeremiah's, Judah's, and God's, throb with pain and reel in desperation.

Prose discourse now shifts almost entirely to poetry. However, the intensity of Yahweh's case against Judah does not diminish. Jeremiah 8:4-13 is a satirical disputation. Yahweh asks the nation and its religious leaders a series of penetrating questions that mock and establish guilt (see 8:4, 5, 8; cf. 8:14, 19, 22). All point to the same conclusion: Judah has done the unthinkable by rejecting Yahweh. When pursuing its "own course" rather than "the ordinance/[justice] of [Yahweh]" (8:7), it departs from reason. The annual migrations of the stork, turtledove, swallow, and crane provide a telling foil for Israel's aberrant behavior. Unlike these migratory birds that follow their instincts, Judah's repudiation of Yahweh and its refusal to return home defy common sense (see Isa 1:2-3). The Hebrew word *šûb*, which basically means "to turn," helps make this point. The word occurs six times in 8:4-6 (translated respectively in the NRSV as "go astray," "turn back," "turned away," "backsliding," "return," and "repents"). Unlike its usage in earlier parts of book (Jer 3–4), the term is no longer a plea for Israel to return to Yahweh. Such invitations are no longer extended. The term functions in the present context to emphasize the people's culpability and their inescapable fate. Judah is adamant about "turning away" from Yahweh for another story; when it does, the nation serves as its own moral compass and so "[plunges] headlong into battle" (8:6). All told, the accused are guilty of both rebellion and torpidity (8:5-6).

Judah's failed leadership is the root cause of the people's insentience (8:8-13). The scribes falsify the Torah and reject the word of Yahweh. Greed blinds prophet and priest to the needs of the community. All three, prophet, priest, and sage, practice falsehood and betray community obligations. They lead the nation down a dangerous road and so stand under the scrutiny of the divine word (8:10-12). These accusations are replete with claims and counter-claims, voices and countervoices, as if Jeremiah is engaged in a heated debate with those he condemns. The prophet recites the words of the "wise" disparagingly—"we are wise and the [Torah] of the Lord is with us." How ridiculous to think of themselves as wise when "[rejecting] the word of the Lord!" Jeremiah lampoons fraudulent prophets and priests who pronounce "peace, peace when there is no peace" (8:11). Because of their leadership, the land is devastated and utterly barren. When God the farmer comes to gather a plentiful harvest, God discovers only ruination and crop failure (cf. Hab 3:17). There are "no grapes on the vine, nor figs on the fig tree; even the leaves are withered" (8:13; see the NRSV footnote for an alternative translation).

To summarize, Jeremiah delivers the (divine) plaintiff's charge with satiric force (8:4-7). He challenges the opposing parties with caricaturing wit (8:8-12). Israel lacks all logic when it rebels against Yahweh; indeed, it betrays natural instincts. It is like "a horse plunging headlong into battle" (8:6) and is less perceptive than "the stork, . . . turtledove, swallow, and crane" (8:7). The *scribes*, who think of themselves as wise, reveal their ignorance by misrepresenting the Torah and rejecting the word of the Lord. The *prophets and priests*, who should have keen insight, are impervious to the true condition of the nation. No one does what ought to come naturally, which takes its greatest toll on Yahweh's "poor people."

A Requiem for Israel (8:14–9:3)

The argument in verses 4-13 triggers a cycle of laments. All of them pulsate with regret, confusion, deathbed musings, and fear. When the people of Judah come to their senses and begin to realize their grim fate, they are flustered and incoherent (8:14-17). Overcome with grief, they head to fortified cities to die. Inconsolable, they conclude that Yahweh has doomed them to perish, poisoning their wells because of their wrongdoing. Their confession, "we have sinned against [Yahweh]" (8:14), is apparently disingenuous for they still think that their suffering is undeserved. "We look for peace, but find no good, for a time of healing, but there is terror instead" (8:15). This statement is likely a veiled declaration of innocence as well as a denunciation of the prophets who had promised peace (cf. 8:11). Unlike these false prophets, Yahweh through Jeremiah braces the people for reality (8:16-17): disaster, not peace, looms on the horizon. A massive cavalry is approaching with such force that the land quakes. Yahweh directs the military offensive, unleashing venomous snakes that will destroy their victims (cf. Num 21:6-9). Mixed metaphors—poisoned water, snorting horses, a land that trembles, and adders—all produce an ethos of death. The city's doom is sure. Any word to the contrary is totally out of touch with the nation's present theopolitical reality.

Jeremiah 8:18–9:3 sustains the chorus of suffering voices. The identity of the speakers is difficult to determine. The first appears to be Jeremiah who bewails Judah's desperate condition. He expresses great sorrow at the unfolding events. As a divine spokesperson, however, it is impossible to separate Jeremiah completely from Yahweh (8:18-22). To be sure, Jeremiah represents Yahweh in word and in deep emotion. "Jeremiah's grief is an embodiment of God's grief" (Fretheim 2002, 155). Nonetheless, by the end Yahweh himself enters the cacophony to express sympathy for the people (9:1-3).

The prophet cries out in anguish as he witnesses the suffering of his people.

> My joy is gone, grief is upon me,
>   my heart is sick.
> Hark, the cry of my poor people,
>   from far and wide in the land:
> "Is the LORD not in Zion?
>   Is her King not in her?"
> "The harvest is past,
> the summer is ended,
>   and we are not saved."
> For the hurt of my poor people I am hurt,
>   I mourn, and dismay has taken hold of me.
>   (Jer 8:18–21)

While the genre of this passage is uncertain, it appears to be a personal lament since "the very first sentence places us inside Jeremiah's thought, and this is where all the essential action takes place" (von Rad 1965, 200). Jeremiah identifies with the suffering people—whom he calls "my poor people"—and mourns over their hopeless predicament. He quotes the people's desperate cry, "Is [Yahweh] not in Zion? Is her King not in her?" These words expose not only their disappointment with God, but more important, the extent of their fatuity. They have been naive about their own situation, in large measure because of the nation's deplorable leadership. Jeremiah has already undermined the belief that Yahweh is unconditionally bound to Zion and that city and shrine will provide unqualified sanctuary from imminent danger. He has declared repeatedly that the presence of God in the temple and in the city is not a given. But sadly the people do not get it; they do not perceive "that the temple claims are dead and have failed (cf. Jer 7)" (Brueggemann 1998, 93). Instead, they maintain the same impudence and false security exemplified in the temple sermon, which evidently informs this passage. One can thus discern in this lament faint echoes of the prose assertion that neither Jerusalem nor the temple will provide refuge from the coming disaster.

The people's unfounded hopes evoke profound sadness and grief. Yet Jeremiah can do nothing but watch helplessly and writhe in heartache and regret. Upon hearing Judah's disconsolate voice—"the harvest is past, the summer is ended, and we are not saved"—the prophet is even more grief stricken. Their powerlessness and bewilderment open the prophetic wound. Although the people are not without fault (8:19), they are still "[his] people." And so Jeremiah expresses intense solidarity with them even to the point of sharing in their suffering and loss. "For the hurt of my poor people I am hurt, I mourn, and [terror grips me]" (8:21). If the prophet is the speaker of 8:22—"Is there no balm in Gilead? Is there no physician there?"—Jeremiah also becomes their voice. He bewails their wounded condition and pleads with God for their restoration. Intercession may make little sense after the surplus of blame and the prohibition to pray, but the prophet's grief is as incoherent as Judah's. One looks in vain for consistency. The same prophet who earlier accuses and condemns now defends and mourns.

Jeremiah 9:1-3 concludes Israel's requiem with the customary rubric "says the LORD." This prophetic formula is significant in that it presents the speech as the voice of Yahweh. With Judah (8:14-15) and Jeremiah (8:18-22), God grieves over the destruction of Jerusalem. In uncontrollable sorrow, Yahweh wishes he could cry his eyes out for his poor people (9:1). God's mourning, however, is juxtaposed with rage. The people's corruption inflames Yahweh. They are adulterers, traitors, liars, and evildoers. What is obvious from the catalog of transgressions is that the people have forsaken God. An exasperated God exclaims, "[Me] they do not know" (9:3). No longer able to tolerate abject rejection and corruption, God imagines a far-away place to escape. Like the psalmist who longs for a safe place in the "[desert]" (Ps 55:7), Yahweh searches for a solitary site. "Who will find me a wayfarer's shelter in the desert, where I can leave my people and go far from them?" (Jer 9:2, my translation).

As a whole Jer 8:14–9:3 bears witness to a convergence of tears. Judah mourns over its own wounded condition, Jeremiah is sick with grief over the plight of his countrymen, and God bursts into tears as darkness descends upon Israel. Although God would like to flee faraway and avoid the pain of intimacy, God instead casts God's lot with a suffering people who are on their way to destruction.

A Community at War with Itself (9:4-11)

Jeremiah 9:4-11 continues the divine speech, first to warn, then to weep, and afterward to rage. Judah is a community at war with itself and on the verge of imploding. Incivility and contempt go unbridled. The absence of honesty and decency creates strife and hostility. By abandoning its timeworn ethic of hospitality, Judah places everyone at risk. Even neighbors and kin can no longer trust one another. The prophet's inventory of avaricious acts includes deception, slander, and other forms of falsehood. Most of these vices involve the misuse of speech in public discourse, which is no minor infraction. The scriptures in general recognize that "death and life are in the power of the tongue" (Prov 18:21). "The tongue is a fire . . . [setting] on fire the cycle of [life]" (James 3:6 in NRSV). Jeremiah's diatribe—"[The] tongue is a deadly arrow"—links the downfall of Jerusalem to its destructive force: "No one speaks the truth." Lies govern marketplace transactions (9:4-6) and infect daily social interaction (9:8). Corruption is systemic. Using a play on the name of Jacob, the prophet accuses the entire community of being deceivers (9:4, lit., "Jacobs"). For Jeremiah, the deterioration of gracious speech and behavior poses a grave threat to the fabric of society. This deterioration is evidence of the nation's loss of God: "[Me] they do not know/ refuse to know" (9:3, 6). Dazed and disorientated by Judah's actions, as a last resort Yahweh resolves to "refine and test" the nation (9:7).

God does not accuse for long before shedding more tears. The Hebrew text of verse 10 (cf. the NRSV which reads with the LXX) suggests that Yahweh again joins the grief-stricken lamenting the destruction of Zion.

> For the mountains I weep and wail,
> For the pastures in the desert (I raise) a dirge,
> because they have been burnt
> and no one inhabits them,
> no one hears the sound of flocks;
> both birds of the air and animals
> flee far away. (Jer 9:10, my adaptation).

In view of the wholesale destruction of life God weeps, wails, and raises a dirge. Then in the very next breath God threatens to "make Jerusalem a heap of ruins . . . and the towns of Judah an [uninhabited] desolation" (9:11). While textual emendations can produce a degree of thematic coherence (see the NRSV), they are unnecessary. All along Jeremiah has entertained the notion that divine anger and divine sorrow are not mutually exclusive. Wrath and sadness embody the anguish of divine grief. God's involvement has demanded vulnerability and vulnerability has led to suffering. The portrait of God that emerges here, therefore, is not congruent and logical but dynamic, discordant, unpredictable, and passionate. Indeed, as O'Connor eloquently notes, "God's tears are more powerful even than the armies under divine command because, for a poetic moment at least, God, people, and cosmos articulate a common suffering and God changes sides" (1998, 184).

Daring Questions (9:12-16)

This brief passage is a prose commentary on Jeremiah's previous oracle. The text reflects the theology and focal concerns of survivors living in captivity, years after the destruction of Jerusalem. Jeremiah 9:12-16 presents itself in the form of a question accompanied by an answer and explanation. An unknown speaker asks three rather audacious queries (9:12) to which Yahweh responds (9:13-16): Who is wise enough to understand this? To whom has the mouth of [Yahweh] spoken [to explain it?] Why is the land ruined, and laid waste like [a desert] [where no one travels?] (Jer 9:12).

The questions treat the destruction of the country as an enigma, beyond the grasp of the sage (9:11-12). Such bewilderment may sound strange in light of the plethora of explanations already given for the city's woes. However, for the exiles in Babylon the destruction of Jerusalem was indeed a conundrum. The loss of their culture along with shattered hopes and an uncertain future torment and perplex them. So they enter the conversation seeking answers to pressing questions.

The divine reply comes with force: The disaster is no accident of history, or sign of divine impotence; rather, the nation has fallen because of its own covenant failures. The people of Judah have rejected God's instruction, stubbornly followed their own paths, and forsaken Yahweh for Baal. Their recalcitrant disobedience has resulted in divine judgment. A series of first-person statements, which are likely cast in the past tense, conveys the devastating effects of Yahweh's punitive actions: Yahweh has fed this people with wormwood, made them drink poisonous water, scattered them among the nations, and sent the sword to pursue them (9:16). The text's reciprocal system of justice interprets Judah's dislocation and humiliating place among the nations as a by-product of it own actions. Put bluntly, Judah has brought the misfortune upon itself by failing to live up to the requirements of the law set before them. Yahweh has only acted according to the stipulations of the covenant (see Deut 29:22-28; 1 Kgs 9:8-9; cf. Jer 16:10-13).

Breaking the Denial (9:17-22)

This elegy formalizes the previous expressions of grief and makes them public and incontrovertible (O'Connor 2001, 497). Yahweh marshals professional mourners to raise a funeral dirge on behalf of the fallen nation. The mere presence of these skilled mourners signals the certainty of disaster. Their conventional rituals excrete an aroma of death. Their words of woe testify to the certainty of Judah's ruin. "How we are ruined! We are utterly shamed . . ." (Jer 9:19). Yahweh instructs them to lead their daughters in a "dirge" over Zion's fate. In their elegy, "death" takes on almost mythological character. The metaphor of death "[ascending] to [the] windows, [entering the] palaces," draws upon understandings from the ancient Near East. Life and death are viewed as fluid and dynamic fields that can interact. When forces of death invade the sphere of life, the outcome is devastating (9:22). And for certain demonic forces of evil have entered the land and destroyed all in their path.

Besides heightening the ethos of death, these "specialists in grief" (Brueggemann 1998) come to shatter all forms of denial, most evident in the unfounded optimism of the nation's establishment. Prophets, priests, and sages still insist that the old city will survive and that business will go on as usual. To shatter such dangerous naiveté, Yahweh summons those skilled at the dirge to join the throng of mourners, which includes Jeremiah and Yahweh. On the streets of Jerusalem they weep over the pain of the world and the end of life as it once was known. Sorrow and anxiety, once bubbling beneath the surface of the text, now explode in public view. The skilled women invite the people of Judah to participate in God's suffering. They entreat the nation to acknowledge its wounded condition and work through its grief. Such liturgical expressions of sorrow facilitate healing. As a prerequisite to any new constructions of reality, the community must come face-to-face with the harsh realities of a fallen world, a failed city, and treasured ideologies gone awry. The liturgy of the dirge, therefore, breaks the illusion of permanence and eventually makes new life possible.

Shattering the Illusion of Wisdom, Power, Wealth, and Privilege (9:23-26)

The final two prose sayings of chapter 9 (9:23-26) are often read as intrusive, but there are good reasons for reading them as an integral part of their present setting. The first saying (9:23-24) draws heavily on wisdom language that informs chapters 8–10. The most obvious is the term "wise" or "skilled" (8:8, 9; 9:12, 17, 23; 10:7, 9, 12). The "wise" (i.e. the scribes), for instance, falsify the law of Yahweh (8:8). They reject Yahweh's word and eventually are put to shame (8:9). Along with prophets and priests, the scribes fail to grasp the gravity of the nation's condition (8:10-12). Jeremiah 9:23-24 further reduces the importance of wisdom in the hierarchy of community virtues. Wisdom along with power and riches are deemed far less important than knowing Yahweh. The second prose statement (Jer 9:25-26) reaches back to the circumcision of the heart motif (4:4). It elevates obedience over religious observance and circumcision of the heart over the physical act.

The prose sayings are rooted in their context in another way. They *respond* to a literary environment that is laden with death and enveloped in tears. Accordingly, they are not propositional statements or universal observations but *reflections* on Judah's particular predicament. As Judah's world unravels (see Jer 2–9), trusted systems and conventional values are exposed as inadequate. As institutions and social structures flounder and collapse, conventional wisdom, military prowess, and the accumulation of goods come up wanting. The old values fail to head off the disaster. They no longer provide even an illusion of security, and they only obscure the importance of trust in God. Although conventional wisdom, power, and riches hold enormous appeal in a stable world, they have little use in a world falling apart. Hence, the exilic community, which is likely the audience addressed, must look elsewhere for meaning and well-being.

In place of the old values of the dynastic state, the speaker instructs the readers to "boast" in understanding and knowing Yahweh, the One who acts with "[constant] love, justice, and righteousness in the [land]/earth" (9:23). "Understand[ing] and know[ing] [Yahweh]" implies an alertness to the character and purposes of God in history as well as a deep personal commitment which affects every aspect of life. In this way, the knowledge of Yahweh is creedal and relational. It involves a confession of faith in the gracious and just character of God, as well as an intimate relationship with this God. It also involves the skill to recognize that God acts faithfully and justly "*in the [land]*" (my emphasis). There is considerable support for reading the Hebrew *bāʾāreṣ* locally and not globally (i.e., "in the land" rather than "in the earth"). While the Hebrew permits either translation, the prepositional phrase in Jeremiah refers most often to national land boundaries. Only rarely does it imply the entire world. That Yahweh "acts with love, justice, and righteousness *in the [land]*" suggests that such overtures are still attendant despite appearances to the contrary. To "understand and know" God is to perceive that the enormous pain and desolation suffered in the land of Judah does not discredit God's core character.

Love, justice, and righteousness not only define God's character but are also ideal virtues for community life: "In these things I delight, says the LORD" (9:23-24). In other words, people who "understand and know" Yahweh *put into practice* love, justice, and righteousness. "Steadfast love" alludes to fidelity and loyalty to one's social and religious obligations, often extending beyond mere duty to gratuitous acts of generosity. A judicial term, "justice" often carries the sense of "gracious justice" as opposed to evenhanded retribution. In this capacity, it delineates the community's social obligations toward those who are victims of exploitation and oppression and consequently are in most urgent need of intervention. The term is thus nearly a synonym for love. "Righteousness" alludes to moral symmetry, integrity, the absence of duplicity, and ethical governance. These principles represent a radical revision of the community's hierarchy of values: the text moves from a royal/urban model that prizes conventional wisdom, military might, and commercial interests (that is, the prominent values of the preexilic dynastic world), to village-based ideals of loyalty, generosity, and integrity.

Jeremiah's counterworld not only subverts establishment morality but also sacred rites that privilege the nation. Specifically, the prophet asserts that physical circumcision carries no special claim upon God and can do nothing to avert divine judgment (9:25-26; see 4:4). By calling the house of Israel "uncircumcised in heart" and lumping it together with other "circumcised nations," the prophet again throws into question Israel's special status as the people of God. Moreover, by focusing upon Israel's place among the nations (9:26; 10:2, 7, 10, 25), this brief prose saying hurtles the reader into chapter 10, which considers the nations and their idolatrous ways.

Yahweh Versus the Gods of the Nations (10:1-16)

Jeremiah 10:1-16 is a hymn in which Yahweh is exalted and praised as the true God. When this text is read in context, it addresses pressing concerns that lie behind chapters 7–9: Who is in control? What can one trust? Which god is truly effective in a world coming apart, Yahweh or the gods of the nations? Beset by forces and circumstances that the community might interpret as an abrogation of Yahweh's power, this responsorial song of praise celebrates Yahweh's supremacy. It lauds the power and wisdom of Yahweh while mocking the impotence (*hebel* in 10:3, 8, 15) and falsehood (*šeqer* in 10:14) of foreign gods. Diagrammed below is the structure of this temple liturgy:

1. Prophetic Charge to Hear the Word of Yahweh (v. 1)
2. Impotence of Foreign Deities (vv. 3-5)
3. Praise to Yahweh, "King of the nations" (vv. 6-7)
4. Impotence of Foreign Deities (vv. 8-9)
5. Praise to Yahweh, "the everlasting King" (v. 10)
6. Impotence of Foreign Deities (v. 11)
7. Praise of Yahweh, the Creator (vv. 12-13)
8. Impotence of Foreign Deities (vv. 14-15)
9. Concluding Praise for Yahweh (v. 16)

The hymn declares that the gods of the nations are mere idols that are unable to "speak, walk, or do either harm or good" (10:5). They are lifeless and powerless to work in nature or history (10:1-5, 14). They are "stupid and foolish" (10:8), utterly "worthless" (10:15), and are merely fabrications of human ingenuity (10:8-9, 14-15). Therefore, they are utterly unreliable and untrustworthy. This caricature serves as a foil for the sovereignty of Yahweh. Yahweh is the sole, universal God, the "King of the nations"

(10:7), the "true God . . . the living God and the everlasting King" (10:10). As creator and lord of history, Yahweh is the power at work forging the destiny of the nations (10:12). All told, Yahweh's stunning power alone evokes praise. Only the Lord is worthy of trust. Reliance upon human institutions and artifacts, whether foreign or indigenous, is a dangerous delusion that leads to death (10:14; cf. 7:4, 8).

Gather Your Belongings and Run for Your Life! (10:17-25)

Determining the speakers, genre, and boundaries of the individual sayings in the second half of chapter 10 (10:17-25) is a formidable task. Verses 17-18 preserve a prophetic oracle of judgment announcing the impending invasion. Verses 19-21 likely represent an individual lament, perhaps placed in the mouth of mother Zion. Verse 22 seems to stand alone as an ominous cry of doom in light of the advancing forces from the north. And verses 23-25, the most problematic section, present themselves ás a composite prayer with several biblical allusions.

The section begins with a command addressed to a people under siege. While time permits they are to pack up their bags and leave the city, for Yahweh is about to cast out the inhabitants of the land. This warning is not unique. Jeremiah 2–6 and 7–10 resonate with the same anxiety and warnings. However, now the danger is closer at hand, if not already underway. The people must prepare immediately for exile. The invading armies are part of Yahweh's military machine mustered to hold the nation's survival in abeyance.

To this point in the prophetic drama, Yahweh's decisive acts of judgment include few explicit prescriptions for life beyond exile. Configurations of hope will eventually emerge, but not until the full effects of judgment are felt. Yahweh's just judgment must first "uproot and tear down" the sacred pillars supporting the state religion. Jeremiah has already dealt the temple a crushing blow; and here, and throughout chapters 2–10, he subverts the promise of land and its capital city. Although Yahweh long ago brought the people of Israel out of Egypt to bring them into the land, now Yahweh hurls the inhabitants out of the land (10:18).

This announcement of siege and exile evokes a response of profound sadness (10:19-25). Commentators are uncertain as to the identity of the speaker(s). Some argue for Jeremiah. Some hear the voice of God in verses 19*a* and 20. Others detect the cry of the people, while still others the city Jerusalem. In character with the dialogical texture of the book, the text probably reflects a combination of individual and collective voices. The prophetic, communal, and divine voices converge in shared anguish and disappointment. The first voice cries out because the pain is too great to bear (10:19). Using the figure of a Bedouin family (Carroll 1986, 261), a second voice, perhaps that of mother Zion, mourns the loss of children and home (10:20). A third voice blames the "shepherds"—that is, the king and those who rule with him—for the hapless state of the people. The leaders' failure to seek Yahweh's guidance has led to their dispersion (10:21). Another voice, ominous and again anonymous, interjects her dreadful premonition of destruction, a tremendous uproar from the north that will leave "the cities of Judah a desolation, a lair of jackals" (10:22).

A composite lament closes the chapter (10:23-25). The wisdom-like prayer reflects on human freedom and evil in the world. The petitioner is anonymous, although the first-person form may point to Jeremiah. If so, he intercedes on behalf of Judah (especially in 10:25) in defiance of Yahweh's prohibition to pray for the nation (see, e.g., 7:16). The appeal falls into three parts. The first acknowledges human frailty and limitation, which are especially evident in a world under assault (10:23). While people would like to think otherwise, they do not control their own destiny (10:23; cf. Prov 16:9). Second, the prophet entreats Yahweh for "[gracious justice]" as opposed to vengeful justice (10:24). Divine justice without restraint leads to irretrievable destruction. Jeremiah cries out for chastisement rooted in mercy. Third, for those who have ravaged the people of Judah and destroyed their homeland, he seeks full-fledged divine vengeance (10:25). By asking for unmitigated judgment on those nations, Jeremiah prays implicitly for Judah's salvation. Judgment upon Judah's enemies establishes moral symmetry and divine justice, and it fashions hopeful possibilities for forlorn Judah. Divine anger against insolent nations, which we find full-blown in Jer 46–51, eventually brings to an end Israel's times of trouble.

Theological and Ethical Analysis

Despite the belief that God is everywhere, people erect sacred buildings to have the advantages of God's proximity (Levine 1970, 71-87). This central concern is as evident in the ruins of ancient Mesopotamia as it is in the plethora of religious structures today. Jews, Christians, Muslims, and others gather at places of worship to be close to God. This same underlying concern—to be close to God—is also present throughout the Bible. Israel built sanctuaries as places where God would be especially near. And when God was near, victory and success were thought to be almost certain. In fact, Israel understood the presence of God at its shrines to be the actual cause of victory and the basis for its well-being. Accordingly, military ventures were often launched at a sacred place or with some form of sacral object in hand (e.g., Judg 6:19-40; Josh 3:1-17; 2 Chr 20:1-30). When the Philistines dealt the army of Israel a terrible blow, for instance, the Israelites fetched the ark, Yahweh's special dwelling place. "Why has the LORD put us to rout today before the Philistines? Let us bring the ark of the covenant of the Lord here from Shiloh, so that he may come among us and save us from the power of our enemies" (1 Sam 4:3). After again suffering defeat in battle, this time with the ark in hand, the people are utterly dumbfounded (1 Sam 4:5-11). In due course the temple of Jerusalem became the primary location of Yahweh's special presence. And many worshipers entered its gates expecting unconditional blessing and protection. The Jerusalem establishment encouraged such confidence. For them the temple was not only the central, organizing, and unifying institution of the state, but also the true source of its security, deliverance, and salvation.

Jeremiah attacks the core belief that the holy place and its systems of worship provide unconditional protection from life's perils. He deems this trusted teaching dangerous and misguided. Not only is it out of touch with the historical realities of its day, but also more important, it puts the people of God into a moral and spiritual stupor. The state's official doctrine makes them numb and nominal. It deadens them to "the weightier matters of the law: justice and mercy and faith" (Matt 23:23; see Jer 7:5-11); it anesthetizes them to social ills that are destroying the fabric of their society. And it blinds them to the stark reality of a world caving in. Indifferent and inattentive to all that is around them, including the voice of God, they carry on as though all were well.

According to Jeremiah, all was not well and no liturgy, doctrine, ritual, or sacred object/place could change that. The prophet is adamant that well-being and blessing are outcomes of a spirituality that expresses itself in love for God *and* neighbor. Love for God cannot be divorced from love for neighbor, just as religion cannot be severed from ethics. "Those who say, 'I love God,' and hate their brothers or sisters, are liars; for those who do not love a brother or sister whom they have seen, cannot love God whom they have not seen" (1 John 4:20). Jeremiah refuses to let worshipers imagine that they can partition worship from social responsibilities. True worship manifests in concrete acts of love and generosity, especially towards those on the margins of society.

The temple sermon implies that anything used to put God at bay is a dangerous distortion of faith—even dazzling temples and trusted doctrines, prized projects and sacred traditions, tested moralities, and beloved institutions. When support systems are exploited to domesticate the free and unfettered God, they are doomed to fail. When they are used as antidotes to confronting God, they become idolatrous. And when religious regiments reduce God to rational discourse and people to mere objects they do more harm than good. Thus, the text urges the listening community to take inventory and tell the truth about itself. It implores us to give up our petty systems of control, and trust in the living God. For only with open hands are we truly free to love as we ought (Nouwen 1972).

Near the end of the literary unit, the dangers of idolatry are dealt with more directly (10:1-16). A liturgy of praise declares that the gods of the nations are "stupid and foolish" (10:8). They are merely the work of artisans (10:3-9). No matter how attractive, they are meaningless, false, perishable, and mere foils for the power and supremacy of the living God, the Lord of heaven and earth. To embrace "the way of the nations" and to worship their gods is thus to play the fool. To cast one's lot with the gods of Babylon is to do the absurd. With such uncompromising claims, the literary unit concludes its critique on idolatry. The text alerts the readers to the perils of idolatry within (7:1-15) and presumably beyond the borders (10:1-16). All forms of idolatry do violence to Israel's relationship with Yahweh. All represent a breach of the first commandment. Whether Israel relies on its own temple and ceremonies or on the gods of Babylon, its actions represent a bold act of infidelity. When venerating the work of human hands, whether foreign or indigenous, Israel abandons the incomparable God for systems that are powerless and unreliable. The nation reveres "the creature rather than the Creator" (Rom 1:25).

In sum, not all worship is acceptable to God. True worship is an expression of profound gratitude and fierce loyalty. It acknowledges God's place and prerogative in the world and in one's life. As such, it demands wholehearted trust in the living God and not in human structures or stale ideologies. True worship *imagines* an alternative world in which generosity and mercy replace violence and greed; and at the same time, it *empowers* congregations to join God in the work of "bring[ing] good news to the oppressed, binding up the brokenhearted, proclaiming liberty to the captives . . . [and] comfort[ing] all who mourn"—all through the power of love (Isa 61:1-2; see also Luke 4:18). Indeed, true worship unites devotion to God with acts of kindness. When the practice of religion seeks certitude, power, and security at the expense of justice and compassion, it becomes dangerous ("falsehood" in 7:4, 8; 10:14; see also 8:8, 10; 9:24). When it anesthetizes adherents to the pain of the world, it becomes skewed. When the worshiping community adopts the values of the dominant culture instead of those of the kingdom of God, it does irrevocable harm to people's lives and to the face of God. In all this, Jeremiah by no means rejects Judah's rituals or organized religion; rather, he denounces worship that is self-absorbed and impervious to the plight of the poor. At the end of the day, what God requires of us is quite simple: to act justly, to be merciful, and to practice faithfulness to God (7:5-7; cf. Mic

6:8). This, Jeremiah insists, is the way of Torah, which is the only basis for well-being amidst turbulent times.

DISMANTLING ISRAEL'S COVENANT RELATIONSHIP (JEREMIAH 11–17)

The third major literary unit in the book of Jeremiah highlights the repercussions of breaking the covenant. From start to finish we encounter a community that refuses to repent and obey God. This defiant autonomy leads to divine judgment: Judah will soon fall into the hands of its enemies. Jeremiah appears here as the Lord's covenant mediator insisting that the claims of the covenant are still urgent matters. The prophet also emerges as a suffering servant who endures the pain of Judah's rejection and bears the brunt of the nation's scorn. Consequently, Jeremiah bears witness to God through his daring message and his terrible ordeal.

Literary Analysis

Chapters 11–17 constitute the third major section of Jeremiah. Like other literary units in Jer 1–25, it is introduced by a prose sermon that exhibits many common features (11:1-17). The prose sermon begins with the formulaic rubric, "The word that came to Jeremiah from [Yahweh]," which constitutes the most basic structural indicator in the first half of the book (11:1; cf. 7:1; 18:1; 21:1). Immediately following this introduction, Yahweh demands that the prophet speak or act in some prescribed manner (11:2; cf. 7:2; 18:2; 21:2). The remaining verses provide the content of the action or message communicated (11:3-17; see also 7:3-15; 18:5-11; 21:3-7). In addition, the initial prose speech introduces the overriding theme of the literary unit: Yahweh takes the community to task for breaking its covenant obligations. Even more critically, the text outlines a script for dismantling another key facet of the nation's preexilic theological systems. Jeremiah 11:1-17 puts the covenant itself under the microscope. Whereas Jer 7:1-15, the temple sermon, destabilized core beliefs related to Israel's long-standing systems of worship and Jer 18:1-12 and 21:1-10 will call into question Judah's election tradition and the Davidic dynasty respectively, Jer 11:1-17 critiques the status of Israel's long-standing covenant with Yahweh.

Jeremiah 11:1–17:27 not only begins with a prose sermon but it also ends with one. Addressed to the "people of Judah and [those who live in] Jerusalem," the introductory speech on covenant and the concluding one on Sabbath observance bracket an assortment of materials, including three of the five major confessions of Jeremiah. These bookends serve three broad literary purposes. First, they establish an ominous tone for the unit by accentuating the grave consequences of disobedience to the covenant regulations. Disloyalty, they claim, will lead to the nation's undoing. Second, the framing texts produce coherence to intermediate chapters laden with dissonance. The predictable categories of the covenant metaphor, and specifically its theology of retribution, tame the literary and symbolic chaos. Third, the prose texts organize the major cycles of the unit: 11:1–12:17; 13:1–15:21; 16:1–17:27. Each of these cycles consists of a prose speech or a prose account followed by a lament. We shall now examine these three features in detail.

First, the prose bookends create a portentous tenor for the unit. The introductory passage, Jer 11:1-17 invokes a Deuteronomic curse upon those who are disobedient to the covenant. As W. L. Holladay and K. M. O'Connor have noted, Jeremiah recites the curse formula to prefigure the fate of Judah (Holladay 1976, 160-61; O'Connor 1988, 131). The prophet proclaims that the present community is no better than the ancestral one: both are guilty of breaking the covenant and both must suffer the consequences (11:8, 11). Jeremiah insists, moreover, that neither God's covenant with Israel nor prophetic intercession (11:14) can turn aside impending disaster (11:11, 12, 14, 17). They are no more able to save the community from judgment than the temple and its liturgical systems. In fact, the covenant only justifies divine judgment and deals a deathblow to any hope associated with Israel's known categories. The concluding passage, Jer 17:19-27, likewise stresses the urgency of covenant obedience and the ramifications of noncompliance. If the people of Judah violate the Sabbath, Yahweh will destroy Jerusalem and its palaces. Although Judah's future *appears* open-ended, the words "not [heed]" leave a foreboding mark on the text. From the standpoint of those living in the aftermath of the fall of Jerusalem, ground zero was stark evidence of the nation's decision: it did "not [heed]" and so sealed its destiny. Thus, Jer 17:19-27 combined with Jer 11:1-17 establishes Israel's guilt beyond reasonable doubt: Israel is responsible for breaking the covenant and must face dire consequences.

Second, the prose bookends create literary and theological symmetry by setting a potpourri of materials within a predictable covenantal framework. That is to say, when the opening and closing texts focus on the covenant between God and Israel, they produce order out of literary and symbolic mess. Like Jer 2–6 and Jer 7–9, much of Jer 11–17 is bumpy, disjointed, and stitched together with materials from different times and places. It consists of a variety of literary genres with limited coherence and thematic unity. And it appears, at least at first glance, to be a patchwork of prose pieces interspersed with poems. Prose sometimes spurs poetry whereas at other times poetry triggers prose. The prose sections are often quite specific: for example, Yahweh threatens to bring disaster upon the people of Anathoth for their plots against Jeremiah (11:21-23) or gives Jeremiah detailed instructions as to what he is to say and do (e.g., 11:1-17; 13:1-11). In contrast, the poetry is usually general, predicting famine and drought as a result of military invasion and occupation. Its images are laced with death and desolation as well as war and hopelessness. Both the poetry and the prose concur, however, that the divine work at this juncture involves "pluck[ing] up and pull[ing] down." Judah's social world is as fragmented as the text that presents it.

Jeremiah's cruel treatment at the hands of his community adds to the dissonance. He is attacked, ostracized, ridiculed, and rejected (see, e.g., 11:18-23; 17:14-18). His ordeal gives rise to raw expressions of rage and poignant doubts about divine justice (12:1-4; 15:15-18). Yet, Jeremiah never responds to his adversity penitentially, as if it were an outcome of his moral failings. Instead, he incessantly declares his innocence and prays for the restoration of moral order (e.g., 17:14-18). *The prose framework is an attempt to tame the raging chaos that Jeremiah encounters.* In context, the prophet's rejection and abuse reveal Judah's culpability. Whereas Yahweh suffers rejection in chapters 2–10, Jeremiah, Yahweh's covenant mediator, is spurned in chapters 11–17. "Now the figure of Jeremiah, typified in his rejection, serves to make plain that Israel has not kept the covenant and must suffer the inevitable curse spelled out in Jer. 11:1-8" (Clements 1996, 115). The prose framework therefore produces moral symmetry for the reader. Not unlike the prologue and epilogue of Job, the beginning and ending of Jer 11–17 create symbolic and literary cohesion. The borders hold together a world falling apart by vindicating the prophetic ministry of Jeremiah—he suffers for no fault of his own—while at the same time exposing Judah's blatant disobedience to God. Henceforth, the suffering of Jeremiah is neither pointless nor arbitrary but serves to justify the divine judgment directed against Judah. The nation will meet with ruin, with no hope for mediation, because it has rejected Yahweh and Yahweh's covenant mediator, Jeremiah.

Third, the prose framework of Jer 11:1–17:27 holds together three composite literary cycles: 11:1–12:17; 13:1–15:21; 16:1–17:27. Each of these cycles begins with a prose speech/account that announces/illustrates divine judgment for disobedience and apostasy (11:1-17; 13:1-11; and 16:1-9) followed by one or more laments (11:18-12:13; 15:15-21; and 17:14-18). Jeremiah 11:1–12:17 revolves around the theme of a broken covenant between Yahweh and Judah followed by prophetic and divine laments. The story of the loincloth and the parable of the wine jars introduce Jer 13:1–15:21. They present a disturbing picture of apostasy and divine judgment, which evokes profound sadness on the part of the people (14:2-9, 19-22), Yahweh (14:17-18), and the prophet (15:10, 15-18). Jeremiah's life experiences serve as a prophetic sign in Jer 16:1-13. To signal the desolation to come, God demands that Jeremiah remain unmarried and without children as well as refrain from other customary social practices. Like Jeremiah, Judah must relinquish all expectations for conventional arrangements. Following these signs of judgment, Jeremiah cries out in pain because of the taunts of his enemies (17:14-18).

The close proximity of lament to a prose speech or symbolic action is significant. In the present form of the text, the two, prose indictment and poetic lament, enjoy a symbiotic relationship that serves several far-reaching purposes. The prophet's screams of pain and his dangerous message of judgment accentuate key facets of the persona of the prophet. As a servant of God, Jeremiah suffers as a direct consequence of Judah's violent reaction to the prophetic indictment. His words and symbolic actions, his frontal attack on the nation's well-established conventional arrangements, provoke rage and concerted efforts to silence the prophetic voice. Thus, the text does not focus primarily upon Jeremiah's *personal* suffering per se but suffering that grows out of his specific situation as a prophet. This suffering becomes an integral part of the divine message to Judah.

After delivering an uncompromising discourse on covenant observance (11:1-17), for instance, Jeremiah complains that he is under attack by community members who would like to destroy him (11:18–12:4). In the face of this persecution, he cries out to God for relief and justice (see esp. 12:1-4), although in a world that is unraveling at the seams, even modest accommodations for safety are not given (12:5-6). The connection of lament and sermon suggests that Jeremiah's grave condition is a direct consequence of the community's offensive against God's covenant mediator. In an effort to nullify the curse pronounced by Jeremiah, his townsmen attempt to cut off the prophet "from the land of the living." Such actions, however, are ineffectual and only expose their malevolence.

Juxtaposing the prose indictment and prophetic lament also demonstrates the utter disparity between the righteous prophet and the idolatrous nation. In the coalescence of lament and divine speech, Jeremiah's every move, his every word, his cries out of the depths, all bear witness to the nation's arrant disobedience as well as to his own "innocence" and alliance with Yahweh. Each prose indictment speaks of various aspects of the nation's wrongdoing, while the adjoining lament clarifies the prophet's integrity and veracity. Accordingly, Jeremiah declares that he was unaware of the community's assault on him and that such aggression was entirely unjustified (11:18-23). The prophet complains that he is a "man of strife and contention to the whole land" (15:10). Though he has "[neither] lent nor borrowed," all curse him (15:10). Though he has been faithful to his prophetic vocation (15:16-17), he still suffers excruciating pain (15:18). He is recompensed evil for good (18:20) and must endure the wrath of those who hate him (18:22). The prophet faces scorn, abject humiliation, and reproach on account of his message of violence and destruction. Jeremiah, especially in his role as a righteous sufferer, unmasks the community's stubbornness, thus justifying the ensuing desolation and exonerating Yahweh of any wrongdoing. This apology was especially pertinent to the survivors of the national tragedy of 587 who were grappling with serious questions about the justice and character of God. It argues that God was neither powerless to prevent the terrible events nor unjust in bringing them to pass.

Finally, the nexus of prose indictment and poetic lament creates a milieu of death in which the guilty community *and* the innocent prophet go down together in apparent hopelessness. In doing so, the prose discourses and the laments descend into near oblivion as they depict the destruction of Judah's world. Whereas Jeremiah's suffering is cast in stark contrast to that of Judah's, both experience shocking devastation. Akin to the prose sermons, which broaden and intensify the scope of Judah's crumbling world, Jeremiah's laments, when read in succession, traverse "a road which leads step by step into ever greater despair" and "threaten[s] to end in some kind of metaphysical abyss" (von Rad 1965, 204). In concert, they testify to the descent of darkness upon the world. And no one—neither righteous nor unrighteous—is exempt from the terrifying reality of cosmic crumbling.

The Confessions of Jeremiah

As one can see from the above discussion, one of the most distinctive characteristics of Jer 11–17 is the presence of Jeremiah's laments (11:18–12:6; 15:10-21; 17:14-18; cf., 14:11-16, and beyond the perimeters of this large unit, 18:18-23 and 20:7-18). Scholars customarily refer to these prayers as "Confessions." Such a designation can be misleading since they are neither penitential pleas nor recitals of faith. Yet, akin to Augustine's *Confessions*, Jeremiah's prayers reflect vacillating moods, trying circumstances, personal suffering, and a robust dialogue with God. Although the prophet addresses his words to God and not Judah, they nonetheless become an integral part of the divine message in written form. Consequently, the prophetic oracle and the prophetic persona together bear witness to God's purposes on earth.

For many, the Confessions are the most engaging part of the book of Jeremiah. In the early part of the last century, scholars read these prayers as the prophet's personal journal, which revealed his inner life and personal struggles. Skinner proposed that the Confessions formed "no part of [Jeremiah's] public message . . . and were probably never published in his lifetime" (1922, 16). Accordingly, their greatest value was their insight into the psychology and personality of Jeremiah. Such a view created an impregnable wall between Jeremiah the person and Jeremiah the prophet. The latter was the repository of the divine message, whereas the former merely revealed a complex and somewhat dysfunctional personality.

Attentive to the similarities between the laments in the Psalter and the Confessions, scholars eventually came to realize that Jeremiah's prayers were more stylized than they once thought. Because of their standard language and conventional features, the Confessions were no longer regarded as an individual expression of a particular human temperament (von Rad 1983, 88-99). They conformed in large part to the lament genre. If the Confessions were not the "personal" prayers of Jeremiah, then perhaps they played some role in his ministry. Berridge argued this very point. He made a convincing case that the Confessions were spoken in public, "constituting a part of his proclamation" (1970, 157). According to him, they enjoyed a "general validity transcending his personal experience" (1970, 131). Taking this line of reasoning a step further, Reventlow went on to suggest that as a spiritual leader, Jeremiah's "I" in the Confessions represented the "personification of the community" (1963, 259). In effect the prayers of the prophet were the prayers of the nation.

Building upon these studies, more recent scholarship has focused on the paradigmatic force of Jeremiah's suffering, arguing that Jeremiah's piety and suffering served as a model for the faithful exiles in Babylon and the repatriates who returned to Judea after the exile. For these wounded people the traditional interpretation of suffering as punishment made little sense. Retributive theology could no longer adequately explain their experience. When wrestling with how to explain their harsh circumstances they appealed to the persona of Jeremiah, a prophet who suffered not because of sin but because of his obedience to God. Innocent suffering found its justification in the person of Jeremiah, and the righteous prophet became an exemplar for all who suffer for no fault of their own. Henceforth, suffering would no longer be viewed as "shameful, resulting directly from wrongdoing . . . but rather as a typical part of life" (Welten 1977, 149).

Another recent development in research is worth noting. Scholars have begun to examine the Confessions of Jeremiah in their literary setting *(Sitz im Buch)*. This tendency is a patent departure from past studies, which have by and large viewed Jeremiah's laments as scattered haphazardly throughout chapters 11–20. By studying the Confessions contextually we now know that the interpretive community of Jeremiah used Jeremiah's laments to demonstrate the guilt of the people and the necessity of exile (e.g., A. R. Diamond, K. M. O'Connor). As such, the Confessions serve the broad purposes of theodicy in the final form of the text: they portray Judah's hardship and misfortune as a consequence of its mistreatment and rejection of Jeremiah, God's spokesperson. By placing full responsibility upon the nation's shoulders, the Confessions free God of culpability and moral mismanagement.

JEREMIAH AS GOD'S COVENANT MEDIATOR (JEREMIAH 11:1–12:17)

Literary Analysis

In the prose introduction Jeremiah indicts Israel and Judah for breaking the covenant (Jer 11:1-17). Infuriated by his message, the people of Jeremiah's village, Anathoth, attempt to silence him. Jeremiah reacts to their plot by crying out to God for help and retribution (11:18–12:6). Not only does God respond to Jeremiah's complaint but God joins the prophetic lament over Israel's utter desolation in Jer 12:7-13. The unit concludes in an unexpected way: God threatens to punish the nations that once ravaged the "house of Judah" and then resolves to show compassion to them (Jer 12:14-17).

Exegetical Analysis

The Covenant Curses for Disobedience (11:1-17)

In some measure Jer 11:1-17 reiterates the prophetic message delivered in the first ten chapters of the book: the people of God have been unfaithful and therefore must brace themselves for a disaster from which they will not escape. The prose sermon, however, expresses this theme in the language, style, and theology of Deuteronomy. Like Deuteronomy, the language of Jer 11:1-17 is prolix and repetitive. Its prose is sermonic and rhetorical. A number of words and phrases in the text are virtually identical to those found in Deuteronomy (e.g., Jer 11:3 = Deut 27:26; Jer 11:4 = Deut 4:20; Jer 11:5 = Deut 7:8, 8:18, 9:5; Jer 11:7 = Deut 4:30, 8:20; Jer 11:8 = Deut 29:1, 9; Jer 11:10 = Deut 8:19, 11:28). Moreover, the prose sermon reflects a Deuteronomic theology in which God promises blessing for obedience and threatens punishment for disobedience (Deut 28). If Israel complies with the stipulations of the covenant, well-being and prosperity will follow. If Israel does not heed Yahweh's commandments, disaster and judgment will ensue.

The structure of Jer 11:1-17 is also strikingly similar to speeches in the Deuteronomistic corpus (e.g., Deut 6, 8; 2 Kgs 17:7-18): it includes an introduction (11:1-2), the word of Yahweh in the imperative, that is, the commandments (11:3-6), a statement of disobedience (11:7-10), and divine judgment (11:11-17). Finally, in the spirit of Deuteronomy, which reinterprets the Sinai covenant in light of pressing concerns of subsequent communities, Jer 11:1-17 re-performs the demands of the covenant in a new setting for a new generation. Covenant, therefore, is not a souvenir from a museum but a living word that makes fresh demands on the people of God. Jeremiah himself recognizes the binding value of the ancient covenant when he replies, "So be it, LORD" (11:5).

In the initial prose sermon Yahweh addresses Jeremiah four times with four distinct commands (11:2-5, 6-8, 9-13, 14-17). Couched in the negative, the first directive follows the letter of Deut 27–28 (11:2-5). "[All are] cursed who do not [obey] the terms of this covenant" (11:3). God instructs Jeremiah to summon the people of Judah to obey the terms of the covenant. The demand for obedience grows out of the exodus story; that is, obedience is the joyous response to God's gracious act of liberation from oppression, "when I brought them out of the land of Egypt, from the iron-smelter" (11:4). God freed the Israelites from Egyptian bondage so that they might obey a benevolent suzerain and enjoy a special relationship with this God. Although God's covenant with Israel is a gift, it does not offer Israel a free ride. Privilege involves responsibility: "From [the one to] whom much [is] given much [is] required" (Luke 12:48). To use Bonhoeffer's terms, grace is not cheap but costly. From the very start, God expects Israel to obey its covenant obligations, and in large measure, Israel's continued status as God's people is dependent upon such fidelity. Obedience is thus in no way ancillary but is the very centerpiece of the covenant relationship. To remain in the land and enjoy the blessings of the covenant, Judah must be a faithful vassal (11:3-5).

The second admonition (11:6-8) builds on the harsh tone of the previous verses. The itinerant prophet calls upon the people of Judah to "hear the words of this covenant and do them" (11:6). Earlier communities had their chance to obey the terms of the covenant but adamantly refused (11:8). God therefore brought upon them "all the words of this covenant." This historical synopsis is another somber warning for the contemporary community. It characterizes Israel's entire history as one of incessant disobedience and infers from this that the present hearers will likely do little to change it. Interestingly, the Septuagint (LXX) almost entirely omits verses 7-8. The shorter Greek text states succinctly, "The Lord said to me . . . hear the words of this covenant and do them, *but they did not*" (my emphasis). Whereas the Hebrew text uses the ancestors' disobedience as a rhetorical device to sway the contemporary people of God, the Greek text hones in only on the unwillingness of the contemporary community to heed the word of God through Jeremiah. Both texts declare that violating the stipulations of the covenant carries grave consequences.

Next Yahweh informs Jeremiah of a "conspiracy" simmering among the people of Judah and the inhabitants of Jerusalem (11:9-13). What makes the conspiracy so dangerous is that it is against God. The Judeans have resolved to follow their ancestors' example of disobedience and unfaithfulness. The first two verbs in verse 10 convey the nature of the "revolt" in stereotyped language: the people of Judah have "*turned back* to the iniquities of their ancestors and have *gone after* other gods to serve them" (my emphasis). The third verb is less common: the house of Israel and the house of Judah have *broken the covenant* made with their ancestors. For the first time in the book, Jeremiah *explicitly* accuses the nation of breaking the covenant. The precise language to "break covenant" occurs five times in Jeremiah (11:10; 14:21; 31:32; 33:20; 33:21), and two of these references identify Judah as the covenant breaker (11:10 and 31:32). Jeremiah 31:32, a principal text for the construction of exilic and postexilic Judaism, states that the establishment of a "new covenant" is necessary since Israel has broken the covenant that God made at Sinai. The reference in Jer 11 is significant because it speaks of a breach that places the future of the house of Israel and the house of Judah in grave danger. This text asserts that one cannot write off the covenant demands without suffering grave consequences, even more so since the people's love affair with "many gods" violates the very cornerstone of the covenant relationship: "you shall have no other gods before me." Furthermore, by associating covenant breaking with the conspiracy against Yahweh (11:9-10), Jeremiah declares that the people's disobedience is a formal and brazen renunciation that will result in the covenant curses (11:11-13). The prophet, therefore, contends that the covenant itself, upon which the community depends for its national identity, has suffered a lethal blow. Long construed as one of Israel's sources of refuge from harm, it can no longer protect the people from disaster. All this contributes to the dismantling of Judah's entrenched preexilic categories.

The final part of the prose discourse intensifies the scope of the divine judgment (11:14-17). Yahweh forbids Jeremiah from interceding on behalf of the apostate people. The command not to intercede in Jer 11:14 is essentially a repetition of Jer 7:16. The people have "[not listened]" to Yahweh (11:8) and now it is Yahweh's turn "not [to] listen" (11:14). By betraying their covenant obligations, the people of Judah have forfeited their covenant claim upon God and their right to enter Yahweh's house. No prophetic intercession or priestly offerings can thwart God's plans to strip away Judah's world (11:14-15). Despite these harsh words, Yahweh still refers to wayward Judah as "my beloved" (11:15), "a green olive tree, fair with goodly fruit" (11:16; see also Hos 14:6) and a people "planted" by God (11:17). As we have seen elsewhere, the text fuses the language of endearment with scathing rhetoric: Yahweh's "beloved" has committed "vile deeds"; the "green olive tree" will be set ablaze "with the roar of a great tempest"; and even though Yahweh has "planted" Judah, Yahweh has now "pronounced evil" against the nation. Although judgment is sure, God cares deeply for the "beloved." Indeed God still loves them even through the worst of times.

Jeremiah's First Confession (11:18–12:6)

The next section (11:18–12:6) shifts from Yahweh's speech to the nation to Jeremiah's speech to Yahweh. That is, we move from sermonic material to the language of prayer/individual lament. While some would isolate Jeremiah's confession from its literary context, hard and fast lines are unnecessary. The prophet's lament is curiously tied to the prose sermon. The prophet's "treasonous" allegation that the covenant relationship is damaged beyond repair incites an impassioned attack upon his life, which in turn inspires his prayer. In an attempt to silence the dissident prophet and ultimately the subversive voice of God, Jeremiah's fellow villagers in Anathoth plot to kill him (11:19). In response Jeremiah cries out to God for help.

The words of Jeremiah's opponents carry considerable legal weight. When they declare, "you shall not prophesy in the name of [Yahweh], or you will die by our hand" (11:21), the prophet's enemies are not merely engaged in a vendetta against Jeremiah or an unauthorized attempt on the prophet's life. Rather, their action constitutes a formal pronouncement of death for offenses that are perceived as detrimental to the social and religious structures of community life. In the judgment of the people of Anathoth, Jeremiah has committed offenses that deserve capital punishment. So they take action to rid the community of one who engages in activities deemed reprehensible to God and society. When Jeremiah invokes the covenant curses upon the nation, he commits an act of violence against Judah's treasured arrangements. His assault on the nation and its covenant relationship with God represents the kind of "antisocial" behavior that the "men of Anathoth" perceive correctly as a serious threat to the status quo. Putting Jeremiah to death, therefore, serves to protect existing structures from collapse. Expunging the "guilty" from the midst of the nation is a desperate attempt to preserve a culture under siege.

When Jeremiah attacks Judah's deep-rooted beliefs and institutions, he relinquishes the legal protection enjoyed by insiders. This lack of social insulation produces distress and vulnerability. "I was like a gentle lamb led to the slaughter. I did not know it was against me that they devised schemes" (11:19). The symbolism of Jeremiah as a "gentle lamb led to slaughter" conveys a sense of innocence and naiveté, as well as defenselessness against the onslaught of enemies. Here and elsewhere in the book, Jeremiah's vocation as spokesperson for Yahweh provokes harsh criticism, threats against his life, and formal legal charges leveled against him. Those who attack Jeremiah imagine that they are acting on behalf of God, which makes the attack all the more dangerous. Like Job, Jeremiah vigorously opposes their efforts and rejects their arguments against him. He is adamant about his innocence and insists that his accusers condemn him unjustly. In this world devoid of legal and social constraints to protect the righteous from evildoers, the prophet can still appeal to God who responds to the cries of the oppressed and vulnerable. Replete with legal language, Jeremiah commits his case or suit *(rîb)* to a God who "judge[s] righteously" and who "[tries] the heart and mind" (11:20). Even the prophet's petition for retribution (11:20*b*) is no more than a cry for justice in a juridical sense, and not only for his own justice, but also for all in Israel who are buffeted by violence and injustice.

As "righteous judge" Yahweh hears Jeremiah's lament and pronounces the prophet's enemies guilty. In doing so, Yahweh vindicates the prophet, exacts vengeance on his behalf, and promises to restore moral sanity to a badly fractured world. God's response (11:21-23) is therefore all that Jeremiah hoped for; it bears out his belief that God acts faithfully on behalf of all those who face intimidation and persecution. God wants justice as much as Jeremiah and so promises to re-establish symmetrical moral categories. With stereotyped prose language, the text announces that God will put an end to the evildoers from Anathoth (11:22-23) and silence those who attempt to subdue Jeremiah. And righteousness will prevail.

Instead of providing peace, however, the assurance of divine judgment only further torments Jeremiah (12:1-6), for his own local context, his own specific situation in life, contradicts such claims. Jeremiah's world is still terribly fractured and in utter disarray. There is no evidence of justice, no visible sign of equilibrium, and no moral logic. The "guilty prosper," the "treacherous thrive," and Yahweh appears blind or even in collusion. "You plant them, and they take root . . . you are near in their mouths yet far from their hearts" (12:2). In contrast, the righteous prophet suffers for no apparent reason ("my heart is with you," 12:3). His charge against God is therefore no theoretical whim about rewards and punishment but a deeply personal cry. His queries are not philosophic but existential; they grow out of raw disappointment and pain. At the same time, his cries of anguish clearly transcend individual experience. Jeremiah the prophet represents all who suffer at the hands of evildoers and who are tormented by the injustices to which the poor fall victim.

Notwithstanding this broad appeal, Jer 12:1-6 is still an individual lament, which employs the lawsuit genre to express serious doubts about God's just rule on earth. Ordinarily the lawsuit genre conveys Yahweh's displeasure over some ethical or judicial infraction committed by Israel. In Hos 4:1-3 and Mic 6:1-2, for instance, *Yahweh takes Israel* to court for violating the terms of the covenant. In Jer 12:1-6, however, the *prophet takes God to court* and blames God for injustice. Jeremiah concedes from the start that the legal proceedings will eventually corroborate Yahweh's innocence, "you will be in the right" (12:1, especially since Yahweh is judge and jury!). Even so, he brings his lawsuit *(rîb)*, which, if proved, would impugn God's character. The essence of Jeremiah's accusation is that the wicked "get away with murder" at the same time the innocent are deprived of justice (Jer 12:1-4). Such ought not to be the case in a morally just universe. In neat and congruent worlds, especially one grounded in Deuteronomic categories, God defends the righteous and punishes the wicked (see Deut 27–28; see also Ps 1 as well as the old proverbial wisdom in Prov 10:1–22:16). However, such a world does not exist for Jeremiah and, therefore, he takes God to task.

The response to the lament of Jeremiah indicates that God hears but ignores his "legal case" (12:5-6). God refuses to "clean up the mess" by answering the prophet's disturbing questions. Instead, God rebukes Jeremiah, warns him that his trials will only intensify, and, as in the book of Job, has a cross-examination readily prepared: "If you have raced with foot-runners and they have wearied you, how will you compete with horses? And if in a safe land you fall down, how will you fare in the thickets of the Jordan?" (12:5). Jeremiah must prepare to face increasing hostility from his "kinsfolk" despite appearances to the contrary ("though they speak friendly words to you," 12:6). In a dangerous world void of moral certitude, God demands of Jeremiah—and all those who dare question divine justice—faithfulness and courage.

God's Lament Over the Beloved (12:7-13)

The catchword "house"—"for even your kinsfolk and the [*house of your father*] . . . " (12:6)—connects Jeremiah's previous lament with Yahweh's lament, "I have forsaken my *house*"(12:7 my emphasis). Uniting these two independent texts holds important implications for interpretation. When the poems are brought together, God's response to Jeremiah's lament no longer concludes with the abrasive words of 12:5-6. Rather, God empathizes with the prophet's plight and mourns over Israel's desertion and distress. God has problems too, and these only further complicate the situation. For now, it becomes altogether clear that Jeremiah does not suffer alone; God also suffers, as do the people of Judah. The whole world is a broken and perilous place. With great sorrow and conflicted passion, Yahweh grieves over Israel's defiance. "My heritage has become to me like a lion in the forest; she has lifted up her voice against me" (12:8). Yahweh casts off his people who are referred to affectionately as Yahweh's "house" (12:7), Yahweh's "heritage" (12:7, 8, 9), the "beloved" of Yahweh's heart (12:7), Yahweh's "vineyard" (12:10), and Yahweh's "pleasant portion" (12:10). The repeated first-person pronouns, "my house," "my heritage," "my heart," and "my vineyard," reveal God's involvement and identification with ravaged Jerusalem. God undergoes enormous pain and sadness over the ruptured relationship with Israel. In addition, the alliteration and cadence of the Hebrew word "desolate" and other sibilants in 12:10-11 (šemāmâ/šāmāh/lešmēmâ/šemēmâ/nāšammâ/ʾîš/śām, which the NRSV translates "desolate/they have made it a desolation/desolate/made desolate, no one lays") creates a dirge-like quality that sets off Yahweh's sorrow. The only thing that torments God more than Israel's abject condition is that "no one [even cares]" (12:11).

It is important to note that when the laments of Jeremiah and Yahweh (12:7-13) are connected, Yahweh still neither answers the prophet's probing questions, nor attempts to repair the badly fractured and tortured mirror of community life. Propositional solutions are not given. Even when acting as Israel's antagonist and judge, God cannot or will not impose moral coherence. In the discordant world of the text, as is the case in our own world, human freedom limits God's justice and God's power. God stands powerless and tormented by the people's (bad) choices. Gustavo

Gutiérrez's commentary on the book of Job applies here: "The all-powerful God is also a 'weak' God. The mystery of divine freedom leads to the mystery of human freedom and to respect for it" (1997, 77-78). Such freedom unites Jeremiah, God, and the exilic readers in suffering and vulnerability.

A Word for Israel's "Evil Neighbors" (12:14-17)

Yahweh's speech in prose employs the term "heritage" from the previous lament (12:7-9) as well as the motto of the book, "to pluck up . . . to build" (1:10). This obscure text seemingly explores the fate of those who have devoured, destroyed, trampled down, and made God's beloved, God's heritage, a desolation (12:7-13). Will these "evil neighbors" get what they deserve? Will God act justly and take vengeance? In a world that has suffered irrevocable harm, matters of justice are complex and conflicting. Yet, God does pledge to "pluck . . . up from their land" those who would even "[lay a hand]" on Israel's heritage. Perpetrators of evil will get what they deserve. In addition, Yahweh promises to "pluck up" or rescue Judah from the midst of the nations. The same word "pluck up" denotes the destruction of Israel's enemies and the deliverance of Israel from the nations. After the "plucking up," God will have "compassion on them," and "bring them again to their heritage and to their land" . . . (12:15).

However, God resolves to show mercy to the people of Israel *and* the other nations. If the nations "diligently learn the way(s) of my people" and "swear by my name" (12:16), God will welcome them into the community of faith. This astonishing message blurs the distinctions between insiders and outsiders. It declares that God's mercy extends beyond national borders to all people on the earth (cf. 12:3). If the first readers hoped to straitjacket God into clear-cut categories of judgment and salvation, judgment for others and salvation for them, they would be sorely disappointed. The text's "astonishing message of 'universal' restoration" heralds that God judges all people by the same covenant standards (Holladay 1986, 291).

Theological and Ethical Analysis

The book of Jeremiah is a thick response to the collapse of Judah's world. In Jer 11:1–12:17 we encounter two dominant understandings of suffering, which are in fact mutually exclusive perceptions of life. The presence of both creates a theologically rich and generative texture. Deuteronomic categories articulate a coherent and symmetrical system, which attends to the construction of a morally exacting universe. In this world, blessing and punishment are purposefully meted out according to conduct. The righteous enjoy blessing from God while evildoers are punished for their wrongdoing. In this predictable and morally unequivocal world, Judah's devastating circumstances are not value-neutral. The nation brings exile and destruction upon itself by refusing to comply with its covenant obligations. God holds Judah accountable for its behavior. And God's people must take full responsibility for their action and eventually come to repentance. Coexisting with this congruent and stable worldview are texts that are wild, explosive, and at times cynical. They throb with anxiety and contend that neatly constructed ethical systems do not fully appreciate the wide range of human experiences. These dissonant texts bring the reader face-to-face with moral ambiguity and innocent suffering. Here one enters a world defined by poignant questions (e.g., 12:1) rather than answers. Some of these queries cast doubt on conventional structures and bear witness to the many postures of evil and the deafening silence of God.

With a clear association to Deuteronomy and the Deuteronomistic History, Jer 11:1-17 articulates the first of these radically different understandings. The covenant sermon is an accusation that Judah has disobeyed the "[terms] of this covenant," indeed has "[fractured]" the ancestral covenant, and therefore must brace itself for inescapable judgment. Jeremiah's assault on the nation is primarily articulated in retributive categories. The prophet predicts that the covenant curses shall befall the nation (such as exile and military defeat) as a penalty for its moral failure and breach of covenant obligations. Just as the ancestral community disobeyed the conditions of the covenant and reaped the consequences of its conduct, so the present nation runs the same risk of suffering these same consequences. Such arrangements dispel any trace of ethical ambiguity. The lines that separate good from evil are well defined. A correlation between conduct and condition is distinctly drawn; acts have definite consequences; and life is predictable. In a universe controlled by a just God who is a faithful covenant partner, evildoers are punished for their wrongdoing, even if they are God's people. In a universe with a meaningful ethical code, suffering is explicable and never beyond the scope of God's just governance. National crisis or disaster and personal suffering are not the product of an arbitrary and chaotic world.

The presentation of Jeremiah's suffering, however, calls into question and then shatters these stable and congruent categories. Immediately following the covenant sermon, Jeremiah cries out to Yahweh concerning his own cruel treatment at the hands of evildoers, who are none other than the "people of Anathoth" (Jer 11:18–12:6). He has done nothing except obey God, yet he is maligned and persecuted. Although Yahweh responds to the prophet's complaint with the assurance of eventual retribution, Jeremiah is still caught in the chaotic interim before justice materializes. So, he accuses Yahweh of wrongdoing and collusion with his enemies (12:1-2). During the interim, between the "already and not-yet," Jeremiah bears witness to the disturbing reality of undeserved suffering and the apparent indifference of God. In stark contrast to his clear-cut proclamation, Jeremiah *lives* in a social environment in which the righteous are denied justice and the innocent encounter real evil. Jeremiah's first confession describes this dangerous world without offering explanation or justification for evil. Here there is no cover-up; no denial of the randomness of suffering, and no easy answers that anesthetize people to the deeply fissured universe. Even innocent prophets, who represent a myriad of tormented people, suffer abuse, bitter opposition, and failure! Thus, Jeremiah has only questions, and these reveal his conflicted character as well as his bold courage to look moral ambiguity in the eye without flinching.

The text, however, does not value the suffering of the prophet over the well-defined covenant arrangements. Rather, Jer

11:1–12:17 affirms the existence of both. Both are held in tension. Admittedly, the shapers of the book attempt to *use* the suffering of Jeremiah to uphold a congruent moral order. They argue that the fall of Judah and the exile to Babylon is in part a consequence of the people's mistreatment and rejection of Yahweh's messenger. Nonetheless, their attempt to *make sense* of Jeremiah's mistreatment is not altogether successful. The moral mess before us in the text is never entirely cleaned up. The prose structure of the book cannot diminish the force of Jeremiah's suffering by placing it in a symmetrical literary milieu. Orderly theological categories fail to censor the prophet's jumbled experience or outbursts of rage. To the contrary, when reading the literary unit (or the book as a whole) in our post-Holocaust context, Jeremiah's screams of pain and protest speak with enormous force. The anguish of the prophet draws attention to the failure of rational understandings to account for human evil. Such suffering puts God on trial, and bold Jeremiah, not unlike Dostoyevsky's Ivan Karamazov, refuses to exonerate God of responsibility for evil. Thus, the prophet, and the communities he represents, must live with disturbing questions, even accusations, rather than neatly construed answers.

CRIES OF DISTRESS (JEREMIAH 13:1–15:21)

Literary Analysis

This section (13:1–15:21) is introduced by two prose stories (13:1-11, 12-14) followed by three poems (13:15-17, 18-19, 20-27). These prose stories and poems accuse God's people of being callous and obstinate, and they continue to portray the dreadful consequences of divine judgment: Judah's world is under massive assault and its culture is on the verge of collapsing. Such claims are not new; nonetheless, they elicit a range of reactions on the part of Judah, Jeremiah, and Yahweh (14:1–15:21). These three voices form a triangular conversation engrossed in a desperate situation. Whereas the earlier chapters of the book typically mute the voice of Judah, the principal antagonist in the saga and the target of the coming military assault, the nation now has its say and becomes a full conversational partner (see, e.g., 14:7-9). In an attempt to avert imminent disaster, it cries out and pleads its case before Yahweh.

An anthology of prose and poetry, Jer 14:1–15:21 consists of literature from different times and places brought together under the heading of public loss and grief. The section's dominant genre is the lament. Indeed, the overall structure of these chapters reveals a surplus of laments, laments by the community, the prophet, and Yahweh. As the following chart indicates, cries of distress and responses to these cries organize the text.

Jer 14:1-9 Community Lament   parallels Jer 14:19-22 Community Lament
Jer 14:10-12 Divine Response   parallels Jer 15:1-4 Divine Response

Jer 14:13 Jeremiah's Lament
Jer 14:14-18 Divine Response

Jer 15:5-9 Yahweh's Lament

Jer 15:10 Jeremiah's Lament   parallels Jer 15:15-18 Jeremiah's Lament
Jer 15:11-14 Divine Response   parallels Jer 15:19-21 Divine Response

The above diagram identifies two parallel community laments in Jer 14:1–15:4. Each, we shall see, has its own complaint, petition, and admission of guilt (14:1-12 and 14:19–15:4). Positioned between these public expressions of sorrow is a lament of Jeremiah to which Yahweh responds by denouncing the false prophets (14:13-18). The accusations leveled against the prophets of peace provide the key for understanding Yahweh's insistence that Jeremiah not intercede on behalf of Judah. Yahweh's own lament over Jerusalem's devastation flanks these materials (15:5-9). Afterward, two parallel complaints of Jeremiah with denunciatory divine responses punctuate the section (15:10-21). The unit's complex structure reflects an intense conversational texture. All parties, including the reader, are involved in the loss of the city. All take part in the hard work of community grief. And all hear again that the old forms will not survive, that a reprieve will not be granted. Such courageous language breaks the denial and paves the way for eventual avenues of newness.

Exegetical Analysis

Jeremiah's Linen Loincloth (13:1-11)

This is the first symbolic act in the book of Jeremiah (see also 16:1-13; 18:1-12; 19:1-15; 28:1-17; 32:6-44). Prophets communicate the message of the Lord through speech and performance (see, e.g., Isa 7–8; Ezek 24:15-27). Hosea's "dysfunctional" family life sheds light on the broken divine-human relationship and God's unconditional love (Hos 1–3). Isaiah parades naked in the streets as a sign of Israel's impending captivity to Assyria (Isa 20). Hananiah breaks a wooden yoke from the neck of Jeremiah as a way of demonstrating his belief that Nebuchadnezzar's hold over Syria-Palestine would soon be shattered (Jer 28). Jeremiah places an iron yoke on his neck to emphasize his conviction that the exile would be a long-term historical reality (Jer 28). The soiled loincloth symbolizes, among other things, the ruin of Judah (Jer 13:1-11).

Narratives of symbolic acts or prophetic theater usually have three parts: (1) divine instructions to perform some deed, (2) the prophet's execution of God's commands, and (3) an explanation of the significance of the action. The "autobiographical" account of the defilement of a girdle/loincloth made of linen—a valuable fabric used for priestly vestments (Lev 16:4)—follows this basic form. God commands Jeremiah to "go and buy . . . take . . . and hide . . . [return and retrieve]" and without hesitation the prophet complies with each of the instructions: he goes, buys, hides, returns, and retrieves. His actions are followed by two interpretations. Just as the loincloth is ruined, so Yahweh will ruin the "pride of Judah and the great pride of Jerusalem" (v. 9). Once devoted to God—"cling[ing] to me" as a loincloth clings to the body—Judah and Israel no longer embrace and "listen" to God (vv. 8-11). Providing more than one interpretation of a symbolic act is unusual and likely represents multiple renderings at different points in the development of the text.

As the story begins we learn that Jeremiah obeys Yahweh's strange command to buy new underwear. He buries his new loincloth in a cliff of a rock according to the divine instructions. "After many days," Jeremiah digs it up and realizes that it is "good for nothing" (13:7). Because a journey hundreds of miles to the Euphrates is implausible, many interpreters have suggested that the Hebrew word *pĕrāt*, which elsewhere in the Bible means the Euphrates River, refers here to a waterbed near the village of *Parah*, only a few miles from Jerusalem (Josh 18:23). Jeremiah could have then actually traveled there and carried out God's instructions literally. Such a rendering, however, is uncalled for since the text is likely a parable rather than a report of an actual journey. And given the Babylonian setting of the first readers of this story, a reference to river Euphrates makes good sense. It may allude to the iniquity or ruination of the Babylonian exiles or perhaps the role of Babylon as Yahweh's instrument of judgment.

As already noted, the text itself interprets the symbolism of the loincloth in two distinct ways (13:8-11). The first exploits the fact that the loincloth is ruined and good for nothing. This soiled undergarment represents the sin of the house of Judah and resulting divine judgment. Just as the linen loincloth has been thoroughly soiled, so also is idolatrous Judah. Its determination to turn away from God and God's ways has made it as useless as the ruined loincloth. Therefore, Yahweh will *"ruin* the pride of Judah and the great pride of Jerusalem" (13:9, my emphasis). The second interpretation of the symbolic act has less to do with the soiling of the undergarment than the fact that loincloths fit tightly or "cling" to the loins. Like the linen loincloth, "the whole house of Israel and the whole house of Judah" (13:11) once "embraced" God and so were God's people, "a name, a praise, and a glory" (13:11). The imagery here conveys a sense of loyalty, devotion, and intimacy (see also Deut 4:4; 10:20; 11:22; 13:4; 30:20; 1 Kgs 11:2; 2 Kgs 3:3; 18:6). Long ago Israel and Yahweh were inseparable. Israel loved Yahweh and was steadfast and obedient (see Jer 2:1-3). Prideful Israel (cf. Jer 48:29), however, no longer clings or listens but goes its own way.

Broken Wine Jars (13:12-14)

In the next section, metaphors shift from loincloths to broken wine jars (13:12-14). Yahweh instructs Jeremiah to utter a proverb that appears self-evident, especially to a drunkard: wine jars are useless unless filled with wine! However, the meaning of this rather amusing aphorism is not what it appears to be: it is actually a sweeping judgment oracle against the nation. Yahweh threatens to "fill all the inhabitants of this land . . . and all the inhabitants of Jerusalem with drunkenness" (13:13). Davidic kings, priests, prophets, and people will drink the potent, perhaps poisonous, wine and stagger and reel in uncontrolled confusion. This imagery anticipates the oracles against the nations when "Jerusalem and the towns of Judah" lead a procession to drink from the cup of Yahweh's wrath (Jer 25:15-29). In addition to language of intoxication, Yahweh threatens to "dash" the citizens of Judah against each other without pity or compassion (13:14). Reading this text of violence brings to mind the dreadful imagery of the "little ones dashed against the rock" (Ps 137:9) or of Yahweh's anointed one "shattering" the nations "in pieces like a potter's vessel" (Ps 2:9). The same Hebrew word "dash[ed]" or "shatter" also occurs nine times in the celebration of Yahweh's fierce judgment against destroyer Babylon (Jer 51:20-23). That text asserts that Yahweh will hammer Babylon with a rapid series of blows from the war club until the nation is beaten to the ground. The object of Yahweh's attack in Jer 13:12-14, however, is not enemy Babylon but enemy Judah, God's own people.

"Dark Clouds Roll In" (13:15-17)

Three oracles follow without interruption, each announcing the terrible fate of the Judean community and its capital city Jerusalem. The first poem (13:15-17) is a faint plea to "listen" and "give glory to the LORD your GOD" [before it is too late]. The possibility of "listening" (13:15) or "not listening" (13:17) suggests that time has not yet run out. Judah still has a chance to repent and shape its future. The depiction of darkness (13:16) and the reference to captivity in the past tense (13:17) obscure this option. The descent of night in incremental stages—from "twilight" to "gloom" to "deep darkness"—paints a grim picture of what is to come. The search for light only to find darkness (13:16) is reminiscent of Amos's inversion of the Israel's popular understanding of the "day of Yahweh" (Amos 5:18-20). This ominous picture of "[nightfall]" is as disturbing to Jeremiah as it is to God. Neither takes pleasure in the people's suffering. Despite their arrogance and wanton autonomy—note the three terms used for the pride of Judah and Israel (Jer 13:9, 15, 17)—the prophet mourns and weeps uncontrollably, mirroring the anguish of God over the captivity of "the Lord's flock" (13:17; see also Jer 9:1).

Fallen King and Queen (13:18-19)

The next brief poem (13:18-19) is a funeral dirge that addresses the royal status of "the king and the queen mother," presumably Jehoiachin and Nehushta (2 Kgs 24:8). Just as the haughty nation was brought down, "stumbl[ing] on the mountains at twilight" (Jer 13:16), so also will those at the pinnacle of the social hierarchy. They will come down from their place of honor and assume "a lowly seat" (13:18) among those deported from Jerusalem to Babylon (2 Kgs 24:12). God "[casts] down the powerful from their thrones, and lift[s] up the lowly" (Luke 1:52), thereby inverting hierarchical arrangements. The king and queen mother, the last representatives of the royal institution, no longer hold a place of power and prominence. Anticipating the critique of unjust politicians and political systems in Jer 21–24, this brief oracle hints at the end of the monarchical structures. The text concludes with two references to exile (13:19), and exile has a strange but effective way of leveling the playing field.

The Royal City's Shame (13:20-27)

With the divestiture of royal power, the poetry departs from the *south* or the Negeb, the site of military occupation (13:19), for the dangerous *north*, from whence the attack originates (13:20-27). These spatial categories tie the humiliation of the royal family (13:18-19) to the brutal images of the country's defeat and the royal city's shame. The dynasty and its headquarters will fall together. Indeed, all Judah will suffer the indignities of military defeat. This third poem develops the central theme of the entire chapter: the downfall and humiliation of proud Jerusalem. Addressed to Jerusalem, as evident by the feminine singular forms and the explicit mention of the city in verse 27, Yahweh asks a number of haunting questions, the first of which probes the whereabouts of the people entrusted to mother Jerusalem. "Where is the flock that was given you, your beautiful flock?" (13:20; cf. 13:17) While the precise meaning of the query in the Hebrew is far from clear, we are reminded of other questions that God asks: "Where are you?" (Gen 3:9); "Where is your brother Abel?" (Gen 4:9); "How can I give you up, Ephraim? How can I hand you over, O Israel?" (Hos 11:8); "How can I pardon you?" (Jer 5:7). The present question is rooted in anger and heartache. Yahweh is deeply concerned over the welfare of the people, "the flock [entrusted] to you, your beautiful flock." Jeremiah has already conveyed divine sorrow when "weeping uncontrollably" over the captivity of his "flock" (13:17). But God also accuses the city and the royal family of defaulting on their obligation to care for their subjects (13:18). It was the responsibility of the royal city to protect, and the duty of the king and queen mother to defend. But both failed miserably and are therefore to blame.

Such anger and disappointment engender harsh charges, bewildering queries, and biting oracles of judgment. Jerusalem is personified not only as a mother bereft of children (13:20), but also as a "woman in labor" (13:21), a ravaged and violated prisoner of war (13:22, 26), and a shameless harlot (13:27). The poet paints a picture of violence and panic produced by military invasion. The city is defenseless before enemy aggression. If Jerusalem should inquire as to why it must suffer so—"Why have these things come upon me?"—the city must know that it has brought the tragic circumstances upon itself. "It is for the greatness of your iniquit[ies] . . . because you have forgotten me and trusted in lies" (13:22c, 25 in part). The text is unflinching in its conviction that military defeat and exile, the "[scattering of] chaff," are neither the consequence of mere geopolitical forces nor a God who is ruthless or indifferent. Jerusalem's total and complete disregard for Yahweh has led to its desperate situation. Arrogance and idolatry have brought down the glorious city. Indeed, at this moment in the drama the prophet has abandoned any hope for conversion or a reversal of Jerusalem's terrible fate. Judah has become so adamant in its rebellious ways, so entrenched in evil, that repentance and transformation are no longer possible. A change in the city's politics of apostasy is as unlikely as a leopard changing its spots or persons their pigmentation (13:23). The hopelessness of the situation demands intense mourning. "Woe to you, O Jerusalem! How long will it be before you are made clean?" (13:27).

Judah Bewails the Devastation (14:1-9)

Chapter 14 opens with a communal lament (14:1-9). According to its editorial heading Yahweh warns Jeremiah of a severe drought (14:1). A narrator reports the details of the disaster in the third person (14:2-6) and then the people speak for themselves in the first-person plural (14:7-10). The drought destroys the social, environmental, and economic aspects of living. The gates of the city languish and lie in gloom. Nobles send their servants for water but they return empty-handed. The ground is so parched that farmers cover their heads in shame and dismay. Even the doe forsakes her newborn fawn for lack of rain and the wild ass pants for air and eventually dies. All search for food and water to survive but there is "no water" (14:3), "no rain" (14:4), "no grass" (14:5), and "no [vegetation]" (14:6). Their absence signals inescapable starvation and impending death.

In anguish and exasperation the people cry out to God. Unlike most communal laments (e.g., Ps 44), their public expression of grief includes a confession of sin rather than a protest of innocence. God's people acknowledge their "iniquities" and many "apostasies" (14:7). In so doing they accept responsibility for their wrongdoing. At the same time, they implore God to intervene on their behalf. Their petition for help is terse and introduces an expression of trust: "O hope of Israel, its savior in time of trouble" (14:8a; see also 17:13; cf. 50:7). But this confession quickly turns into a complaint about God's inactivity:

Why should you be like a stranger in the land,
    like a traveler turning aside for the night?
Why should you be like someone confused,
    like a mighty warrior who cannot give help? (Jer 14:8b-9a)

139

Echoing the bold language of Jeremiah elsewhere in the book (e.g., 12:1-4; 20:7-12) as well as the despair expressed by the exiles in Isaiah (e.g., Isa 40:27), Israel complains that God is inattentive to its plight and unable to help. As Brueggemann so aptly suggests, Israel accuses Yahweh of being "a helpless giant" (1998, 135). But such cynicism is not really a denial of God's power or covenant relationship with Israel. Israel is certain, perhaps all too certain, of God's presence and its own status as God's people (14:9). What perplexes the nation is that God's power and its own special standing before God have not prevented the devastation.

In many respects, this communal lament is an ideal prayer. Even its disputatious language reflects the most robust and compelling aspects of Israel's spirituality. One might, therefore, expect a favorable response to the plea for help. To be sure elsewhere in the Hebrew Bible, God responds to prayers for help in the affirmative. When Hannah prays for a child at the shrine in Shiloh, Eli the priest recites the encouraging words, "Go in peace; the God of Israel grant the petition you have made to him" (1 Sam 1:17). When threatened by neighboring armies King Jehoshaphat prays for deliverance and victory (2 Chr 20:1-12), and Jahaziel delivers an oracle of salvation. "Thus says the LORD to you: 'Do not fear or be dismayed at this great multitude; for the battle is not yours but God's . . . take your position, stand still, and see the victory of the LORD on your behalf . . .'" (2 Chr 20:15, 17). Then again, God does not always answer prayer the way people desire. God refused to spare the child of David and Bathsheba (2 Sam 12:13-23). King Zedekiah does not receive divine assistance to defeat Nebuchadrezzar (Jer 21:2). And God does not restore equilibrium to Jeremiah's chaotic world as he wished; in fact God only rarely responds to Jeremiah's complaints with words of assurance (e.g., 12:1-6; 15:10-12; see also 15:15-21 for a rather complex oracular response).

God's Disconcerting Reply (14:10-12)

The divine reply to Israel's complaint (in 14:7-9) corroborates the point that God does not always answer prayer in the affirmative. God will not be railroaded. The anticipated oracle of deliverance is not given. God rejects the nation's plea for help and forgiveness, and reminds Israel of its idolatrous ways. The people have wandered far from the Lord and have shown little inclination to curb their infidelity (see 2:20-25). Therefore, God will "remember their iniquity and punish their sins" (14:10). There will be a time when God will "forgive their iniquity and remember their sin no more" (31:34), but now is not that time. At this moment covenant law governs the divine-human discourse and so judgment is the nation's penultimate reality. Judah must face its grim circumstances, take responsibility for its actions, and embrace its stark realities before counter-realities of hope can be formulated. The text thus forcefully rejects any attempt to validate the status quo or diminish the force of God's justice.

To emphasize divine judgment, Yahweh again forbids Jeremiah from interceding for the people (14:11-12). This is the third prohibition on prophetic prayer (7:16; 11:14). Jeremiah must do nothing to mitigate the sting of Yahweh's stance against the nation. God has rejected Israel's appeal for help, so Jeremiah must not pray for "the welfare [i.e., the good] of this people" (14:11). Yahweh also warns the worshipping community that fasting, prayer, burnt offerings, or grain offerings will not sway him or assuage the devastating effects of "the sword, famine, and pestilence." Judgment is sure and nothing will mitigate this position.

A Defiant Prophet and a Defiant God (14:13-18)

It is now Jeremiah's turn to voice his lament (14:13) and Yahweh is no less sympathetic to his plea (14:14-16). Jeremiah refuses to acquiesce and relinquish his role as advocate for Israel. In blatant disregard for the divine command not to intercede, he shifts the blame from Israel to the (false) prophets. They have deceived the people by prophesying, "You shall not see the sword, nor shall you have famine, but I will give you true peace in this place" (14:13). The prophets have been promising peace when disaster was approaching and therefore are at fault. When Jeremiah excuses Israel and blames the prophets, he indirectly blames the One who sends prophets and commands them to speak, sometimes deceptively (see 1 Kgs 22:1-28). Hence Jeremiah

141

implies that *God is ultimately responsible* for Israel's plight. And if this is the case, how can God hold the people accountable for matters beyond their control? What can people do when God sends prophets to deceive?

This is a bold and intriguing stance, for rarely in Jeremiah is God blamed, even tacitly, for Israel's terrible suffering. God is generally let off the hook and Israel is found guilty. Such a strategy contributes to one of the primary purposes of the book, which is to establish a reasonable defense for God's character in the face of Israel's suffering—especially for exilic and postexilic readers. As we have seen, Jeremiah construes the national calamities experienced between the years 598–582 as a direct result of Israel's sin and Yahweh's just punishment. Israel breaks covenant, forsakes Yahweh for other gods, rejects God's spokesperson Jeremiah, and so reaps the consequences of its misconduct. Israel's harsh realities are not the result of divine impotence, capriciousness, or malevolence. Nor do the nation's hardships nullify God's mercy and great love for the people.

Despite these arguments, there are counter arguments that contend that the crushing of Judah is too devastating and too complex for any singular explanation. Jeremiah 14:13 represents one of these dissenting voices. That Yahweh might be responsible for Judah's ill-founded optimism and wretched condition is an astounding insinuation. Yahweh, however, refuses to accept it. Rejecting Jeremiah's premises and implied blame, Yahweh retorts emphatically,

> I *did not* send them,
> I [*did not*] command them,
> [I *did not*] speak to them. (Jer 14:14, my emphasis)

The threefold use of the first person with the negative underscores the divine assertion that the prophets' message of peace is wholly unauthorized. It is "a lying vision, worthless divination" derived from "the deceit of their own minds" and not from Yahweh. This rebuttal is unambiguous, as is the ensuing judgment: the prophets will meet the very fate that they deny. They, along with many people in Jerusalem, will die "by the sword and famine" without honorable burials (14:14-17). Yahweh in turn will be acquitted of complicity.

The prose indictment of false prophets, which probably derives from the exilic period, helps explain the uncompromising posture of Yahweh toward the nation. It sheds light on both the crushing divine rejection to the people's prayer for help (in 14:2-9 and 14:19-22) and the prohibition on prophetic intercession (14:11-12; 15:1-4). The false prophets soothe the people's pain with salve and illusions of *shalom*. In their falsehood, they render what the people desire: coherence and continuity. But their message of peace spells disaster for the nation. Their words of hope, though extraordinarily attractive, are nearsighted. Their belief that Israel's mess can be easily cleaned up and that life will soon return to normal is a flat denial of the nation's profound loss and bereavement. Offering such hope not only contradicts geopolitical realities, but it also does violence to the character of God who is *just* and *forgiving* and who insists that the destruction of the city is a necessary and irreversible turn for Judah. Yahweh will not respond in kind, no matter who asks, be it Jeremiah, the people, or even Moses and Samuel (Jer 15:1). To grant a reprieve now would be nothing less than collusion with those who misrepresent social and symbolic realities. Instead, Yahweh demands that Judah look suffering right in the face, without illusions or pretensions. Only then will God's people discover God's hidden gift of hope and salvation. To break the denial is to trust that there is something beyond the collapse of safe human categories.

Prose turns to poetry as Yahweh continues to respond to Jeremiah's (and Judah's) lament (14:17-18). In utter contradiction to the prophets' message of peace (14:13), Yahweh presents a realistic picture: war ravaging the land. Yahweh's "virgin daughter" suffers a crushing blow that causes a grievous wound (14:17). Wherever God looks, God sees sick and wounded people. City and countryside are full of the dead. The sword and siege have done their work well: they have produced starvation, confusion, and defeat. Responsibility for the massive devastation lies in large measure with prophet and priest, the nation's leaders, who ply their trade without knowledge.

The people's plight is a source of great sadness.

> Let my eyes run down with tears night and day,
>   and let them not cease,
> for the virgin daughter—my people—
>   is struck down with a crushing blow,
>   with a very grievous wound. (Jer 14:17)

The voices of grief are so intertwined that any sharp distinction between Jeremiah and God risks misrepresenting the text. Both suffer with the people; both are dismayed at the nation's downfall. Both are overcome with pain. As T. E. Fretheim has observed, "Jeremiah's mourning is an embodiment of the anguish of God, showing forth to the people the genuine pain God feels over the hurt that his people are experiencing" (1984, 161). In unison, God and Jeremiah join the requiem for the fallen city.

Judah's Agonizing Question for God: "Why Us, Lord?" (14:19-22)

In a parallel lament Judah again participates in this symphony of mourning. The community cries out in sorrow, acknowledges its wrongdoing and pleads for God's mercy and help (14:19-22). The prospect of divine rejection is a reality too painful for Israel to fathom. Therefore, the nation hurls at Yahweh a battery of questions. The community poses these queries in order to understand its own bewildering situation. Following Jeremiah's lead (in 14:13), Judah intimates that its present situation makes no sense at all in light of the prophetic message of peace (14:19). It has heeded the words of the prophets, and yet nothing good has come of them. "We look for peace, but find no good, for a time of healing, but there is terror instead" (14:19; see 4:10; 6:14; 8:11, 15; 14:13-16). This cryptic allusion to the nation's trust in Yahweh's prophets is a veiled declaration of innocence.

The people of Judah also try to motivate God to respond favorably to their petition. They desperately appeal to whatever might persuade God to act on their behalf, including God's name, throne, and covenant (14:21). Surely, God would not want God's name maligned among the nations! Dishonoring God's "glorious throne," likely a reference to the Jerusalem temple and its ritual, would tarnish God's reputation. Perhaps it would be even more embarrassing if God were to violate the covenant with Judah, although elsewhere Jeremiah insists that Judah is the one who breaks covenant with Yahweh (11:10; 31:32). The last rhetorical question is actually a confession that Yahweh is the only One who can save and bring rain to the land (14:22). Neither the "idols of the nations" nor the impersonal forces of nature can end the drought and save Israel (14:1-9, 17-18). In making this profession of faith, Judah offers to God what God has long desired: loyalty and devotion. But the rejoinder (15:1-4) makes it painfully clear that the nation's confession is too little and too late.

Not Even Moses and Samuel Could Change God's Mind (15:1-4)

The divine response to the community's petition is structurally parallel to the earlier ban on intercession and offerings in Jer 14:10-12. Both reply to Israel's prayers with a definitive "No!" However, the statement in Jer 15:1-4 is even more emphatic. Yahweh outright dismisses the possibility of intercession. Even Israel's greatest intercessors, Moses and Samuel, would fail to persuade God to turn toward "this people" (15:1). Neither could prevent the disaster soon to befall the nation. The logic is straightforward: if these preeminent figures could not alter Israel's course, surely the people's own prayers (14:7-9, 19-22), even Jeremiah's mediation, will fall to the ground.

The allusion to Moses takes on another meaning. The verb "send out" (15:1) is the same Hebrew verb in Moses' declaration to the Pharaoh, "Let my people go" (see, e.g., Exod 5:1; 7:16; 8:1). In an inverted use of this core tradition, Yahweh threatens to "send" Israel away from his presence. "Send them out of my sight, and let them go" (15:1). Also reminiscent of Moses and the exodus story is the second verb which the NRSV translates, "let them go." This familiar word is used in Exodus and Deuteronomy to describe Israel's "departure" from Egypt. However, instead of "going forth" to "a land flowing with milk and honey," Jeremiah is to "bring Israel out" of the promised land to revisit the house of bondage. The fourfold credo, "to pestilence . . . to the sword . . . to famine, . . . to captivity" (15:2), as well as the "four destroyers" (15:3) all depict Judah's horrific "exodus." The nation will indeed "go out," but it will go forth to meet inescapable disaster. This disparaging recital of death, which answers the probing question, "where [should] we go" (15:2), replaces the saving formulations of old (e.g., Deut 6:20-24).

Israel's fate (15:3) is linked directly to "what King Manasseh . . . did in Jerusalem" (15:4). Placing collective responsibility on the shoulders of one person is unusual in the book of Jeremiah. Typically, the multiple voices of the text condemn either the nation's failed leadership or the entire people. Here, however, the writer identifies one king, Manasseh, as the principal protagonist in the nation's downfall. This intriguing identification is too often dismissed as a later, intrusive allusion. While the reference to Manasseh may be a gloss, it nonetheless functions typologically in the present form of the text. Manasseh is no longer merely a historical figure whose social and religious reforms adversely affected the nation. He represents all that is wrong with Judah's monarchic arrangements. Here and in 2 Kgs 21:1-18, the Judean king is the embodiment of Torah defiance and the antithesis of his grandson Josiah.

Second Kings 21:1-18 uses highly charged hyperbolic language to describe its antipathy for Manasseh. According to the text, the king's establishment of forbidden practices ruined the promising reforms of his father Hezekiah (21:2-6). Manasseh's Torah-condemned rituals defiled the sacred temple (21:7). His violence toward the innocent pervaded all Jerusalem (21:16). Manasseh deceived the people of Judah into doing "more evil than the nations had done that the Lord destroyed before the people of Israel" (21:9). Based on this record of moral and religious failings, the writer of 2 Kings concludes that the evil king single-handedly brought down the city of Jerusalem (21:10-15). Jeremiah 15:4 not only concurs with this judgment but employs it to validate

Yahweh's final rejection of Judah's plea for help in Jer 14:19-22. (For a more positive assessment of Manasseh, see 2 Chr 33:10-25 as well as the penitential "Prayer of Manasseh.") Thus the text uses the best (Moses and Samuel), and the worst (Manasseh) of Israel's tradition to stress the certainty of judgment.

Yahweh's Complex Reaction to Jerusalem's Fate (15:5-9)

Flanking the two parallel communal laments and their oracle responses in Jer 14:1–15:4 is a divine lament in which disconsolate Yahweh grieves over Jerusalem's destruction (15:5-9; see also 8:18–9:2; 14:17-18). Rejected Yahweh first addresses Jerusalem directly (15:5-6) and then speaks to another about the end of the beloved city (15:7-9). Every word of Yahweh's speech enunciates disaster, although expressions of mourning are so intermingled with rage that it is difficult to tell the two apart. This complex reaction to Jerusalem's condition embodies the work of grief that Yahweh, Jeremiah, and the people of Judah must do together. Such grief, which sometimes erupts as anger, sometimes as bewilderment, and at other times as uncontrolled sadness, is the first step on a long journey toward wholeness. Before any configuration of hope is possible, however, all must recognize that the city will never be the same, that its collapse is not episodic but long-term.

The rhetorical questions of the poem (15:5-9) indicate that nobody is paying attention to the destruction of Jerusalem.

> Who will have pity on you, O Jerusalem?
> Who will [have compassion for] you?
> Who will turn aside
>   to ask about your welfare? (Jer 15:5)

Forlorn Jerusalem (*yršlm*) is all alone. No one consoles the fallen city. No one cares enough "to ask" *(lš'm)* about its "welfare" *(lšlm)*. The consonants of the Hebrew word "to ask" *(lš'm)* can also mean "to(wards) Sheol." Thus, even to "inquire" *(lš'm)* about Jerusalem's *(yršlm)* "wellbeing" *(lšlm)* is to utter the word "Sheol" *(š'm)*, the place of the dead, which is the present abode of the nation.

The lament enlists into its service multiple images of Jerusalem's end. Its dominant metaphor is that of a helpless woman who is easy prey for her assailant. Defenseless Jerusalem is desperate, disgraced, and in utter ruins because Yahweh has stretched out his hand against her (15:6). But she is not innocent. Mother/wife Jerusalem has "rejected" Yahweh, "gone backward" (15:6), and has still not "turned" (šûb) from her recalcitrant ways (15:7). The poet imagines that when Jerusalem acts in unseemly ways, she threatens her own survival. To emphasize this point, two other metaphors are used to depict the ravages of war. Both transform traditional images of life into images of death and ancient promises of blessings into curses (15:8-9). The first exploits the ancestral promise of progeny: "I will make your offspring [more] numerous . . . [than] the sand . . . on the seashore" (Gen 22:17; 32:12; see also 1 Kgs 4:20). It is difficult not to hear echoes of this ancient promise in Yahweh's cry, "their widows [have become] more numerous than the sand of the seas" (15:8). What was once offered as divine assurance of survival now portrays the decimation of Jerusalem and its inhabitants. Widows populate the land instead of offspring. The second image personifies Jerusalem as a languishing mother of seven (15:9). She is no longer able to bear children and gasps for her last breath; she is "shamed and disgraced," and ultimately bereft of her young. The maternal blessing of seven, which customarily represents fertility and favor (Ruth 4:15; 1 Sam 2:5; cf. Exod 2:16), now symbolizes barrenness, bereavement, and rejection.

Persecuted for the Sake of Righteousness (15:10-14)

Two individual laments, almost universally associated with Jeremiah, bring closure to the mournful voices of this complex (Jer 13:1–15:21). Internally, Jer 15:10-14 and 15:15-21 comprise confessional material that parallels each other. Each consists of an individual lament that bemoans the absence of justice (15:10 and 15:15-18) and a disconcerting response from God (15:11-14 and 15:19-21). Externally, the two laments and the accompanying divine oracles balance the earlier communal laments in Jer 14:2-12 and Jer 14:19–15:4 (see chart on p. 133). However, whereas the first two community laments acknowledge wrongdoing and take some responsibility for misfortune, the concluding laments are indignant about the prophet's innocence before God and the community. In the war-torn world of the text, however, the righteous and unrighteous face an identical fate. War rains down on the just and the unjust ! The earliest readers of the text understood this all too well, as do all who suffer through no fault of their own.

In the lament in 15:10-14, Jeremiah's contemptuous treatment at the hands of persecutors takes center stage. He is so distraught over his condition that he wishes he had never been born (15:10). The prophet has done all that God has asked; he has faithfully fulfilled the responsibilities of his call and has neither "lent . . . nor borrowed." Yet he encounters nothing but "strife and contention." Despite his integrity, the whole land curses him. Instead of goodwill there is enmity. Rather than acceptance there is widespread rejection. The treatment he receives from his community and the dearth of moral order torment Jeremiah. However, this conflict is not the prophet's alone. It brings into full view the pain and protest of the oppressed.

This lament is full with interpretive challenges and possibilities, as evident in Jeremiah's scream of pain: "Woe to me, my mother, that you ever bore me, a man of strife and contention to the whole land! I have not lent, nor have I borrowed, yet all of them curse me" (Jer 15:10). The vocative "my mother" links Jeremiah's lament to the "mothers" of 15:8-9. Whereas the imagery of mothers giving birth typically conveys joy and blessing, here and in the previous passage it conveys deep regret and sorrow. Mother Jerusalem is emotionally and physically spent at the loss of her children and Jeremiah has endured such contempt that he wishes his mother had never given him birth (cf. Job 3). This maternal motif adds force to the somber tone of the text. But the proximity of Jeremiah's cry to languishing Jerusalem raises a number of questions. Does Jeremiah see himself as one of mother Jerusalem's bereaved children? If so, does he call out to her in anguish or anger? To be sure the prophet and the city are on the verge of going down together and thus have much to grieve over. However, the city has also been the source of his pain. Jerusalem has been Jeremiah's nemesis; it has made him "a man of strife and contention."

Then again, the prophet's reference "my mother" may be no more than an "apostrophized element" (Carroll 1986, 326) or a cryptic allusion to his call during which Jeremiah learns that Yahweh had chosen him before he was formed "in the womb" (1:5). In the latter case, the figure of speech reveals a crisis of vocation: the prophet expresses profound disappointment, even despair, over his seemingly failed mission. This despair eventually reaches its lowest point when the prophet curses the day when his "mother" bore him (20:14-17).

The subsequent verses of the lament (15:11-14) are equally puzzling. The almost unintelligible rendering of 15:11 in NRSV illustrates the problematic nature of the Hebrew text. It is difficult to determine whether the divine response to Jeremiah's lament is positive, negative, or some combination of the two. Craigie and others contend that Yahweh supports Jeremiah in 15:11-14, promising personal protection and the defeat of his enemies (1991, 209-10). Less sure, Carroll suggests that in verse 11 "Yahweh . . . presumably reassures the speaker of divine protection against the enemy" (1986, 327). Thompson, however, proposes that verses 11-12 are "Yahweh's word of rebuke" which is only reinforced in verses 13-14 (1980, 393-94). To compound the problems, the boundaries of the speeches are porous. Most limit Jeremiah's words to 15:10, although others, following the LXX, include 15:11 as part of Jeremiah's prayer. However, since the LXX and MT are two distinct editions of Jeremiah, it seems unwise to conflate the texts in the hopes of arriving at a harmonized reading. Finally, it is difficult to ascertain the intended audience of 15:13-14, which is a variant of Jer 17:3-4. In the latter context, Yahweh addresses Judah, but in 15:13-14 it is unclear as to whether Yahweh is speaking to Jeremiah, the people, or both.

The exegesis suggested here follows the MT and views 15:11-14 as Yahweh's "discordant" response to Jeremiah's lament in 15:10. Yahweh has supported and intervened on his behalf throughout his life, perhaps even during times of persecution (esp. in 15:11a). Yet iron and bronze cannot break iron from the north (15:12).

That is, neither tenacious Jeremiah nor the "iron-willed people" (Fretheim 2002, 236, who interprets the text slightly differently) will be able to prevent the advance of Babylon, the foe from the north. If 15:13-14 is directed to Jeremiah, and this is by no means certain, then Yahweh reiterates that the prophet and the people will have to deal with the same grueling future. Their enemies will plunder their possessions and subjugate them in a foreign land. Jeremiah's claim of innocence and his assumption that faithfulness should provide sanctuary from evil (15:10) are rejected. Even though Yahweh has "intervened in [his] life for good," Jeremiah is no less subject to the dangerous forces and shifting winds of geopolitics (15:12). No one, not even a faithful prophet, is granted immunity. Along with his adversaries, Jeremiah will have to endure the pangs of war and exile (15:13-14).

"Your Words Were Found and I Ate Them" (15:15-21)

The final prayer in chapters 13–15 conforms to the structure of the lament genre more closely than the prose outburst in 15:10-14. Still Jer 15:15-21 does not exhibit all of its characteristics, as set forth by C. Westermann and others.

1. Address or Invocation: "O LORD, you know" (v. 15a)
2. Lament: "Your words were found, and I ate them . . . Why is my pain unceasing, my wound incurable?" (vv. 16-18)
3. Expression of Confidence/Praise: Absent
4. Petition: "Remember me and visit me . . ." (v. 15).
5. Motivations: Same as lament which includes a testimony of innocence (vv. 16-18)
6. Oracular Response: "Therefore thus says the LORD" (vv. 19-21)
7. Vow to Praise: Absent

Lacking from 15:15-21 are the expression of confidence and the vow to praise. While the expression of confidence is only occasionally attested in the Psalter, the vow to praise or anticipatory praise is virtually always present. Both components are not only missing here but in all the laments in Jeremiah (see, however, 20:13). Their absence is telling. The omission of praise and confidence bears witness to an erosion of hope, and this palpable hopelessness calls into question the trustworthiness of God (O'Connor 1988, 41-42).

Similar to other laments, Jer 15:15-21 functions on several levels. On the surface this lament gives voice to the suffering and disillusionment of Jeremiah, as well as the apparent failure of the prophetic mission. The battered and tormented prophet cries out to God in distress and complains that he has been faithful despite his wretched condition. Jeremiah asks God to hear and act on his behalf: "remember me and visit me . . . in your forbearance do not take me away" (15:15). When God "remembers," God intervenes (e.g., Exod 2:24), and Jeremiah needs divine intervention immediately or else he will not survive. At the same time he prays for retribution against his enemies. When praying against his enemies, Jeremiah asks that perpetrators of injustice reap the consequences of their deeds. This is necessary for the restoration of social and symbolic equilibrium. To motivate God, Jeremiah reaffirms his dedication to his prophetic call. "Your words were found, and I ate them, and your words became to me a joy and the delight of my heart; for I am called by your name, O LORD, God of hosts" (15:16; see also Ezek 3:1-3). The prophet, who is Yahweh's voice, has done all God expects of prophets (15:17-18). He has internalized the divine message (15:16), avoided "the company of [scoffers]" (15:17; cf. Ps 1:1), and "[sat alone under the weight]" of Yahweh's hand (15:17b). Nonetheless, he still suffers excruciating pain and persecution. For the distraught prophet, God has failed. Thus, he likens the Lord to a "deceitful brook" (15:18), a figure that draws on the image of a desert mirage that tricks a parched wanderer into believing there is water when the brook is dry. Yahweh has sorely disappointed and such disappointment leaves the prophet incurably wounded (15:18).

Although Jeremiah's condition makes little sense in terms of personal suffering, it is fully intelligible as a theodicy. And this lament functions as such in its literary context. The mistreatment of the prophet provides incriminating evidence against the nation and exculpatory evidence for Yahweh and Yahweh's spokesperson Jeremiah. When Judah rejects and brutalizes the prophet it corroborates the truth of divine judgment and establishes beyond doubt God's innocence. Hence, the text accounts for Jeremiah's anguish. Rather than revealing moral incoherence and excessive evil, such suffering creates well-proportioned and symmetrical arrangements. Suffering is rationally manageable and testifies to a just God and a morally coherent universe. Jeremiah's pain, therefore, is meaningful.

On still another level Jeremiah's pain and protests of innocence (15:15-18) represent the experience of persecuted sufferers of the exilic and postexilic communities. Jeremiah speaks for and on behalf of those who suffer at the hands of evildoers. Although Yahweh's inactivity raises doubts about divine reliability, the suffering service of Jeremiah takes on paradigmatic force and becomes a "modicum of hope" (Smith 1990, 67). Suffering is not a consequence of turning away from God but turning to God; it is not punishment for disobedience but an outcome of steadfast faithfulness and devotion. Jeremiah, and those he represents, suffers for God's sake. In stark contrast to retributive understandings of life, suffering and staunch opposition are now characteristic of the righteous life, the outgrowth of service to Yahweh.

The response to the lament confirms this new theological development (15:19-21). God offers Jeremiah, and the community for whom he speaks, little hope for a reprieve from conflict (15:19). Conflict is a given and is not to be construed in any sense as atypical. Even the assurances of divine aid (15:20-21) assume a steady flow of adversity and opposition. Yahweh, therefore, does not scold Jeremiah for his expressions of pain and bewilderment, but rather for his scandalous position against him, a position that Yahweh will not tolerate. Although the tradition in some way sanctions this rhetoric by its very presence, Yahweh opposes it and insists that Jeremiah cease uttering "what is worthless" (15:19). For the prophet to "stand before [Yahweh]" and "serve as [Yahweh's] mouth," Jeremiah must "return" to God and embrace

God's point of view. The disturbing oracle of Yahweh uses the word "(re)turn" *(šûb)* and its derivative forms four times in verse 19:

> If you turn back,
> I will [turn back to you] . . .
> It is they who will turn to you,
> not you who will turn to them.

At the core of Jeremiah's preaching has been the admonition that Israel must "turn" or "return" to Yahweh. Now Yahweh demands that Jeremiah return to his prophetic work instead of complaining about it (Martins 1986, 114). Jeremiah's solidarity with the people, his immersion in the world, is so intense and so thoroughgoing that Yahweh uses the same denunciatory language to address both him and Judah. "It is they who will turn to you, not you who will turn to them." Even though his life is forged with the nation, the nation must not subsume him under its regime. While sharing in the misfortune and suffering of the people, Jeremiah is still to speak and embody the divine message. Jeremiah must live betwixt two worlds, the human and divine, without forsaking either.

When Jeremiah returns to Yahweh in faithfulness, Yahweh assures him of protection and the divine presence: "I am with you to save and deliver you" (15:20). The oracle given in this context echoes the words of assurance that accompany the call narrative (1:18-19). The prophet will still encounter opposition and hostility but he will emerge victorious. His enemies will fight against him, "but they shall not prevail." With language reminiscent of the exodus story, Yahweh promises to "save," "deliver," and "redeem" the wounded prophet (see 15:18; cf. 14:17) "from the grasp of the ruthless" (15:21).

Theological and Ethical Analysis

It is difficult to arrive at this point in the prophetic book without noticing the prominent role of the lament genre in these chapters. All of the central players are painfully involved in a maelstrom of suffering. Jeremiah 13:1–15:21 is made up of prose and poetic materials that depict a mournful prophet and people, and more intriguingly, a grief-stricken God who participates in their distress. While this particular cycle enjoys a unique place in Jeremiah, it actually only adds a fresh layer to Israel's collective memory of suffering. Large sections of the Bible speak of Israel in a perilous world, vulnerable and at risk to forces beyond its control. The epic literature envisions the ancestral community as a people on the fringe of society without land or legal rights. In Egypt, Israel first encounters a policy of genocide (Exod 1:8-14). The ruthless empire forces the Israelites into abject slavery and then attempts a systematic extermination of the Hebrew population. In this crucible of pain, the "Israelites . . . cried out, and God heard their [cries] and God remembered his covenant" (Exod 2:23-25). Once freed from Egyptian domination, the former slaves eke out an existence in the wilderness. Here too, however, suffering and adversity beset the community. When entering the land, Israel encounters an array of cultural and religious wars that pose a grave danger to the integrity of community life. While combating these internal forces, Israel must also negotiate dangers from the outside. The imperialistic exploits of powerbrokers on the Euphrates are a source of hardship and trouble. Assyrian dominance in the mid-eighth century eventuated in the destruction and dispersion of the northern state (722). Some years later, the Neo-Babylonian Empire brought the Judean nation to its knees in three decisive offensives beginning in the year 598.

Signs of encroachment, marginalization, and loss can thus be encoded in much of the Old Testament. Besides the epic and historical books, the laments of the Psalter and the Confessions of Jeremiah exhibit deep-seated anxiety over contact with dangerous insiders and outsiders. In these prayers, petitioners frequently face peril and social chaos. The reasons for this environment of vulnerability are complex, although certain geopolitical and social realities clearly play a decisive role. Foremost, Israel often lacked the capability of insulating itself from enemies beyond its borders as well as from those living within them. Unlike the stories of the empires, however, the literature of ancient Israel rarely denies these "embarrassing memories." The Bible does not suppress

Israel's vivid sense of scarcity and powerlessness. On the contrary, its moments of weakness become an integral part of Israel's story and the milieu for Yahweh's presence and solidarity with the people (cf. 2 Cor 12:9-10). This is particularly evident in Jer 13:1–15:21 where Jeremiah discerns the presence of God in personal and communal suffering rather than in an ideology of triumphant nationalism. Yahweh weeps at the wounded condition of the people and grieves over their bleak fate (see esp. 15:5-9). God is deeply moved by Judah's crisis.

The texts that speak of these painful experiences are not merely prophetic oracles or national sagas. That is to say, they are *more than story or proclamation; they are liturgy*. As M. Biddle has argued, it is quite likely that Jer 13:1–15:21 and other poetic texts in Jer 7–20 figure in the liturgical life of the exilic (or postexilic) community (1996). The nonmelodic voices of Jeremiah, Judah, Yahweh and others represent facets of Israel's public worship, which eventuate in a workbook for community worship. As such, the community's grief and hardship become a vital part of the nation's liturgical tradition. We know that earlier creeds include particular memories of suffering. At pivotal junctures in its history, Israel would recall these events as a way to bring to mind its own great need for Yahweh, as well as Yahweh's faithful provision (e.g., Deut 26:4-11; Josh 24). Now, exile and the other national calamities that occurred between 598 and 582 are transformed into salient parts of the community liturgy. Exile, thereafter, was not only a historical datum, a real historical experience, but also a living reminder of the cessation of Judah's long-standing national-cultic identity. It symbolized the end of one world and the possibility of a new one; the death of an old generation and the birth of a new one!

Reading these texts as liturgy has far-reaching implications. First, it shows that Judah was not ashamed of times of distress and failure. Human frailty did not shock the community. Although battered and bruised by events over which it had little control, the nation was not in denial. Instead, its "off-centered" experiences gave rise to *public* grief. Unlike many of our modern liturgies, Israel's public worship provided the people a venue in which to grieve the loss of a world. As a direct consequence, Israel was empowered to face displacement and national humiliation and eventually move on. Second, its language of prayer is far more textured than that of conventional prayers. Israel's liturgy is immersed in pain and is engaged in combative dialogue. It eschews faking and pretension. It resists safe categories, and it affirms that suffering is real and significant. Although this language is at times offensive to modern readers (e.g., 13:22-27), it nonetheless pulsates with authenticity and passion. Finally, the liturgy of Jer 13:1–15:21 is polyvalent: it articulates an array of emotions, concerns, and theological understandings. Besides cries of distress, one finds exonerations of God, accusations of blame, utterances of hopelessness, and glimpses of hope (15:20-21). All of these disparate voices revolve around events that defy melodic speech. The framers of the text refuse to reduce the rich, albeit dissonant dialogue to any singular category.

In stark contrast to the interpretive community of Jeremiah, the lament and its language of engagement are largely absent from the life of the middle-class church in the United States. This disparity between sacred text and ecclesial culture creates an enormous chasm. The church reads a sacred text that is foreign. Contemporary worship, for instance, often construes faith in the "major key." It is melodious, symmetrical, congruent, and primarily attentive to peace and equilibrium rather than distress and disorientation. In many worship services, there is little place for public sorrow. Grief belongs to the privacy of one's home! With the exception of massive events, such as the tragedy of 9/11, human failure and suffering are usually seen as an affront to the religious claims of community life. Unfortunately, removing "off-centered experiences" from the public arena creates an exclusive (rather than inclusive) church. It nurtures a culture for mainstream people who are content and well positioned in the dominant culture. Those who live on the fringes of society or who are in social or personal chaos are foreigners. Their cries of distress do not ring true. Their presence is unwelcome. Their pain disturbs a pleasant and comfortable setting. Ironically, public worship for the well and not the sick, for the whole and not the broken, is strikingly anti-evangelical. It not only misses opportunities for healing and compassion but also refuses a hand of solidarity toward the poor.

THE FORECLOSURE OF HOPE (JEREMIAH 16:1–17:27)

Literary Analysis

Jeremiah 16:1–17:27 brings closure to the larger literary unit (11:1–17:27). The organization of this material is problematic, and many call attention to its disjointed character. Yet, one can detect signs of literary order amid the chaos. Jeremiah 16:1–17:27 intensifies the overall theme of "plucking up and pulling down, destroying and overthrowing" (see Jer 1:10). With disturbing images and raw emotion, its prose discourses and poetic oracles reinforce the harsh and unrelenting cadence of terror that we have seen in the previous chapters. The alarming shadow of death is now all-pervasive. The rhetoric of dismantling and cosmic crumbling permeates nearly every section of the cycle. God unleashes a torrent of judgments in order to bring Judah to its senses, albeit with little success. Because of the depth of its sin, the nation's destiny is all but certain. Its culture will not survive (16:1-13). While one can discern isolated voices of hope (e.g., 16:14-15), these faint echoes are again submerged beneath an ocean of despair. Disobedience and divine judgment thus unify these chapters.

Besides thematic coherence, certain familiar literary patterns are apparent in Jer 16–17. First, an initial prose passage announcing judgment upon Israel (16:1-13) incites an array of reactions including a lament of Jeremiah (17:14-18). We have observed the pattern of prose discourse triggering laments in the previous chapters and it appears here as well. Second, a prose border (16:1-13 and 17:19-27) holds in check the complex and sundry parts. Specifically, this border surrounds jumbled psalmic and wisdom pieces (16:14–17:18). Third, this frame reflects the diction, style, form and theological perspective that are peculiar to the Deuteronomic literature. Characteristic of this literature, for example, it explains destruction and exile as a result of widespread apostasy: the people of God have served foreign gods and will therefore reap the consequences of their actions (Jer 16:10-13 and Deut 29:24-29; Jer 17:19-27 and Deut 5:12-15). Judah's predicament is thus not a quirk but is God's just retribution: the ruin of Jerusalem results from breach of covenant observance. Once again, we see an editorial hand at work organizing the text's untidy landscape.

The placement of this introductory prose account itself reveals editorial intentionality. Connecting words or catchwords tie Jer 16:1-13 to the preceding unit. The "mother motif" joins this text to its larger literary setting. In Jer 15:8-9 Yahweh declares that "Mother-Jerusalem" has ceased bearing children and breathed her last breath. Immediately afterward Jeremiah mourns that his "mother" gave him birth (15:10). Now Yahweh commands Jeremiah not to marry or have children because "mothers" and their children who live in the land will soon perish (Jer 16:3-4). On all three occasions, the maternal motif, which is usually associated with progeny and hope, conveys bereavement and barrenness. Also connecting Jer 16:1-13 to its literary terrain are the destructive forces of the "sword and famine" (16:4; see also 14:12, 13, 15, 16, 18). This common formula points to the ravages of war and thus heightens the dirge-like quality of the introductory passage. Finally, the eradication of "peace" *(šālôm)* in Jer 16:5 hearkens back to the false prophets' message of "peace" (see 14:13, 19). The word of God delivered through Jeremiah contradicts the message of the popular prophets. Jeremiah asserts that Yahweh shall not only remove "peace" from the people but also "[covenant] love and mercy" (16:5).

Besides lexical links, several themes tie 16:1-13 to the broader context. The introductory prose discourse develops the prophetic persona. Yahweh makes additional demands upon the prophet that clarify his prophetic vocation. In the previous chapters, we read of the prophet's social isolation, his mistreatment, and the injustice he endures. We encounter one who is under siege from above and from below and who is sick with despair. This man is an object of scorn and mockery, and God does little to lighten his load. In fact, God divests Jeremiah of everything, strips him of all of his securities, until the prophet stands naked before all (see esp. 15:12-14, 19). To add to Jeremiah's humiliation now Yahweh prohibits him from getting married and having children (16:2). Moreover, Yahweh forbids the prophet from participating in customary mourning practices (16:5) and community celebrations (16:8). Jeremiah must embody the sad realities of his message. Yahweh's spokesperson incarnates the message of doom that he proclaims by mouth. One wonders if "eating" God's word is still a source of joy (15:16) to Jeremiah.

As a whole, the texts in this literary unit appear as an extended dialogue. Yahweh is the sole speaker in 16:1-18 and this speech stirs up an array of reactions in 16:19–17:27. *Each strand, each participant, grapples with Yahweh's ability to see and act appropriately.* Throughout the exchange, Yahweh maintains that his actions toward Judah are just and necessary. However, the speakers, each representing their own concerns and social positions, are not easily persuaded. The collage of voices can be broken down as follows:

A Speaker from the Nations	16:19-20
Yahweh's Response	16:21
An Indictment of Judah	17:1-4
A Sage's Instructions on Two Ways of Living	17:5-8
A Counter Statement	17:9
Yahweh's Rebuttal	17:10
An Aphoristic Saying About Injustice	17:11
A Zion Liturgy	17:12-13
Jeremiah's Third Confession	17:14-18
A Deuteronomic Discourse on the Sabbath	17:19-27

The speakers express a range of perspectives on the scope and character of Yahweh's justice. Among the participants one can discern the voices of the wise, the priests, the so-called Deuteronomists, and the nations, as well as pious Judahites who suffered at the hands of Babylonians (represented by the lament of

Jeremiah). In light of events that defy conventional explanations, all are engaged in a theological conversation as to whether Yahweh can be trusted to rule the world justly.

Exegetical Analysis

The Stripping Away of Ordinary Human Activities (16:1-13)

The prohibition to marry or attend funerals and weddings in Jer 16:1-13 is especially shocking. It signals the suppression of the most visceral human emotions—joy and sorrow—and the most basic social and symbolic structures in Israel. Marriage and children were regarded as part of the very order of creation (Gen 1:27-28; 2:18-25). Progeny were a token of God's blessing (see Deut 28:4, 11). The birth of a child could transform despair into joy (Ps 113:9; Gen 21:1-7). Descendants would perpetuate one's life and memory beyond the grave. To have children was thus to circumvent death (2 Sam 18:18). So important was the concern for progeny that the community implemented social mechanisms to ensure that a person would not die without (male) offspring (see Deut 25:5-10). For this reason celibacy and childlessness express more than the cessation of conventional social interaction. They represent a fundamental reversal of the natural order of life. No wonder barrenness and sterility evoked great sadness and mourning in Israel and throughout the Near East (1 Sam 1:9-18; see also the Babylonian story of Atrahasis). The deprivation of children was considered a sign of divine displeasure (Gen 16:2; 20:18). In light of this social matrix, celibacy and childlessness indicate the interminable death of the nation. Not unlike the vision of the created world returning to its primeval state of chaos (Jer 4:23-26), the terrifying picture of human carnage (16:4-6) with no prospect of propagation marks the collapse of the order of creation.

The text leaves little doubt about the meaning of the symbolic acts. An interpretation accompanies each sign command, which essentially echoes the same message: the end has come and all semblance of social and symbolic order will cease. Jeremiah is to refrain from marriage in view of the imminent military attack, which neither "son nor daughter" will survive (16:3-4; see also 15:8-9; cf. 1 Cor 7:25-26 for an intriguing point of correspondence). He is not to take part in mourning rituals because Yahweh has withdrawn his peace and blessing from the people (16:5). What is more, the prophet is to avoid the "house of feasting" (16:8) as a sign that God will banish joy and pleasure from the land (16:9). The ban on all forms of public celebration and consolation symbolizes the end of community life as it was known. Jeremiah is to reveal in his body the woeful destruction of structured life, Judah's hour of darkness.

In view of these "apocalyptic" portents, the people yearn for understanding, and Yahweh commands Jeremiah to provide it (16:10-13). To give greater insight into the ominous events, the poet uses a question-answer-restatement form that is attested elsewhere in Jeremiah (5:19; 9:12-16; 22:8-9) and in other parts of the Old Testament (Exod 13:14-15; Deut 6:20-25; 29:22-29). The didactic form is used to teach children about the significance of religious practices. It serves to explicate the meaning of past events for those who did not participate in them. In response to Judah's three-part question ("Why, What, What"), Jeremiah instructs the present generation ("this people") that Yahweh's pronouncements of judgment are in no way fickle or unfounded (see also 1 Kgs 9:8-9). The entire history of the nation, past and present, testifies to its accountability. In traditional terms Jeremiah declares that the ancestors have

"forsaken" Yahweh
"gone after other gods"
"served them"
"bowed down to them" and
"not kept" Yahweh's law.

By acting in this manner, the nation has brought the tragic circumstances of exile upon itself (16:11-13). Its refusal to "listen" constitutes a flagrant breach of covenant. Because it has committed the gravest of offenses, Yahweh sentences Judah to banishment from the land. The question-answer-restatement form reiterates a principal conviction of the prose tradition: the tragic experiences that befell Judah between 597–587 and beyond are the outcome of Judah's ill-chosen choices. Hence Judah must take full responsibility for its own actions.

A Promise of Return from Exile (16:14-15)

In an abrupt change in content and tone, a (editorial) prose voice shifts from indignation to momentary hope, perhaps as a way to temper the harsh judgment previously announced (16:14-15; see also 23:7-8). Indeed the balance of chapter 16 moves back and forth between condemnation and approbation, massive destruction and the promise of deliverance. Against a background of widespread destruction (16:1-13), Yahweh assures survivors that exile and displacement are not the final words. God's dispersed people will not come to total end. The text looks beyond the present moment to a future when they will return to their own land. Once "[hurled] out of [their] land" (see 16:13), Yahweh will gather them from the north for a stunning homecoming. This promissory act of deliverance and restoration is so massive and so unexpected that old speech forms break down ("it shall no longer be said"). Confessions of faith from the past fail to capture the magnitude of God's gracious act on Israel's behalf. With Isa 40–55, the exilic voice speaks of a new exodus which makes the first obsolete (cf. Isa 43:16-21; 51:9-11). Israel's deliverance from the north (Babylon) will totally eclipse its earlier liberation from Egypt.

Yahweh's Search-and-Find Mission (16:16-18)

Salvific language vanishes and grim metaphors mount up as the text resumes its denunciation of Israel. No longer does Yahweh gather Israel from the nations for a joyful homecoming but rather for judgment. In order to locate those scattered far and wide, Yahweh disposes a company of fishermen and hunters on a search-and-find mission. "I am now sending for many fishermen . . . and they shall catch them; and afterward I will send for many hunters, and they shall hunt them from every mountain and every hill, and out of the clefts of the rocks" (16:16). The image

COMMENTARY

of fishermen being summoned to catch people occurs in other places of the Bible (see, e.g., Ezek 29:4-5; Hab 1:14-17; see also Amos 4:2; cf. Matt 4:19; Mark 1:17). The figure of the hunter stalking his prey is not as well attested, although Amos 9:1-4 depicts Yahweh on the hunt for Israel. In Jer 16:16 the imagery of "fishermen" and "hunters" tirelessly tracking down their game represents God's fierce pursuit of Judah. No one can evade God's detection. No one can hide from the all-knowing and all-seeing God (16:17). Yahweh pursues not to save but to pounce and punish, and Judah, once caught, will pay in full (i.e., "double") for "polluting" the land with its "detestable idols" (16:18).

To review, the sign commands at the beginning of chapter 16 set in motion an array of penetrating questions regarding the propriety of God's harsh justice.

Why has [Yahweh spoken] all this great evil against us?
What is our iniquity?
What is the sin that we have committed against [Yahweh] our God? (Jer 16:10)

These probing questions imply that Yahweh has acted vindictively and beyond appropriate measure. The next three texts attempt to answer the charge of injustice. Using Deuteronomic categories, Jer 16:11-13 claims that Yahweh's harsh pronouncements are neither misdirected nor excessive. Judah's long history of rebellion warrants divine judgment. Exile is the consequence of the people's unfaithfulness and disobedience. Next, a salvation oracle softens the sting of Judah's fate with a promise of future restoration (16:14-15). Though the nation suffers catastrophic events, God will one day repeal the sentence and bring Judah back to its land. In the meantime, Yahweh hunts down and captures sinful Judah in order to exact appropriate measures of punishment (16:16-18). Yahweh sees "their ways" and repays "their iniquity" appropriately.

For those tormented by the historical realities of a post–587 world, the three prose texts (16:10-13, 14-15, 16-18) do little to satisfy the deep-seated concerns about the scope and character of God's justice. As a result, Jer 16:19–17:27 delves further into the penetrating question of divine justice: Do the "eyes of God" (see 16:17) actually see into the human heart and comprehend human ways (for the word "heart," see 17:1, 5, 10)? And if God does see, does God judge human behavior fittingly or is God's judgment excessive and unwarranted?

A Conversation Between Yahweh and the Nations (16:19-21)

An unexpected expression of worship interrupts the prophetic discourses that dominate chapter 16. The source of the poem is uncertain. Many commentators attribute it to Jeremiah. Carroll, however, suggests that the psalm derives from a "pious speaker" (1986, 347), while Mark S. Smith notes that it represents "a dialogue between Yahweh and the nations" (1990, 53).

The thanksgiving song appears in its present context because of its attention to "false gods" (see 16:18) as well as the "ancestral" motif ("our fathers" in 16:11, 12). It professes trust in Yahweh as a source of strength and refuge in the day of trouble. Once trust is professed, the prayer shifts to an intriguing affirmation about the nations and their conversion. The nations will gather before Yahweh from the ends of the earth to acknowledge the "falsehood" and "inadequacy" of their idolatrous ways (see especially Jer 10:1-16; Isa 44:9-20; Ps 115:3-8). This confession of faith is primarily a polemic against idolatry. "Can mortals make for themselves gods? Such are not gods" (16:20). In contrast to Judah, which continues to "pollute" the land and fill Yahweh's inheritance with abominations (16:18), the "nations" come to their senses and recognize that manufacturing idols is absurd. This song of thanksgiving also deals with the principal concern of the entire unit: God's justice. It asserts that God will deal fairly with the repentant nations and will one day afford them the opportunity to worship the true God.

In the oracle response (16:21), Yahweh declares to the nations—contextually, the antecedent of "them" is the nations— "I am surely going to teach them, this time I am going to teach them [about] my power and [strength]" (16:21a). Unlike the gods of the nations, which are weak and ineffectual, Yahweh is strong and mighty (cf. Jer 10). Yahweh reveals this power not to coerce or intimidate but to make known his name. The disclosure of the divine name is the necessary prerequisite for a relationship with the living God (cf. Exod 3:13-16).

Wisdom Perspectives on Divine Justice (17:1-11)

Jeremiah 17:1-11 consists of materials that enjoy a distinctively wisdom orientation. Alert to the many exigencies of life, each part deals with the problem of God's justice by using the language and theology of the sages. The first prose speech (17:1-4) contends that Judah's sin is engraved with an "iron pen" and a "diamond point" on the "tablet of their hearts" (17:1). The term "iron pen" occurs only in Job 19:24 and Jer 17:1. The phrase "tablets of the heart" appears twice in the Wisdom literature (Prov 3:3; 7:3). In Prov 3:3, the sage exhorts the pupil to write "loyalty" and "faithfulness" on the "tablet of your heart." In Prov 7:3, a teacher urges students to write "Yahweh's commandments" on the "tablets of the heart." The second speech (17:5-8) is a wisdom reflection on two opposing views of reality, despite the introductory prophetic formula (which is not present in the LXX). The wisdom poem pits reliance upon human resources or flesh against trust in Yahweh (cf. Ps 1). The three subsequent sayings in 17:9, 10, 11 are general statements with a wisdom orientation as well. Verse 11, for instance, is a proverb that compares the ill-gotten gain of the partridge with the prosperity of the wicked.

The text moves briskly from the song of thanksgiving to a condemnation of Judah for idolatry (Jer 17:1-4). Whereas the nations will one day turn from their idols to Yahweh, Judah continues to turn from Yahweh to idols. The irony of this indictment is biting. Inscribed indelibly on the tablets of the people's hearts and the horns of their altars is the sin of Judah. The metaphor of engraving sin with an "iron pen" and inscribing it with a "diamond point," an instrument used to carve steles (stone inscriptions), alludes to the permanence and deep-seated character of Judah's sin. Once Yahweh inscribed the words of the covenant on two tablets of stone (Exod 31:18; Deut 5:22; 10:1-2), but now Yahweh etches Judah's wrongdoing on the "tablets of their hearts, and on the horns of their altars" (17:1). Moreover, the "horns of the altar," which once provided atonement for sin and protection from pursuing adversaries (Exod 29:12; 30:10), now serve as a constant reminder of Judah's guilt before Yahweh. The text transforms the symbols of salvation and sanctuary into emblems of guilt and danger.

Canaanite fertility rituals are so ingrained in the national psyche that children "remember" the stories of strangers rather than their own narrative (17:2). Much of Israel's life as a religious community revolves around the act of holy remembering. One of the fundamental obligations of the people of Yahweh is to remember what they have received and already know. Such remembering gives rise to life. Amnesia, or remembering the stories of strangers, results in death (Deut 8). When the community forgets its own narrative and identifies with some foreign story, it loses its identity as the people of God. When it participates in heterodox religious practices, whether they are indigenous or imported, it violates sacral law. Therefore, Judah's apostasy leads to plunder, loss of land, and exile (17:3-4). In other words, Yahweh indeed sees and requites human behavior with justice.

Jeremiah 17:3-4 is a variant of 15:13-14, although the former is addressed unequivocally to Judah. Images of pillage and despoilment, banishment and servitude are associated with Judah's syncretistic worship. The text claims that false worship is not an ancillary problem in Judah but one that jeopardizes the very fabric of community life. Jeremiah 17:3-4 insists that the nation's adulterated practices will eventuate in destruction. Such an argument is disturbing to many readers who are often more comfortable with prophetic injunctions against acts of violence and oppression than with those against false worship. Nonetheless, here and elsewhere in Jeremiah, the importance of correct worship is stressed, and the distinction between acceptable and unacceptable expressions of worship carries serious implications for the future of the community. These concerns in part grow out of a conviction that false worship misrepresents the character of God and adversely shapes human behavior. Idolatrous practices not only violate the essence of Judah's covenant with Yahweh, but they also distort the image of God.

While one can detect traces of a wisdom influence in Jer 17:1-4, the reader enters more fully into the sapiential world in Jer 17:5-11. There are good reasons why the wisdom tradition comes into full view in a literary setting that deals with concerns such as impartiality, human motivation and outcome, as well as the morality of Israel, the nations, and God. The sages were at home reflecting on these pressing issues (see, for example, Job, Proverbs, Qoheleth, and Ps 37). They were interested in the individual as a human being and not merely as a member of a national-religious community. B. S. Childs observes that the canonical association of wisdom with Solomon, Israel's patron sage, suggests that its proper interpretive milieu is international rather than national-cultic (1979, 551-52). Wise men and women studied the "world." They were curious about human behavior, morality, suffering, and other conundrums that engage human thought and imagination. The goal of their literary enterprise, however, was not primarily theoretical but actually pragmatic: the sages desired to help people live meaningful and productive lives, empowered to negotiate the many obstacles that life presents.

Jeremiah 17:5-11 reflects the "central interpretive and organizing principles of the material in [chapter] 17" (Diamond 1987, 167). The conversation begins with a wisdom saying that divides the world into neat and well-defined categories (see also Ps 1). It contrasts the destiny of two kinds of people who represent *all people*. One trusts in "mere mortals" and the other trusts in "the Lord." One values human autonomy, the other prizes trusting obedience to God. Those who "trust in mere mortals and make mere flesh their strength" are "like a shrub in the desert." They are barren and unproductive. When "good" ("relief") comes their way, they are unable to perceive it. In contrast, the godly are those who "trust in [Yahweh] and whose [security] is in [Yahweh]" (17:7). They are "like a tree planted by water, sending out its roots by the stream." People who rely on God enjoy blessings and favor. Even during seasons of drought, they do not "cease bear[ing] fruit" (17:8).

This wisdom saying points out that the object upon which one trusts, that is, the fundamental commitment one makes, shapes her or his destiny. Trust is inevitable. *What* one trusts makes all the difference. Relying on "flesh" or human categories commonly denotes seeking refuge and security in political alliances, military intervention or one's own resources. It represents dependence on and loyalty to power structures that stand apart from God. Such trust is misplaced, ineffectual (Ps 108:12) and impermanent (Ps 146:3-4). It results in defeat, trouble, shame, and ultimately death (see, e.g., Isa 31:1-3; cf. 30:1-5). Reliance on human props, whether they are military machines, power people, charisma, or ingenuity, is doomed to failure. On the contrary, trust in the invisible God involves confidence in God's core character. It relies on the most fundamental commitments of God and God's ability to see those through. This kind of trust is a vital expression of faith. To trust in Yahweh is thus to acknowledge that Yahweh is truly trustworthy.

Although Jer 17:5-8 divides the world into two camps, it does not support the "expectation of prosperity as a reward of faith" (McKane 1986, 394). Those who trust in Yahweh still face times of difficulty and deprivation ("when heat comes" and "the year of drought"). Conversely, those who forsake God come upon relief ("good"), even though they fail to recognize God's blessings. Yet, in the general course of events, the text affirms that life is meaningfully arranged and God judges justly. Acts have consequences, and core commitments profoundly influence human experience. The faithful are able to endure life's contingencies without undue anxiety and fear, while the ungodly "live in the parched places of the wilderness" (17:6a). In light of the overriding concerns of the literary unit, the text may imply that Judah, which is accused of turning away from Yahweh (5:23; 6:28; cf. 2:21; the same Hebrew word used in 17:5) has reaped what it has sowed.

Jeremiah 17:9 does not stand on its own, as is often suggested. It is the voice of a dissident who takes offense at the conclusion of the wisdom poem. Whether uttered by Jeremiah or a sage from the exilic or postexilic congregation, someone contends that the human heart is too iniquitous, too deceitful, to be grasped. "The heart is devious above all else; it is perverse—who can understand it?" Inner motivation and intentions are murky and problematic. Sensitive to the complexities of the human mind or heart *(lēb)*, the speaker proposes that life is not so well organized and unambiguous as to comprise two all-inclusive categories. The heart is devious (the same root used for the name Jacob) and thus is beyond understanding. To posit this is to suggest that the ways of humans are intractable. Jeremiah 17:9 may even go a step further by intimating that the heart and the actions that emanate from it are beyond human control. If such is the case, this terse rejoinder to 17:5-8 asserts that people cannot be held entirely responsible for their actions since interior motivation is ultimately imponderable. How then can God judge people as they deserve?

In Jer 17:10 Yahweh speaks for himself in the first person. "I, [Yahweh], test the mind and search the heart, to give to all according to their ways, according to the fruit of their doings." Yahweh does not dispute the premise that bolsters the previous observation. The *lēb* is indeed too deep, too evil to comprehend and control. Nonetheless, it does not elude the probing eyes of God, who both sees (that is, "tests and searches") and rewards according to conduct. Righteous and appropriate judgments are therefore possible because Yahweh, unlike humans, can search the depths of interior motivation and the actions that spring from the *lēb*. God is able to penetrate the impenetrable. Unlike humans, God is not deceived by appearances. "[Mortals] look on the outward appearance, but [Yahweh] looks on the heart" (1 Sam 16:7*b*). One can hear in this dialogue the voice and concerns of those struggling with the nagging and seemingly insurmountable questions concerning Yahweh's justice and the plight of the innocent.

In Jer 17:11 another discrete voice enters the dialogue, interjecting a proverbial saying based on the popular belief that the hen "visits a neighbor's nest and adopts the eggs" (Jones 1992, 242). The ill-gotten gain of the partridge, a partridge gathering a brood not its own, is compared with a person who amasses goods unjustly. The guilty party will not get away with it, which essentially repeats the dominant position that God governs the world justly. Spasms of injustice occur, but they will be resolved in the end. Like the wisdom saying on two ways of life (17:5-8), the proverb concedes a certain degree of ambiguity in the moral sphere. But these glitches, it suggests, will soon be rectified. Dishonest gain is a momentary state soon to be resolved in a moral universe. Wealth gained dishonestly will not last. Life will eventually exact its due punishment on evildoers (which is a stance also affirmed by Job's comforters).

Shame Awaits Those Who Forsake the Fountain of Living Water (17:12-13)

Still another enters the dialogue in Jer 17:12-13. The anonymous participant no longer speaks from a wisdom point of view but as one enamored of the Jerusalem temple and its national-cultic theology. It is strange to hear this perspective after Jeremiah's diatribe against the temple in Jer 7:1-15. Nonetheless, Zion theology is still a prevailing view with its own staunch supporters (see, e.g., Hananiah as an advocate for this position in Jer 28) and the Jeremiah tradition refuses to suppress it. Moreover, as many exegetes have argued, Jeremiah is not anti-temple per se; he only attacks the belief that the temple is an unfailing safety net. The prophet's trenchant criticism pertains to an ideology that views Jerusalem and its temple as Judah's ultimate hope.

The metrical structure of Jer 17:12-13 loosely follows a conventional form used for elegies in which the second line is shorter than the first. This rhythmic device suggests that the words of praise actually function as a funeral dirge: it eulogizes God's "glorious throne," the splendid Jerusalem temple. For Judah the temple was Yahweh's unique habitation on earth, founded at creation (i.e., "exalted from the beginning"; see Jer 3:17; 14:21; cf. Exod 25:22). In Zion Yahweh takes his place on a glorious throne upon the cherubim on the ark of the covenant (Pss 80:1; 99:1-2). From there Yahweh rules the earth and maintains the stability of the universe. The destruction of the temple thus disrupts Judah's link between earth and heaven, thereby threatening the order of all creation. In the wake of Zion's ruin, a poet-priest cries out that "[all who forsake] the fountain of living water" (cf. 2:13), referring likely to Yahweh as worshiped in the Temple, will suffer disgrace. All who "turn away" (the same verb is used in 17:13 and in 17:5) shall be "written in the dust" (see Jer 17:13 NIV) (rather than in "the book of the living"; see Ps 69:28; cf., Exod 32:32; Dan 12:1). Judah's sin has already been "[inscribed] with an iron pen . . . and engraved on the tablets of their hearts and on the horns of their altars" (17:1), but now is also "recorded in the underworld." Such a profession echoes the view that grave consequences await those who depart from the worship of Yahweh for competing loyalties (see 17:2, 5-6).

"Heal Me, O Lord, and I Shall Be Healed": Jeremiah's Third Confession (17:14-18)

Thus far the various voices in Jer 16–17 generally concur that Yahweh rules the world justly and equitably. From their own distinct perspectives, priestly, wisdom, and prophetic voices claim that Yahweh indeed sees the subtleties that drive human actions and judges appropriately. Even so, the participants in the textual liturgy recognize a degree of moral ambiguity (17:6, 8, 9, 11). Life is not mechanistic; ethical "anomalies" are part of human experience. One day, however, these "glitches" will be rectified (cf. Ps 37); God will right the present wrongs and justice will prevail. In the meantime, Jeremiah suffers unjustly and cries out to God for healing and deliverance (17:14-18). As is typical for the Confessions, the prophet locates himself in this unsettling interim period, when signs of injustice are still present, when enemies place the welfare of the faithful in grave danger, and when social and symbolic chaos is not yet overcome. This "in-between" world is unstable, fraught with danger, and on the verge of collapsing. It is especially perilous because God is seemingly oblivious to the schemes of the wicked. The first readers of the text were all too familiar with this conflicted world. It was their own and one of their central concerns was: "If YHWH can be trusted to punish and reward any and all individuals with such fidelity, how does one understand . . . the incidental disasters which befall the righteous when YHWH punishes the wicked? Surely some pious Jerusalemites suffered the common fate at the hands of the Babylonians" (Biddle 1996, 107). Jeremiah stands in for these suffering people and voices their anxiety.

Accordingly, the third Confession is not only a prophetic cry to God for healing and help. As a part of the extended liturgical dialogue on divine justice, Jeremiah speaks for the faithful who suffered at the hands of the Babylonians. This double reference is characteristic of many psalms where the speaker's "I" represents some corporate dimension of community life. In addition, Jeremiah's lament reflects apologetic interests. It is concerned about Yahweh's sovereignty and justice in light of events that cast grave doubt upon these core attributes. Does God govern the world with fidelity and requite in due measure? Do the disasters of 597 and 587 impugn the integrity of Yahweh? Resembling other texts in Jer 16–17, the third Confession of Jeremiah is preoccupied with problems that arise from the disparity between theology and social reality.

The prophet's prayer begins without the customary address. The lament bursts forth with a petition (17:14), followed by a complaint (17:15), a pronouncement of innocence (17:16), and a prayer for divine intervention (17:17-18). While suffering persecution at the hands of his opponents, the prophet cries out to God for healing and salvation. Jeremiah's condition of anguish is a result of the taunts of his opponents. "Where is the word of the LORD? Let it come!" Their pejorative words torment Jeremiah. His enemies ridicule him for his announcement of judgment. They reject his ministry, insinuating that he is a false prophet. Jeremiah insists that their claims are unfounded. He had taken no pleasure in announcing the day of disaster, but has merely proclaimed the message entrusted to him by Yahweh. Furthermore, he has faithfully carried out his role of "shepherd" (17:16). The term "shepherd" is a title usually given to the king and the leaders of the nation. Jeremiah 17:16 is the only place in the Old Testament where a prophet is referred to as a "shepherd." Traditionally, shepherds strengthen, defend, and feed the flock (see, e.g., Ezek 34). They do not abandon their sheep at the sign of danger, but protect them from predators. Motivated by love and not self-interest, good shepherds "execute justice and righteousness in the land" (Jer 23:5). By identifying himself as a shepherd in Yahweh's service, Jeremiah stresses his concern for justice and his commitment to the welfare of the nation. These claims serve as the basis for his defense against the allegations of his adversaries.

The prophet prays for protection and vengeance (17:17-18). He asks God to shield him from the onslaught of his enemies and take decisive action against his persecutors. Jeremiah prays that his adversaries will "be shamed . . . be dismayed," and that they will not escape the "day of disaster." Indeed, the prophet pleads that Yahweh will mete out "double destruction" upon his opponents (17:18). The vindictive character of the petition is disturbing. The language of hostility toward one's enemies counters a piety of nonviolence that other parts of the Jewish and Christian Bible espouse. Without necessarily viewing this hostility as paradigmatic, as a model for piety, it "bespeaks the courage and candor of prayer that is characteristic in Israel" (Brueggemann 1998, 163). Moreover, the petition for retribution is more than a self-centered cry for revenge. Jeremiah also speaks for those who suffer derision on account of their faithfulness to God. Jeremiah's cry for vengeance is thus a cry that justice should prevail, that the righteous be vindicated, and that the wicked be thwarted. In other words, the prophet pleads that God would act in character and not be indifferent to the plight of the needy. During the interim of uncertainty and moral ambiguity, when the pious endure the same fate as the wicked, the prophet yearns for the establishment of God's just rule.

This is the first complaint of Jeremiah that is not accompanied by a divine response (cf. 12:1-6; 15:15-21). It is, of course, impossible to interpret this silence. Nonetheless, the silence of God is noteworthy. While the nonresponse may simply be incidental and carry no great weight, it may represent both a widening chasm between Yahweh and the prophet and an intensification of isolation and despair. If so, Jeremiah must live with disturbing silence, for God chooses no longer to respond to questions about justice and the suffering of the innocent.

All Hinges on the Sabbath Observance (17:19-27)

Like other prose homilies in the book of Jeremiah, the Sabbath sermon has a distinctly Deuteronomic flavor. Scholars have long recognized its association with Deuteronomy and the editorial parts of Joshua, Judges, and books of Samuel and Kings. They base this judgment upon diction (Rudolph), structure (Nicholsen), style (Hyatt), and theology (Thiel and others). As is characteristic of this literature, elevated or artistic prose calls for obedience to God's word and expresses the conviction that the destruction of Jerusalem has occurred because Israel has violated the covenant. Like other homilies in the Deuteronomistic historical work, moreover, the prose sermon on the Sabbath includes a synopsis of Israel's history that characterizes its entire past as one of hardheartedness and disobedience. It also reflects a typical covenant form. The basic structure of this form includes: an introduction (17:19-20), a call to obedience (17:21-22), a description of communal guilt (17:23), and a pronouncement of judgment (17:24-27). Finally, Jer 17:19-27 incorporates an "alternative speech form" (17:24-27; see also 18:7-10) in which salvation and destruction stand side by side as two options for the people of God.

As the passage opens (17:19), Yahweh commands Jeremiah to stand at the "People's Gate" and "in all the gates of Jerusalem" in order to speak to the inhabitants of the city. All must hear the message, for all have a stake in Jerusalem's future. The explicit mention of "the kings of Judah" among those addressed is striking, since the reaction of kings to the prophetic word has particularly profound consequences for the life of the community. So they too must hear. The message to Jeremiah is urgent and indeed a matter of life and death (17:21). Yahweh demands covenant obedience in the form of Sabbath observance. "Keep the Sabbath day holy, as I commanded your ancestors" (17:22; cf. Exod 20:8, 11; Deut 5:12, 15; Neh 13:22). In this context, Sabbath adherence involves not carrying a burden or working on the holy day (17:21-22), and the fate of Jerusalem and its temple is dependent upon the nation's compliance. Accompanying this injunction, however, is the chilling reminder of the ancestors' refusal to "hear" and "[accept correction]" (17:23).

In large measure, the cards are stacked against the present community, at least if the past is any measure of present performance.

Why should the contemporary community be different from the previous generations? Nonetheless, the prophet presents the nation with a choice that will indelibly shape its future: If the community sanctifies the Sabbath day, the city and its temple will survive. The apodosis (the "then" part of the sentence) in 17:25 suggests that "the key to the stability of city and land, royal house, and people is grounded in keeping the Sabbath" (Carroll 1986, 367). If, however, the nation violates the Sabbath, Yahweh will kindle an unquenchable fire that shall devour Jerusalem's palaces (17:27). Amos uses the image of fire in his oracles against the nations (Amos 1:4, 7, 10, 12; 2:2, 5). Jeremiah employs it for defiant and nonobservant Judah. Like Israel on the plains of Moab (Deut 30:19-20), Jeremiah presents Judah with two paths from which to choose: one leads to life in the form of national restoration, and the other leads to massive destruction. Such clear-cut categories correspond in large measure to Jer 17:5-8, which divides the world into two distinct groups: those who trust in mortals and those who rely on Yahweh. What is at stake is nothing less than national survival, the future of Israel.

Identifying the historical setting of Jer 17:19-27 is fraught with difficulties. While some consider Jer 17:19-27 to be Jeremianic in origin and thus preexilic, the majority of scholars more convincingly assign it to a period well after 587. Prose discourses that reflect a Deuteronomic character, such as Jer 17:19-27, are commonly associated with the exilic period. It was during this period that scribal theologians developed Jeremiah's sayings (and created their own ad hoc materials) under the influence of the Deuteronomic tradition. They did so not only to preserve older material but also to address the focal concerns of their own local context. Moreover, it was during the exilic period that the Sabbath began to blossom in importance. Even though the origins of the Sabbath go back to the preexilic period, it was not until the exilic period and beyond that Sabbath observance became a defining part of community life. Indeed, at that time, nonobservance was considered a serious violation of the covenant (see, e.g., Ezek 20:1-21). The priestly tradition viewed refusal to keep the Sabbath as an omission that endangered the community and thus carried the threat of grave consequences (Exod 31:14-15).

While an exilic dating seems plausible, some assign Jer 17:19-27 to the time of Ezra when Sabbath observance played an even greater role. During this time, Sabbath adherence became the mark of a special relationship with God. It was during the early second temple period that the Sabbath, along with circumcision and endogamy, became distinguishing marks of the Jewish community (see, e.g., Neh 13:15-22, 23-27).

Whether exilic or postexilic, whether compatible or incompatible with Jeremiah's theology, Jer 17:19-27 represents another facet of the prophetic collage of voices in the book. Each voice in the symphony has an interest in Jerusalem's status and in the ongoing life of the community after 587. Each expresses its own convictions regarding the catastrophes of 598 and 587 and speaks from and for its own local context. Jeremiah 17:19-27 sees the survival of the national-cultic community as contingent upon its attitude toward the Sabbath. The text blames the destruction of Jerusalem and its temple on the nation's failure to keep the Sabbath. In the aftermath of the predicted events, the writer concludes that Sabbath violations had led to the disappointments and vicissitudes of the community's new marginal social location. In taking such a stance, the prose discourse asserts that Sabbath observance is essential to the maintenance of the "cosmos." As long as the Sabbath is sanctified, the community enjoys some measure of blessing, protection, and order. When it is violated, the social and symbolic order is jeopardized. Understood this way, Jer 17:19-27 not only provides an interpretation of the past but also an exhortation directed to the contemporary audience: obey the Sabbath regulations "for the sake of your lives" (17:21*a*). In other words, what were imagined options for the preexilic community, which had already sealed its fate, were real options for those listening after 587. This is another way of buttressing the broad and sweeping contention that Yahweh is not responsible for the suffering of the nation. In harmony with others' views, it affirms that the nation's failure to obey the stipulations of covenant played the decisive role in its downfall. Jeremiah 16–17 thus ends with a stern warning about covenant observance and the fate of Jerusalem. Before new formulations are possible, Judah must take full responsibility for its own breach of covenant observance.

Theological and Ethical Analysis

God's refusal to allow Jeremiah to participate in normative community life broaches the terrifying possibility of the end of Judah's world. Yahweh forbids the prophet from marrying and having children as a sign of death and devastation. That Jeremiah may not attend funeral services or public celebrations only reinforces the vision of cosmic crumbling. For the first readers of this text such images were anything but foreign. Living in the aftermath of war and deportation, Jewish refugees in Babylon understood all too well that trusted social structures could collapse overnight. Residing in camps in a faraway land, they could see through past illusions of permanence. Even those who held out hope for the return of the old world could hardly deny the dreadful consequences of military invasion. And so, the text's portrait of horror rang true in ways that would once have been unimaginable. The exiles' disenfranchised social location, at least initially, was as bleak as Jeremiah's haunting imagery. A world had fallen, a beloved city lay in ruin, and the disaster was beyond conventional categories.

Not long ago such "apocalyptic" language would have been completely foreign to many modern readers, especially those well situated in the United States. "Our world" was stable and insulated, with only a few bumps in the road. Only yesterday, it seems, one could make a case for a new spirit of international cooperation, and for progress in curbing the proliferation of weapons of mass destruction. But all that has suddenly changed and so the text's haunting language resonates in strange and unexpected ways. It now takes little effort to imagine the mass slaughter of people (16:4) and the resulting palpable disease (16:9). It is far too easy to envision plowshares beaten into swords, pruning hooks into spears, and nation lifting the sword against nation (Joel 3:10; cf. Isa 2:4). One need think only of massive jets crashing into twin towers, preemptive military strikes creating unspeakable social

178

and personal chaos, seemingly unending cycles of violence treating human life with disdain, refugee communities emerging at shocking rates, and the brazen disregard for international law and morality. We now live in a world destabilized by terrorism as well as by imperial exploits. All this leads to unprecedented global vulnerability.

Jeremiah's portrait of the end of culture elicits a maze of reactions from various constituents in the community. It is instructive that the interpretive community of Jeremiah does not flatten the literary terrain and allow only one voice to speak. In fact, the conversational nature of the text with its range of perspectives discourages monolithic explanations. It insists that all have a say, that all have questions to pose, and that all have a right to mourn the losses. While the presence of many speakers produces an unwieldy text, it at the same time candidly addresses events that defy conventional rationality. In this way the text, as Brueggemann notes, reads the "abyss" (Fall 2002, 349-50). This polyvalent text also calls into question our own singular readings of the present world crisis. Along these lines, economist Clyde Prestowitz challenges "American exceptionalism." He argues that "Part of the shock of September 11 was the shattering of the myth that bad things happen only to other people. It was the shock of joining the world. It doesn't mean that we should be fatalistic, but in an age of globalization we need to recognize that others' problems are our problems too and that we don't have all the answers" (2003, 284).

One of the numerous responses to Judah's crisis focuses on the Sabbath. For many years Christian interpreters have dismissed Jer 17:19-27 as "mere legalism" from the second temple period. Such a reading shows little appreciation for the value of the Sabbath in ancient Israel's spirituality, not to mention its role in the history of Judaism. The Sabbath is rich and layered with spiritual and social significance (Muller 1999). Its origins are associated with creation (Gen 2:1-3), the wilderness period (Ezek 20:8-26), and Mt. Sinai (Exod 20:8-11; 31:12-17). Its purpose is humanitarian (Exod 23:12; Deut 5:14): all members of the community, regardless of their social status, are entitled to its benefits. It serves as a sign of the covenant (Exod 31:12; Ezek 20:12, 20), a marker for holy days (Lev 23:12, 15, 16), and a reminder of servitude in Egypt and God's gracious deliverance (Deut 5:15). It is observed in a variety of ways, which include keeping God's "ordinances" (Ezek 20:12-20), performing certain Levitical and priestly duties (Lev 24:8; 2 Chr 23:4, 8), and offering prescribed sacrifices (Num 28:9-10). Most often, it involves a sacred abeyance of economic activities (e.g., Exod 20: 10; Neh 13:15-22; Deut 5:14) because God "rested on the seventh day" (Exod 20:11).

It is exegetically significant that "keep[ing] the Sabbath holy" involves not carrying a burden out of one's house (17:22; see also Neh 13:15-22) or "through the gates of [the city]." As customary, work is prohibited on the Sabbath (17:24). The cessation of work emphasizes that Israel is not owner but steward of God's creation. All that Israel has is theirs on loan. The Sabbath, moreover, is a living reminder that life is more than economics, that the sum total of existence is greater than the accumulation of things, unbridled consumption, and feverish accomplishment. Work can cease and life will go on. Indeed work must cease to cause the community to remember that its *raison d'être* is not merely to produce and acquire. While work is fundamentally good (Gen 2:15) and not to be disparaged, the Sabbath observance as formulated in Jer 17:19-27 asserts that people are not commodities, to be used and discarded; nor are they mere players in an economic and geopolitical world. Humans have inherent worth as people created in God's image. All God's children have immeasurable value apart from their utility.

The Sabbath says "yes" to the sacred, to compassion, to human dignity, and to economic propriety. At the same time, it says "no" to self or national aggrandizement, the insidious need for more, exploitation, and frenzy for upward mobility. As such, it cultivates a just and fair society. To keep the Sabbath, therefore, is gratefully to affirm God's lordship of creation. When Israel observes the Sabbath, it acknowledges that it belongs wholly to God. To profane the holy day is a flat denial of God and Torah values. It stands to reason that Jer 17:19-27 envisions the fate of the city hanging in the balance until it says "yes" or "no" to the Sabbath.

DISMANTLING INSIDER-OUTSIDER CATEGORIES (JEREMIAH 18–20)

Bracketed by prose discourses (17:19-27 and 21:1-10), Jer 18–20 stands on its own as the fourth literary division of the book (following chs. 2–6, 7–10, and 11–17). This unit redefines another core tradition of the preexilic world: Judah's election as God's chosen people (e.g., Exod 19:4-6; Deut 14:2; 26:18). The people of Judah firmly believed that God had chosen them to be a special nation. Indeed, one of their most cherished claims was that the God who created the earth had set them apart to be God's "treasured possession out of all the peoples" (Exod 19:5). This belief now comes under the methodical scrutiny of the prophetic word. By the end of the unit, it is plain to see that election is no entitlement.

Literary Analysis

Like other major sections in Jer 1–25, the fourth literary unit of the book begins with a standard superscription, which then introduces a prose narrative written in autobiographical form (18:1-12). This carefully crafted narrative encapsulates the dominant motifs of Jer 18–20, and, as is typical of other opening prose discourses, it subverts a fundamental assumption of Judah's symbol system: the nation's status as chosen and blessed. Jeremiah 18:1-12 takes on the popular belief that Judah's election provides unqualified protection. Such insider status, the text asserts, is not an unconditional claim. Judah's refusal to (re)turn to Yahweh compromises its privileged position and earns it a place alongside the recalcitrant nations. In making this astonishing statement, the prose tradition continues its systematic critique of every belief, practice, and institution that Judah might use to prop up its fallen world. Judah cannot cling to the old systems, no matter how familiar and comfortable. While the old forms worked in the old context, now something altogether new is necessary. Because of its new social reality, the community in exile must be amenable to the new workings of God. Written for post–587 readers, Jer 18:1-12 not only undermines entrenched readings of reality but also calls for radical trust in a God who is still "shaping" the world.

This introductory prose story is made up of several layers, which together create an embroidered texture: (1) The customary introduction, signaling a new editorial unit and the divine authority of the account (18:1); (2) a symbolic act and its initial interpretation: Yahweh, the divine potter, is utterly free to destroy and reform Israel as he sees fit (18:2-6); (3) a series of "if . . . then" sequences that outline the conditions for salvation or judgment (18:7-10); (4) an invitation to circumvent disaster (18:11); and (5) an unqualified refusal to "return to Yahweh" that seals the fate of the nation (18:12).

The remaining parts of the fourth block of material are not difficult to determine. Following the prose sermon is a poem that presents an editorial commentary on the preceding text (18:13-17). Usually prose interprets poetry, but here poetry elaborates prose. The poem functions as a divine response to Judah's abject repudiation in 18:12. Its prophetic formula, "therefore thus says Yahweh," connects Judah's formal rejection of Yahweh to a divine accusation/lament (18:13-16) and declaration of judgment (18:17). Furthermore, the foreign nations, who have just been given an opportunity to turn from their evil and receive God's blessings (18:7-10), are now summoned to witness Israel's inconceivable act of infidelity, and ironically, are first to witness the resultant dissolution of Judah's special status. God interrogates these wayward (or perhaps repentant!) nations regarding the propriety of Israel's conduct. It is plain for all to see that Israel's stubborn stance against Yahweh is pure folly. Also connecting the prose and poetic passages is an intriguing play on words: $\check{s}^crrt$ ("a most horrible thing" in 18:13) and $\check{s}rrt$ ("stubbornness" in 18:12). The alliteration suggests that Judah's cardinal vice, its "[horrible act]," is its defiant autonomy (18:12).

The next passage of the unit is the fourth Confession of Jeremiah (18:18-23). A brief prose statement (18:18) introduces the Confession proper (18:19-23) and provides the occasion for it. This editorial preface connects the lament to its broader literary environment by utilizing the "conspiracy" motif. The word "conspiracy," also translated "plan," or "plot," appears in several places in chapter 18. In 18:11, Yahweh reveals that he is "[plotting a plot]" against "the people of Judah and the inhabitants of Jerusalem." In 18:12 the people insist on following their own "plans/[plots]," instead of Yahweh's. And in 18:18, the people (?) take dead aim at Jeremiah by "plotting" against him. The conspiracies and counterattacks, reactions and counteractions, occur within a dialogical context.

Yahweh's "scheme" against Israel, 18:1-11
Judah's determination to follow its own "scheme," 18:12
Yahweh's accusation and declaration of judgment, 18:13-17
Judah's "scheme" against Jeremiah, 18:18
Jeremiah's complaint, 18:19-23

The interaction among Yahweh, the people, and Jeremiah serves several objectives. It illustrates that Yahweh's "scheme" of judgment against Judah is fully justified in light of Judah's "scheme" to follow its own evil way (18:11). Moreover, when the nation devises its "schemes" against the prophet (18:18), it betrays its own recalcitrance and culpability.

Jeremiah 19:1–20:6 is the longest continuous narrative in the first half of the book. The material is related to its larger context by the potter-clay metaphor and by the announcement of inevitable judgment on Jerusalem. Taking its lead from Jer 18:1-12, which deals the nation's election status a devastating blow, Jer 19:1–20:6 subverts the promises centered on Jerusalem's invincibility. Although the narrative is a literary unity in its present form, a close reading reveals that it consists of three independent strands almost seamlessly woven together. The first is a brief account of a symbolic act (19:1-2a, 10-11a) that uses the pottery motif of the last chapter as its point of departure. Inserted into this brief account is a (later) sermon that fills out the details with Deuteronomic categories (19:2b-9, 11b-13). Following the symbolic act and its interpretation is a story about Jeremiah's imprisonment, which puts the final touches on the literary mosaic (19:14–20:6).

The fourth literary unit closes with Jeremiah's final two confessions (20:7-13, 14-18). The literary setting of these poems is not fortuitous. The previous story of Jeremiah's incarceration by the Jerusalem establishment provides the occasion and catalyst for the laments. Again, prose account and prophetic lament are integrally related. The use of the key phrase "Terror-all-around" (20:3 and 20:10) confirms this literary arrangement. First used as Pashhur's new name in the judgment oracle in 20:3-6, Jeremiah's enemies now turn his own words against him when they whisper scornfully, *Magor-missabib*, "[Terror-all-around]" (20:10). According to Jeremiah's foes, the prophet, not Pashhur, is the real scourge among them.

Jeremiah 18–20 introduces several new motifs: (1) Jeremiah is persecuted and explicitly rejected by a representative of the upper-tiers of the religious hierarchy. This rejection serves as a transition to the fifth major unit, Jer 21–24, which focuses on Judah's leadership. (2) Babylon—the once rejected and now accepted nation—is mentioned for the first time by name. It is the instrument of God's judgment against Judah and the faraway place of Judah's captivity. The reference to Babylon suggests that disaster looms even closer on the horizon. (3) Judah's election tradition is challenged and is in fact rescinded as a result of the nation's propensity toward evil; and finally, if W. L. Holladay is correct, (4) The nation's salvation history and particularly its ancestral covenant is overturned (1972, 305-20). The only core belief not yet addressed is the royal theology, which claims that the Davidic king and his resident city, Zion, will last forever. This powerful ideology is the focus of attention in the next major block of material (Jer 21–24).

Exegetical Analysis

God the Potter (18:1-12)

Jeremiah 18:1-12 reflects the diction and style of the prose sermons in Jeremiah. Phrases such as "[hearken] to my voice" (18:10), "[to do that which is] evil [in the sight of Yahweh]" (18:10), "the men of Judah and the inhabitants of Jerusalem" (18:11), to "turn now, all of you from your evil way" (18:11), "amend your ways and your doings" (18:11), and "[to build and plant, to pull down and uproot]" (18:7, 9) occur regularly in this literature. Moreover, like other prose discourses in Jeremiah, the prose heading (18:1) is followed by a divine command addressed to the prophet (18:2) and the prophet's obedience to God's instructions (18:3-4).

The notion of God as potter and people as clay unifies the text. This metaphor is widely attested in the biblical literature and in other ancient Near East texts. The ram god Khnum appears on Egyptian reliefs forming diminutive people on a potter's wheel (Boadt 1982a, 139). In the Babylonian creation epic *Atrahasis*, the gods fashion humans from a piece of clay made out of the flesh and blood of a slain god. The earliest creation account in the Bible pictures Yahweh as a potter who shapes humanity (ʾādām) from the ground (ʾādāmâ). The imagery of potter and clay also appears in the book of Isaiah (29:16; 45:9; 64:8), in the late Wisdom literature (Sir 33:13; Wis 15:7-8), and in the New Testament (Rom 9:19-21). It commonly conveys the idea of human frailty and divine power. In addition, the image "reveals a God who focuses closely on the object to be created and takes painstaking care to shape each one into something useful and beautiful" (Fretheim 1994, 349).

As the narrative begins Yahweh instructs Jeremiah to visit ("go down to") a potter's workshop where he will receive a divine message (18:2). Jeremiah obeys the command (18:3) and witnesses spoiled clay being reworked by a potter (18:4). The potter refashions the blemished clay into another shape, "as seemed good to him" (18:4). It is unclear as to whether the clay or the design of the potter was flawed, though the former seems more likely. The prophet perceives in this ordinary encounter an extraordinary message (18:5-6). Like the potter who is at liberty to shape the clay as he wishes, so Yahweh can refashion Israel at will (18:6b). God is free, unrestrained, and in control of Israel's destiny. However, Yahweh's freedom is not absolute, nor is it arbitrary. Verses 7-10 qualify the divine prerogative. Although Yahweh is at liberty to remold Israel and the nations, Yahweh does so based on their conduct and response to prophetic speech. Mercy and justice temper (and limit) divine sovereignty. Yahweh will accept any nation against whom he has decreed judgment (to "pluck up and break down and destroy") should that nation "turn from its evil" (18:7-8). And Yahweh will reject any nation that he has promised to "build and plant" if it "does evil in his sight" (18:9-10). The divine potter can accept the once-rejected and reject the once-accepted. In the topsy-turvy world of the text, "insiders"—once chosen, protected, and blessed, that is to say, those whom God has "built and planted"—can become "outsiders." Conversely, outsiders, if responsive to the word of Yahweh and repentant, can be transformed at any time into insiders (cf. Jonah). Verse 11 makes it clear that the option of blessing or curse, rejection or acceptance, pertains specifically to those whom Yahweh has chosen. Yahweh the potter is "shaping evil" against the people of Judah and the inhabitants of Jerusalem, but at the same time is offering them a final chance to avoid judgment.

Jeremiah 18:1-12 concludes with a blanket renunciation of Yahweh placed in the mouth of the people of Judah (the antecedent of the phrase "but they say" in verse 12 is evidently "the people of Judah and the inhabitants of Jerusalem" in verse 11). Whether out of defiance or despair, the nation refuses to reform its "evil ways." "It is no use! We will follow our own plans, and each of us will act according to the stubbornness of our evil will" (18:12). This rejection makes it entirely clear that the community has missed yet another opportunity to "return" to God. O'Connor is even more emphatic when she observes that the people respond here to their *last exhortation to repent . . . with a dramatic and definitive no"* (emphasis mine) (1988, 143-44). This final and unequivocal "no" overshadows all previous possibilities of repentance in the book. While the future of Israel hangs in the balance in 18:1-11, the appended verse 12 spells out in no uncertain terms that the story of the potter is ultimately about the forfeiture of Judah's position of privilege. Consequently, Judah emerges from the text as a nation with no special claim upon God.

God's Response to the People's Decision (18:13-17)

In the next poem the writer poses two rhetorical questions. The NRSV translates the difficult Hebrew text:

Does the snow of Lebanon leave
the crags of Sirion?
Do the mountain waters run dry,
the cold flowing streams? (18:14)

Both queries are self-evident: The snow on the high mountains of
Lebanon, perhaps Mt. Hermon, will always be there (literally, will
not *"forsake* the crags of Sirion"), and its cool mountain streams
will never dry up. One can count on these regularities of nature.
They are givens, ever present and always reliable. In sharp contrast, fickle Israel lacks all constancy and fidelity. That Israel can
so easily transfer its loyalty to "another" is shocking (see also Jer
2:9-12; 8:7). To Yahweh, however, Israel's apostasy is not only
shocking but a source of great anguish. The dirge-like refrain, "my
people have forgotten me" (18:15; see also 2:32; 3:21; 13:25),
expresses Yahweh's distress. It is not surprising that "forgetting
Yahweh" lies at the heart of the lament/indictment. To forget is so
devastating because it is a manifestation of callous apathy.
Forgetting Yahweh trivializes and disregards the voice of love.
Israel no longer even cares! Such forgetfulness coupled with abject
idolatry catapults the nation down a dangerous and rocky road.
The Hebrew construction of 18:15-17 suggests that Israel's apostasy sets in motion a series of devastating events including humiliation, military defeat, and the withdrawal of Yahweh's gracious
presence. "I will show them my back, not my face, in the day of
their calamity" (18:17).

Due to the intermingling of rage and sorrow, it is again difficult
to determine whether this poem is a lament or an indictment. In a
world whose fundamental social structures and literary forms are
crumbling, such distinctions are blurred at best.

Jeremiah's Fourth Confession (18:18-23)

The fourth confession of Jeremiah illustrates the terrible nature
of Israel's rebellion. It describes a conspiracy or plot to silence
Jeremiah, God's principal spokesperson (18:18). Once again the
prophet finds himself the target of an intense attack, which
attends to the construction of theodicy. When Judah denounces

Jeremiah, Yahweh's messenger, it rejects Yahweh. The total dismissal of both serves to justify the coming devastation, vindicate Jeremiah as a true prophet, and absolve Yahweh of any malice. When Jeremiah asks God to punish his enemies (18:19-23), prophetic intercession takes a backseat to judgment, which is fitting for a community bent on dismissing the prophetic word.

The brief-yet-important prose report in 18:18 sketches the contours of the plot against Jeremiah. Unnamed people, perhaps associated with the Jerusalemite authorities (though the antecedent of "they" is not identified), conspire against the prophet from Anathoth. They scheme against him, bring false charges, disregard his words, and attempt to silence the troubling prophet. Such reactions, as we have seen, are not unexpected. Daring utterances often elicit heated, and at time murderous, responses from stakeholders in the establishment. But the motivation behind the contemptuous treatment of Jeremiah is still rather ambiguous: "For instruction [Torah] will not perish from the priest, nor counsel from the wise, nor the word from the prophet" (18:18).

There are at least two ways to interpret the enemies' words. They may grow out of *arrogant confidence and complacency.* The conspirators are convinced that the fundamental power arrangements of the existing conditions will remain intact despite Jeremiah's attack. The three authority figures of the nation, priest, sage, and prophet, will withstand the weight of Jeremiah's predictions of woe and will be able to continue communicating the knowledge of God. As such, the speech of Jeremiah's rivals represents the antithesis of Jeremiah's conviction that the dominant structures will collapse. That is to say, their ideology openly defies Jeremiah's announcement that instruction shall indeed perish from the priest, counsel from the sage, and the word from the prophet. A slightly different interpretation is also possible. The words of the opponents may represent the *staunch determination of the schemers not to allow* Jeremiah to destroy their cherished way of life, as personified by the priest, sage, and prophet. To thwart Jeremiah's assault upon the status quo, they unite to stop him in his tracks. To prevent Jeremiah from ruining all that they hold dear, his enemies bear false witness and relegate him to be a figure of no significance ("let us not heed any of his words"). Fueled by patriotic and religious fervor, these unidentified schemers will do anything in their power to stop the iconoclastic poet from weakening the state and its religious systems.

Regardless of the motivation behind their mean-spirited measures, Jeremiah's opponents appeal to the three legitimate forms of authoritative speech in the exilic and postexilic communities, the priest, sage, and prophet. The curious absence of the "shepherd" (usually the king) may indicate a late dating when Judah no longer lived under its own monarchic systems. The priest, sage, and prophet are the repositories of divine knowledge and as such "control" the dissemination of divine communication. They hold a monopoly on the religious establishment. It is, therefore, no coincidence that Jeremiah's assailants appeal to their positions when facing a fundamental threat to the establishment structures.

Priests were associated with "instruction" or "torah." They were guardians of the sacred times, places, and traditions as well as the representatives of the establishment par excellence. The priests viewed all of life as "organized along structural lines emanating from the Temple" (Neusner 1997, 42). It was their responsibility to offer sacrifices to God, to give instruction in matters of ritual holiness, and to make juridical decisions at the central sanctuary (e.g., Deut 17:8-13). In these capacities, the pattern-maintenance leadership of the priests commonly recognized the institutional structures of the state. The sages, whose writings are preserved in Proverbs, Job, Qoheleth, and elsewhere, were learned individuals who gave "counsel," teaching people how to cope and negotiate the many vicissitudes of life. Also allied with the temple and the Jerusalem elite, the sages had a wide range of responsibilities, including providing guidance to heads of state. Prophets, of course, delivered the divine "word." They did so in a variety of social contexts. While some maintained a fundamental detachment from the control of the temple and the royal court, others practiced their "trade" within this framework. Prophets were thus capable of functioning as advocates (e.g., Hananiah) or detractors of the state and its dominant ideologies.

Whether Jeremiah's opponents include him in the latter category is unclear. It is possible that they do not consider Jeremiah a prophet at all. Either way, they regard him as a menace to their venerated institutions. They recognize that Jeremiah is capable of breaking their monopoly on divine knowledge and communication. Their assessment is well founded. This iconoclastic figure does not follow the party line, does not knuckle under, and possesses the *true* word of God. Over and against priest, sage, and prophet, the power brokers and spokespersons of the state, the text claims that Jeremiah communicates the will of Yahweh. He is a true prophet who undermines the peoples' confidence in the state's official leadership. Consequently, he incites furious opposition.

The enemies' taunts and ill-treatment enrage Jeremiah (18:19-23). In response he calls on Yahweh to repay them for their malicious acts. His prayer reflects the rudimentary components of the lament psalms, although without the vow to praise.

Address, 18:19
Lament, 18:20*ab*, 23*a*
Petition, 18:20*cd*, 21-23
Motivation, 18:20*cd*

In addition to these form-critical elements, the language and piety of supplication are similar to the laments in the Psalter. However, unlike the psalmists, Jeremiah's declaration of innocence pertains specifically to his prophetic office (18:20).

In a world that is unresponsive to his words (characterized by "not heeding"; see 18:18, "let us not heed"), Jeremiah begs Yahweh to "give heed" to him and "[pay attention]" to what his adversaries are saying (18:19). The prophet complains that his opponents mistreat him (18:20) and plot to kill him (18:23). Their attacks, Jeremiah insists, are unjust, for he has faithfully discharged his prophetic responsibility of intercession (18:20). The persecuted prophet has maintained in previous laments that he has served Yahweh faithfully. He has "eaten" Yahweh's words (15:16) and has suffered social disdain and solitude (15:17). He has neither attempted to elude his role as shepherd (17:16) nor longed for the day of judgment (17:16). Now Jeremiah adds to this litany that he has fulfilled his intercessory duties as well. Even in defiance of the divine charge not to intercede, he has stood before Yahweh as an advocate for the masses. Yet, he is still the target of harassment. For that reason, he seeks revenge, or as seems plausible, the reestablishment of justice. While many commentators regard Jeremiah's words as vindictive, it is at least worth noting that his plea largely echoes Yahweh's announcements of judgment against Israel (e.g., Jer 6:11-12). When the prophet asks that his enemies die by famine, sword, and pestilence (18:21), he actually reiterates the "evil" that Yahweh threatens to bring upon the nation and its rulers (16:4; 21:7, 9; 27:8, 13; cf. 14:15). One could therefore make a case, as a number of scholars have already done, that Jeremiah's shocking prayer *to God* functions in the book as a word *from God* aimed at the perpetrators of injustice.

Several important features become clear in Jeremiah's prayer. First, despite the use of stereotypical language, the lament grows out of a social world in which dangerous persons coexist with the righteous within the borders of the state. Deviant persons are present and wield enough clout to place the welfare of good insiders in jeopardy. This type of setting indicates a society under a great amount of pressure from within its boundaries. Such an environment is perilous not only because it lacks social constraints but also because God appears to be silent. Nonetheless, even in a world vexed with problems and persecution, the prophet trusts in Yahweh his covenant partner for help and for the restoration of moral sanity. Presumably, he prays because he believes that Yahweh can and will intervene. Second, Jeremiah *expects* a certain degree of moral order to exist in the world and is profoundly disappointed when it does not. "Is evil a recompense for good?" His understanding of reality, governed by covenant categories, demands a universe that is in large measure coherent and orderly. Jeremiah must cope, however, with a social reality that is at variance with this conviction. Third, the prophet's prayer is rather egocentric. Jeremiah is concerned about his own welfare and thus desires the punishment and downfall of his enemies. Whereas some prayers in the Bible are theocentric and submit human needs to God's will, the plea of Jeremiah, like so many others, grows out of desperation. Jeremiah prays in order to eke out a life on the margins.

In addition, the entreaty reflects a piety that does not accept suffering passively as the will of God. One can find a range of human attitudes and responses to suffering in the Bible including acceptance, repentance, submission, and even worship. However, Jeremiah responds in anger and protest. He kicks, screams, curses, and appeals to God for deliverance. Jeremiah, like Job, will not accept responsibility for his misfortune, as if it were the consequence of some personal failing. Instead of remorse, Jeremiah expresses rage. Finally, Jeremiah's petition functions as the word of God. Although Jeremiah's prayer derives from his own hardship and is by itself somewhat provincial, it is nonetheless transformed into Yahweh's message of judgment against Judah and its leadership. In this way, the entire chapter speaks of the reversal of the election tradition and the inescapable consequences of "not turning."

Broken Beyond Repair (19:1–20:6)

In chapter 19, the symbolic action concerning the potter/pottery continues to take shape. It becomes visible that the "clay jar" is no longer amenable to "re-formation" but must be shattered and destroyed (19:11). Whereas the clay is still pliable in chapter 18, the earthen jar, now fired, is fixed and brittle. Brueggemann observes in this regard that "the broken flask is a parabolic assault on imagination. The coming judgment is a firm resolve on the part of God. That resolve is all the more ominous because 'it can never be mended' (v. 11). This is the point of no return" (1998, 177).

The "first" layer of this complex text presents the symbolic action and its interpretation in a concise and straightforward manner (19:1-2a, 10-11a). Yahweh instructs Jeremiah to buy a "potter's earthenware jug" in the presence of some of the community elders and senior priests, the custodians of the community (19:1). Together they are to go to the valley of the son of Hinnom at the entrance of the Potsherd Gate where Jeremiah will smash the ceramic flask. When he breaks the jug, the prophet will announce the meaning of the act (19:10-11*a*). "Thus says [Yahweh] of hosts: So will I break this people and this city, as one breaks a potter's vessel, so that it can never be mended" (19:11). The shattering of the hardened clay flask represents a bold demonstration of Jerusalem's demolition. While a trace of hope is present in the earlier symbolic act (18:1-10), none exists here. The broken jar is beyond repair, signaling the irreversible condition of Israel. The fate of Jerusalem and its inhabitants is sealed (Jer 19:11).

The sign of the broken flask contradicts the assurances of previous prophets that with God's help Jerusalem would withstand the onslaught of its enemies. In the final years of the eighth century, for instance, Isaiah prophesied that Jerusalem would survive the terrible offensive of Sennacherib's armies. The Assyrian king had already captured most of the cities and towns in Judah before turning his attention toward Jerusalem. At that point, he sent his representatives to King Hezekiah with an ultimatum: surrender or face humiliating defeat. Isaiah encouraged fearful Hezekiah with words of hope. God would protect the city, and therefore the military campaign of the Assyrian ruler would not succeed (Isa 37:21-29). "For I will defend this city to save it, for my own sake and for the sake of my servant David" (Isa 37:35). As the incident unfolds in 2 Kgs 19:35-37, an angel of Yahweh destroys 185,000 troops laying siege to Jerusalem, and eventually the Assyrian king withdraws. The deliverance of Jerusalem convinced many that the city would stand forever. When Jeremiah qualifies this belief, we again come face-to-face with the historically conditioned nature of prophecy in ancient Israel. Prophetic utterances are not abstract and timeless truths, but words, oral then written, that address particular people who live in particular places at particular times. To extricate the message from its local context is to do violence to the essence of prophecy. As Yahweh's spokesperson, Jeremiah smashes the earthenware jug to demolish the venerated belief that Jerusalem would remain forever the invincible city of God.

In its earliest form, the pottery story is scant in details. It predicts only that the city and its inhabitants will suffer a terrible and irreparable blow. It says nothing about motivation or rationale, and as such is more declarative than explanative. A prose sermon provides these details with Deuteronomic categories (19:2b-9, 11b-13). The two originally independent narratives now appear as a relatively unified story. Following an introductory word that beckons "kings of Judah and the people of Jerusalem" to hear the word of Yahweh (19:2b-3), the "inserted" text provides a catalog of offenses (19:4-5). The offenses provide the reasons for a declaration of divine judgment upon the ritual site of Topheth, Tal Hinnom, and upon Jerusalem itself (19:6-9, 11b-13). Jeremiah accuses the people of:

> Forsaking Yahweh, 19:4
> Profaning this place,19:4
> Making burnt offerings to other gods, 19:4
> Filling this place with the blood of the innocent, 19:4
> Erecting high places to Baal, 19:5

Following these accusations, the verbs shift from the third-person plural (they, they, they) to an infinitive construct, "[in order] to burn their children in the fire as burnt offerings to Baal" (19:5). The transition indicates that Israel's apostasy culminates in the revolting practice of human sacrifice. According to the Deuteronomists, the ritual act of child sacrifice, which was associated with the ill-fated reign of Manasseh, the most deplorable of Judah's kings, had erupted anew in the valley of the son of Hinnom (cf. 19:3-5 and 7:31-33). In their judgment, this horrific act had brought down the Judean state. Using Deuteronomic covenant curses, the sermon describes the once thriving Topheth and Jerusalem as a massive grave (19:6-9, 11b-13).

The opening of the third section of the narrative (19:14–20:6) shifts from the speech of Yahweh to Jeremiah (19:1-13) to Jeremiah's speech to the nation (19:14). The prophet departs from Topheth for the temple in Jerusalem where he delivers a synopsis of the previous sermon. Within the temple precincts, Jeremiah addresses "all the people" rather than certain cross sections of elders, senior priests, and kings of Judah (see, e.g., 19:1, 3). This brief "temple sermon" reiterates the threat of imminent judgment against "this city and uponall its towns" (19:15). Jeremiah condenses the grounds for the indictment into a single accusation: Israel has refused to hear Yahweh's words. That is all that Jeremiah needs to say. By not listening, Israel has broken covenant with Yahweh (Deut 6:4). By ignoring Yahweh's words, Israel essentially reiterates its bold assertion: "We will follow our own plans, and each of us will act according to the stubbornness of our evil will" (18:12). "Not hearing," according to the prophet, is tantamount to idolatrous autonomy (1 Sam 15:22-23), which ultimately leads to death.

While Jeremiah is delivering his message in the temple, its chief administrative officer Pashhur takes notice of his "seditious" oracles. Actually, he "hears" (20:1) without truly "hearing" (19:15), which has been the problem all along. Jeremiah has prophesied that Yahweh is against the city, and that it will suffer severe, even irrevocable, consequences for its infidelity (19:14-15). "Thus says [Yahweh]: I am now bringing upon this city and upon all its towns all the disaster that I have pronounced against it" (19:15). Pashhur will not tolerate such words; he cannot endure such a frontal attack on the nation and its beloved institutions. So the priest strikes the prophet and puts him in stocks at the upper Benjamin Gate of the temple (20:2).

Although highly charged, the details of the confrontation are again few and leave much to the imagination of the reader (see 20:1-6). As chief officer in charge of policing the temple for troublemakers and madmen (see also 29:26), Pashhur, in all likelihood, acts only in accordance with the Deuteronomic law when he beats and imprisons Jeremiah. Deuteronomy 25:2-3 orders flogging for the party at fault in litigation disputes, and there are considerable grounds for reading the altercation as a legal dispute. In his role as temple overseer responsible for maintaining order, the priest is to thwart any attempt to violate existing systems of control. His intense opposition to Jeremiah, although misguided and injudicious, makes sense, for Jeremiah dares to speak against the state's treasured ideologies and institutions. As guardian of the state and its sacred systems, therefore, Pashhur must act against this untamed, undomesticated "outsider." Reminiscent of other trustees of the empire including Amaziah, the priest at Bethel, who

COMMENTARY

attempted to control disturbing Amos (Amos 7:10-17), Pashhur seeks to silence Jeremiah's anti-establishment rhetoric.

His attempt fails. Jeremiah's enemies cannot shackle Yahweh's word. The prowess of the nation's power people cannot frustrate Yahweh's sovereign purpose. One can imprison Jeremiah but not the word of God. When released from his confinement, Jeremiah delivers a scathing oracle against Pashhur and the nation (20:3-6). He renames Pashhur "Terror-all-around" (20:3) and then explains the meaning of his symbolic action. Yahweh is making Pashhur a "terror" to himself and his priestly associates (his "friends"). Moreover, all Judah will suffer the terror of the king of Babylon, who is mentioned for the first time in the book. This foreign ruler will plunder and pillage the land of Judah (20:4-5). In the end, Pashhur and his fellow priests will find themselves in Babylon where Pashhur will eventually die (20:6).

Jeremiah's inflamed speech is far more than a personal vendetta against the man who incarcerated him. When Jeremiah addresses Pashhur, he speaks the word of Yahweh. "Yahweh has named you not Pashhur but 'Terror-all-around'" (20:3). Like others whose names are changed (see Hos 1:4–2:1; Isa 8:1-4), Pashhur becomes a prophetic sign that broadcasts Yahweh's message. Once an agent of supposed salvation by virtue of his priestly office and his prophetic oracles (which Jeremiah reckons "false" in 20:6), Pashhur now symbolizes the destruction to come. Whether Jeremiah uses a wordplay when he gives Pashhur the symbolic name *Magor-missabib* is difficult to know. No linguistic correlation is obvious, but Holladay has made an intriguing suggestion. He notes that Pashhur is formed from two Aramaic words, "fruitful" and "all around" (Holladay 1986, 544). By naming him "Terror-all-around," Jeremiah essentially reverses the priest's name as well as Yahweh's promise of fruitful progeny to the ancestors (Gen 17:5, 20; 35:10, 11; 48:4).

When Pashhur rejects the messenger who comes in the name of Yahweh, he joins the throng who says "no" to God's gracious invitation to "turn from [its] evil" (18:12). When vilifying the prophet, he aligns himself with the party engineering a plot to destroy Jeremiah (18:18). Pashhur echoes the response of his townsmen who threaten Jeremiah with death (11:18-23). Moreover, he anticipates the reaction of King Jehoiakim to the prophetic scroll in chapter 36. In this way the priest's ruthless action in the temple provides both the setting and rationale for the last Confessions.

Jeremiah's Final Confessions (20:7-18)

The prayers of the prophet are commonly divided along the lines of 20:7-13 and 20:14-18, although some scholars, such as Rudolph, treat 20:7-18 as a singular unit. The first prayer is an individual lament that exhibits most of the constitutive elements of the genre. It begins with an invocation or address (20:7*a*, "O Yahweh") and then sets forth the complaint itself (20:7*b*-10). A brief petition is present in verse 12*b* where the prophet pleads for retribution upon his foes. Unlike the other Confessions of Jeremiah, this lament includes both a word of confidence (20:11-12*a*) and a concluding expression of praise (20:13). Because of the abrupt shift in moods, some view the exclamation of praise in verse 13 as intrusive and secondary. However, though this component is unknown in Jeremiah, it is present in all but two individual laments in the Psalter. Consequently, a sudden change of disposition, while problematic, does not by itself provide adequate grounds for such an argument.

The second passage (20:14-18) is a curse that is similar to Job 3. While Jeremiah expresses some hope for vindication in the first lament (20:7-13), he plunges into the depth of despair in the second. In this passage, Jeremiah's hopelessness reaches its most critical level. He curses both the day of his birth (20:14) and the bearer of news of his birth (20:15-17). As a target of terrible abuse, the prophet bemoans his own "toil and sorrow" (20:18). Here we see what von Rad calls the "lowest point in the suffering of Jeremiah" (von Rad 1983, 96). "Night has now completely enveloped the prophet" (von Rad 1983, 95). All hope for tomorrow has dissolved. In total isolation, the prophet grieves "the past forever gone" (a phrase coined by Dan Daley and made popular by the Charlie Daniels Band in a song entitled "Still in Saigon"). Yet, Jeremiah does not grieve alone. He stands beside and amid a community that must also face the loss of temple, covenant, election privileges, land, and king—that is to say, the deprivation of all past certainties and national prestige.

So understood, the first twenty chapters of Jeremiah travel a road that begins with the prophet's call ("before I formed you in the womb" in 1:5) and ends with his longing for death (20:14-18). Intriguingly, both the call and death wish of Jeremiah are associated with the "womb" (1:5 and 20:17, 18). The womb, as a place of birth and as an abode of death, forms the symbolic boundaries for the persona of Jeremiah in the first half of the book. Jeremiah's prophetic vocation has led him into "the valley of the shadow of death." Along with the Judean people, he must endure enormous hardship. And so, by the conclusion of this chapter, darkness has thus engulfed the words *and* the persona of Jeremiah. Both testify that God's dangerous work of "pluck[ing] up and pull[ing] down, destroy[ing] and overthrow[ing]" is well underway.

Jeremiah's cries of distress, therefore, grow out of his mission as a prophet (see also 15:16, 18:20). He perceives his social victimization as a repercussion of his message. On account of Yahweh's dangerous word, he suffers "reproach and derision all day long" (20:8). Because he has waged war against Pashhur and the Jerusalem establishment, his friends and foes alike denounce him (20:10). To his opponents Jeremiah has become the community pariah. They attempt to overpower and subdue him, all in the name of justice (20:10).

With raw emotion and astonishing boldness the prophet holds Yahweh responsible for his maltreatment. Jeremiah accuses God of "betraying/enticing/seducing" and "overpowering" him.

> O LORD, you have *enticed* me
> and I was enticed;
> you have *overpowered* me,
> and you have prevailed.
> I have become a laughingstock all day long;
> everyone mocks me. (20:7, emphasis mine)

Such language pushes the lament genre to the limits, and in fact fractures conventional forms. Although other laments are daring enough to question the reliability of Yahweh, none does so in such a frontal manner. The verb "overpower" in verse 7 has a wide semantic range, which includes seizing, compelling, strengthening, taking hold of, and even raping (Deut 22:25). The Hebrew word translated as "deceive/entice/seduce," depending on the English translations, has a more narrow range. It occurs in about twenty-five texts in the Hebrew Bible. Besides its use in Jer 20:7, Jeremiah claims that his adversaries attempt to "entice" him to do evil (Jer 20:10). The same verb occurs in Judg 14:15, 16:5, and in 1 Kgs 22:20 where it denotes a type of trickery or deception. For instance, the Philistine lords ask Samson's wife to "coax" him into revealing the secret of strength so that they can "overpower" him (Judg 16:5). In Prov 1:10 and 16:29, the word conveys the idea of enticement of the innocent by violent people. The term also signifies sexual seduction. The Sinai covenant makes provisions for a "virgin" who has been "seduced" into having sexual relations (Exod 22:16; Sir 42:10; see also Deut 11:16). Also interesting is the presence of the word in Ezek 14:9, which proposes that prophets sometimes deliver a word because Yahweh has "deceived" them (cf. 1 Kgs 22:19-23). In spite of the divine participation in the "deception," Yahweh still threatens to stretch out his hand against such prophets and destroy them from the midst of Israel.

Heschel understands the imagery in Jer 20:7 as predominantly sexual (see also McKane 1986). According to him, Jeremiah's extraordinary confession conveys the idea of sexual enticement (Exod 22:16; cf. Hos 2:14) and forcible rape (Deut 22:25) (2001, 144-45). Jeremiah feels coerced and violated by God. To convey his sense of shame and powerlessness, the prophet deploys metaphors of sexual violence. Taking a different position, O'Connor argues that the imagery communicates the idea of Yahweh as "Jeremiah's deceitful opponent" (1988, 71). Based on contextual similarities with Ezek 14:9, O'Connor concludes: "Jeremiah is accusing Yahweh of deceiving him as a prophet, making him a false prophet by sheer domination . . . and superior strength" (1988, 71).

From either perspective, the prophet's complaint revolves around what he perceives as a terrible abuse of power

COMMENTARY

(Brueggemann 1997, 359-72). Jeremiah feels duped and besieged by the power and purposes of Yahweh, forces over which he has little control (e.g., 20:9). At the outset of his prophetic ministry, Yahweh had assured him that "kings, princes, priests, and the people of the land" (1:18-19) would not "prevail" against him. But now all victimize him. Pashhur beats and imprisons him, his enemies slander and mock him (20:7c-8), and his "close friends" attempt to "prevail" against him (20:10). Even Yahweh, his ally, has "crushed" him and "prevailed" (20:7b). Such malevolent actions and fractured promises evoke a deep sense of rage and betrayal. All seems bleak and hopeless. Yet, amidst the persecution, the prophet approaches Yahweh and expresses enormous faith in Yahweh's trustworthiness. Jeremiah affirms that Yahweh is with him "like a dread warrior" and as a result his "persecutors . . . will not prevail" but "will be greatly shamed" (20:11). Moreover, he declares that Yahweh has "[rescued] the needy from the hands of evildoers" (20:13), which harkens back to the divine promise at his commissioning (see 1:8, 19).

In all, the lament and the spirituality that produced it throb with pain and ambivalence. The prophet accuses and acclaims, celebrates and despairs, denounces and extols, doubts and hopes. Simultaneously, Jeremiah views Yahweh as both "deceiver" and "dread warrior," trustworthy and capricious, one who "test[s] the righteous" and sees "the heart and the mind" (20:12) and yet who coerces and exploits. Like his ancestor Jacob, Jeremiah strives with Yahweh and entrusts his problems to God all while God *is* his problem. Such understandings are complex, and reflect a piety that is comfortable with ambiguity and protest, as well as with public displays of grief. This piety, moreover, bears witness to a fresh understanding of misfortune: suffering and persecution are no longer associated with wrongdoing but with doing God's will. Jeremiah suffers *because* he has faithfully fulfilled his service to Yahweh.

Theological and Ethical Analysis

Perhaps no dilemma has perplexed people of faith more than the matter of human freedom and divine sovereignty. Is life a collage of human choices, the product of the superimposing divine program, or some combination of the two? Does God intervene in human affairs? And if so, who ultimately controls human destiny, people or God? Both modernity and postmodernity take human freedom and responsibility with utmost seriousness. For the playwright and novelist Albert Camus, freedom to choose one's destiny is what sets us apart from every other living creature. As such, freedom is not illusory in any sense of the word; it is real and not only real but an essential part of what it means to be human. For the philosopher Søren Kierkegaard, God's ultimate blessing is "the ability to choose." According to him, religion is not merely a system of beliefs and set of behaviors, but the acceptance of responsibility, moral obligation, and ethical freedom. Permeating the very fabric of our present moment is the awareness that we possess the mammoth potential to destroy or preserve our planet. We are free to choose life or death.

The biblical literature expresses a wide range of beliefs regarding human freedom and divine prerogative. Some texts accentuate the far-reaching significance of human accountability to God. "Now therefore revere the LORD, and serve him in sincerity and in faithfulness . . . choose this day whom you will serve" (Josh 24:14*a*, 15*b*). "Know that all lives are mine . . . it is only the person who sins that shall die. If a man is righteous and does what is lawful and right . . . he shall surely live, says the LORD God" (Ezek 18:4, 5, 9*b*). Others stress the sovereign purposes of God at work both in observable and hidden ways. When God breaks through ordinary categories in abrupt and intrusive ways or is at work in the world in more subtle and natural ways, transcendence, to varying degrees, overshadows human autonomy. "The human mind plans the way, but the LORD directs the steps" (Prov 16:9). "Even though you intended to do harm to me, God intended it for good, in order to preserve a numerous people, as he is doing today" (Gen 50:20). This stunning affirmation that God is capable of undoing human evil concludes the Joseph novella.

Jeremiah 18–20 enters the fray on the subject of divine sovereignty and human freedom, a conundrum that still perplexes religious communities today. It does so not to satisfy some philosophical curiosity but to address the concerns of survivors of the destruction of Jerusalem. When confronted with the starkness of their ground zero, they surely wondered, "Who is responsible for this mess and who is in control?" When undergoing great hardship as refugees, they questioned the character and purposes of God. Is God truly sovereign, and if so, does this sovereignty violate God's benevolence? These anxieties almost certainly lie beneath the surface of this layered literary unit.

In response, the initial prose narrative asserts that God, the divine potter, is capable of doing whatever God wishes, even reversing divine decrees (18:7-10). Nothing can constrain God. As clay, Israel (like other nations) is utterly dependent and powerless. The metaphor of potter and clay emphasizes the sovereign prerogative of God. As a potter working with clay, God is free to shape and reshape human lives and human history as God sees fit. Such a notion is, of course, not new, but only echoes a claim that is made throughout the book: Yahweh reigns and controls the destiny of all nations. From beginning to end, Jeremiah testifies to Yahweh's rule on earth. In chapter 1, Yahweh calls and commissions Jeremiah (before he was born) as "a prophet to the nations" (Jer 1:5) with the intention of accomplishing the divine purpose on earth: "to pluck up and to pull down, to destroy and to overthrow, to build and to plant" (Jer 1:10). This mission statement puts all subsequent events in perspective. The disastrous geopolitical policies of Babylonia over Syria-Palestine and the resultant reordering of Israel are not beyond the divine scope, but rather are part of the disturbing purposes of God. The dismantling of the state religion and its social institutions represents Yahweh's sovereign program of "plucking up and pulling down." The plans of Yahweh, "the true God, the living God, and the everlasting King" (Jer 10:10) cannot be foiled. No power structure lies outside the sphere of Yahweh's reign. Yahweh is in charge of the earth despite the power games and vicissitudes of geopolitics. Indeed the book concludes with the triumphant note that Yahweh will both establish justice among the nations and subdue every arrogant and oppressive system on earth (Jer 46–51).

While the metaphor of potter and clay attends to the assertion that Yahweh holds sway over the destiny of all nations, it at the same time qualifies Yahweh's freedom and sovereignty in poignant ways. The text maintains that divine actions are neither unilateral nor unqualified but are in fact deeply affected by human choices: God acts in direct measure to people's actions (18:7-10). As Hyatt observes, in contrast to the claims of sovereignty in Jer 18:1-6, Jer 18:7-10 affirms that "the fate of the people depends upon what they do, not God" (Hyatt 1951, 83). Accordingly, human autonomy is real and impinges on the purposes of Yahweh. Israel possesses the power to change its course and "shape" (like the potter) its destiny. The sovereign program of God is, therefore, not a closed, predetermined system. On the contrary, Jeremiah bears witness to the inherent openness of God to human choices.

All this is well and good. In the face of disaster, the text asserts that the sovereignty-freedom dilemma is not an "all or nothing" proposition. History is not a closed continuum governed solely by divine decree or by human action. The potter-clay analogy is an effective means of showing that "though [Yahweh] is sovereign, the people have a will of their own which they exert against him" (Holladay 1986, 515). God rules the world, and yet humans enjoy a degree of freedom and thus are fully accountable for their actions.

However, when we reach the end of the literary unit, we discover that the sovereignty-freewill conundrum is even more complex than the introductory parable of the potter suggests. Now we encounter a prophet who is *unable to exert himself* against Yahweh (20:7-18). Yahweh's behemoth control on his life deprives him of freedom, leaving him weak and wounded, although not without words of protest (20:7*ab*). Yahweh's robust rule restrains and subdues a combatant Jeremiah (20:7). Sovereignty now eclipses human autonomy. For Jeremiah, there is no evading the purposes of Yahweh (20:11-13). They are too powerful and too sure. Although Jeremiah can at times assert that Yahweh's power is reliable and Yahweh's promises are trustworthy (20:11-12), he nonetheless must still live with a keen sense of powerlessness. Thus, by the end of chapter 20, we find little openness of God to human initiative. This infringement on human freedom coincides with the foreclosure of hope, for at this stage in the prophetic drama all must travel in darkness down a road of anguish and relinquishment.

DISMANTLING KINGSHIP IN ISRAEL (JEREMIAH 21–24)

Chapters 21–24 mark the final literary unit of the first half of the book, Jer 1–25. This cycle of material divides into four complex parts. The first is a prose narrative in which King Zedekiah sends envoys to Jeremiah to seek respite from the Babylonian siege of Jerusalem (21:1-10). The second takes up matters related to the Davidic dynasty and the fate of the final kings of preexilic Judah (21:11–23:8). Following a series of judgment oracles for breaches of royal duties, it concludes with a promise of a new exodus and a "righteous Branch" in David's line who will execute justice, practice righteousness, and usher in a time of salvation for God's people. The third block of material renounces prophets who speak unauthorized words (23:9-40). The condemnation of these prophets casts Jeremiah in a positive light, representing him as a true spokesperson of Yahweh. The final section is a vision report of two baskets of figs (24:1-10). The rotten figs in one basket symbolize Zedekiah and his court officials as well as Judeans who remain in this land or migrate to Egypt. The good figs in the other basket represent the refugees in Babylon (24:4-7). Exile to Babylon apparently represents the kind of abrogation of the past that is necessary for the introduction of new symbolic arrangements.

Literary Analysis

Jeremiah 21:1-10 introduces the literary unit. The language, style, and outlook of this prose discourse betray significant points of correspondence with Jer 7:1-15, 11:1-14, 18:1-12, and 25:1-14. The text begins with the conventional introductory formula (21:1a) and exhibits the verbose style and alternative speech form (21:8-10) that is characteristic of other prose discourses. Jeremiah

21:1-10 also operates as a *hinge* that holds together rhetorical sections denouncing priest, prophet, shepherd (king), and sage, namely, the major shareholders in the old world order (18:18–20:18 and 21:11–23:40). Furthermore, the prose account introduces the major theological motifs present in the unit as a whole. First, it puts the reader on notice that the Davidic monarchy is in grave danger. God's determination not to intervene on behalf of Zedekiah, the last king of the Davidic line in Jerusalem, creates a portentous aura for the remainder of the unit. Second, it depicts the predicted downfall of the royal city as now underway. No longer presented in purely mythic terms, the narrative assumes that the Babylonians have begun their assault on Judah. Third, the prose discourse declares that the destiny of Judah rests on its response to Babylonian subjugation. In an unexpected departure from traditional expectations, the text asserts that the future of Judah does not lie with those who escape deportation and remain in the land but rather with those who peacefully surrender, abandon the land, and "go out" to Babylon.

These three themes, the announcement of the cessation of the historical dynasty, the role of Babylon as Yahweh's instrument of judgment, and preferential place afforded the exiles in Babylon over the remnant in Jerusalem, are taken up again as principal motifs in the concluding chapter of the unit, the vision of the baskets of figs (24:1-10). In this way the prose introduction and the prose ending create a thematic *inclusio* (envelope) that surrounds the unit's material. This framework also brings to a close the prose program aimed at dismantling Judah's social and sacred worlds. Prose sermons have already demonstrated that the temple and its liturgical systems, the covenant, and the election tradition will not sustain Judah in the days to come. Now it is clear that the royal theology and the imperial modes of reality will be equally ineffectual. None of these familiar categories will save Judah from national humiliation.

Situated between the opening and closing prose narratives are a series of oracles concerning kings and prophets. The largest of the two blocks of material, Jer 21:11–22:30, calls into question the unconditional nature of God's promise to David (2 Sam 7:1-29).

While the prose framework only hints at the demise of the historical dynasty, the litany of allegations against Davidic rulers in Jer 21:11–22:30 exposes the bankruptcy of monarchic systems of governance. Jeremiah contends that these systems have fallen miserably short of acceptable Torah standards of justice and are in fact the root cause of the community's state of disorientation. Because Davidic rulers have failed so shamefully in their community responsibilities, Jeremiah can no longer envisage their continuation. In their place, God resolves to appoint good shepherds/rulers (23:1-4) and to establish a "righteous Branch on King David's throne" (see 23:5-8). Notwithstanding these promissory words regarding the distant future ("the days are surely coming"), the text emphasizes the conditionality of kingship and its present shortcomings. By the end of the entire literary unit, Judah's last kings are all condemned: Jehoahaz or Shallum (22:11-12; cf. 1 Chr 3:15), Jehoiakim (22:13-19), Coniah or Jehoiachin (22:24-30), and Zedekiah (24:1-10).

Also accountable to God are the false prophets (23:9-40). In perhaps the most inflammatory polemic in the book, Jeremiah declares that God is against the prophets for leading astray the people of Judah. Instead of turning the nation to God, the false prophets only make matters worse: they corrupt society, ignore injustice, and blind the nation to its true condition. With faithless kings, the prophets therefore must bear the brunt of responsibility for Judah's predicament. It is no accident that the text condemns prophets alongside kings. They belong together as constituent partners in Judah's failed leadership. In the account of Israel's royal history (1 Samuel–2 Kings), prophets first appear at the inception of the monarchy. From the start their role was to bridle the authority of the king. Prophets were supposed to be living reminders that power has its limits, that kings are not gods, and that political arrangements are provisional. They were to testify to an alternative social reality in which every power structure is ultimately critiqued by the living God. No wonder Yahweh takes such an aggressive stance against prophets who "speak visions of their own minds, not from the mouth of the LORD" (23:16). In the twilight of the Judean monarchy, it becomes painfully apparent that they had fallen dreadfully short of their high calling.

Exegetical Analysis

Here Comes the King of Babylon (21:1-10)

One encounters few texts in the first half of the book that refer to precise events. In Jer 21:1-10, however, the narrator begins to speak more directly of identifiable dates and persons. We read of the word of the Lord coming to Jeremiah during the reign of King Zedekiah while Babylonian forces are blockading Jerusalem. Although Jer 21:1-10 does not mention the specific year of Zedekiah's reign or indicate whether the incursion of Jerusalem occurred in 597, 587, or sometime in between, the storyteller depicts the invasion of Judah in lifelike, historicized terms. Babylon's king is even mentioned by name for the first time (21:2). This shift is not from theological to historical discourse; the text continues to be dense with symbolic overtures (Hill 1999). But now the threat of divine judgment becomes concrete and geographic.

With the king of Babylon breathing down his neck, Zedekiah sends a delegation to Jeremiah to inquire of Yahweh. His envoys, Pashhur—not the same Pashhur as mentioned in 20:1, but a curious link nonetheless—and the priest Zephaniah, plead that God will lift the Babylonian siege by performing "a wonderful deed for us." As we have already seen, petitions for divine intervention are common in the Bible, and God usually responds favorably to them. Indeed, God delights in defying the odds and rescuing people in times of great need. The Lord "works wonders" (Ps 77:14) and accomplishes great feats, especially during times of duress (Ps 107:8, 15, 21). On many occasions psalmists declare that God has performed "marvelous acts" on their behalf and on behalf of their ancestors (see, e.g., Pss 26:7; 71:17; 75:1; 98:1; 106:22). When the children of Israel were enslaved in Egypt, God rescued them by performing a "miracle" (Exod 3:20; Mic 7:15). Isaiah rejoices that God does "[such] wonderful things . . . [planned from long ago and now accomplished]" (Isa 25:1). Jeremiah himself exclaims, "nothing is too hard" for Yahweh (32:17). Zedekiah asks Yahweh to act, therefore, because Yahweh "often" (21:2) performs extraordinary acts of deliverance on behalf of Israel. His appeal is based on a strong precedent, and so there is ample reason to believe that God will rescue the king from his formidable foes.

Yahweh, however, refuses to help. The request for a hearing is granted, but the petition for divine intervention on Zedekiah's behalf is denied. Jeremiah declares in stern resolution that nothing will abort the Babylonian invasion since Yahweh is the one waging war against Zedekiah and the royal city (21:3-7, my emphasis):

> "*I am going* to turn back the weapons of war . . . " (v. 4)
> "*I will bring* them together into the center of this city . . . " (v. 4)
> "*I myself* will fight against you . . . " (v. 5)
> "*I will* strike down the inhabitants of this city . . . " (v. 6)
> "*I will* give King Zedekiah . . . into the hands of King Nebuchadrezzar . . ." (v. 7)

The surplus of first-person forms underscores Yahweh's decisive action. Yahweh is involved, yet not as Zedekiah had hoped. The inversion of the Israel's sacred creed and holy war traditions draws attention to Yahweh's antipathy for the city and its king: Yahweh's "outstretched hand and mighty arm" no longer represent God's power to deliver Israel, but God's power to oppose the Davidic monarch and the royal city. Several triads drive home the divine resolution to destroy: Yahweh wages war on the city and its king "in anger, in fury, and in great wrath" (21:5). If Zedekiah and others in Judah survive "the pestilence, sword, and famine" (21:7), they will fall "into the clutches of King Nebuchadrezzar of Babylon, into the clutches of their enemies, into the clutches of those who seek their lives" (21:7). When they do, King Nebuchadnezzar "shall not pity them, or spare them, or have compassion" (21:7). Jeremiah's reply to the delegation leaves no room for doubt: Yahweh will act as judge and adversary rather than as savior and deliverer.

The ill-fated oracle against Zedekiah is followed by a short alternative prophetic message that addresses the people of Judah

(21:8-10). Initially, the language *appears* to qualify the preceding message of judgment by offering the community safe passage, or at least a choice between life and death. In Deuteronomy, Israel is given such an opportunity on the plains of Moab (Deut 30:19; cf. Josh 24:15). If obedient to Yahweh, Israel will enjoy God's blessings in the land promised to the ancestors. If disobedient, the nation will "perish and not live long in the land across the Jordan." As Deuteronomy sees it, life and death relate to the land that Yahweh promises Israel. Life involves living peaceably *in the land*, even as death implies exile *from the land*. In Jer 21:8-10, these Deuteronomic options are inverted. "The way of life" no longer means living "in the land" of Judah (Deut 30:16) but rather "in the land" of Babylon. Yahweh promises life for (obedience that is expressed in) *surrender* to Babylonian rule and *exile* to a faraway place. Moreover, continued residence in "this city" is tantamount to "the way of death." By reconfiguring traditional categories, Jeremiah dashes all expectations for deliverance. In order to "live," the people of Judah must "die" to any hope of perpetuating social policies that support the power structures of the state. To survive, they must relinquish their privileged place for displacement in a foreign country. To do this is no doubt daunting, but it is the only way to escape with "their lives as a prize of war" (21:9).

Jeremiah's Third Response to Zedekiah (21:11-14)

Jeremiah 21:11-14 may be read as the third response to Zedekiah's petition for divine assistance (the first two appearing in 21:3-7, 8-10). Jeremiah has already delivered two distressing oracles to Zedekiah's envoys. Now he adds fuel to the fire by lecturing the king on the fundamental responsibility of the monarchy. The most important work of the king is to maintain justice in the community (21:12). The power and policy of the king are to protect and defend citizens from exploitation. The phrase "in the morning" may refer literally to the time when legal cases are settled, or it may point to the priority and urgency of judicial decisions in the affairs of kings (cf. Exod 18:14-16). A serious warning accompanies the admonition. If Torah justice is neglected, then disaster, envisioned as a consuming fire (Jer 21:12, 14; cf. Amos 1–2), will ensue. Unlike kings who avert their eyes from the practice of oppression and thus become co-conspirators, God will not disregard the politics of injustice. God holds leaders responsible for their silence in the face of extortion. There is no excuse for abdicating fundamental moral duties. Though Judah's kings think that they are insulated from harm, Yahweh will penetrate their fortresses (21:13). Like the Jerusalem temple, the royal palace is no bulwark from the blast of Yahweh's anger. When the demands of justice are ignored, even kings find no refuge from "fire [that enflames] the forest and devour[s] all that is around it" (21:14).

Kings and Their Weighty Responsibilities (22:1-9)

Jeremiah 22:1-9 gives further details on the king's judicial role in community life as well as on the dire consequences of not fulfilling this responsibility. Yahweh instructs Jeremiah to visit the royal residence and deliver a message that will hold enormous consequence for the nation. To be sure, the future of the dynasty will ride on whether the Davidic king and his entourage will "listen to" Yahweh's admonition concerning the practice of justice in the public arena (22:3, 5; cf. Deut 6:4). Drawing again on Deuteronomic categories, the sermon spells out what "executing justice" actually entails. For the king to "do justice" he must protect the downtrodden and disenfranchised and serve as their advocate. It is his sacred duty to deliver the oppressed from the oppressor, to "do no wrong or violence to the alien, the orphan, and the widow, or shed innocent blood in this place" (22:3; see also 7:5-7; Ps 72:1-4). Even as Moses pronounced a covenant curse on anyone who would deprive "the alien, the orphan, and the widow" of justice (Deut 27:19), Jeremiah makes the continuation of the dynasty contingent upon compliance to this categorical imperative (22:4). If, however, the king should not obey, then the "house," which is an ambiguous allusion to the royal palace and the dynasty (see Jer 22:5-6 as well as 2 Sam 7:1-17), will be destroyed (22:5). Like the conditional construction in 21:8-10, the larger context of 22:1-5 reveals that the choice Jeremiah offers is really no choice at all, for Judah's final rulers have already sealed their own fate. Verses 6-9 expel all doubts to the contrary when

Jeremiah depicts the total decimation of the "royal palace" and the "city." Note the allusion to the "choicest cedars" from Lebanon in this context (22:7) and as building materials in the construction of the temple and the palace (see 2 Sam 7:1-17; cf. 1 Kgs 5-7; and Jer 22:14).

Scathing Oracles of Judgment Against the Kings of Judah (22:10-30)

A series of prose and poetic pieces flesh out the denunciation of kings (22:10-30). What holds these oracles together is not only disdain for Judah's rulers but also the language of lamentation. Images of death and the funeral dirge frame the denunciation of Judah's kings, now often mentioned by name. The collection begins with a brief poem and prose interpretation that speaks of the fate of Shallum (Jehoiahaz) as more distressing than the death of his father, King Josiah (22:10-11). Whereas Josiah died gallantly at Megiddo in 609, that is, *in the land*, his son was "carried [away] captive . . . never to see this land again" (22:12). Mourners are therefore not to weep for the dead but for their captive king, whose fate is worse than death.

This lament leads into a scolding condemnation of King Jehoiakim, another of Josiah's sons (22:13-19). The indictment of King Jehoiakim, who is portrayed elsewhere in Jeremiah as a despicable man who loathes the word of God (Jer 36), begins with a cry of "woe" which is customary in funeral processions. The judgment speech concludes imagining the grim and hopeless end of the king. Cast down from his lofty place, he will die in disgrace, without mourners, tears of sadness, or the usual pomp and ceremony (22:19). Instead, there is relief that the wicked king is dead.

According to Jeremiah, Jehoiakim represents the antithesis of a good king. Jehoiakim has built "his house by unrighteousness and his upper rooms by injustice" (22:13). The relative clause, "who builds his house," is usually interpreted literally as a reference to the construction of the royal residence. A detailed description of the palace in verse 14 supports such a reading. However, the poet may use "house" figuratively with the empire in mind, or as a reference to both the palace *and* the empire. In the previous text, Jer

21:11–22:9, "house" carries a double meaning—alluding to the Davidic dynasty and royal palace. In this context too, the text likely employs intentional ambiguity: the prophet blasts the king for building his "residence" and "his kingdom" on the backs of people. He has withheld wages (22:13; see also 1 Kgs 5:13; 11:28; cf., however, 1 Kgs 9:22; note also the prohibitions for withholding wages in Lev 19:13 and Deut 24:14-15), shown ruthless disregard for his "neighbors," and indulged in unbridled "pleasure without conscience" (Gandhi). With no concern for Judah's citizenry, Jehoiakim exploits the resources of the nation to erect his own monument, which, according to Jeremiah, divulges only greed and self-absorption.

In 22:15-17, the prophet rhetorically addresses Jehoiakim in the second person and asks three revealing questions. Each contrasts the diminutive legacy of Jehoiakim with that of his father Josiah. According to the poet, one glance at King Josiah's character and reign shows that true greatness is not measured by amassing goods or personal assets but by practicing justice and championing the cause of the poor. Unlike Jehoiakim, who builds a kingdom for himself at the expense of the poor (22:17; cf. Amos 2:6; 4:1; 8:4), Josiah employed his power and position (he "ate and drank") on behalf of those in need. "Is not this to know me? says the LORD" (22:16; cf. James 1:26-27). "Knowing God" or the "knowledge of God" is manifest here in the vigilant observance of justice for the weakest members of the community. In so doing, Josiah is set apart from his self-serving son.

Positioned between the condemnation of Jehoiakim and Coniah is an obscure poem addressed to an unidentified female figure (22:20-23). The poem is apparently connected to its context by the catchwords "shepherds" (see 22:22 and 23:1-4 and the critique of Judah's shepherd in 21:11–22:30) and "cedar" (22:23 and 22:7, 14, 15). It also draws upon the wayward wife motif of earlier chapters in the book (especially Jer 2–3). Yahweh presumably addresses unfaithful Jerusalem, who still insists on following her many lovers. As suggested by the parallel construction of shepherds (rulers) and lovers in 22:22, her lovers are not "other gods" but Judah's corrupt kings. These lovers/rulers will be crushed and deported, even while Yahweh's wife, headstrong and insubordinate since youth (22:21), shall be humiliated (22:22). It is unclear who the poet has in mind when addressing the "inhabitant of Lebanon, nested among the cedars" in 22:23. If the image refers to the proud capital city Jerusalem (Holladay 1986, 600-03), then the text stresses the futility of seeking refuge in grandiose edifices.

Next in the series of judgment oracles against kings is one leveled against (Je)Coniah son of Jehoiakim, whose throne name was Jehoiachin (22:24-30). Actually, the text consists of a prose judgment (22:24-27) and a poetic counterpart (22:28-30). Both belong to Yahweh and both speak in no uncertain terms of Coniah's demise (cf., however, 52:31-34). Yahweh declares under solemn oath that Coniah shall be deported to Babylon and shall never return to the land of Judah. The fourfold incantation, "into the hands," "into the hands," "into the hands," "into the hands," (22:25), drives home Yahweh's resolve to "hurl" Coniah and the queen mother (Nehushta) out of the land. Language of divine rage, however, is still mingled with sorrow (22:28-30). The poet speaks of Coniah as "a despised broken pot, a vessel no one wants" (22:28). Both he and his descendants are outcasts in a foreign country. In effect, Yahweh mourns over one in whom so many had placed their hopes for the restoration of the kingdom (see 2 Kgs 25:27-30). Yet "this man" (22:28, 30) will be left without an heir to sit on the throne of David. In a passionate plea, the land is summoned to behold the wretched news. "Land, land, land, hear the word of the LORD" (Jer 22:29). As customary for covenant ceremonies and covenant lawsuits, an element of nature is invoked to witness solemn announcements (Deut 32:1; Josh 24:27; Mic 6:1-2). Here the land is called upon to attend to the dissolution of a promise, the end of an era. For the implied reader, the unthinkable has happened: the four-hundred-year Davidic dynasty is over (22:30).

At this point, all looks hopeless for the nation and the future of the monarchy. The oracles concerning Coniah are a portent of failure and cessation. With no heir to the throne, the family dynasty will surely die out. Indeed, kingship itself will end.

Interestingly, however, the "childlessness" of Coniah does not signal the ultimate demise of the promise to David but only its suspension. Though the promise appears in grave danger, it is actually held in abeyance. Like the "childlessness" of Sarai and Abram, barrenness is not the end of the line (Gen 15:2 and Jer 22:30 use the same rare Hebrew word for "childless"). In spite of seemingly insurmountable odds, God will still accomplish God's purposes. God will act unilaterally to fulfill the ancient Davidic promises and accomplish what Judah's shepherds had failed to do.

Bad and Good Shepherds (23:1-8)

These saving overtures in no way excuse the conduct of bad shepherds (23:1-2; cf. 22:22). They will get their due. God will "attend to" (i.e., punish) them for not "attending to" (i.e., caring for) the sheep (23:2). But after a period of judgment, God promises to mend and restore. God pledges to gather those scattered and return them to the fold. Then God will provide leaders who treat the sheep with kindness and genuine concern. Behind this assertion lies the ancient theocratic notion that God is Israel's true shepherd-king (see Ps 23; Ezek 34:1-16). Next God will place on the throne a "righteous Branch" of the line of David who shall act with wisdom and execute justice in the land (23:5). The idea of the righteous branch or rightful scion also appears in Isa 4:2, 11:1, Jer 33:15, and indirectly in Ezek 17:22. During the postexilic period, the shoot imagery became a formal messianic title (Zech 3:8; 6:12). In the present literary context, the metaphor signifies the survival of the Davidic tree (dynasty) when taken for dead. Out of the devastation, life would sprout, albeit barely, from that which is cut off. Although the last of the heirs is childless, the text claims that God will nonetheless fulfill the promise to David. As such, the present salvation oracle qualifies and reconfigures the utterances of blanket judgment leveled against the dynasty. Furthermore, the announcement of "a shoot for David" contrasts Judah's last kings, especially Zedekiah, with a coming ruler who will embody the qualities of the ideal king: wisdom, justice, and righteousness (23:5-6). Unlike the disappointing Zedekiah, who belies the meaning of his name,

"[Yahweh] is my righteousness," Yahweh's coming ruler will fittingly bear the title "[Yahweh] is our righteousness" (23:6).

The final prophecy of hope in 23:7-8 (essentially a doublet of 16:14-15) envisions a time when the dispersed people of God will return to the land. Homecoming from exile will be so astonishing that it will overshadow the memory of the ancient exodus from Egypt. While these brief oracles of salvation receive only scant attention here, they will receive far greater consideration in the second half of the book (Jer 26–52), which focuses on the divine program of "building and planting."

Yahweh Is Against the Prophet (23:9-40)

This section is the longest discourse on prophecy in the Bible (23:9-40). The unit consists of six prose and poetic sections that scrutinize prophets who speak under the guise of divine authority. The individual parts are 23:9b-12, 13-15, 16-17, 18-22, 23-32, and 33-40. As is often the case in the first half of the book, the prophecies lack circumstantial details. They are neither tied to specific times or places, nor mention by name any of the prophets who are accused of wrongdoing. As literature, the oracles present a social world that is laden with danger. By virtue of their role as intermediaries between heaven and earth, prophets possess enormous authority in ancient Israel. They communicate the divine message, a message upon which the nation relies. When prophets distort this message, as Jer 23:9-40 claims some do, they jeopardize the very existence of community life. Indeed, the Deuteronomic law code states that prophets who proclaim unauthorized oracles commit an offense that is punishable by death (twice mentioned in Deut 13:2-6 and 18:15-22). The very formulation of false prophecy as a capital crime in the Deuteronomic law code reveals the gravity and intense fear that surrounds this activity.

The six denunciations of false prophets in Jer 23:9-40 are diverse, but together they produce a treatise on the conduct, message, origin, and fate of prophets who do not speak at Yahweh's command. First, a comparison between prophets who embellish the message with one (Jeremiah), who faithfully proclaims the word of Yahweh, sets the tone for the larger discourse (23:9*b*-12). As a true prophet Jeremiah is fully engaged in Yahweh's purposes on earth. He is brokenhearted and drunk with the wine of Yahweh's holy words (23:9). His heart is crushed and his bones shake because of the message he must speak. This emotional involvement not only reveals aspects of the prophetic psychology, but also, more important, validates the divine authority of Jeremiah's prophecy. Unlike prophets who fabricate their message, he speaks at the bidding of Yahweh, grieves deeply over human evil, and suffers beyond words on account of his prophetic charge. Jeremiah, however, is not the only one overcome with despair. The land also mourns because of the terrible state of affairs (23:10-11). Summoned earlier to witness the dissolution of the royal covenant with David (22:29), the land now endures a "curse," perhaps in the form of a drought, as a result of Judah's blatant disregard for Yahweh (see Deut 27:15-26).

The next oracle likens the prophets of Jerusalem to the prophets of Samaria who speak in the name of Baal (23:13-15). The damning comparison claims that the former, who presumably prophesy in the name of Yahweh, are even worse than their northern counterparts. The Judean prophets betray their very *raison d'être*. They "commit adultery," perhaps a reference to their participation in forbidden religious practices; they "walk in lies" instead of the truth and they "strengthen the hands of evildoers" rather than expose the nation's corruption (23:14). Their moral indifference and turpitude earns them a place alongside the people of Sodom and Gomorrah (Gen 18–19). And these prophets will come to an end that is no less ruinous. Yahweh will feed them wormwood (a bitter-tasting shrub) and poisoned water (23:15).

Jeremiah 23:16-17 exhorts the community to reject prophets whose message is void of ethical content and whose vision of the future is one of complacency and unabashed nationalism. Prophets that do not warn the people of Judah of the consequences of their behavior are deluded and do not utter the word of the Lord. They are no longer the conscience of Israel, but are rather co-conspirators in evil. Worse, they sanction covenantal disobedience in the name of Yahweh. When they give assurances of peace, "It shall be well with you" (23:17), they only perpetuate the lie that calamity will not come upon the nation. They deaden the people to the gravity of their predicament. Their message of peace does not create peace, as they perhaps suppose, but the very opposite.

Jeremiah 23:18-22 also stresses the moral vision of prophecy. Prophets who stand in the council of Yahweh and "heed his word" (23:18, 22) explode with Yahweh's wrath in the face of evil rather than wince at it. As messengers of God, privy to the divine purposes, they convey Yahweh's fierce displeasure with sin (23:19). Having seen and heard God's word in the heavenly assembly (23:18; see also 1 Kgs 22; Isa 6), these confidants of the Lord do not cower or cringe at their awesome responsibilities. They are intent on turning people from their evil ways (23:22). Quite the opposite is true of the optimistic prophets. They do not stand in the divine council and are indifferent to the nation's social evils. Although they prophesy, they are neither sent nor authorized by God to speak. They speak solely on their own volition. These prophets know nothing of divine rage, which is the means by which God accomplishes "the [purposes of his heart]" (23:20).

In the next to last denunciation (23:23-32), God asks a series of questions that call attention to one incisive point: God sees and holds the guilty accountable (cf. 7:11). As one who fills "heaven and earth" (23:24), God is not a domesticated patron deity (i.e., "near by" in verse 23) who cannot observe from "far off" the despicable practices of prophets and dreamers. Yahweh is privy to their falsehood and disparages their dreams and oracles. These opponents of Jeremiah are nothing but impostors. Yahweh has not sent them. They fabricate their messages, mimic the words of others, and want only to deceive their audiences. Their announcements are merely human invention masquerading as truth. But they are not harmless. Under the semblance of divine authority, they lead God's people astray (23:32). They contradict the fundamental direction of Israel's religious heritage and distort divine justice. Therefore, Yahweh derides them with a haunting threefold declaration—"I am against the prophets. . . . I am against the prophets. . . . I am against those who prophesy lying dreams" (23:30-32).

Jeremiah 23:33-39 broadens the scope of Yahweh's diatribe to include prophets, priests, and the people (23:33-34), that is, anyone who seeks or offers a divine utterance. The interpretation of the passage depends in large measure on two factors: (1) whether one adheres to the Hebrew or Greek of verse 33, and (2) how one translates the Hebrew homonyms of *maśśā²*, which means "oracle" or "burden." The NIV follows the Hebrew text in verse 33: "When these people, or a prophet or a priest, ask you, 'What is the *oracle* of the LORD?' say to them, '*What oracle?* I will forsake you, declares the LORD.'" The NIV consistently translates *maśśā²* as "oracle." Such a rendering reads as a treatise on the silence of God: any attempt to inquire of Yahweh, even through Jeremiah (note the second-person singular in 23:33) is absolutely pointless. God is no longer speaking, or at least, *speaking words of salvation.* God has resolved not to shore up Judah's present world with words of support and approbation (as Zedekiah so desperately desired in 21:1-2).

The NRSV consistently translates *maśśā²* as "burden" and renders verse 23 (emphasis mine) according to the LXX: "When this people, or a prophet, or a priest asks you, 'What is the *burden* of the LORD?' you shall say to them, '*You are the burden,* and I will cast you off, says the LORD.'" The NRSV plays on the double meaning of *maśśā²,* oracle or burden. Those who seek or deliver an "utterance" *(maśśā²)* of Yahweh discover to their dismay that they are a burden *(maś śā²)* to Yahweh. Eventually a divine oracle is delivered (23:38-40), but not as the community had hoped. In an announcement of inescapable judgment, the play on the word "burden" is developed a step further. Jeremiah declares that Yahweh will "lift up" (the verb *nś²* is akin to *maśśā²*), and "cast away" *(nṭś)* those who have defiantly uttered "the burden [*maśśā²*] of Yahweh" (cf. Gen 40 for a different play on the verb "lift up"). If Zedekiah's earlier petition for divine aid, "inquire of Yahweh on my behalf," is still in the province of the present text (see 21:1-2), the reply is again unmistakable: none will be granted.

Baskets of Figs (24:1-10)

This concluding text of chapters 21–24 recapitulates motifs that appear in the opening text (21:1-10): the cessation of the historical dynasty of David, the role of Babylon as Yahweh's instrument of judgment, and preferential place afforded the exiles in Babylon over the remnant remaining in Jerusalem. Set in the years after the first deportation to Babylon in 597, Jer 24:1-10 is a simple vision report (formally similar to 1:11-12, 13-15) in which Jeremiah sees two baskets of figs: one is rotten and the other ripe and delicious. The baskets of figs are quite commonplace, even though they are placed in the temple of the Lord (24:1) as "an offering of the first-fruits" (Rudolph 1947, 134-35). Yet Jeremiah sees what others do not. He discerns in this ordinary scene the destiny of Israel. The "good figs" symbolize the Judean exiles in Babylon to whom Yahweh promises blessings and restoration (24:4-7). They are the recipients of Yahweh's covenant blessing (24:7). Yahweh will act graciously toward these exiles, pledging to bring them back to their land, to "build them up and not tear them down," and "to plant them and not pluck them up" (see 1:10). With this group of survivors lies the future of Israel (see also 21:8-10). In stark contrast, the bad figs represent those who remain in Judah or flee to Egypt (see 21:3-7), including King Zedekiah of Judah and his officials (24:8). They shall become a spectacle and object lesson for all to see. This remnant residing in Jerusalem and in Egypt (24:8) will suffer the curses of the covenant, which ultimately spell death.

Theological and Ethical Analysis

While the meaning of this vision is quite clear, its theological and ethical rationale is not. Why should Yahweh accept one community and not another? The text is silent. It simply asserts that Yahweh opposes the communities in Judah and Egypt and bestows favor on the survivors in Babylon. Such a position, it should be said, is thoroughly consistent with the general direction of the book. The interpretive community of Jeremiah is convinced that exile is a crucial and inescapable part of the divine program. Because of the nation's covenant disloyalty and unfaithfulness to Yahweh, Israel must face divine judgment. The land must be evacuated, and its systems of governance, institutional life, and theological vision must be totally abandoned. Consequently, exile represents the kind of rupture with the past that Yahweh requires. Without this complete break the inauguration of the new workings of God is impossible. Thus, those who leave the land for Babylon do so in accordance with the divine will; conversely, those who remain there or escape to Egypt act in defiance of God.

Another dynamic may factor in the text's polarity. The reader might construe residence in the land of Judah as a sign of God's favor and banishment to Babylon as divine judgment. Such a conclusion would be easy to make in light of Jeremiah's view of exile as divine punishment and the Deuteronomic claim that land occupation is a blessing for obedience. The text, however, turns this assumption upside down by insisting that those who remain in the land "unscathed" are rejected whereas those who suffer the pangs of exile are exalted. In other words, God lifts the downtrodden, gives hope to the hopeless, and brings low the exalted. Though displaced and humiliated, the dispirited exiles cannot be dismissed as rejected and cursed. To the contrary, these Judean refugees are the true custodians of God's promises.

The prose report of the vision of baskets of figs is far more than a political tract that endorses one community, the Babylonian group, over rival communities in Judah and Egypt. While partisan politics likely lie beneath the surface of the text, the present form of the text is governed by theological concerns. We find here an attempt to speak about God in a meaningful way in the midst of tragedy. The text transforms massive devastation and hardship into constructive categories. Like the bitter memory of slavery in Egypt, exile is reconstrued as a disturbing yet potentially positive pattern of meaning. This is not to deny the devastating impact of forced relocation. The text only affirms that exile does not seal its victims' fate. God will be faithful to those who experience the physical and emotional wreckage of displacement and will bring good out of their suffering (see also 29:10-14; cf. Gen 50:15-21). Though banished far from their country, God will watch over and care for them. Even in Babylon, perhaps the least likely place for the presence of God, the Jewish refugees are able to find God (24:7). There they will be given a new heart so they can know and return to the Lord. Hence, exile in no way nullifies God's commitment to the people.

While these assurances fail to do justice to the hardships of the remnant in the land and those who fled to Egypt, they eventually transcend sectarian interests and become paradigmatic for survivors everywhere. These hopeful overtures claim that dispersion to the uttermost places cannot separate the faithful from the love and presence of God.

Jeremiah 21–24 is foremost a treatise on leadership. According to the text, the fundamental well-being of people depends in large measure on their leaders. In the ancient world as well as in our modern settings, leaders wield enormous power to influence for good or ill. Jeremiah bears witness to this by cataloguing the terrible abuses of those in authority (see also Deut 17:14-20; Ezek 34:1-31). With damning evidence in hand, the text concentrates on the failure of Israel's leadership and its devastating consequences for the community. Rather than attending to the needs of the poor and needy, Judah's rulers cater to their own whims and desires. Rather than maintaining justice and defending the most vulnerable members of society, they abuse their power, are self-absorbed, and exploit the state's resources for their own economic advantage. Indifferent to the moral demands of the covenant, they build their kingdoms to the detriment of others. To ensure their own standard of living they rob and oppress. Such acts are not only crimes against humanity but also crimes against God. God sees and condemns because God is a father of orphans and protector of widows (Ps 68:6). God defends the cause of the poor, delivers the needy, and crushes the oppressor (Ps 72:4). Thus God will topple diminutive kingdoms for the sake of the victims.

The text does not say that leadership—even in its monarchic form—is doomed to failure. There are cases in which Judah's kings use their political power for the good of the community. Josiah is a case in point. He is one who rules justly and champions the cause of the poor and needy (22:13-17). Notwithstanding the success of this one, the self-serving policies of Judah's final leaders leave a bleak legacy of greed and egotism.

The diatribe against kings is interrupted by a strong denunciation of false prophets. Like kings, these prophets fail to fulfill their divinely appointed duties. God raised them up to be spokespersons and covenant mediators who would turn the people away from evil and back to God. But the prophets are worse than the people. They lie, steal, and spread wickedness through the land (23:14-15). Instead of telling the truth, they disseminate hollow promises and follow an evil course. They lead Judah astray and narcotize the community to its true condition. These prophets are God's burden.

When prophets fail, kings go down in ruin. When prophets flounder, alternatives to royal power cease. Without the prophetic presence there is no poetry, imagination, generosity, or testimony to transcendence. Kings avert their eyes to human needs, economic inequities, and broken social systems. And there remain only "horses and chariots," unbridled greed, brutality, technology, and stinginess (see, e.g., Deut 17:14-20). When prophets fail no one sees beyond the superficial to grasp life at its depth (which is what Vincent van Gogh the painter said that he tried to do in his work). No one introduces God's viewpoint and God's passion into public discourse. Life flattens into settled categories, undisturbed and insensitive to what is truly going on. When prophets avoid the divine counsel and compromise their vocation, nations have their way and no one dares to bring them to their senses. When prophets cease being God's voice, sweatshops make sense, gaps between the rich and poor are merely the result of market forces, murdered civilians are collateral damage, and landmines tearing off arms and legs are just security burdens. Some celebrate the demise of prophets. Who wants to hear their disturbing speech? Yet when dissident and oppositional voices are silent, when accommodation wins out and ethical angst is soothed, all suffer, including kings.

THE END HAS COME (JEREMIAH 25)

Chapter 25 plays a vital role in the architecture of Jeremiah. It brings to a close the written account of the first phase of

Jeremiah's public life. The text summarizes the prophetic activity of Jeremiah from its inception (627) to the fourth year of King Jehoiakim (605/4), which adds up to twenty-three years of prophetic speech (25:1-14). The reference to the fourth year of King Jehoiakim's reign is fraught with meaning. It signals the first year of the reign of Nebuchadnezzar, the principal agent of Judah's dismantling (25:1). The divine program of "plucking up and pulling down, destroying and overthrowing" defines this pivotal chapter.

Literary Analysis

In conjunction with the first chapter of the book, chapter 25 provides an editorial framework for the first half of the book (Jer 1–25). Chapter 1 foreshadows the dominant themes of the first twenty-five chapters. It introduces Jeremiah as a "prophet to the nations" (1:5), who is appointed "over nations and kingdoms to pluck up and pull down, to destroy and overthrow . . . " (1:10). It affirms that Yahweh's word is trustworthy (1:11-12) and transcends Judah's sectarian interests (1:13-14). And it prepares readers for an imminent invasion by unnamed northern invaders (1:15-16). The opening chapter also puts Jeremiah on notice that he will face his own war, not with foes from distant lands but with Judah's own kings, princes, priests, and people (1:17-18). These motifs culminate in chapter 25. Here Jeremiah emerges as a prophet who turns his attention beyond Judah to other peoples (25:9, 11-26; see also the Oracles Against the Nations in Jer 46–51 which occur after Jer 25:13 in the LXX). After twenty-three years of rejection, Jeremiah delivers a devastating message of divine judgment to Judah *and* "all the nations" (25:13). Furthermore, chapter 25 identifies the cryptic reference to the "north" (1:14-15) as the armies assembled by King Nebuchadnezzar of Babylon (25:9). The devastation that Nebuchadnezzar produces, however, is not outside the scope of Yahweh's purposes. It is part of Yahweh's sovereign plan "to pluck up and tear down." Babylon advances to punish headstrong Judah for not heeding the prophetic message (25:3-11).

There are other indications that chapters 1 and 25 function as an envelope that holds in check the intervening chapters. First, the framing texts share the same chronological arrangements: Both refer to the reign of "King Jehoiakim son of Josiah of Judah" as the background for the coming of the word of Yahweh, and both assign the beginning of Jeremiah's prophetic activity to "the thirteenth year of King Josiah son of Amon of Judah" (1:2; 25:3). Second, chapter 1 and chapter 25 focus on the rejection of the prophetic word. The initial chapter intimates that the prophet will face opposition and rejection (1:8, 17-19), while the concluding one looks back on twenty-three years of opposition and rejection (25:3-7). Third, one can discern a movement from orality to writing, that is, from prophecy as *speech* to prophecy as an authoritative body of *writing*. Chapter 1 is the *written* account of the genesis of the *oral* proclamation, "I have put my words in your mouth" (1:9) and "and you shall speak whatever I command you" (1:7). Accordingly, the "word" is placed symbolically in the mouth of the prophet in preparation for his *oral* proclamation. Chapter 25 presents a *written* synopsis of twenty-three years of prophetic proclamation. Moreover, whereas chapter 1 appeals to the oral proclamation for authority, chapter 25 shifts its focus to writing as a primary source of authority. "I will bring upon that land all the words that I have uttered against it, *everything written in this book*, which Jeremiah prophesied against all the nations"(25:13, my emphasis). Fourth, the two framing texts give the same reason for Yahweh's displeasure: Judah's disobedience and apostasy, expressly its worship of other gods (1:16; 25:4-7). Although the entire community is culpable before God, chapter 1 singles out Judah's leaders for their opposition to the prophetic message (1:18-19) and chapter 25 identifies these leaders as the first to drink from the "cup of the wine of wrath" (25:15-18).

In addition to these thematic connections, there are also lexical links. Note, for instance, the frequency of the term "word(s)" in the two chapters (Jer 1:1, 2, 4, 9, 11, 12, 13 and Jer 25:1, 3, 8, 13, 30). Also observe that the words "hand," "send," and "north" occur in both chapters. In the first chapter Yahweh stretches out his "hand" and touches the mouth of Jeremiah (1:9). In chapter 25 Yahweh commands Jeremiah to take from his "hand" the "cup of the wine of wrath" (25:17). In chapter 1 Yahweh "sends" Jeremiah (1:7) and commands him to speak; in chapter 25,

Yahweh "sends" forth his servants the prophets (25:4) as well as his devouring sword (25:16). Finally, it is worth noting that high incidence of the word "north" contributes to the ominous tone of the intervening chapters (1:13, 14, 15; 25:9, 26).

Jeremiah 1 and 25, therefore, serve as "bookends" for the first half of the book. They frame the intervening chapters and provide symmetrical arrangements for them. Together these bracketing texts create a theological scaffold for the many dissonant voices and themes. Supported by this framework, the first half of the prophetic drama announces in bold and unflinching terms that Yahweh rules the world and judges all nations.

On its own, Jer 25 consists of three main parts: A prose sermon which summarizes the prophetic activity of Jeremiah from the thirteenth year of King Josiah to the fourth year of King Jehoiakim (25:1-14); a symbolic action concerning the cup of Yahweh's wrath (25:15-29); and a final oracle against the nations (25:30-38).

The initial sermon of Jeremiah reflects the language and structure that is standard for the prose tradition in Jeremiah (see also, e.g., 7:1-15; 11:1-17; 18:1-12; 21:1-10). Like other material in this tradition, Jer 25:1-14 has a clear affinity with Deuteronomy and the Deuteronomistic History. Besides linguistic parallels (esp. prominent in 25:4-7), the text is structurally akin to pivotal passages in the historical epic (e.g., Josh 1, 23; Judg 2; 1 Sam 12; 1 Kgs 8; 2 Kgs 17). Its major parts include:

a. An introduction that describes the setting and speaker, 25:1-3*a*
b. A warning to heed the word of the Lord, 25:3*b*-6
c. A statement announcing Israel's disobedience, 25:7
d. A declaration of Yahweh's judgment, 25:8-14

As is customary of prophets in the historical work, God sends Jeremiah to warn the people of the consequences of their recalcitrance. Israel refuses to "listen" or "turn" and so Yahweh brings the curses of the covenant upon the nation.

The concluding words of the prose sermon broaden the scope of Yahweh's judgment to include Judah's enemies, namely, King

Nebuchadrezzar and Babylon (25:11-14). The reference to Babylon serves as a natural transition to the next section of the chapter (25:15-29). In one of the most disconcerting texts in Jeremiah, God commands the prophet to intoxicate the nations with the wine of divine wrath. The symbolic action envisions the world under the dreaded judgment of God. Starting with Judah and its capital city Jerusalem, Yahweh metes out to all peoples unmitigated judgment and devastation. The final oracles of judgment (25:30-38) amplify the message of universal devastation. As a roaring lion, Yahweh will devour the "inhabitants of the earth," with the "shepherds" (rulers of the nations) being the main targets of Yahweh's fierce anger.

Exegetical Analysis

Despite Human Failure the Lord Reigns (25:1-14)

The setting of Jer 25:1-14 is significant. The word of God comes to the prophet at a crucial moment of Judah's world. As suggested by the synchronous allusion to the first year of King Nebuchadrezzar's regime, the reference to the fourth year of King Jehoiakim's reign is far more than a mere historical allusion (25:1). It represents the end of an epoch and the emergence of another. The nation of Judah will soon fall and become a displaced community within the great Neo-Babylonian Empire (25:1-3). The seemingly innocuous date signals the arrival of Nebuchadrezzar's reign of terror and the end of Judah's preexilic world.

In this perilous setting, the prophet preaches a sermon in which he accounts for the crushing defeat of Judah by Babylon. The sermon begins with a retrospective on Jeremiah's prophetic activity and Judah's persistent recalcitrance. Like other key figures in Judah's history (see, e.g., 1 Sam 12), Jeremiah appears as one who looks back on events of his lifetime in an attempt to interpret the present course of life (25:3). Now the amalgam of voices of chapters 2 through 24 converge and speak with clarity that the destruction of Judah is the consequence of an entire history of obduracy and disobedience to prophetic words. With one bold stroke, twenty-three years of prophetic speech are reduced to "not hearing." Indeed the words "not listen" occur four times in this sermon (25:3, 4, 7, 8). Judah has rejected repeated invitations to "return" and as a result will be uprooted from the land and relegated to the status of subject people. At the same time, Jeremiah is vindicated as a true prophet. He has spoken the word of the Lord faithfully, though his message has gone unheeded.

Whereas the main part of the homily accentuates collective blame and prophetic vindication, its final verses take aim at Judah's nemesis (25:12-14). The text's coherent system of reciprocal justice cannot tolerate Babylon, the symbol of raw and indiscriminate power, to go unchecked. After seventy years of dominance, Yahweh will punish the king of Babylon and his land. Not unlike the domestication of Pharaoh (in Exod 1–15), Yahweh will thoroughly tame and subjugate "his servant," King Nebuchadrezzar (25:9). He and his kingdom must be held accountable for their actions.

Cup of Divine Wrath (25:15-29)

The remainder of chapter 25 extends the range of God's judgment to include all facets of the created order. A symbolic act first drives home the message of universal judgment. Yahweh commands cupbearer Jeremiah to make the nations drink the cup of divine wrath (25:15-29; see also Num 5:11-31). At this chilling banquet of death, all who drink from the poisonous cup will eventually die (McKane 1986, 634-35). The force of God's anger is overwhelming, and none can resist it (25:28-29). The wine of divine wrath reveals the terrifying power of Yahweh and the diminutive might of "all the kingdoms of the world that are on the face of the earth" (25:26). The One who controls the destiny of the world is able to send the once-powerful nations away reeling in pain.

Oracles against the nations often imply the triumph and salvation of Israel (see, e.g., Jer 46–51; Ezek 25–32). This is not the case here. Jerusalem and the towns of Judah are first to drink the cup of divine wrath (25:18). God's own people do not have the antidote for the poison and therefore suffer the fate of the nations

(25:29, 30). Next in line to drink is "pharaoh king of Egypt," Israel's first oppressor, followed by nations that border Israel and then those far away. The last on the roster is "Sheshach," a cryptic reference to Babylon (25:26). The significance of this cryptogram eludes us. Perhaps the mere mention of Babylon is too odious to utter in public. Perhaps the poet intends to mock. Perhaps the predicted downfall of the empire is too dangerous to bring up. Regardless, the presence of Babylon on the list levels the playing field: Even mighty Babylon, triumphant in power and seemingly invincible, will be called to judgment for its terrible deeds. *Yahweh, not Babylon, rules!* The miniature collection of oracles against the nations, which appear at this point in their entirety in the Septuagint, reveals God's sovereignty over all nations and Jeremiah's special role as "prophet to the nations" (Jer 1:5).

Cosmic Disaster (25:30-38)

The metaphors shift in the final oracles of the chapter (25:30-38). Yet, multiple images of Yahweh's advent convey the dominant theme of the chapter: God's universal judgment. First, Yahweh roars like a lion ready to devour the nations (25:30). Next, the tumult of battle resounds throughout the world (25:31). Finally, a violent storm stirs the very ends of the earth (25:32). The divine roar, the terrible battle cry, and the great tempest culminate in an apocalyptic battle in which the slain fill the earth. The magnitude of God's judgment has global repercussions: its force leads to cosmic desolation (25:33). The apocalyptic theatre of war evokes cries of desperation from the rulers of nations (25:34-38). Stripped of their pride and power, they wail at the sight of earth's wasteland (25:37-38).

Theological and Ethical Analysis

The prophetic treatise on the dismantling of Judah's preexilic tenets of faith and institutional life is complete (1:10). The first half of the prophetic drama (Jer 1–25) has successfully subverted conventional understandings of worship (7:1-15), covenantal categories (11:1-13), and the tradition of Israel's election as God's chosen people (18:1-12). It has delivered a mortal blow to any hope for the uninterrupted occupation of the land as well as for the continuation of monarchic structures (21:1-10). All evidence attests to the same disconcerting conclusion: long-standing institutions and testimonies of God's reality will not sustain the community in its new social order (in Babylon). For an assortment of reasons ranging from human sin to geopolitical realities to divine prerogative, Jeremiah testifies to the end of Israel's most cherished beliefs and social institutions, especially those associated with the dynasty and its capital city. As a result, nothing is sure. All is fluid and emptied of meaning. Life becomes riddled with anxiety. The text has accomplished its goal of hurtling the reader into the strange world of exile with few support systems in place. Its objective all along has not been to console but to shatter certitude and various forms of denial. God's program of uprooting and pulling down involves afflicting the comfortable, not comforting the afflicted.

To underscore this agenda, Jeremiah now serves a cup of wrath to all nations. The ferocious Lord roars against "all the inhabitants of the earth." The cry of cosmic war is heard "to the ends of the earth." A mighty tempest shakes the world and corpses cover the earth. These alarming apocalyptic images drive home the fact that nothing would ever be the same again, for Judah or the nations. The entire world lies under the dread judgment of God.

While these images of violence are disturbing, they must be examined against a particular historical setting: the short-lived but destructive Neo-Babylonian conquest of Syria-Palestine in the late seventh century and first half of the sixth century. Within a span of a few decades, Babylonian battalions had done irrevocable harm to the small Judean nation. The invasions and deportations, the destruction of Jerusalem and its temple, and the immense havoc wrought on human lives were the most devastating experiences of Judah's history. This massive evil raised poignant theological questions about the scope of Yahweh's power. Grappling with the national tragedy, Jeremiah affirms that the power politics of Babylon do not immobilize the living God. In spite of the domination of the Neo-Babylonian Empire, God is still in control. Yahweh rules in and through the wreckage of the nation. Furthermore, Jeremiah declares that the perpetrators of evil will not get away with murder. In God's just universe, evildoers receive their due punishment. Babylon will pay. While such a confession of faith runs smack in the face of a world where injustice, plunder, and death prevail, it boldly asserts that evil and exploitation are not the final word. Not unlike the psalmist who experienced the presence of God while passing through "the valley of the shadow of death," (KJV; "the darkest valley" NRSV). Jeremiah testifies to the reign of God amidst a world gone awry.

People of faith and religious communities sometimes undergo periods of enormous upheaval and loss, when conventional modes of faith and trusted institutions fail and settled categories give way. During such times, what is left? How is one to cope? Is there hope amid a crumbling world? At this stage in the prophetic drama, the text has little to say about constructing new worlds out of the rubble of fallen ones. It is more concerned with tearing down rather than building up, with judgment rather than salvation. No doubt it would be easier to navigate through the wreckage with safe categories, with answers rather than questions. Yet, few are given at this point and the best one can do is to "live the questions." Jeremiah has to live the questions, perplexed by his own turmoil and a world spiraling out of control. The people of Judah have to face a future yet inscribed, without the familiar props from the past. Even Zedekiah and his administration must reconstrue their most basic views of life and death: in order to live they must leave the land and surrender to the enemy.

This dangerous process of dismantling is still instructive. In the first place, it reveals that the people of God must let go of what is gone and cannot be retrieved. Attempts to recapture bygone days are destined to fail; and running from the pain of lost worlds provides only a temporary anesthetic. Second, it shows how important it is to face the failure of the old forms. Candor is certainly difficult; it is far easier to return to familiar arrangements and attempt business as usual. In some respects, this is exactly what Judah's kings and prophets were doing, and Jeremiah exposes their efforts as futile. Finally, embedded in the process of dismantling is the conviction that when denials are broken and false hopes are dispelled, fresh expressions of faith are possible. While the first half of Jeremiah does little to lay down these hopeful forms, it provides fertile ground for their development in the second half of the book. Yet even at this moment of the prophetic drama, we know that the end of the known world is not the end of God. Though it may appear that way and even feel that way, God is present in and through the wreckage.

COMMENTARY
BOOK TWO: JEREMIAH 26–52

THE EMERGENCE OF HOPE OUT OF
SHATTERED WORLDS

Survival depends on hope. When hope is gone, life becomes unbearable. There are only faint traces of hope in Jer 1–25, and these vestiges are obscured by reams of divine judgments. Instead of inspiring hope, the first half of Jeremiah dismantles configurations of hope that are based on a building and on a king; on a land and on political autonomy. Jeremiah attacks a temple theology that had become an idolatrous system (Jer 7). He employs the covenant to curse rather than to bless (Jer 11). Jeremiah assaults the community's privileged position (Jer 18) and its seemingly inviolable dynastic rights (Jer 21). He even subverts ancient land claims by insisting that the land must be abandoned before the inception of new era. The prophet demolishes these long-held understandings of reality allied with the old preexilic world, insisting that they stand under the "wrath of love." By this means, the text's rhetoric of judgment frustrates every argument that God is inextricably tied to Judah's conventional religious systems. Hence, nothing remains to support the toppling world. The few islands of hope in Jer 1–25 have been submerged in an ocean of death.

Jeremiah 26–52 is altogether different. While the fall of Jerusalem occupies the center of interest in the second half of the book (see esp. 39:1–40:6), the text begins to articulate strategies for new beginnings beyond the fateful events of 587. Overtures of salvation and hope are no longer muted, as they were in chapters 1–25, but now play a central role in the literary organization and theological message of Jer 26–52. For the first time in the book,

233

extensive sections paint the future of Judah in a positive light. Major collections envision a time of renewal following national humiliation. The most stunning of these is the "Book of Comfort" (Jer 30–33), which is the centerpiece of Jer 26–52. Here God reverses the judgments against Judah and maps out in their place a "hope-full" script for the future. Also, for the first time, the text introduces individuals who are receptive to the message of Jeremiah. These faithful few come to Jeremiah's aid when his life is on the line in the temple (26:16-19), when he is thrown into a cistern (38:7-13), during the Babylonian siege of Jerusalem (39:11-18), and before Baruch reads his dictated scroll to Jehoiakim (36:9-19, 26). In each case, supporters not only rescue Jeremiah from harm's way, but they protect the nation from "bringing innocent blood" upon itself (26:15). For the reader, the faithful few provide a dramatic foil for the multitudes that will come under divine judgment.

The multiple endings of Jeremiah, each representing different points in the development of the book, likewise point to better times for the suffering people of God (Jer 45, 46–51, 52). The first is an oracle response to Baruch, Jeremiah's scribe and confidant (45:1-5). Amidst a world under siege (45:4), Baruch is promised his "life as a prize of war" (45:5). Although this individual salvation oracle is certainly modest, it nonetheless represents a pledge of a future when none seemed possible. Emerging from the ruins of old systems destined for destruction (45:4) are signs, however tenuous, of survival. The Oracles Against the Nations (Jer 46–51), another ending of the Hebrew text of the book, punctuate the book with implicit oracles of hope for exiled Judah. The announcement of Babylon's defeat particularly signals salvation for Judah (Jer 50–51). Not unlike Isa 40–55, the triumph of Yahweh over arrogant Babylon provides the conditions necessary for the restoration of those banished to distant lands. Finally, a historical appendix winds up with the kind treatment of King Jehoiachin in Babylon (Jer 52:31-34). King Evil-merodach of Babylon shows favor to Jehoiachin and releases him from prison. The Babylonian monarch treats him kindly and gives him an honored position above the other vassal kings in Babylon. Moreover,

Judah's deported ruler is afforded a place of preeminence at the king's table (52:33) and is given a "regular daily allowance . . . by the king of Babylon . . . to the day of his death" (52:34). The allusion to Jehoiachin's survival and kind treatment, which is essentially a repetition of 2 Kgs 25:27-30, apparently implies that the future of Judah has not come to an irrevocable end.

Although configurations of hope in Jer 26–52 are neither unified nor systematic, their broad outlines are still evident. From the literary arrangements of the second half of the book as well as from its recurring motifs, we find that hope is rooted in suffering. Every buoyant overture appears against a background of exile. Hope requires letting go of the old world and its systems of security. To hang on to the old leaves little room for the new workings of God. Hope is found on the margins and not at the center. That is, it is found among the "losers" and not the "winners." Hope involves building genuine community in a place of risk. Ironically, the community established in Babylon became one of the three great centers of Jewry in the ancient world. Hope takes shape in the form of a new spirituality based on internal renewal, forgiveness, and an awareness that God cares deeply about suffering people and their disappointments. Hope is textual. Its various expressions and authorization derive primarily from a scroll. Hope looks forward to homecoming. It anticipates a time when refugees will return home and enjoy God's blessings. Finally, hope emerges within the context of worship, the place where new social and symbolic visions develop and gel.

A GLIMMER OF HOPE (JEREMIAH 26)

Modern Jeremiah scholarship has focused largely on the historical development of Jer 26 and its relationship to Jer 7, commonly referred to as Jeremiah's temple sermon. Discussions of authorship and dating have dominated the field. While these discussions have clarified the history of composition, they have shed little light on Jer 26 as a literary reality that occupies a particular position in the book. Jeremiah 26 is not merely an isolated text or an elaboration of Jer 7. Moreover, it is more than a prefix to the collection on true and false prophets in Jer 27–29. When reading the text holistically, one discovers that Jer 26 plays a strategic role in the overall architecture of the book.

Literary Analysis

This biographical text introduces part two of Jeremiah in a manner analogous to the first chapter of the book: it presents the dominant motifs of the second half of Jeremiah in cryptic and anticipatory terms. According to Ronald Clements, "chapter 26 uses the prophet's temple address [of chapter 7] to provide a thematic introduction to the sequence of reports concerning the message of the prophet" (1988, 154). The introduction to the second half of the book encapsulates the central themes that follow: (1) Jeremiah encounters intensified efforts to thwart his message. (2) This opposition sets in motion a series of events culminating in the destruction of Jerusalem and its holy shrine. (3) Despite prophetic persecution and national devastation, a faithful few emerge to defend Jeremiah, heed his message, and become the nucleus of a new community.

While Jer 26 sets the tone for subsequent chapters, it also functions as a hinge text anchored in the past. As a bridge to the earlier chapters of Jeremiah, the passage continues to mount an attack against the capital city and its central shrine. It also presents Jeremiah as a true prophet who speaks the words of Yahweh. The "officials and all the people" (26:12), "some of the elders of the land" (26:17), and the testimony of the dead prophet Uriah (26:20-23) all bear witness to the veracity of Jeremiah's message. He is a faithful witness whose life is placed in grave danger by a community on its way to destruction. Moreover, the text emphasizes the importance of repentance and obedience as the only means of skirting disaster. Finally, the introductory chapter highlights the culpability of the nation's leadership. The opposition waged by the power brokers of the nation to Jeremiah's message is not surprising given their role in the social order; they run the risk of losing the most if the old systems of control are overthrown. They will have to forfeit their status and power base in the reformulation of the community.

236

The opening scene of the second half of Jeremiah is broken down into five parts. Verses 1-6 recount Jeremiah's abbreviated temple sermon. Verses 7-11 narrate the hostility that his words evoke. Tensions escalate to the point that priests and prophets seize Jeremiah and sentence him to death. In verses 12-15, Jeremiah defends himself before his accusers, insisting that he is only speaking the message entrusted to him by God. Unexpectedly, certain officials come to his defense in verses 16-23. They argue that Jeremiah's message is not inconsistent with other prophets in Israel, such as Micah of Moresheth who appeared during the reign of Hezekiah and Uriah of Kiriath-jearim who prophesied against the city and land during the reign of Jehoiakim. The chapter concludes with Jeremiah's remarkable escape, in large measure due to the intervention of Ahikam son of Shaphan (26:24).

Exegetical Analysis

Jeremiah's Disturbing Temple Sermon (26:1-6)

Jeremiah's sermon is delivered in the temple of Jerusalem at the beginning of King Jehoiakim's reign (26:1). The great temple is both the arena for hearing the word of the Lord and the tribunal for determining the fate of Jeremiah and the nation. The association with Jehoiakim is more than a mere historical reference: the allusion to Jehoiakim, who is a prototype of infidelity and disobedience, functions as a code word for cosmic crumbling and the collapse of moral courage. Unlike Zedekiah, who is in part a victim of circumstance, Jehoiakim squanders his many chances to obey the prophetic word. His very name eventually becomes associated with treason and alarm. The setting in the Jerusalem temple is also significant. The temple is the nation's principal source of security and sanctuary. It is the center of community life, the sacred place that anchors the present community in holy history and shared story. The temple also represents the nation's illusion of permanence. It follows that at the start of the second half of the book the temple should provide the field of schemes upon which the future of Israel is to be determined.

God instructs Jeremiah to enter the temple and address those who come to worship (26:2). Should his hearers "turn from their evil way," they can still forestall the coming disaster (26:3). Notwithstanding this opportunity, the sermon itself (26:4-6) is cast in the negative: the temple and the city face a grim future if the community continues its defiant posture. Disobedience to the prophetic message holds grave consequences: Yahweh will "make this house like Shiloh," and Jerusalem will become "a curse for all the nations of the earth." Echoes of the ancestral promise of Israel's birth resound here: "In you [the descendants of Abram] all the families of the earth shall be blessed" (Gen 12:3). Now, however, Jeremiah reverses the promise of life to intimate the death of Israel, a death that will be visible to "all the nations of the earth." In Jeremiah, Yahweh's dealings with Israel are never hidden from the masses.

Jeremiah Is Sentenced to Die (26:7-11)

The remainder of the chapter elaborates the charges brought against Jeremiah (26:7-11), as well as his self-defense (26:12-15), corroboration (26:16-23), and eventual acquittal (26:24). The disproportionate attention given to the various responses to Jeremiah's sermon suggests that they carry more weight than the sermon itself. When Jeremiah finishes his address, the priests, prophets, and people bring charges against him. It is instructive to note the frequency of the terms "house" and "city" (see 26:2, 6, 7, 9, 11, 12, 15, 20). The opponents of Jeremiah evidently interpret his message as a frontal assault on the national-cultic state and its conceptions of reality. To thwart his subversive words, they sentence him to death, which brings us to a crucial point in the drama. What is at stake at this juncture of the book is more than another instance of the community rejecting the word of the Lord. Chapter 26 presents leading sectors of the nation attempting *ritually and legally* to silence the voice of God.

We have already noted that the death penalty is reserved for offenses that are perceived as the most detrimental to the social and symbolic order. Persons engaged in such acts are expunged from the state so that it can survive. The temple priests and prophets sentence Jeremiah to death because they believe that his message poses a grave threat to existing structures. By putting Jeremiah to death, they hope to protect insiders and existing structures from harm and even collapse. Unfortunately, these "defenders of God" and custodians of the status quo fail to recognize that it is not Jeremiah who is against the temple and the capital city, but Yahweh!

Jeremiah's Defense (26:12-15)

Jeremiah appreciates the gravity of his accusers' charges and defends himself before them. He does so by testifying that his words are not his own but God's (26:12). Furthermore, Jeremiah perceives the enormous repercussions that his potential death sentence holds for the future of Judah. If he is put to death, his executioners will bring bloodguilt upon the nation (26:15). The language employed here, "bringing innocent blood upon," echoes Jeremiah's earlier words (7:6; see also Deut 19:10; cf. 1 Kgs 2:31; 2 Kgs 21:16; 24:4). The reference to shedding innocent blood in the first temple sermon is *implicitly* related to loss of land and shrine. In the abridged sermon, Jeremiah's fate *explicitly* and inextricably involves the future of the city and its inhabitants (26:14-15). If Jeremiah is executed, his innocent blood will cry out in vengeance against the community (cf. Gen 4:10). If his sentence is commuted, the city will be granted yet another reprieve (26:13).

Officials to the Rescue! (26:16-23)

The narrative takes an unexpected turn following Jeremiah's declaration of innocence. The court officials adjudicating the case reverse the decision of the temple priests and prophets (26:16). Some of the community elders who come to Jeremiah's defense strengthen their decision (26:16-23). They appeal to written prophecy to show that Jeremiah's position is entirely tenable. The prophet Micah, they contend, prophesied during the reign of King Hezekiah that God would destroy Zion. Rather than putting Micah to death, King Hezekiah feared the Lord and entreated divine favor. Because of his repentance, God spared Jerusalem.

COMMENTARY

Moreover, Uriah son of Shemaiah from Kiriath-jearim delivered a message virtually identical to that of Jeremiah. Despite his assassination by Jehoiakim's henchmen, Uriah's oracles add weight to Jeremiah's defense. In effect, textual authority, that is, written prophecy, and historical precedence (26:20-23) vindicate Jeremiah.

For the first time in the book, and strategically placed at the beginning of the second half of the prophetic drama, the message of Jeremiah receives an ambivalent reception. Until this point, concerted and unilateral efforts had been made to silence Jeremiah. Now, something startlingly new takes place: while some accuse Jeremiah of treason, others defend his innocence and, by implication, accept the plausibility of his searing critique. Thanks to the "officials," "elders," and particularly Ahikam son of Shaphan (26:24), the innocent blood of Jeremiah is not shed and the future of the community is spared. The court proceedings, however, are not yet finalized. Certain parties still seek Jeremiah's life and certain kings still execute innocent prophets. Such ambivalence foreshadows the nation's response to God's word. A few will hear and be receptive to the words of the prophet, while others remain defiant.

Theological and Ethical Analysis

At first glance chapter 26 appears to continue the saga of Jeremiah's rejection and persecution. Jeremiah proclaims God's message and he encounters the usual adversity. The leaders of the nation arrest him and demand his execution. There is little new here, except that the stakes for the nation and the prophet increase. Then when all looks hopeless for Jeremiah and Judah, the tide changes and seeds of hope take root. The narrative begins to hint at the possibility of a new beginning for a community whose old world is on the verge of ending. Although the story is anchored in the old regime, during the reign of Jehoiakim and in the temple precincts, the power base of the old world, it still introduces signs of hope that transcend the coming disaster. These hints of better times for the people of God are present in the following:

240

(1) Although Jeremiah suffers unjustly, his life is spared and his sentence of death is commuted; as a result, the voice of God is not silenced.

(2) With this deliverance, the community is extricated from bloodguilt and the resultant retribution.

(3) A group of faithful supporters of Jeremiah emerges, first among the royal officials of Judah and the community elders, but more important in the person of Ahikam. Although Ahikam receives no explicit commendation for his sympathetic treatment of Jeremiah, he (and his family) enjoys a significant place in the text. His actions not only save Jeremiah's life but also prevent the nation from making a tragic mistake (26:24).

(4) For the first time in the prophetic drama, some entertain the possibility that Jeremiah may be telling the truth, despite the disturbing character of his message.

(5) Jeremiah is vindicated not only by faithful supporters but also by a prophetic text. Written prophecy adjudicates the legal dispute, and in some sense takes precedence over spoken prophecy. We have already seen indications of a shift from spoken to written prophecy in the first half of the book. Now at the start of the second half, a prophetic text is again employed as a primary source of authority, this time to corroborate Jeremiah's spoken words. The prophecy of Micah demonstrates that Jeremiah's scathing critique is consistent with an emerging prophetic tradition.

Overtures of hope are connected to suffering, exile and dislocation. While the narrative begins to fashion new beginnings, it does so in a world under assault. The people who hear Jeremiah's message recognize that he is speaking against this city and against this land (26:20). Indeed, the heart of his sermon is that the temple and the city will end up like Shiloh, "desolate, without inhabitant" (26:9). Jeremiah is certain that the old arrangements must give way before new ones emerge. In addition, the convergence of hope and hardship crystallizes in the prophetic persona. The story presents Jeremiah as a suffering servant whose affliction is inseparably related to the people he represents as well as to the God who sends him. No one here gets off scot-free. All will face unbearable loss. Henceforth, all viable constructions of hope in the second half of the book grow out of and are tied to communal (and divine) suffering. To divorce hope from suffering is to fashion a quixotic world that is shallow and deceptive. Although such a world has a host of supporters, it does not ring true to a refugee community that knows better.

The narrative is a case study of *hope in action*. Its anatomy of hope is in large measure dependent on those who "hear" the prophetic word and speak out on behalf of one who is at risk of being deprived of justice. To stem the tide of injustice, people at the center must come forward and take action on behalf of those on the margins. In this particular case city officials bring evidentiary grounds for the legitimacy of Jeremiah's claims, even though his oracle subverts set ways and cultural givens. Their defense is based on scripture and historical precedent, and it is rooted in courage and truth-telling. They appeal to Micah's prophecy to show that prophecies of woe are not extraordinary. Like Jeremiah, Micah prophesized that Jerusalem would "become a heap of ruins" (26:18). King Hezekiah recognized the veracity of his words and in response entreated Yahweh to save the city from disaster. In addition, we are told of another prophet, Uriah, who spoke "against this city and against this land" (26:20). In this case, however, King Jehoiakim tracked down the fleeing prophet in Egypt and put him to death. To conclude, the story introduces Ahikam son of Shaphan who appears long enough to deliver Jeremiah from harm (26:24). In contrast to his king, this important royal official uses his position to save and protect rather than to exploit and destroy. Taken as a whole, the story speaks of hope as inextricably related to the actions of faithful people who take great risks to ensure that justice does not falter and prophetic speech is not silenced. "The only thing necessary for the triumph of evil is for good men to do nothing" (Edmund Burke). In this opening chapter of Jer 26–52 we encounter a few who dare speak up and act. Due to their courageous deeds hope is born.

CONFLICTING THEOLOGIES OF HOPE
(JEREMIAH 27–29)

Jeremiah 27–29 assumes that the nation of Judah has already experienced the first pangs of captivity and that the armies of Babylon have plundered the articles of the temple in Jerusalem and deported many of Judah's leading citizens to Babylon. Within a decade, the city and its temple would be burned to the ground and still others would be led off to the east. During the interim period, that is the time between the first and second deportation, the Judean people must grapple with pressing matters that would irreversibly influence their future. Even after 587, when these chapters were likely composed, the exiles continue to wrestle with burning questions about the charter of the new community. Jeremiah 27–29 speaks to these central concerns.

Most important, the Judean people and their leaders struggle to understand the tragic events that had interrupted their lives. That Jerusalem had been invaded and ravaged by Babylonian forces was an established fact. But what the invasion meant theologically and politically was not yet determined. Would their status as refugees be brief or a harsh reality that they would have to tolerate for many years? Would Babylonian subjugation permanently alter the ongoing nature of the community? Would the community essentially remain the same after Babylonian subjugation or undergo some kind of metamorphosis? Fueled by political unrest in Babylon, the accession in Egypt of Psammetichus II, and nationalistic fervor, violent opposition to Babylonian domination surfaced. Certain coalitions encouraged insurrection and bolstered the belief that the political crisis would be over before long. Soon, they maintained, life would return to normal. Jeremiah 27–29 vehemently opposes such a position, arguing instead for a lengthy exile and a deep-seated transformation in the character of the people of God during and after the exile. This ideological rift materializes most visibly in prophetic conflicts.

Prophetic controversy is present everywhere in Jer 27–29 and to a large degree holds this collection together. Jeremiah cautions the community in Jer 27 not to accept the oracles of prophets who predict a speedy resolution to the Babylon problem. According to him, prophets who foster the belief that Babylonian domination will be short-lived and who encourage insurrection present a clear and present danger to the community. A specific prophetic tussle arises when Hananiah challenges the fundamental direction of Jeremiah's oracles (Jer 28). In the final chapter of the unit, Jeremiah writes a letter in which he encourages the exiles in Babylon to prepare for a long stay in Babylon. They too must not believe opposing voices that raise hopes for an early return to Jerusalem (Jer 29).

Literary Analysis

The first major literary unit of the second half of the book, Jer 27–29, is comprised of biographical and autobiographical accounts of symbolic actions (Jer 27), prophetic conflicts (Jer 28), and letters written by prophets (Jer 29). This prose collection is set in the period between the first deportation in 597 and the fall of Jerusalem in 587, although it is likely intended for those who lived after the tragic events. Chapters 27 and 28 are related directly to the reign of Zedekiah (the Hebrew reference to Jehoiakim in Jer 27:1 is an error) and Jeremiah's correspondence in chapter 29 to the years immediately following the first deportation in 597.

Much of the unit's language reflects the style and diction characteristic of other prose sections in the book (Stulman 1986, 87-94). Moreover, Deuteronomic understandings of prophecy are ubiquitous here. The kings of Syria-Palestine, for instance, are implored not to listen to prophets who proclaim rebellious oracles, which in this case involves inciting insubordination to Babylonian rule (see, e.g., 27:9-11; cf. Deut 18:9-12). And the consequence of proclaiming treasonous oracles is death (Deut 13:1-5; 28:17; see also 29:29-32). Overall, stylized language and style as well as Deuteronomic nuances are all employed to point out the dangers of resisting Babylonian sovereignty. The unit's uncompromising message is that foreign rule is a geopolitical reality with which the community will have to deal for years to come. Any attempt to circumvent it will end in disaster.

The Hebrew text of Jer 27–29 (MT) is considerably longer than the Greek text (LXX). The majority of additions are somewhat inconsequential. For example, the MT adds divine epithets, fills out personal names, and extends serial clauses, generally for the sake of clarity or emphasis. However, in chapter 29, we encounter one of the longest texts to appear only in the MT (vv. 16-20). There is considerable debate as to why verses 16-20 are not attested in the LXX. Many scholars argue that the Greek represents a shorter underlying Hebrew text, thus conforming to the character of the LXX of Jeremiah as a whole. However, it is possible that the passage is missing in the LXX due to a scribal error. Since verses 15 and 20 end with identical words ("in Babylon"), it is possible that the scribe omitted the first of these references and the accompanying material. To complicate matters, verses 16-20 are clearly intrusive; they disrupt the continuity existing between verses 15 and 21 and appear to be secondary. If this is the case, the text provides another witness to the growth and development of the tradition as it was read and interpreted by later communities.

Exegetical Analysis

To Submit to Babylon or Not (27:1-22)

The first narrative in the unit is composed of three parts: a divine message addressed to emissaries from Edom, Moab, Ammon, Tyre, and Sidon that they should surrender unconditionally to King Nebuchadrezzar (27:1-11); a divine message to King Zedekiah of Judah that he should capitulate to King Nebuchadrezzar (27:12-15); and a warning to the priests and the people not to believe the prophets who promise an immediate return of the temple vessels (27:16-22).

The chapter opens with dramatic action on the part of Jeremiah (27:1-11; see also 13:1-11; 16:1-9). God instructs Jeremiah to wear an ox-yoke on his neck to symbolize the political subjugation of the nations to Babylon. With the yoke of straps and bars on his neck, Jeremiah delivers Yahweh's message to emissaries from the Transjordan and Phoenicia who have come to Jerusalem to meet with Zedekiah. The text gives no reason for the meeting, although it appears that the envoys have gathered in Jerusalem to plan a revolt against Babylonian control. The message that Jeremiah delivers to them is exceptionally disturbing: any nation that will not "put its neck under the yoke of the king of Babylon" will suffer complete destruction (27:8). Babylon's world domination is no accident of geopolitics but is part of God's ordained plan. Yahweh has willed the rise of Babylon as well as its eventual fall. The nations are to remain faithful vassals of King Nebuchadnezzar, "[Yahweh's] servant" until "the time of his own land comes; then many nations and great kings shall [enslave him]" (27:7). To submit to Babylon's rule is thus to submit to the will of God. Any utterance to the contrary is false and will result in prolonged pain.

Jeremiah essentially reiterates this message to Zedekiah (27:12-15). Zedekiah is to squelch any conspiracy against Babylonian rule and resolve to serve the king of Babylon. Any oracle that inspires hope for Babylon's immediate defeat is untrue and not from Yahweh. In contrast to these encouraging prophecies, Jeremiah demands the unconditional surrender of Zedekiah to the king of Babylon. But this admonition is accompanied by a promise: "Serve him and his people, *and live*" (27:12, my emphasis). Jeremiah offers the Judean ruler the possibility of circumventing total destruction by bowing to the yoke of vassalage. Ironically, this distressing stance, which accepts the scandalous role of Babylon as an instrument of divine punishment, provides far greater hope for a viable future than the optimistic words of competing prophets. To deny or resist Babylonian rule would lead only to more suffering.

Jeremiah addresses the priests and people of Judah in the third section of the autobiographical account (27:16-22). The message from the Lord again demands unconditional surrender to the king of Babylon as a prerequisite for survival (27:17). Once more Jeremiah takes on prophets who contradict his message by impugning the character of their words: "they are prophesying [lies] to you" (27:16). Now, however, the matter at hand is related specifically to the temple equipment plundered in 598. Certain prophets announce that the stolen temple treasures will soon be returned to Jerusalem. Jeremiah disagrees and warns the priests and people not to believe their seductive oracles. In fact, according to Jeremiah, the sacred objects still housed in the temple will soon be carried off to Babylon (see 2 Kgs 25:13-17). In other words, things will get far worse before they get better! Judah's historical contingencies can neither be played down nor denied; they represent harsh realities that the community will have to come to terms with in order to survive. Jeremiah's warning, however, is not entirely bleak. He prophesies that the sacred vessels yet pillaged will eventually be returned to the temple, although he leaves undetermined when this restoration will occur (see Ezra 1:7-11).

Jeremiah the Prophet Versus Hananiah the Prophet (28:1-17)

Jeremiah 28 is a continuation of the previous chapter. The text is dated to the same year as Jer 27, at the beginning of the reign of Zedekiah, although it pinpoints the time: "the fifth month of the fourth year" of his reign (594–593). The interlude between the first and second deportation of exiles, during which anti-Babylonian sentiment among vassal states was intense, sets the stage for the narrative. The "yoke" motif still dominates the story, as do questions regarding its significance for the community. Now the general controversy over prophetic messages takes shape in a specific confrontation between Jeremiah and a Judean prophet by the name of Hananiah son of Azzur. No longer are Jeremiah's opponents nameless and faceless. Jeremiah and his opponent Hananiah give two contradictory interpretations of Judah's crisis. Hananiah, whose name means "Yahweh is gracious," speaks out of a conviction that the length of the exile will be short, and so he urges the populace to resist Babylonian hegemony. Jeremiah feels just as certain that the Neo-Babylonian power of Syria-Palestine will be a continuing political reality. Thus, he calls upon the Judean community to submit willingly to Babylonian rule as to God's will.

The clash between the two prophets takes place in the temple before the priests and the people. Hananiah renders a stunning interpretation of the yoke around Jeremiah's neck. According to him, Yahweh will break the stranglehold of the king of Babylon; within two years the temple treasures as well as those taken captive to Babylonia will return to Jerusalem. Jeremiah would like to believe Hananiah's message (28:5-9) but is reluctant to do so for several reasons. First, Hananiah's utterance contradicts the message entrusted to him, and prophets dare not compromise their own convictions (see 1 Kgs 13). Second, Hananiah's buoyant message does not conform to prophetic oracles of the past, which typically predict "war, famine, and pestilence" (28:8). Finally, Hananiah's message of salvation must meet stringent criteria before Jeremiah can embrace it: prophecies of peace must be fulfilled to validate their divine origin (28:9).

Jeremiah's refutation does not intimidate Hananiah in the least. He takes the yoke from Jeremiah's neck, breaks it, and brazenly reiterates his message, at which point Jeremiah leaves in silence (28:11). Only later does Jeremiah return to the scene with a word from the Lord (28:12-17). With new confidence, Jeremiah declares that Yahweh has replaced the wooden bars that Hananiah had broken with an iron yoke. The iron yoke, which cannot be broken, symbolizes the certainty (and protracted length) of Babylon's world domination and Judah's exile. Now certain that Yahweh has not commissioned his opponent, Jeremiah predicts Hananiah's imminent death (28:16). In fulfillment of Jeremiah's prediction and the Deuteronomic penalty for false prophets (Deut 18:20), Hananiah dies in the seventh month of the fourth year of Zedekiah's reign (28:17). Hananiah's death provides further proof of the falsehood of his oracles as well as the truthfulness of Jeremiah's.

The disagreement between Jeremiah and Hananiah is one of the most poignant prophetic face-offs in the Bible. It highlights the difficulty involved in discerning true from false prophecies, especially for contemporaries of the prophets. The matter is perplexing because both oracles are delivered by recognized prophets. Only the Septuagint describes Hananiah as a "false prophet," which it mistranslates from the Hebrew word "prophet." Jeremiah himself never questions his opponent's sincerity, nor impugns his integrity. He apparently considers Hananiah a genuine prophet, although not sent by Yahweh on this particular occasion. Hananiah introduces his message with the customary messenger formula, "thus says the LORD," and practices the customary symbolic action (28:10). Thus, his form and delivery follow conventional patterns. His message, moreover, in no way contradicts the general direction of Israel's religious heritage, which Deut 13:1-3 advances as the primary criterion for distinguishing the true from false prophet. In fact, quite the contrary is true. Hananiah proclaims a theological perspective that is similar to Isaiah's, that Zion will survive the onslaught of its enemies.

Yet, obviously something is wrong with Hananiah's prophecies. The basic problem apparently lies in his indiscriminate recital of Isaiah's Zion theology without discerning a profound difference in the present historical and existential predicament (Overholt 1970, 41). Hananiah adequately recites the tradition, yet without using critical lenses to address the current crisis of the community (Osswald 1962, 21-22). Although he speaks out of the authoritative traditions of ancient Israel, he is out of touch with the political and spiritual subtleties of his moment in history. Hananiah does not understand that rebellion against Babylonian rule could only result in further oppression and hardship for God's people. In contrast to Jeremiah, who has the right word for the right people at the right time and place, Hananiah speaks out of place and thereby misses the mark.

Letters of Jeremiah: Settle Down in Babylon (29:1-32)

Jeremiah 29 is related to the previous two chapters chronologically and thematically. It deals with matters that are peculiar to the period between the first deportation of Judean exiles to Babylon in 597 and the destruction of Jerusalem in 587 (29:1-2). Specifically, the text addresses members of the community whom Nebuchadrezzar had taken into exile to Babylon (29:1). The parenthetical reference to the deportation of King Jeconiah, the queen mother, the court official, and other leading citizens (29:2) adds force to the circumstantial background. As for its central themes, chapter 29 develops the controversy over the length of Judah's captivity and deliberates over the character of community life in the years immediately following 597. Just as in Jer 27–28, Jeremiah tries desperately to convince the community that it must embrace Babylonian rule as a long-term reality ordained by God. Even so, Jeremiah is not incapable of fostering hope among the Judean refugees. He speaks of a time in due course when the exiles will enjoy a grand homecoming, when Yahweh will "restore the fortunes" of Israel. But his primary concern is to dispute prominent members of the community whose insistence on an early return from Babylon would lead the people of God down a destructive road.

Whereas Jer 27–28 develops these themes in biographical and autobiographical prose accounts, Jer 29 takes the form of a narrative that comprises portions of letters and prophetic oracles. The major part of the chapter embodies a letter written by Jeremiah in Jerusalem to those carried off to Babylon (29:4-23). Along the lines of many of Paul's letters in the New Testament, Jeremiah's epistle addresses specific situations in the life of the community. Jeremiah first tackles the question as to how the exiles are to live their lives while residing in Babylon (29:4-9). Next, he deals with what they are to anticipate in the future (29:10-14). Interrupting the continuity of the epistle is a pronouncement of judgment upon Zedekiah and those with him in Jerusalem (29:16-20). Attested only in the MT (see the literary analysis above), this prose piece is probably a later expansion intended to encourage the exiles in Babylon to see themselves as recipients of God's gracious promises (cf. Jer 24:1-10). Jeremiah then turns his attention to two prophets in Babylon whom he denounces for misleading the people (29:15, 21-23).

The remainder of chapter 29 contains portions of two other letters: the first is an excerpt written by a prophet identified as Shemaiah of Nehelam (29:26-28) and the second is a rejoinder by Jeremiah (29:31-32). From Babylon Shemaiah writes to the temple overseer Zephaniah in Jerusalem, accusing him of failing to arrest Jeremiah for his subversive words (29:28 is a quotation of 29:5). Instead of taking punitive action against Jeremiah, however, Zephaniah reveals the content of Shemaiah's scathing letter to him (29:29). Upon hearing it, Jeremiah writes another letter at

Yahweh's instruction in which he assails Shemaiah and predicts his demise (29:30-32). Like his counterpart Hananiah, Shemaiah has preached rebellion against Yahweh and therefore will suffer the same fate as his contemporary (Deut 13:5; 18:20).

Jeremiah's first letter is delivered to the exiles in Babylon by royal couriers, Elasah son of Shaphan and Gemariah son of Hilkiah (29:1-3). These two men are mentioned only here, although Elasah is perhaps the brother of Ahikam, who rescued Jeremiah from near death after his trial in the temple (26:24), and Gemariah may have been the son of the high priest who discovered the book of the law during the reign of Josiah (2 Kgs 22:4, 8). At the outset of the letter, Jeremiah declares that the dire situation of the exiles is not outside the divine compass. God has sent the Judeans to Babylon and there they must stay (29:4). In this way, Jeremiah immediately dashes any hope for an early release from captivity. The exiles are to settle down, unpack their bags, and attend to domestic affairs of life (29:5-6). Building houses, planting gardens, establishing families, and increasing in number convey both the disturbing notion of long-term residence and the creation of a new community in a faraway land (Gen 1:28). The exiles must in some respects begin anew on foreign soil, and this reordering demands accepting their lot in Babylon and building a life together there. According to the rules of warfare, those who have recently "built a new house," "planted a vineyard," or "become engaged" are exempt from military service (Deut 20:1-20). Therefore, Jeremiah may also be exhorting the exiles to refrain from any form of violent resistance to Babylon sovereignty (Holladay 1989, 141). Such a belief clearly lies behind the prophet's instruction that the community should seek the welfare (peace) of Babylon and pray to Yahweh on its behalf (29:7). This radical counsel is fraught with political realism, for it concedes that the future of the exiles is tied to the interests of their captors. The text's language of accommodation is not, however, a directive to assimilate into the dominant culture and embrace its maxims, values, and patterns of behavior. On the contrary, the epistle merely acknowledges that the refugees can only survive if they transcend their own provincial categories, refrain from any form of insurrection, and create a meaningful communal life within the empire.

To this point, Jeremiah has only addressed the relationship of the exiles to Babylon. A far more rudimentary issue still exists: is there a future for the people of God apart from Babylon or must the people of God always live in the shadow of their oppressor? While discouraging false confidence in a speedy return to Palestine, Jeremiah asserts that Babylon's hold on its captives will not last forever. Eventually the Judean refugees will leave for Jerusalem (29:10, 14). In "seventy years"—which likely symbolizes a lifetime—Yahweh will fulfill promises made to Israel and bring the Judeans home. In this fashion Jeremiah urges the exiles to see their present situation as an interim and not as a permanent state. During this interim period of waiting, he assures them that the Lord's intentions are gracious, not malevolent (29:10). Despite present appearances, Yahweh has not forsaken the suffering community, nor broken his word. Amid all the devastation and wreckage, God is present and accessible (29:12-13), and God's purpose prevails. With these words of assurance, Jeremiah encourages patience and bolsters the flagging faith of the refugees.

The editorial comment on Jeremiah's letter adds force to the prophet's words of hope for the Babylonian exiles (29:16-20). When this passage is read contextually, it strengthens the stance that the exiles in Babylon are the heirs of God's gracious promises (see 29:10-14) whereas the remnant in Palestine is the object of Yahweh's displeasure. Such a critique inverts *prima facie* assumptions about each community (see also Jer 24): Yahweh denounces those who escape exile and might be deemed favored. And, Yahweh champions the cause of those who suffer the pangs of exile and might be considered as good as dead. This theological inversion is again more than a confession of faith: it is an astute assessment of geopolitics. While the Davidic king and some of the residents of Jerusalem elude banishment in 597, they would not escape the devastating events of 587. Pursued by "sword, famine, and pestilence" and made "an object of cursing, horror, hissing, and derision among the nations," the remnant in Judah would reel under the weight of fallen Jerusalem.

Only one reason is given for this massive judgment: the text claims that the community in Judah has "not listened to" Yahweh's word spoken through the prophets (29:19). King Zedekiah and those with him remain in the land in total defiance to Yahweh's directive. These "rotten figs" (see 24:1-10) are so entrenched in the structures of dynasty and state that they cannot "hear" Jeremiah's message to evacuate the city. Like Lot's wife, they refuse to leave. This reproof of the Jerusalem establishment is germane to the letter's condemnation of "lying" prophets in Babylon, for they too are deeply rooted in national-cultic arrangements that have blinded them to Yahweh's purposes.

Jeremiah identifies three such prophets. Mentioned first are Ahab son of Kolaiah and Zedekiah son of Maaseiah (29:21-23) whom Jeremiah denounces for prophesying falsehood in Yahweh's name. Like Hananiah in Palestine, Ahab and Zedekiah mislead the community with anti-Babylonian rhetoric and with false hope of an imminent return of the deportees to their homeland. These two nemeses of Jeremiah instigate such political turmoil among the Judean exiles in Babylon that they eventually incur the wrath of Nebuchadnezzar. The text is altogether clear: Ahab and Zedekiah will pay for their deceptive oracles in accord with Deuteronomic law (Deut 13:5; 18:20). Then Jeremiah takes aim at the prophet Shemaiah of Nehelam (29:24-32). To Shemaiah Jeremiah is a "madman who plays the prophet" in Jerusalem. He is nothing but trouble and therefore must be dealt with. This belief motivates Shemaiah to take Zephaniah the temple overseer to task for not putting Jeremiah in shackles (29:26-28). Zephaniah's "dereliction of duty" frustrates his attempt at silencing him. To add fuel to the fire, Zephaniah exposes Shemaiah's malicious words to Jeremiah. In the end Shemaiah is foiled; under the curse of the covenant, neither he nor his offspring will enjoy Yahweh's restoration (29:32). And again, Jeremiah emerges from the controversy as victor.

Theological and Ethical Analysis

The present form of Jer 27–29 is a coherent literary body organized around a theological nucleus. While prophetic conflicts leave a lasting mark on the unit, they are not of primary interest. Instead, Jer 27–29 explores two competing scripts for the future of Judah. Both articulate new configurations of hope and salvation. Both grapple with questions of meaning amid social and emotional upheaval. And both claim to be authorized by God and vie for preeminence. The first minimizes the dreadful impact of the Babylonian conquest by appealing to traditional categories of continuity. Its theology of continuity accepts the networks of temple and state as enduring and trustworthy. In contrast, the second sees the events of 597 and 587 as major crossroads in the history of Israel, crossroads which demand radical disordering before any reordering of social arrangements and religious meaning is possible. The text is entirely clear as to its assessment of the two understandings of reality: it views the former as dangerous, even malevolent, and the second, the theology of discontinuity, as authorized by God.

Hananiah, Shemaiah, and probably Zedekiah and Ahab are proponents of the theology of continuity. They perpetuate the ideologies and social realities associated with the dynasty and the temple as fundamental doctrines of the state. In political terms, these advocates of continuity envision the first deportation to Babylonia to be only a momentary interruption to life. Afterward, they expect the Davidic kingship to be reestablished, Jerusalem and its representative institutions to return to normal, virtually unscathed by exile, and the sacred vessels brought back to the Jerusalem temple. As follows, the nation's encounter with Babylon leaves no lasting imprint on the community and requires no essential changes in community life. Since God upholds the old networks of meaning, few social and religious transformations are necessary. The future takes shape in large measure with Judah's a priori belief systems and social structures in tact. Exile is thus a glitch rather than a defining moment in the life of the community.

Jeremiah 27–29 takes dead aim at this theological framework, dismissing and caricaturing it as a violation of all that is true and sensible. Jeremiah contends, for instance, that the prophecies of Hananiah are both misinformed and potentially disastrous. In the first place, they are totally out of step with the will of God. As lord of nations and the power that supports and opposes governments, Yahweh has established Nebuchadrezzar, "his servant," to mete out judgment upon the nations. Resisting Babylonian rule is, therefore, tantamount to rebellion against Yahweh. In addition, Hananiah's theology of continuity is a blanket dismissal of all that the first twenty-five chapters advocate, which is that "plucking up and pulling down, destroying and overthrowing" must *antecede* the redemptive work of "building and planting." According to Jeremiah, Yahweh demands a radical break from the past as a prerequisite to fresh networks of hope. Judah can no longer depend on the old props once considered crucial to its identity: temple and sacrifices, military and court, political autonomy and king, land and election. The absence of these "old friends" is a reality with which the community must come to terms. Thus, the wrenching experience of exile must be faced squarely and embraced before *any* future is possible. Indeed, the future must be constructed upon the ruins of the national catastrophe. Before any formulation of viable hope, Judah must accept its plight, submit to Babylonian hegemony, and recognize the hand of God in its present predicament.

For Jeremiah, Hananiah's appeal to traditional categories of continuity is not only dangerous and deceptive but also a demonstration of profound denial. Hananiah is in fact a metaphor of denial. He shows a propensity to reject the painful dimension of human experience. Blinded by unfounded optimism and false expectation, he would like to forget personal and national traumas and live as if they did not really happen. However, by not remembering them, Hananiah and others like him "cut down [their] own history to a pleasant, comfortable size and try to make it conform to [their] own daydreams. Forgetting the past," Henri Nouwen suggests, "is like turning our most intimate teacher against us" (1977, 22).

The fabrication of a fictitious world precludes healing and restoration. With apparently the best of intentions, Hananiah would remove the angst from the Judean community. He would distract the people of God from their pain and dislocation. Jeremiah's opponent would numb Israel to their encounter with suffering, which is, unbeknownst to him, an encounter with the God who "plucks up and pulls down." No wonder Jeremiah calls Hananiah's optimism "deception." Judah cannot run from its pain without running from God. In order to hear God it must listen attentively to its own struggle. The misery of exile, the crumbling of familiar categories, the reality of loss must be acknowledged as the *magnalia dei*, the acts of God. Only then, with the shaking loose of conventional certainties, can the community begin anew with fresh categories of meaning. Contrary to Hananiah's high hopes, there can be no retrieval of the old systems; they are lost forever.

Jeremiah's critique of the theology of continuity evolves into a discourse on hope through community building. Although the new world of exile pulsates with anxiety and vexation, it presents unique opportunities. Jeremiah encourages the exiles in Babylon to seize the moment to create genuine community. "Build houses and live in them; plant gardens and eat what they produce . . . multiply there, and do not decrease . . . For surely I know the plans I have for you, says the LORD, plans for your [shalom] and not for harm, to give you a future with hope" (29:5, 6d, 11). During their time of displacement the people of God might be tempted to sit back and do nothing or hastily follow the guidance of those who promise an imminent return to Jerusalem. But Jeremiah presses the exiles to put down roots, affirm the bonds of family, and work toward peace and community building in their own neighborhoods, that is, in their own local settings in Babylon (29:7). Such instructions would not have been welcome. To pray for the welfare of the state, to set up homes in Babylon, and to forgo, at least for a long time, their aspirations to return to Jerusalem would be anything but good news. Nonetheless, Jeremiah insists that the key to survival and hope is to join God in creating a just and compassionate counterculture, a place of new shapes and social alternatives.

In all, Jeremiah entreats the deportees to become a viable subcommunity within the Babylonian Empire. To do this they must abandon their identity as a national-cultic community and immerse themselves in another world. Relinquishment of the old identity and acceptance of their marginal status in Babylon is the first step to survival and hope. Surrendering the treasures of the past makes room for the newness of God. All this, of course, requires enormous courage. Yet, when the community lets go of past certainties, transformation takes place. When it stops clinging and gives itself wholly to God, mercy and grace rush in to fill the void. Sprouting from the desolate place of Babylon is a stunning new piety. No longer defined by the old forms of institutional life, the faithful enjoy a new and intimate relationship with God (see, e.g., 29:11-14). This new spirituality, which Clements describes as "intense inwardness of religion," takes on more definitive shape in the so-called "Book of Consolation" (1988, 173).

THE BOOK OF CONSOLATION (JEREMIAH 30–33)

We now cross the threshold to the most detailed treatment of hope in the book. This welcome respite interrupts the somber tone of the text and shatters its anatomy of judgment. It is as if the pangs of exile disappear for a moment, although even a superficial reading reveals that despair and hardship still sculpt the backdrop for the announcement of good news. God promises to reverse the judgments against Judah and Israel and restore their fortunes. When all signs of hope disappear, the exiles are surprised by "grace in the wilderness" and are embraced by the loving-kindness of God (31:3). While sporadic oracles of salvation appear in the first part of the book, the sheer volume of dread-filled oracles mutes their voice. Now the converse is true. A surplus of hope subdues the announcements of judgment. The shift from judgment to salvation, however, does not appear unexpectedly. It comes into view in Jer 26 when Jeremiah is vindicated in a legal case brought against him. It develops in Jer 27–29 when Jeremiah triumphs over opponents who contest his script for Judah's future. Now, it appears as a lush garden in bloom in Jer 30–33, inasmuch as Jeremiah lays out a full-scale treatment of God's program for the eventual restoration of Israel and Judah.

Literary Analysis

Because of their positive content and overarching theme of restoration, scholars often refer to chapters 30–33 as the "Book of Comfort" or the "Book of Consolation." Notice, however, that the chapters are neither unified nor homogeneous. One encounters an anthology of poems and prose pieces that form a tapestry of hope. In their present form, the chapters divide into three major parts: Jer 30–31, Jer 32, and Jer 33. Jeremiah 30–31 is technically the book of consolation proper. Following a prose introduction (30:1-4), it breaks down into several smaller units: 30:5-11, 12-17, 18-24, 31:1-6, 7-14, 15-26. At the end is a chain of eschatological utterances announcing Israel's coming restoration (31:27-40). Some date this collection to an early period in Jeremiah's career, even to the time of Josiah, when the prophet supposedly spoke of the reestablishment of northern Israel. The multiple references to incursion and deportation as well as the emphasis on homecoming and restoration, however, make a later provenance more plausible. The text offers hope to those whose present situation is sated with anxiety and adversity and whose future is vastly uncertain. It is more likely that the implied audience consisted of Judean exiles residing in Babylon during the sixth century.

Standing on its own, Jer 32 is a narrative of Jeremiah's purchase of a family field in Anathoth from his cousin, Hanamel son of Shallum. The acquisition is actually a symbolic action conveying God's resolve to bring back the people of God to the land from where they were deported. The chapter comprises our parts: the setting in 32:1-5, the land purchase in 32:6-15, the prayer of Jeremiah in 32:16-25, and Yahweh's response to Jeremiah's prayer in 32:26-44. The story is set in the days immediately before the fall of Judah to Babylon in 587; that is, in the tenth year of Zedekiah and the eighteenth year of Nebuchadnezzar's reign. Similar to other prose materials, however, the text likely represents a recasting of Jeremiah's words in the years immediately following his prophetic career. Along the lines of chapters 30–31, Jer 32 attempts to engender hope in a marginalized and disenfranchised community betwixt and between two worlds: the old dynastic state in Palestine and one which is not yet in hand. According to this narrative, the creation of a new future, a new symbolic world, is inconceivable without the restoration of land.

Jeremiah 33 is an addendum to the collection. The chapter divides into two equal sections and both elaborate the theme of renewal: 33:1-13, 14-26. The latter verses are entirely absent from the Greek version of the Old Testament. This omission in conjunction with the general character of the text indicates that 33:14-26 is likely a late addition to the book. The link between David and the Levitical priests, which is similar to that made in Zech 12:12-13, suggests that the passage may have originated during the time of Ezra and Nehemiah (ca. the mid-fifth century). Given this post-Jeremianic dating, some dismiss the passage as inconsequential. However, the elaboration of Jeremiah's preaching in a subsequent time is indicative of the vitality of the word and its continued relevance in the ongoing life of the people of God. Moreover, the developed tradition contributes to the *text's* portrait of the new people of God and its charter of salvation.

Collectively these four chapters enjoy a strategic location and function in their literary setting. R. E. Clements has shown that the oracles of hope in chapters 30–33 form "the *pivotal center* for the entire book" (1988, 8, my emphasis). They are located between prophecies that predict the destruction of Jerusalem and those that depict the actual fall of the capital city. As centerpiece of the book, this literature serves at least two purposes. First, it encourages the suffering refugees to look ahead to a new chapter of God's dealings with Israel. Or, to say this in another way, Jer 30–33 declares that the exiles' time of hardship is not the concluding episode in salvation history. Like Isa 40–55, this anthology seeks to console and support a community that can no longer bear the weight of its present situation. In this manner, the text strengthens the floundering exiles so that they can go on living through their present turmoil. Second, Jer 30–33 presents the most concrete picture in the book of the character of a new Israel. This portrait is not a blueprint for the future but a vision intended to shape theological imagination and social reality. The prophet envisions a future in which God overturns the bad fortune of the people and heals their fractured lives. The picture of Israel's new beginnings transforms or reverses motifs, metaphors, and deep-rooted beliefs that served as the basis for the world that was in place before 597–587. These transformations and inversions now form the heart of Israel's new order. The following diagram provides examples.

God's Reversals of the Judgments Against Judah/Israel

The Old World Order Dismantled Jeremiah 1–25	The New World Order Envisioned Jeremiah 30–33
exile to the north (6:22)	deliverance from the north (31:8)
the temple threatened and its systems of worship rejected (7:1-15)	a new piety that is not dependent upon temple and system of worship (read widely)
an "old" (Sinai or Deuteronomic) covenant (11:1-13)	a "new covenant" or "everlasting covenant" (31:31–34; 32:40)
the election understandings dismantled (18:1-12, 13-18)	the election of Israel reaffirmed and guaranteed (31:35-37; 33:23-26)
the dynastic state dismantled, the dethronement of the Davidic king, and an emphasis on the conditional nature of the dynasty (21:1-10)	the dynastic state redefined with more attention to the social and judicial role of the Davidic king; the enduring covenant with David and unconditional nature of the promise accentuated (30:8-9, 21-22; 33:14-26)

The Old World Order Dismantled Jeremiah 1–25	The New World Order Envisioned Jeremiah 30–33
the condemnation of the priests or priestly representatives (6:13; 8:10-12; 20:1-6; 23:11-12)	the enduring covenant with the Levites; unconditional nature of promise stressed (33:14-26)
land claims rescinded (read widely Jer 1–25)	land claims reestablished (32:1-44)
depopulation of the land (13:19; 16:4)	repopulation of the land (30:19; 33:22)
Jerusalem threatened with ruin (read widely Jer 1–25)	Jerusalem's restoration promised (30:18; 31:6, 38-40; 33:10-13)
exile and scattering (read widely Jer 1–25)	homecoming and gathering (30:3, 10-11; 31:1-14; 32:36-37)
God threatens Israel with "evil"/"disaster" (read widely Jer 1–25)	God promises to treat Israel with benevolence (32:39-42; 33:9, 14; cf. 29:10)
"to pluck up and tear down . . ." (1:10; 18:7-10)	"to build and to plant" (31:4, 28; 33:7; see also 42:10)
intercession on behalf of Israel prohibited-prayer unheeded (11:14; 14:11-12; 15:1-2; cf. 20:14-18)	prayer and relationship restored (33:3)
the end of celebrations (7:34; 16:9)	the return of thanksgiving and joy (30:19; 31:4; 33:10-11)

The preceding chart illustrates that the new age envisioned by Jeremiah is never far removed from the collapse of the old order described in Jer 1–25. Jeremiah draws upon many of the uprooted assumptions of the preexilic systems as a way to imagine a new Israel. For instance, the land of Judah, once evacuated, is repopulated; the north, the faraway place of banishment, is the locale of deliverance. The covenant, once broken by the people of God, is now renewed. The election of Israel, once rescinded, is now reestablished on sure footing. Images of hope and new life make sense only against the background of Jer 1–25.

Yet, while the promissory material in chapters 30–33 employs traditional imagery, it does not merely rehash the old forms, however idealized. God's work on behalf of Israel is creative and new, and totally surpasses the grandeur of the former world. The divine program involves a radical break from the old structures for fresh, bold arrangements. Indeed, the transformations of the coming age, which the prophet often describes using eschatological language such as "the days are (surely) coming" and "at that time," are so massive that a new world may be said to be born. The community that lives through the wreckage will no longer depend upon the temple and monarchic structures of authority as God's primary vehicle of blessing. Those who survive the sword will enjoy alternative forms of worship, government, and community life.

Exegetical Analysis

Instructions to Record God's Words in a Book (30:1-4)

The Book of Consolation opens with Yahweh instructing Jeremiah to record in a "book" the promises of the eventual return and restoration of God's people (30:1-4). This is not the first time in Jeremiah that a written source functions as a means of expressing the divine will. Jeremiah testified that God would punish Babylon and its king according to the judgments recorded in a "book" (25:13). In defense of Jeremiah, the elders of the community appeal to the presumably written and authoritative words of Micah (26:17-19). While in Judah, Jeremiah sends a letter containing divine instruction to the exiles in Babylon (29:1-14). Also, Yahweh will demand that Jeremiah preserve on a scroll all the prophecies he has spoken from the reign of Josiah to the fourth year of Jehoiakim (36:1-3). When Jehoiakim destroys the scroll, the prophet is to create another scroll with the help of his assistant Baruch (36:32). And at the conclusion of the Hebrew text of Jeremiah, the narrator reports that the ultimate fall of Babylon is to be inscribed on a scroll, which Seraiah will cast into the Euphrates (51:59-64).

In the present context, the written word serves multiple functions. In the first place, it testifies to the survival of the dispersed people of God and their eventual homecoming. The Hebrew particle *kî* that introduces 30:3 (sometimes translated "for" or "because") connects the creation of the "book" to the promised redemption of God's people. There would be little need for this document if the refugees had no future. Its very presence, therefore, generates hope and preserves for the scattered people of God a written pledge of their restoration. The prospect of a future rests on the word of God and not on political or military maneuvers, such as an uprising against Babylon. The "book," however, does more than bear witness to life beyond the present tragedy. It is the primary medium though which God will address future generations. No longer limited to the physicality of the prophet, the written word now enjoys independent authority; it guides, instructs, inspires, and creates (cf. Gen 1:1-3). Jeremiah can now address an audience that he is not among. More important, an authoritative scroll empowers the people of Judah and Israel to see beyond their own decimated dreams to a brighter future.

Liberation from Oppression (30:5-11)

The initial words in the "book" are far from idyllic (30:5-11). There is no luminous vision of happiness, no ideal notion of justice and peace. Rather, one encounters a whirlwind of trouble and multiple images of distress conveying the miserable conditions of the people. An anonymous voice signals an alarm (30:5). Battle cries, panic, and symbols of excruciating pain, such as warriors suffering the pangs of childbirth, ensue. The poet refers to the dreadful moment as "the day of the LORD" (30:7-8). The day of the Lord is a complex idea in the Old Testament, but it most often denotes a time of judgment and/or blessing when God intervenes decisively in human affairs. At its core is the belief that God will one day right the wrongs of human history and establish moral order and symmetry. Thus, the day of the Lord defines God's reign on earth. In the present literary context, the "day" refers to a time of great suffering and retribution, as well as salvation for Israel and Judah. God promises to intrude into history in order to save people from their trouble and liberate them from their oppressors. For a brief moment, the poet returns to the metaphor of the yoke (30:8; see also Jer 27–28) to announce the end of political servitude. In place of foreign rulers, Yahweh will raise up a Davidic figure as king. Henceforth, the community will enjoy peace, security, and blessing. With words echoing the call of Jeremiah (1:8), God assures Israel of God's presence and protection (30:11). At the end of the poem, we learn that the oracles of salvation will not absolve the community of moral responsibility. When Yahweh punishes the nations, Jacob, or Israel, must also face divine chastisement (30:11).

God Heals Judah's Incurable Disease (30:12-17)

The second lyrical poem at first recounts the plight of the exiled people of God (30:12-17). Their condition looks hopeless. Their wound is fatal. Their grievance is beyond compensation. Their lovers, or political allies, upon whom they once turned for help, have forsaken them. It is no use crying out to God; no intercession or cry of protest can change the deplorable situation (30:12-15). It is simply too late! The people's great and many transgressions have dealt them a mortal blow. Jacob, the name now used for the community, stands guilty and defenseless before all. Then, all of a sudden, the poem takes a most unexpected turn (30:16). Instead of announcing judgment, as one would expect given the magnitude of Jacob's sin, the text heralds God's plan to save daughter Zion. God will plunder those who plundered her and despoil those who made spoil of her. What is more, the Lord promises to heal Zion's incurable disease and restore her to health. Such gracious language thoroughly transcends categories of justice and moral symmetry, sin and judgment, expectation and rationality. Yet, verse 17 explains the underlying motive: the nations' contempt for daughter Zion inspires God to act. When they call her an outcast for whom no one cares, they fail to grasp that Zion, although chastised by Yahweh, is still the object of God's affection. This is a family matter and God will not let outsiders ridicule God's beloved wife. Thus, Yahweh resolves to come to Zion's aid, helping the helpless and comforting the downtrodden. In so doing, the text turns conventional categories upside down in a robust demonstration of mercy and unexpected grace.

Joy and Honor Restored (30:18-24)

The Hebrew word "return" or "restore" *(šûb)* brackets the poem in 30:18-24, although each occurrence carries a very different meaning. At the start, the prophet announces that Yahweh will "restore" *(šûb)* the fortunes of Jacob's ruins (30:18). The restoration of the people of God anticipates a time of renewal and transformation that would have been inconceivable under the conditions of exile. In a grand display of divine compassion, God promises to rebuild ancient ("tents of Jacob"; see Num 24:5) and recent ("a city and citadel") dwellings, to restore joy to the community, to add to the dwindling numbers of the exiles, and to honor those who long suffered humiliation and defeat. Community worship and political autonomy will be reestablished, albeit without a temple or monarchy. Jeremiah refers only to a worshiping "congregation" and a prince/ruler (not king) who will enjoy access to God's presence (30:20-21). The allusion to a "prince/ruler" draws on traditions from the distant past when Yahweh's theocratic rule precluded the installation of a human king (Judg 8:22-23; see also 1 Sam 8:1-9). This string of prophecies culminates in the most far-reaching development of all: the restoration of Israel's broken relationship with Yahweh. While Israel has strained the divine-human relationship to its breaking point, Yahweh renews it by sovereign decree (30:22).

The word "return" appears again at the end of the poem (30:24). The prophet declares that Yahweh's fierce anger will not "turn back" or "return" *(šûb)* until the divine purposes are accomplished. The reader is not yet informed as to the nature of these intentions but will understand them in the future. The previous image of the "storm of the Lord," "a whirling tempest bursting on the head of the wicked" (30:23), in tandem with the allusion to Yahweh's "fierce anger" more than suggests that the mystery pertains to divine judgment. Hence, by the close of chapter 30 judgment and salvation, uprooting and planting, and wrath and love once again merge.

Discovering Grace in the Wilderness (31:1-6)

Chapter 31 develops the theme of restoration. The covenant formula, "I will be the God of all the families of Israel and they shall be my people," and an eschatological marker, "at that time" (31:1), serve as a literary bridge to the subsequent oracles of hope. These oracles express the conviction that all the dispersed clans of Israel will one day unite and enjoy a renewed covenant relationship with God. The phrase "at that time" designates a period in the unforeseen future when God would transform present circumstances to such a degree that they represent a new epoch or paradigm in human history.

The first poem of chapter 31 (vv. 1-6) exploits several key traditions of Israel's epic literature to construe the present suffering of the people of God and the new work of God on their behalf. The language in 31:2-3 recalls the time when God delivered Israel from slavery in Egypt, cared for the people in the wilderness and appeared "from far away," perhaps at Sinai. These echoes from the past now allude to the disaster inflicted by the Babylonians and the future return of the exiles to their land. In this way, the text relies on traditional language and formative memories to structure the experience of exile and homecoming. After surviving "the sword," the refugees in Babylon will discover the provision of God in the wilderness before they return home to the promised land (cf. Deut 8:2-4).

The desert imagery in this construction is particularly striking. The "desert" or "wilderness" in the Bible is a place of danger, trial, and vulnerability, as well as divine provision and judgment. In Jeremiah, the wilderness is the place where Israel once followed Yahweh faithfully (2:2). It is part of the nation's forgotten past (2:6). Jeremiah likens Israel to a nomad and a wild donkey accustomed to the desert (2:24; 3:2). He speaks of a terrible desert wind that will destroy Israel (4:12) and of enemies who will come by way of the desert to devour the land (12:12). In a demonstration of judgment, Yahweh will turn lush and productive land into uninhabited desert (4:26; 9:11; 12:10; 22:6; 23:10). Eventually Babylon, the instrument of destruction, will itself become a desert (50:12). In the meantime, Yahweh is so sick with pain over Israel's unfaithfulness that the forsaken lover longs to dwell in the desert (9:2). It is there that Yahweh weeps for his disloyal people (9:10). Interestingly, only in Jer 31:2 does the "desert" imagery have an unmistakably positive sense. The people who "survived the sword" (see also 51:50) will "find favor in the desert." God transforms the once treacherous wilderness into a place of hope and liberation.

The force behind God's act of renewal is immediately recognizable (31:3): God's boundless love for Israel and resolve not to abandon his suffering people. God loves "with an everlasting love" and draws [Israel] up (the same Hebrew word is used in 38:13 for Ebed-Melech's rescue of Jeremiah) in faithfulness (31:3). Such love sees the beloved only through the eyes of mercy. Israel is no longer "faithless" (3:11, 12; see also 31:22) or promiscuous but is now "virgin Israel" (31:4; see also 18:13; 31:21). Such benevolence, moreover, flies in the face of well-defined Deuteronomic categories of blessings and curses (Deut 27–28); despite the many failures of the nation, Yahweh remains loyal and embraces unconditionally. God's saving deeds, thus, have little to do with Israel's piety, virtue, or prestige (cf. Deut 4:37; 7:8) and everything to do with mercy. Divine love transforms the exiles' suffering and sorrow into happiness, and it alone will provide a home for the survivors of war. Because of divine compassion, displaced people shall return to the land with jubilation, singing, and dancing as they hear the call to worship at Zion. In this joyous world the sentry need no longer concern himself with approaching enemies. Instead, he plays a priestly role of calling the returnees to prayer: "Come, let us go up to Zion, to the LORD our God" (31:6).

A Joyous Homecoming for All to See (31:7-14)

The next section elaborates the theme of homecoming by using striking images of joy. The poem opens with a liturgical call to worship and then enumerates the reasons for praise (31:7-9). As the captive community prepares for the journey to Zion, Yahweh, the principal speaker, invites the exiles to "sing aloud with gladness" and plead for deliverance, "Save, O [Yahweh], your people, the remnant of Israel" (31:7). After that, Yahweh resolves to gather the scattered people of Israel/Jacob from the land of the north (31:8). The assembled include the most vulnerable members of community: the blind, the lame, pregnant women, and those in labor (31:8). On their journey Yahweh will sustain the needy delegation, leading them by brooks of water and on level ground. The motivation behind Yahweh's plan is clear: Yahweh is "[Israel's] father" and Ephraim is his "firstborn [son]" (31:9).

Yahweh summons the nations to witness the grand homecoming (31:10-14). Though they once mocked Zion by calling God's people "an outcast for whom no one cared" (30:17), they soon will see how wrong they were. Four verbs create visuals of the Lord's saving acts toward Israel. Yahweh will *gather* the scattered flock and *care for* them like a good shepherd, and will *ransom* Jacob and *redeem* him from his enemies. The last two italicized words have a particularly rich theological background. To ransom conveys the sense of rescue or liberation from the bullies of this world (Deut 7:8; 9:26; 15:15; 1 Sam 14:45; 2 Sam 4:9). Among other things, the word "redeem" carries a technical sense of fulfilling a familial obligation through a monetary transaction (Lev 25:48-52; Ruth 4:4-6; Jer 32:8). Both verbs, "ransom" and "redeem," often describe Yahweh's liberation from Egyptian slavery (Exod 6:6; Pss 74:2; 77:15; and Deut 7:8; 9:26). In the tradition of Isa 40–55, Jeremiah portrays the return of the exiles to their homeland as another glorious exodus from repression. No longer will praise attend only the former acts of God; the people of God will hereafter celebrate God's present victory over "[those stronger than they]" (31:11).

The rich images of Yahweh's triumph over Israel's enemies and of the captives' return to Zion resonate with radiant joy (31:12-14). The exiles' life will be a well-watered garden that will never wilt (31:12; see also Gen 2; Gen 13:10; Isa 51:3; 58:11; Ezek 36:35). In this edenic world, lives flourish, crops and livestock thrive, gladness supplants sadness, and priests and people feast on God's goodness (the Hebrew word "good," *ṭôb,* occurs in 31:12, 14). Such a celebration of God occasions praise, and indeed men and women, young and old sing and dance with uninhibited delight. Here and elsewhere in the Bible, dancing is an expression of great joy (see, for instance, the poetic parallelism in Ps 30:11-12; Lam 5:15). When the Israelites cross the sea and escape from the Egyptians, Miriam and the women of Israel dance in jubilation (Exod 15:20). When David retrieves the ark of God, he "danced before the LORD with all his [strength]" (2 Sam 6:14). At the festive dedication of the temple, God turned the psalmist's mourning into dancing (Ps 30:11; see also Ps 149:3). When the Babylonians destroyed Jerusalem and carried off many of its residents to a foreign land, the dancing stopped (Lam 5:15; see also Ps 137:1-4). Now the dancing begins again (Jer 31:12-13).

God Comforts Forlorn Rachel (31:15-26)

A voice of uncontrollable wailing interrupts the homecoming celebration (31:15). Anonymous voices ring out throughout the book, often with reports of approaching military danger and lamentation (e.g., 4:15, 4:31; 9:18, 10:22; 30:5; 48:3; 50:22). The voice here is that of Rachel weeping bitterly for her lost and presumed dead children (see 1 Sam 10:2; cf., however, Gen 35:16-20). Like Yahweh, the father of Israel/Ephraim (see 9:1-3; 31:9, 18-20), Rachel, the mother of Joseph and the grandmother of Ephraim (and hence the people of Israel), is utterly heartbroken. The early epic literature remembers the ancestress of Israel as one who was tortured by her longing for children. Her barrenness and her sister Leah's multiple births (Gen 29–30; see also Gen 35:16-29) drive her to such despair that she demands of her husband Jacob, "Give me children or I shall die!" (Gen 30:1). Ironically, after Yahweh "opens her womb" and she gives birth to her first-born Joseph, Rachel dies delivering her second son Benjamin. Her screams of anguish still linger in Jeremiah. Yet, unexpectedly she receives astonishing news: her lost children are not dead after all! Soon they will return home from exile (Jer 31:17). Only in this way can Yahweh comfort distraught Rachel. The consolation of the grieving mother of Ephraim provides another telling portrait of hope rooted in suffering. We now add to earlier images of transformation a bereaved mother embracing her lost sons and daughters.

Rachel's (grand)son interjects his own voice into the dialogue (31:18-20), and apparently both God/father and mother Rachel are present to witness the extraordinary confession. Ephraim, whose name often is used as a synonym for Israel, acknowledges both the disgrace of his youth (cf. Jer 2:2) and his stubborn resistance to Yahweh's discipline. He accepts his appropriate punishment and pleads for reconciliation. Rachel's lost son, Yahweh's firstborn child, is ready to return home and receive mercy: "Bring me back, let me come back, for you are the LORD my God" (31:18*b*). Like the prodigal son (Luke 15:11-32) and faithless Israel (e.g., Hos 2:2-9; Jer 3:22-25; 8:14-15), Ephraim recognizes the folly of his way and longs for reunion. The contrition of Ephraim moves Yahweh deeply. The waiting father "remembers" (see also Exod 6:5) and absolves his dear son of all wrongdoing.

In the final two verses of the poem (31:21-22), Yahweh no longer addresses mother Rachel or her son Ephraim but "faithless" virgin Israel who is part of the same broken family. Like her brother, she personifies the exiled people of God whom God/husband/father summons to return to their country. On her way back, she is to "set up road markers," make "[sign]posts," and pay close attention to the "highway" that leads home. Despite the invitation and the promise of safe travel, daughter Israel wavers and is reluctant to join the processional. Her ambivalence, which may actually hint at the unwillingness of many families to leave Babylon in the Persian period, cannot thwart the new work of God (31:22). What is the new thing that Yahweh has wrought on earth? God, the husband and father, tracks down Rachel's (and his) lost children, and thereby consoles the disheartened mother. Ephraim, once rebellious and unresponsive, comes to his senses and returns home. Faithful daughter Israel, though wayward and promiscuous in times past (Jer 2:17-25; 2:33–3:5; 18:13), at last embraces or "encompasses" her God. Another report adds that Judah will one day join Israel in the land of their ancestors and bask in God's blessings (31:23-26). Farmers and shepherds, although traditionally antagonistic, will live in harmony, as God refreshes the faint-hearted and replenishes those who languish (31:25). Thus, Yahweh's new work on earth involves the healing and restoration of the broken and dysfunctional family of God (O'Connor 2001, 514).

These oracles of newness set the stage for four eschatological promises (31:27-30, 31-34, 35-37, 38-40). The common formula, "the days are surely coming," introduces the prophetic announcements. Each one reverses particular aspects of the process of destruction involved in judgment and sets forth in their place facets of the symbolic and social charter for the restored community. All four oracles use declarative language to convey Yahweh's determination to rebuild the fortunes of Judah and Israel. First-person speech, "I will," is so dominant that it almost eliminates the openness of God to human choices (see, however, 31:30). The new creation does not depend on raw human grit or faithfulness; nor is it contingent upon military might or political prowess. Israel and Judah's new life is again a manifestation of God's resolute love.

God's Renewal of Israel and Judah (31:27-30)

This eschatological piece envisions the renewal of the house of Israel and the house of Judah in the aftermath of invasion. The threat of extinction makes it necessary to replenish the "seed of humans and the seed of animals." Yahweh therefore decides to repopulate a desolate earth and a war-torn community. Ecological renewal is a crucial facet of God's intent to rebuild and replant. The time for plucking up and breaking down is now over; the era of judgment is past. As God had attended to the work of judgment with the watchful eye (31:28; see the use of the word "watch" in 1:11-12), so God sees to the second stage of the divine plan: the creation of a new people, a new life, and a new covenant.

Despite this claim, some still question the vigilance of God and entertain serious doubts about divine goodness and justice. "The parents have eaten sour grapes, and the children's teeth are set on edge" (31:29). In the present context (cf. Ezek 18:2), the ancient proverb reflects the despair of certain survivors who have endured enormous pain for no apparent reason except as punishment for the sins of previous generations. Jeremiah rejects the proverb's assumption that children are accountable for the moral or ritual failings of their parents. Moreover, he contends that such complaints against God's governance will cease in the restored community of faith. In the future people shall no longer recite the ancient proverb, for every member of the community will be accountable to God for his or her own deeds, and justice will not miss its mark (31:30).

A New Covenant with Israel and Judah (31:31-34)

Jeremiah 31:31-34 is certainly the best-known eschatological text in the Book of Consolation. For Christians the promise of a new covenant is one of the most crucial claims in the Bible (see Heb 8:8-12; 9:15; 10:16-17; 1 Cor 11:25; Matt 26:28; Luke 22:20). Unlike other passages cited in the New Testament, however, Christian commentators often treat Jer 31:31-34 in complete isolation from its literary and historical setting. That is to say, they read this particular text as the exclusive property of Christians. Such exegesis creates a rigid dichotomy between Jews and Christians, relegating Judaism to the inferior province of the "old covenant." In its present literary context, Jer 31:31-34 forms an integral part of the identity of the post–587 Jewish community. Christians are clearly latecomers on the scene (Brueggemann 1998, 291-92).

Jeremiah 31:31-34 envisions another stunning reversal of Israel's distressing condition. Whereas earlier parts of the Book of Consolation concentrate on the joyful homecoming of the scattered people of God, Jer 31:31-34 focuses on the rapprochement of Yahweh and Israel and the advent of a new spirituality. As part of the nation's restoration, Yahweh resolves to "make a new covenant with the house of Israel and the house of Judah" (31:31). This new covenant resembles the old one in certain ways—the demands and effects of the Torah are the same—but it is not merely a "renewal" or a "modification" of the Sinai covenant. The new covenant represents an entirely distinctive mode of action with fresh understandings of the divine-human relationship. "*It will not be like* the covenant that I made with their ancestors when I . . . [brought] them out of the land of Egypt" (31:32). The new covenant is new because God initiates the relationship in the face of the people's abject infidelity and recalcitrance. Verse 32 reinforces the contention of Jer 1–25 that the people of God have been unfaithful covenant partners. By violating the commandments, they have rendered the covenant null and void. Thus, the exiles are not only landless in Babylon but also without any special claim on God. In a bold and unprecedented move God offers those who have broken the covenant a fresh start.

The new covenant is also distinctive by virtue of God's intent to inscribe divine law/instruction on people's heart, which is the seat of the will. In the first dispensation God wrote the terms of the covenant on tablets of stone at Mount Sinai (Exod 24:4, 12; 31:18; 32:15-16); now God pledges to engrave the law of the covenant on the inner being of the men and women who make up Israel. The internalization of the law empowers Israel to love and obey God. It allows Israel to break out of its cycle of failure and fulfill the demands of the covenant. In the old, pre–587 world, Judah's transgression was indelibly engraved on the tablets of the heart so that the nation above all desired to sin (17:1-2). Now divine instruction is written within them so that they delight in doing God's will.

When God has performed this internal operation, there is no longer a need to teach others to know God. All will know the Lord (31:34). Young and old, women and men, the poor and the powerful will enjoy direct and immediate access to God independent of priestly mediation. The knowledge of God is a key piece of Jeremiah's theological construction. In the old world, the knowledge of God was conspicuously absent; neither priest nor people knew Yahweh (2:8; 4:22; 9:3); neither rich nor poor understood the ways of God (5:4, 5). This dearth of knowledge led the community down a treacherous road of corruption. In the new world, regardless of social or economic position, all know God; that is, the entire community enjoys an intimate relationship with the Lord and practices justice (see 22:16).

COMMENTARY

Finally, the new covenant offers unqualified forgiveness to broken people who can no longer bear the burden of their guilt. Interestingly, absolution of sins comes with no strings attached or without reference to the temple or sacrifice. Yahweh merely declares it so: "I will forgive their iniquity and remember their sin no more" (31:34). The syntax of verse 34 suggests that forgiveness is more than a characteristic of the new covenant; it is the very basis of the astonishing workings of God. Divine forgiveness makes possible inner transformation, intimacy with God, and an inclusive community that delights in faithful living.

Israel Is God's Beloved Forever (31:35-37)

Jeremiah 31:35-37 represents another reversal of the dismantled pre–587 world. It overturns God's blanket rejection of Israel. The text consists of two "if-then" statements that guarantee God's enduring faithfulness to Israel. The first (31:35-36) appeals to the established order of the universe as grounds for the continued existence of the "offspring of Israel" (31:36). The regularities of nature henceforth attest to the permanence of the restored community. The second (31:37) relies on the incalculability of the cosmos to establish the salvation of the restored community. Only if one could fathom the mysteries of creation—an absolutely impossible feat—would God reject the "offspring of Israel." The catchword "offspring" in verses 36 and 37 (see also 31:27) is reminiscent of God's promise to Abraham that his "offspring" would be "like the dust of the earth" (Gen 13:16). Throughout the first half of the book, Jeremiah challenges the election tradition and presses the prophetic imagination to the limit by declaring God's rejection of Israel (see, e.g., 15:1-4; 18:1-17; 20:1-6). Now the text repeals this stance and reestablishes the election of Israel on solid ground: a divine oath asserting that nothing will be able to separate God's people from God's love, not even "all they have done" (31:37).

A New Jerusalem (31:38-40)

The vision of a new people and a new covenant is incomplete without the creation of the new Jerusalem. Jeremiah 31:38-40

274

reverses the former judgments against Jerusalem (see, e.g., Jer 7:30–8:3) and imagines its restoration. Yahweh maps out the topographical details for its reconstruction, including its northern and southern boundaries: the Tower of Hananel and Corner Gate to the north and Gareb and Goah, presumably in the south (cf. Zech 2:1-5). Places that were once defiled by the dead, such as the Wadi Kidron and Horse Gate, are set apart for the Lord. Like the offspring of Israel, the city will remain forever (31:40). Although God had once waged war on the stronghold of Judah's apostasy, now Yahweh exalts Jerusalem and transforms its ruins into the city of God.

Confinement in a Worthless Place (32:1-5)

Jeremiah 32 belongs chronologically to the extended narrative in Jer 37–39, which depicts incidents in the final years of King Zedekiah. The chapter appears in its present context because of its dramatic message of hope. Although the form of Jer 32 differs from preceding chapters, its theme is essentially the same: the eventual restoration of the fortunes of the people of God. The account, however, is set during one of Judah's darkest hours (32:1-5): only months before the fall of Jerusalem (see 39:2). It is the tenth year of Zedekiah's botched reign, the eighteenth year of Nebuchadrezzar's leadership, 588. By now the siege of Jerusalem is well under way. The enemy is at the gates ready to attack. The Babylonian army has already overrun the country and threatened the city's flow of supplies. A weak and vulnerable Zedekiah has sought military aid from Egypt, but to no avail. And, Jeremiah is under house arrest in the palace of the king. He is a political prisoner accused of sedition.

While confined there, Zedekiah approaches Jeremiah to inquire why he has prophesied against the city and the king. Actually, the anxious king pleads for help as his kingdom spirals out of control. Jeremiah is silent and renders no assistance. Readers hear only the words of Zedekiah. Nevertheless, when quoting Jeremiah, the king unwittingly becomes the bearer of God's word. That is, the storyteller places in Zedekiah's mouth Yahweh's incriminating message: Nebuchadnezzar shall destroy Jerusalem and take him prisoner to Babylon (32:3-5). Jeremiah, therefore, need not utter another word. Although he is restrained, the word of God is not. It rings out loud and clear through the mouth of Judah's failed leader.

An Outrageous Real Estate Offer (32:6-15)

Zedekiah's voice fades as the text zooms in on Jeremiah. In autobiographical form, Jeremiah tells the story of another meeting in the court of the guard, this time with a member of his own family. At first, the encounter appears private and unrelated to either Zedekiah's query or the siege of Jerusalem; soon it becomes clear that the conversation is both public and prophetic in character. To prepare Jeremiah for the meeting, the Lord alerts him that his cousin Hanamel will soon arrive with a request that he buy a piece of family property. In accordance with the law of redemption, it was the obligation of the next of kin to purchase family property when a relative fell into economic difficulty (Lev 25:25-28). This practice prevented the forfeiture of land, which ultimately belongs to God and on which the Israelites lived only as tenants (Lev 25:23). The potential loss of land, therefore, was both a violation of economic justice and an infringement on Yahweh's domain.

Just as Yahweh had said, Hanamel visits Jeremiah and asks him to fulfill his duty as next of kin redeemer. The "serendipitous" meeting is enough to convince the prophet that the request is indeed wrought by God (32:8). Hanamel wastes no time on small talk; immediately he attends to the legal details of the public transaction. Jeremiah purchases the field and weighs the money on scales, seventeen shekels of silver. He signs and puts his seal on the deed of purchase, and in the presence of witnesses gives Baruch, his secretary and faithful friend, two copies of the deed. Baruch signs the official, sealed copy of the deed of purchase, which contains the terms and conditions of the legal transaction. Then Jeremiah charges Baruch to deposit both the sealed and open copy in an earthen jar so that "they may last for a long time" (32:14). Verse 15 discloses the purpose of the transaction: the business deal functions as a sign that "houses and fields and vineyards shall again be bought in this land." This "contrary-to-fact" pronouncement imagines a future beyond the present disaster. It envisages rebuilding and planting after the present plucking up and tearing down. One day, life will return to normal in the land for it still belongs to Yahweh.

Jeremiah's Candid Prayer (32:16-25)

When the transaction is completed, Jeremiah offers a prayer of praise. His prayer generally conforms to the style and structure of psalms of praise in the Old Testament (Pss 104, 105, 136; Neh 9:6-37; Ezra 9:6-15). Psalms of praise customarily exalt God for two divine attributes: majesty and mercy or greatness and goodness. Worshipers recognize the greatness of God in the splendor of creation and in God's sovereign rule in the world. God's mercy is evident in gracious acts of deliverance and provision. Although Jeremiah celebrates God's might and mercy, he is mostly concerned with God's ability to intervene in human affairs and keep promises, especially in light of his outrageous land acquisition.

The prophet looks first to creation as a sure sign of God's power. For the One who has made heaven and earth "nothing is too hard." Jeremiah then acknowledges the outpouring of covenant love and righteous judgment in God's dealing with the world. God's "eyes are open to all the ways of mortals" (32:19). Such love and involvement bear witness to God's compassionate and just rule. In particular, God's mighty deeds on behalf of Israel reveal divine mercy and might. With great power, the Lord brought the people of Israel out of the land of Egypt and gave them the land promised to their ancestors (32:22). More than any other moment in Israel's history, the exodus deliverance out of Egypt and the gift of the land of Canaan establish the claim that "nothing is too hard for [Yahweh]." But God's wondrous acts are not to be relegated to the distant past: God's "signs and wonders" and self-disclosure continue "to this very day" (32:20).

To this point, Jeremiah has focused entirely on God's acts in creation and history. Now he shifts his attention to the people's transgressions, which he sees as the cause of the community's dire circumstances (32:23-24). Because the people refused to obey God's voice or follow divine instruction, Yahweh brought upon them the existing disasters: the siege ramps erected against the city, the Chaldeans breathing down their necks, and the "sword, famine, and pestilence" that is the fulfillment of the prophetic message. Everything points to the same conclusion: "What [Yahweh has spoken] has happened . . . " (32:24). God is trustworthy and God's word is certain. The splendor of creation, the exodus out of Egypt, the settlement in the land, and even the present judgments are compelling evidence that nothing is too hard for God.

Despite his profession of faith, doubts linger (32:25). Jeremiah's recital of God's wonders culminates in candid skepticism. He entertains no suspicions about God's previous acts of mercy or God's present acts of judgment. They are well established. However, given the present exigencies, Jeremiah has serious misgivings about the future and regards any stake in it as ridiculous. Specifically, the purchase of a worthless piece of land and the claim that "houses and fields and vineyards shall again be bought in this land" make absolutely no sense in light of Babylonian occupation. For the moment, Jeremiah is captive not only to the palace guards but also to his own qualms about God's ability to create a future beyond the present chaos and disarray.

"Is Anything Too Hard" for Yahweh? (32:26-44)

Yahweh's reply neither rebukes nor reprimands Jeremiah for his doubts but rather addresses his fears and focal concerns. Following a solemn declaration of self-identity, resembling the preamble to the Sinai covenant (Exod 20:2), Yahweh returns to Jeremiah's opening affirmation that "nothing is too hard for you." Although Jeremiah had uttered these words at the beginning of his prayer, it is obvious by the end that he is still struggling with their implications. Because of the terrible devastation, he questions whether God can really create newness out of the fissured world. Yahweh thus turns Jeremiah's affirmation into a rhetorical question—"Is anything too hard for me?"—and then demonstrates that the answer is an indisputable "no."

Yahweh first considers the present crisis of Judah (32:28-35). Jerusalem will soon fall into the hands of the king of Babylon who will set it on fire. The "burning" of Jerusalem, however, is no indication of divine impotence or injustice. Yahweh is going to give the city over into the power of Judah's enemies because of the people's sinfulness. Developing the book's theodicy, the divine speech emphasizes Judah's moral responsibility in the disaster. The people are not victims of a capricious deity or a political powerhouse but are shapers of their destiny. Yahweh is angry because they have

- done nothing but evil from their youth, v. 30;
- done nothing but provoke Yahweh to anger by the work of their hands, v. 30;
- aroused Yahweh's anger and wrath, v. 31;
- turned their backs to Yahweh, not their faces, v. 33;
- refused to listen or accept correction, v. 33;
- set up their abominations, v. 34;
- built the high places for Baal to offer their sons and daughters to Molech, v. 35.

The catalog of sins justifies the capture of the city. It exonerates God of wrongdoing and places full blame on the people. As important, it establishes that Judah's predicament is not outside the reach of divine scrutiny.

The second half of Yahweh's reply moves from the certainty of judgment to an uncertain future. Yahweh speaks directly to the question of whether newness and hope are possible (32:36-44). To start, Yahweh acknowledges the dreadful plight of the people. The king of Babylon is indeed about to take the city by "the sword, by famine, and by pestilence." However, Judah's suffering is not the end of the road. God is in the business of willing new beginnings and fresh shapes out of the fallen worlds. After the collapse of the old, a new Israel shall emerge by the power of the divine word (cf. Gen 1:1–2:3). By a series of verbal commands, God speaks the unimaginable into being.

(1) Yahweh will rescue the scattered exiles and gather them to their homeland where they will live in safety, v. 37

(2) When returning to the land, Yahweh will reestablish a relationship with them and give them a new heart that makes obedience possible, vv. 38-39

(3) Yahweh promises to make an "everlasting covenant" with the exiles, v. 40

(4) Yahweh resolves to treat the people compassionately and "plant them" in the land, v. 41

Nothing is impossible for the One who executes judgments on earth and breathes life into a dead and hopeless people (cf. Gen 18:14 and Luke 1:37).

After marshaling an impressive array of evidence, the divine response directly tackles the issue at hand, Jeremiah's qualms about God's intentions (32:42-44). Yahweh can now assert with force: "fields shall be bought in this land." Regardless of the desolation wrought by the Babylonians, community life in its fullness will resume throughout the territory of Judah. Yahweh will bring form to a situation that appears formless and will rebuild the wastelands of Judah. This determination to restore is rooted in nothing but God's power and faithful utterance. The people of God must only look beyond their present contingencies to see the coming intervention of God.

God Will Restore the Fortunes of Judah and Israel (33:1-13)

The setting in the "court of the guard" (33:1; see also 32:2) ties chapter 33 to the preceding one. Jeremiah is still under house arrest in the palace precincts when the word of Yahweh comes to him a second time (33:1-3). Yahweh invites the prophet to discover certain mysteries through prayer. "Call to me and I will answer you, and will tell you great and hidden things that you have not known" (33:3). Presumably, the oracles to follow disclose these secrets. The first oracle begins by echoing a theme found throughout the book (33:4-13): Babylon is going to inflict an enormous toll on Jerusalem. The description of the carnage is terse but striking (33:5-6). Dead bodies will line the streets, turning the city of God into a place for the dead. To fend off the enemy's siege ramps, the people of Judah tear down houses including those of the kings of Judah. Such efforts, however, are useless for "Yahweh has hidden his face" from the city because of its wickedness. The Hebrew idiom "to hide one's face" often denotes turning away from an undesirable situation. When Yahweh hides his face, Yahweh withdraws divine presence. As a result, chaos and disarray ensue and hope for salvation vanishes (see Deut 31:17; Pss 30:7; 143:7).

This somber tone is suddenly interrupted and an unexpected turnaround occurs. Whereas verses 4-5 assert that God has abandoned the city, verses 6-9 announce the city's healing and restoration. God will again inhabit Jerusalem. The One who had plucked up and pulled down now promises to reestablish and rebuild the people "as they were at first." The God who had earlier "hidden his face" here decides to cleanse the guilty and forgive the rebellious. As is true elsewhere in the Book of Consolation, mercy not only tempers judgment, but eclipses it. The reserve of first-person pronouns reveals God's gracious intent to heal, restore, rebuild, cleanse, and forgive. In response, the inhabitants of Jerusalem stand amazed, trembling not out of fear but in delight at the cascade of divine goodness and peace showered upon them. God turns the city of ruins into a city of joy and renown (33:9). Uninhabited Jerusalem rediscovers the sounds of joyous celebrations (33:10-11). The desolate places now overflow with flocks and pasture.

The Restoration of King and Priest (33:14-26)

The final oracle in the Book of Consolation uses both traditional and innovative imagery to depict the re-establishment of king and priest (33:14-26). To start with, it envisions a society ruled by a royal savior from the house of David (see also 23:5-6). A scion will spring up from the line of David who will finally do what kings were supposed to do all along: execute justice and save their people from threatening foes. Under the leadership of the promised ruler, Judah will be saved, and Jerusalem will be called "[Yahweh] is our righteousness," a title previously bestowed on the king (Jer 23:6). In addition, Levitical priests will play a dominant role in this vision of the community (see also Deut 18:1-5). They will resume their role as mediators between God and the people, presenting to God burnt offerings, grain offerings, and sacrifices. Since self-absorbed priests and mercenary shepherds failed so miserably during the preexilic world, it is necessary that their sacred duties be fulfilled in the ideal world order. Thus, God authorizes the future status of king and priest and expresses a lasting commitment to them. God's faithful pledge to the Davidic ruler and the Levites is based on the unchanging order of creation—"my covenant with the day and my covenant with the night"—and on the ancestral promise of progeny (33:19-22; cf. Gen 15:5; 22:17). Hereafter, creation itself along with God's trustworthy promise to Abraham and Sarah testify to their enduring place in the life of the community.

Jeremiah 33:23-26 refutes the contention that God has rejected the people of Judah and Israel. To be sure, Jeremiah has done much to encourage such an inference. The prophet has proclaimed that Judah's disobedience and unfaithfulness have jeopardized its relationship with God. He has even dared to imagine the annulment of Judah's special claim as God's people and insisted that the election of Judah would not shelter the nation from impending harm. Notwithstanding these troubling prophecies, the final oracle in the Book of Consolation is adamant that the status of God's people is a "family matter" which is off-limits to others. Outsiders have no right to butt in and ridicule. To counter their attacks, Yahweh pledges enduring support for the offspring of Jacob and the descendants of David. While the election of Israel and Judah may once have been in doubt, it is now rooted in the basic order of existence, Yahweh's "covenant with day and night," and in the boundless mercy of God.

Theological and Ethical Analysis

The Book of Comfort represents the most sustained treatment of hope in Jeremiah. Its vision is not seamless or comprehensive, but it does render an impressive portrait of Israel's charter of salvation. In the first place, Jer 30–33 unites all expressions of hope with suffering and marginality (Clements 1988, 180). The very starting point for a hopeful future is the acknowledgment of brokenness, loss, refugee status, and massive upheaval. Accordingly, the text is beset with images of siege and military assault (30:4-7), abandonment and oppression (30:12-17), communal devastation and despair (30:18-24). Almost every articulation of hope is located against the background of exile and death. Consequently, there is no ecstasy without mourning, no homecoming without exile, no salvation without judgment, no joyous celebrations without the scars of survival. For Jeremiah any vision of the future that avoids the real world of human suffering makes a travesty of the past and can never deal with the emotional and symbolic pain of exile. It is therefore no accident that the Book of Comfort depicts the people of God as "survivors." They have endured war, amputated hopes, splintered families, and the travail of a shattered world. Now, by the power of the word, God empowers these broken and shipwrecked people to imagine a future when none seemed possible.

According to the Book of Comfort, hope requires a genuine break from the old world. There is a powerful temptation during times of fear and uncertainty to cling to the past. We have seen this propensity in prophets, priests, and kings who live as though their crisis were only a momentary disruption. For dear life, they hang on to familiar categories confident of their return. But Judah cannot return to its life before exile. The old world and the old scripts are forever gone. Only when one recognizes this reality can hope begin to take shape.

A daring expression of the text's radical break with the past is its treatment of the temple and the dynasty, as well as its construal of community life and the divine-human relationship. First, Jeremiah no longer envisions the temple and its systems of worship as the foundation of Israel. Although some scholars overstate the case when they argue that Jeremiah advocates the idea of a spiritual cult, devoid of public rites (Lindblom 1962, 373), Israel's future pilgrimage to Zion is often to a place without temple and offerings (Jer 31:6, 12; cf. 33:11, 18). In a number of places, the restored people of God receive forgiveness of sins without priestly mediation or sacrificial system (31:34; 33:8; see, however, 33:18).

Israel's new piety thus shows far less reverence for the Jerusalem temple and its ceremonies. These definitive components of the past are relegated to, at best, a secondary role in the life of the community.

Second, the Davidic ruler of the restored Israel represents a fundamental departure from earlier monarchical systems of governance, which the text considers partially responsible for the downfall of the nation. The newly imagined leader is no longer one who wields interminable military authority. The promised king does not rule God's people with an iron fist; nor does he lead a great and powerful nation into battle. Judah's king does not rape and plunder, like the rulers of other nations (see 1 Sam 8:5, 20). Instead, the descendant of David envisioned by Jeremiah is a just and righteous upholder of the social and judicial order without the traditional pomp and circumstance. The royal savior of Israel is committed to preserving justice and peace within the community (see 30:9, 21; cf. 33:14-26).

Third, in support of this simpler way of life, Jeremiah advocates the notion of community as inclusive and unified. Israel's homecoming, for example, includes the northern and southern kingdoms. The scattered people of Judah and Israel one day return to the land of promise. All God's people are invited to the banquet, especially the most vulnerable and needy (31:7-9). The knowledge of God is available to all persons, often without priestly mediation (31:34); and God bestows joy and dignity on everyone (e.g., 30:18-19; 31:1-6; 32:36-41). Hierarchical arrangements of community life, while not abandoned, are diminished in the text.

Fourth, the restoration of the loving relationship between Israel and Yahweh is not a replication from the past. The spirituality of the new world has a profoundly "personal" texture. While the text does not promote a piety that divorces the individual from the group (which is clearly a modern notion), it does envisage a community in which individuals enjoy a close relationship with God, where people's lives and personal affairs matter to God. The "new" relation, described in one place as a "new covenant" (31:31-34) and in another place as an "everlasting covenant"

(32:36-44), carries with it the assurance of full forgiveness (31:34; 33:6-8), divine favor and protection (30:10-11; 32:36-44; 33:1-9), deliverance from captivity (30:10-11, 18-21; 31:7-14, 23-25), joy (30:18-19; 31:3-6), and inner transformation (31:33; 32:39-40). Unlike the old piety, which emphasized Israel's responsibility in the divine-human relationship, this new spirituality depends far more on the extraordinary workings of God. The "if" of the divine-human relation takes a backseat to the declarative speech and the gracious activity of God. In other words, God assumes the responsibility for creating the "new Israel" and the humane conditions of the new world order.

All told, while the Book of Comfort employs beliefs, practices and memories of the past to describe the "world-to-come," its new spirituality and social structure represent a deep and penetrating break from the old systems. The temple and its forms of worship, the king as traditionally understood, and the royal city—the major symbols for and evidence of God's presence in the life of Israel—no longer enjoy their central place in the new epoch. Governing assumptions of the dismantled world, such as covenant and election, are now reconfigured. Israel's "new covenant," inaugurated because the "old" Sinai covenant has been broken (31:32), involves a radical transformation of the community life. Israel's election, forfeited in the old epoch, is reconfigured and enjoys a more firm and enduring foundation (33:23-26). This reconstructed world represents a new mode of action, a new narrative, and a new program by which God can succeed in fulfilling the divine purposes.

The Book of Comfort sees all expressions of hope as grounded in God's mercy, love, and sovereignty. Hope is not the result of human virtue, human ingenuity, human grit, or human imagination. Nor does it derive from success, military might, technological prowess, or even the elimination of scars and memories of loss. Hope is God's gracious gift to suffering people who are at their breaking point. It is the promise of life when none is expected.

MORAL INSTRUCTION FOR THE EXILIC COMMUNITY (JEREMIAH 34–35)

Chapters 34 and 35 have been united to tell a poignant story of two communities. One treats its formative sacred traditions with contempt and the other with utmost respect. One blithely dismisses its core beliefs while the other complies wholeheartedly. These stark contrasts function primarily as a word of judgment for Judah, but they also authorize a script for the ethical character of the exilic community. In the most uncompromising terms, they reveal values to be adopted and vices to be avoided at all cost.

Literary Analysis

Much as Jer 34 and 35 represent two distinct texts, together they present an object lesson on fidelity and infidelity, obedience and disobedience (Brueggemann 1998, 323-37). The story divides neatly into parallel parts.

Jeremiah 34:1-7 Introduction

Jer 34:8-11 Description of Disobedience	Jer 35:1-11 Description of Obedience
Jer 34:12-16 Condemnation for Disobedience	Jer 35:12-16 Commendation for Obedience and Condemnation for Disobedience
Jer 34:17-22 The Verdict	Jer 35:17-19 The Verdict

Jeremiah 34:1-7 introduces the literary unit with a stinging message of judgment against Jerusalem and its king. Jeremiah declares that both will fall into the hands of the king of Babylon. The sections that follow ground the judgment in a particular covenant violation. Judah is in breach of the commandment that demands the release of Hebrew servants after six years of service (34:8-11). At first, the people make a covenant to liberate indebted slaves and cancel their debts in accordance with God's command. Shortly afterward, they reverse that decision and reclaim their servants. Jeremiah indicts Judah for this inhumane act, which is

particularly heinous in light of God's gracious deliverance of Hebrew slaves from bondage in Egypt (34:12-16). The balance of the chapter (34:17-22) pronounces the sentence for national disobedience: the people of God will come under the curses of the covenant in the form of conquest, deportation, and exile.

In Jer 35:1-11 the scene switches to Jeremiah's interaction with the Rechabites. As instructed by Yahweh, Jeremiah offers the Rechabites wine in the temple. In faithful adherence to the commands of their founder Jonadab, they reject Jeremiah's offer. Jeremiah 35:12-16 explains the significance of the symbolic action. Unlike the people of Judah, the Rechabites do not compromise their principles. They remain loyal and resolute. The accolades lavished upon this nomadic sect illustrate Judah's offense by stark contrast. Jeremiah 35 concludes with the verdict in hand: judgment on Judah for "not listening" and mercy on the Rechabites for "listening" to the command of their ancestor Jonadab (35:17-19).

Exegetical Analysis

Jeremiah's Warning to Zedekiah (34:1-7)

The narrator employs historicized and symbolic terms to describe the siege of Jerusalem. The king of Babylon and his army have begun their campaign against the city. Nebuchadrezzar marches in step with "all the kingdoms of the earth and all the peoples under his dominion" (34:1). While this language clearly has historical underpinnings, referring to the assembly of Babylon's vassals gathered in Jerusalem to aid their suzerain in 587, it also imagines the assault on Jerusalem as a massive cosmic battle (cf. Dan 3:2-4). The results are devastating. Only Lachish and Azekah, two cities west of Jerusalem, remain standing. Soon all will be reduced to rubble. To exacerbate the conflict the storyteller insists that Yahweh commissions Judah's invader. Thus, the king of Babylon is no mere military figure, as we have previously learned (e.g., 27:1-15), but an ally of Yahweh in the judgment of Judah. Nebuchadrezzar and his forces are Yahweh's instruments procured to exact punishment upon a rebellious people and their rebellious king. As God's agent, Nebuchadrezzar will capture Zedekiah and deport him to Babylon. Although the Judean king learns that his life will be spared (34:4-5; cf. 21:7), desperation and fear still pervade all that is said. There is no time to forestall the coming events, no opportunities to repent. All is set in motion and about to go down.

Short-lived Obedience (34:8-11)

During the siege of Jerusalem, Zedekiah proclaims the manumission of Hebrew slaves. The proclamation of freedom is carried out in compliance with the ancient teaching that calls for the liberation of fellow Israelite slaves after six years of service (see Exod 21:2-11; Deut 15:1, 12-18). In an effort to combat poverty and unbridled greed, covenant law demands that the community forgive debts and give the poor a new start. By making provisions for those who have been disenfranchised because of debt, tight-fisted economic pragmatism yields to the covenantal ethic of compassion and generosity. It is uncertain whether this "law" was actually practiced in Israel or whether it only represented an ideal moral vision of community life. It likely serves a wide range of symbolic and historical interests.

As the story unfolds, the people respond decisively to the royal edict: everyone obeys and enters into a covenant to set debt slaves free. The language is inclusive and unequivocal. Twice in verse 10 the narrator reports that all the officials and all the people "obeyed" the king's proclamation. There is little time for commendation, however, before the people "turn around" and repossess their slaves. The use of the Hebrew word "turn around" (šûb) is significant. Jeremiah has repeatedly called for Judah to "turn" to Yahweh in repentance, but Judah's only "turning" is away from Yahweh and Yahweh's commandments. The accusation could not be more damning.

The main events of the story thus far are straightforward: the king makes a covenant, which the people obey and then defy (34:9-11). It is not at all clear, however, whether their misguided actions are done with or without the king's consent. That is, Zedekiah's role in the debacle is rather ambiguous. Equally puzzling are the motives behind the royal edict and its reversal. Attentive to these queries, some commentators suggest that Zedekiah initially acts in good faith, motivated by genuine interest in the welfare of his fellow Israelites. The dangerous times provide Zedekiah and his administration an opportunity to rectify long-standing systemic injustices. Other scholars propose that Zedekiah enacts the legislation for short-term economic and military gains: during a period of severe food shortages he attempts both to alleviate the burden of feeding enslaved persons and to increase the numbers for military engagement with Babylon. Still others put forward that Zedekiah may have proclaimed freedom as an attempt to placate Yahweh. By acting upon his fundamental responsibilities toward the needy, the king tries to motivate the Lord to lift the siege of Jerusalem and save the city. Interestingly, if Zedekiah does seek to appease Yahweh in this way, his eleventh-hour plea seems to work. When the Egyptian army under the leadership of Pharaoh Hophra approaches Jerusalem, the Babylonians momentarily withdraw (34:21; see also 37:4-12, which is contemporary with the events of 34:8-22). As soon as the emergency is over and all is well again (34:11), however, Judah resubjugates its disadvantaged people. For a brief moment, when it is convenient, Judah "listens" only to "turn around" and take back the male and female slaves they had set free.

An Indictment for Broken Vows (34:12-16)

The duplicity enrages God. The decision to rescind the cancellation of debts represents a brazen breach of covenant law. But it is far more. The act of infidelity is a violation of all that Israel stands for. Jeremiah builds this case by mounting two rhetorical lines of attack. First, he draws a hard and fast distinction between God and the Jerusalemites. God is the covenant-keeper; the people are covenant-breakers. God is trustworthy; the people are faithless. When the people "do not listen" or "incline their ears," they follow the lead of their faithless ancestors. When they "turn away," they profane Yahweh's name, or reputation. Second, Jeremiah reminds the Judeans of their roots as an oppressed people whom the Lord delivered from the house of bondage. Indeed,

Yahweh is identified with the liberation of Israel. "Thus says the LORD, the God of Israel: I myself made a covenant with your ancestors when I brought them out of the land of Egypt, out of the house of slavery" (34:13). The memory of the exodus lies at the heart of the law requiring the freedom of slaves every seventh year (see Deut 15:15). The Judeans are to free their fellow slaves because God freed their ancestors from their oppressors in Egypt. The conviction that God is aligned with the oppressed against oppressors frames the full gamut of Israel's moral vision. It is evident not only throughout Jeremiah but also in covenant formulations in Exodus and Deuteronomy. The story of Israel's beginnings as an enslaved people and God's act of emancipation introduces the divine commandments (Exod 19:3-4; 20:2; Deut 5:6). In Deuteronomy, Israel's history of slavery provides the basis for observing the Sabbath (Deut 5:15; cf. Exod 20:11). Without doubt every ethical mandate is rooted in this story of weakness and helplessness. Here lies the crux of the people's wrongdoing. By reclaiming their freed slaves, both the king and the people exploit their place of privilege. By withholding mercy, the recipients of divine mercy become "hard-hearted or tight-fisted" (Deut 15:7). By treating people as mere commodities, they do violence to their core identity as God's people: the once oppressed now become oppressors.

The Divine Sentence (34:17-22)

Yahweh holds both king and people accountable for their actions. An ill-boding "therefore" coupled with a conventional prophetic speech formula, "thus says the LORD," introduce two searing pictures of divine judgment. Both use the covenant metaphor as their reference points, and both use wordplays to illustrate the harsh and sweeping sentence. A play on the word "release" or "liberty" creates the first image. Because Judah failed to "release" its slaves from their debts, Yahweh will "release" Judah. However, Yahweh will not "release" Judah *from* bondage or disaster, as in the past, but "to the sword, to plague, and to famine" (34:17-18). The nation is now "free" to suffer the penalties of the covenant, eventually becoming a "horror to all the kingdoms of the earth" (34:17; cf. Deut 28:37). A play on the word "cut"—the conventional term for "making" a covenant—is even more grievous (34:18-22). All those who "cut" a covenant with Yahweh to free their slaves and then reneged on their oath (see 34:8, 15; see also 34:13) will suffer the same fate as a sacrificial animal that is "cut" into halves. This imagery derives from covenant rituals in which the parties would walk through the dismembered parts of an animal and pronounce a similar fate on themselves if they violate their oath (see Gen 15:7-21). Jeremiah proclaims that covenant offenders in Judah will bear the curse of that covenant—death, captivity, and exile.

The Telling Story of a Fringe Group's Fidelity (35:1-19)

The story of the Rechabites is set in the reign of King Jehoiakim (609–598), a decade earlier than the previous chapter. By this time, the destruction of Judah's world was well underway. Nebuchadrezzar had already begun his military campaign in the west, and Babylonian troops were in the process of occupying the land of Judah. The invasion forced a small nomadic community called the Rechabites to take up temporary residence in Jerusalem. We know very little about this group. Late genealogical lists associate them with the Kenites (1 Chr 2:55). According to the book of Judges, the Kenites were relatives of Moses who lived in the Judean wilderness south of Hebron (Judg 1:16). In a zealous attempt to eliminate the religion of Baal from the borders of Israel, Je(ho)nadab son of Rechab, the famous ancestor of later Rechabites, participated in the massacre of the house of Omri under King Jehu (2 Kgs 10:15-27). Whether Je(ho)nadab's descendants followed his example of violent resistance is not known. Jeremiah 35 only implies that the protest community rejected urban and agrarian conventions for a more austere lifestyle. The Rechabites apparently lived in tents and practiced a form of Yahwism frozen in the distant past before Israel became a sedentary community. Symbolizing their rejection of settled agriculture, they abstained from drinking wine (cf. Num 6:1-8). For Jeremiah their staunch adherence to the teachings of their ancestors became a telling contrast to the flaccid piety of the Judeans.

The narrative begins with the Lord instructing Jeremiah to approach the Rechabites and bring them to the temple precincts (35:1-11). There Jeremiah is to offer them wine to drink. Jeremiah obeys the Lord's command and invites Jaazaniah and his family to one of the temple chambers where he sets before them large bowls full of wine. The Rechabites turn down Jeremiah's offer. They explain that they are acting in line with their ancestral commandments, which forbids them from drinking wine or building houses, sowing seed, or owning vineyards. In compliance with Jonadab's teaching, they have rejected the values and practices of the dominant society and have embraced instead the life of sojourners in the wilderness. Their presence in Jerusalem is only an emergency measure taken for fear of the Babylonian and Syrian armies (35:11). Otherwise, they live in tents as their ancestors have done for centuries.

Jeremiah 35:12-19 interprets the symbolic act: the faithfulness of the Rechabites serves as "a lesson" for recalcitrant Judah. The term "lesson" (35:13) is used for "instruction that the older generation offers to the younger as part of inculcation and socialization into the norms of the community" (Brueggemann 1998, 332-33). In this case, the inculcation of values comes from a most unlikely source. Instead of insiders instructing insiders how to behave, a strange group of outsiders teaches the people of Judah how to live as God's people. The Rechabites are indeed an odd lot, perhaps even a byword, to the sophisticated Jerusalem urbanites. These strangers fail to grasp the importance of "progress"; they reject the advantages of new technologies and show little appreciation for the attractions of the modern world. As hardcore traditionalists, they live in the old days, embracing the old ways, and adhering to outdated customs, or so it must have seemed to the city folk. Accordingly, they are easy targets. Yet Jeremiah flip-flops conventional ways of thinking and places these nonconformists on a pedestal. Now they become models of faithful living. By their example, Jeremiah drives home the importance of fidelity and obedience to God, which is what God has long desired from the people of Judah. Nothing more and nothing less!

All along, the Rechabite lesson has been an indictment for infidelity. Unlike the descendants of Jonadab who carry out ancestral commandments, the people of God refuse to follow divine teaching. Yahweh has spoken persistently to them but they have not listened. Yahweh has sent prophets but the people of Judah have "not inclin[ed] [their] ear [to listen]" (35:15). The Hebrew word "hear" or "obey" organizes and fuels the prophetic denunciation. The probing question, "Can you not learn a lesson and *obey* my words?" (35:13, my emphasis) is answered no less than four times (35:14, 15, 16, 17). The people of Judah have flunked the test and *"not obeyed"* (35:14, 15, 16, 17, my emphasis). The obedience of the Rechabites (35:14, 18) only accentuates this failure. In this way, the text presents the two communities as opposing ways of life—a life of faithfulness and one of infidelity—and implicit in each are contrasting destinies. One leads to blessing (35:18-19) and the other to disaster and death (35:17).

Theological and Ethical Analysis

Such clear-cut, unambiguous categories of "good guys" and "bad guys" are easy to fault. People are complex and ethical decision-making is rarely so neat and symmetrical. However, the storyteller does not employ these categories to make ontological judgments but rather to address two central concerns: one deals with the disaster that befell Jerusalem in 587, which was likely past for the implied audience, and the other grapples with the future of the surviving community of faith in exile. Regarding the first, the Rechabite-Judean lesson makes sense of the initial announcement of judgment against the citizens of Jerusalem and their king Zedekiah (34:1-7). It shows that Judeans deserted their covenant obligations, treated the poor cruelly (34:17-22; see also 35:12-17), and therefore reaped what they sowed. The text claims that mistreating the marginal and disadvantaged is an act of obscenity with far-reaching consequences. Contempt for the vulnerable provokes divine anger and brings about the loss of city and king. God is not mocked. Perpetrators of injustice will suffer the consequences of their actions. To strengthen this argument,

Jeremiah highlights the obedience of Jaazaniah and his family to their principles. Their fidelity provides a glaring contrast to the infidelity of Judah. As in other parts of Jeremiah, the story seeks to make sense of the destruction of Jerusalem in a way that does not compromise the integrity of God.

As for the second matter, the Rechabite-Judean story is a lesson for those who could still shape their future. Specifically, it addresses the moral formation of refugees who had undergone enormous hardship and were facing the challenge of forging a new identity. In this capacity, the story is a study of cardinal virtues and vices; it attempts to inculcate certain ethical principles for the purpose of survival while discouraging other types of behavior as detrimental. The narrative makes the point that the most indispensable value for exiles is faithfulness/obedience to covenant law and prophetic utterance. Conversely, the conduct most destructive is insubordination to traditions that demand compassion toward those in greatest need. Of course, both points are essentially the same. To survive and flourish, God's people must be faithful and obedient to the Lord, and especially attentive to those who are most vulnerable to economic exploitation. To live this way is to renounce nationalistic arrangements of raw power and control. With biting irony, the case study contends that a fringe religious group, not Israel, embodies the cardinal virtues of faithfulness and obedience. Its unflagging loyalty to its founder's ideals not only exposes the failure of the people of God but also reveals the unwavering obedience that God desires.

Overall, Jer 34–35 is didactic in intent. The unit points out what went wrong in the past so it will never happen again. Perhaps the central moral claim of the text is that abuse and exploitation of the "nameless" will sink a nation. Jeremiah asserts that God sees and condemns acts of violence against those who have no voice. Such acts may seem economically expedient or entirely innocuous, but they are serious enough to attract God's attention. This conviction is clearly not unique to Jeremiah. It is in fact one of the principal beliefs of the scriptures. In order to be God's people, the community of faith must incarnate fidelity, justice, and compassion—the core attributes of Yahweh.

THE ENDURING WORD (JEREMIAH 36)

Jeremiah 36 tells the story of the rejection and triumph of the prophetic word. The wonderfully crafted narrative consists of three main parts. The first introduces the storyline and sets the stage for the action (36:1-8). At the command of Yahweh, Jeremiah dictates to his scribe Baruch a scroll of prophecies that he had spoken to Israel, Judah, and all the nations from the time of Josiah until the fourth year of Jehoiakim's reign (605). Afterward, Jeremiah instructs Baruch to read the scroll in the temple since he can no longer enter the Lord's house. In obedience, Baruch follows the directives of Jeremiah (36:8). The second part describes the action (36:9-26). In the winter of 604, Baruch reads the scroll publicly in the temple and then privately to a small group of state officials. Eventually, the scroll is read before Jehoiakim who cuts it into pieces and burns it. The final section departs from the king and his court to Jeremiah whom Yahweh commands to rewrite the oracles (36:27-32). With the aid of Baruch, the prophet creates another scroll that condemns the king and reiterates God's resolve to dismantle the kingdom. Despite Jehoiakim's attempt to thwart God's will, the word of God prevails.

Literary Analysis

Jeremiah 36 plays a strategic role in the organization of the book. This pivotal passage relates specifically to three other key texts: Jer 25, 26, and 45. Chapters 25 and 36 are complementary texts that refer to the same year (605). Both summarize oracles that Jeremiah had delivered from the period of Josiah until the fourth year of King Jehoiakim (25:3; 36:2). Accordingly, the chapters mark the end of the first stage of Jeremiah's prophetic career, a period in which repentance and submission to Babylon could still temper the oracles of judgment against Judah. Both texts now appeal to written prophecy to signal the end of that possibility (25:13; 36:1-3, 27-32).

Links between chapters 36 and 45 are no less important. Jeremiah 36 and Jer 45 create a literary frame around the so-called "Baruch Narrative." The chapters allude to the production of a scroll written by Baruch at the dictation of Jeremiah in 605 (36:2, 4; 45:1). This "scroll motif" reveals one of the collection's dominant themes: namely, the proclamation of the word of God, its rejection, and fulfillment in the history of Judah. Furthermore, the two chapters describe events related to the "fourth year of King Jehoiakim son of Josiah of Judah," the year in which Nebuchadrezzar became king of Babylon and overtook the Egyptian army at Carchemish (36:1, 45:1). It is as if the events of that year, that is, the accession of Nebuchadrezzar and Jehoiakim's contempt for the scroll, set in motion the tragic events narrated in chapters 37–44. Finally, Jer 36 and Jer 45 contrast Baruch's tortured though faithful response to the divine word with King Jehoiakim's hostile reaction to the word of God. Whereas the defiant king seals the fate of the nation—Yahweh resolves to destroy the "land" (36:29; 45:4)—the righteous suffering of Baruch (and Yahweh's ambivalent response to his complaint) leaves open-ended the possibility of hope and a new beginning, at least for a few (45:1-5).

Most clearly related are Jer 26 and Jer 36. These chapters function as bookends to Jer 27–35, a composite collection of poems and narratives. Lexical and thematic parallels between the two framing texts (chapters 26 and 36) are significant enough to be noted. First, the *superscriptions* of both chapters locate the stories in the time of Jehoiakim. The events in chapter 26 are said to take place "at the beginning of the reign of King Jehoiakim son of Josiah of Judah" (26:1), whereas those in chapter 36 in "fourth year of King Jehoiakim son of Josiah of Judah" (36:1). Within a brief period of four years, Jehoiakim's regime nails the coffin shut on the Judean nation.

Second, the temple provides the *geographical setting* for large segments of both chapters. In Jer 26, Yahweh instructs Jeremiah to "stand in the court of [Yahweh]'s house and speak to all the cities of Judah that come to worship in the house of [Yahweh]" (26:2). In Jer 36, four years later, Jeremiah is no longer permitted access to the temple (36:5) and must send Baruch to read the words of Yahweh from the scroll in Yahweh's house (36:6). The officials who hear the case against Jeremiah in chapter 26 assemble at "the entrance of the New Gate of Yahweh's house" (26:10), which is later the location for Baruch's first reading of the scroll (36:10).

Third, the *purpose* of Yahweh's word is to give the hearers/readers the opportunity for repentance and forgiveness. Yahweh fervently hopes that those who hear the message will "turn from their evil way(s)" so that the predicted disaster can be averted (26:3 and 36:3). In contrast to most other narratives in the second part of the book, the two framing texts declare that it is not too late to repent and avoid disaster. Nevertheless, most formulations of hope in the intermediate chapters take for granted that Babylon's assault is already underway.

Next, the "edifying prose stories" (Nicholson) reflect a *literary structure* encapsulated in 2 Kgs 17:13-18 and elsewhere in the book of Jeremiah. Yahweh warns Israel "by my servants the prophets" (26:4-5; 36:1-8); Israel rejects the message (26:5; 36:9-26); and Yahweh brings judgment upon Israel (26:6; 36:27-31).

Finally, the two narratives express the same *theme*: the mixed responses to the word of God by the Judean establishment. In chapter 26, priests, prophets, and officials attempt to sort out whether dissident words against the state are grounds for capital punishment. Their decision is inconclusive and their reaction to Jeremiah's message is mixed. In chapter 36, the reading of the prophetic scroll is equally perplexing, and the reaction by the government officials is likewise ambivalent. Not so with regard to Jehoiakim! The two framing texts paint this king in the worst possible light. In chapter 26, officials (?) tell the story of Uriah's execution at the demand of Jehoiakim (26:20-23). In chapter 36, Jehoiakim destroys the sacred scroll and seeks to arrest Baruch and Jeremiah (36:20-26). Despite attempts on his life, Jeremiah survives. A few supporters from the family of Shaphan rescue him and speak on his behalf (26:24; 36:25). Thus, while certain people attempt to silence Yahweh's prophet (26:11; 36:26), others are willing to listen and ultimately God's word triumphs (26:17-18; 36:27-32).

In sum, chapter 36 functions as a hinge/seam text that connects major sections of the book. It shares striking features with Jer 25 and so forms a bridge to the conclusion of the first half of Jeremiah. At the same time, it unites two divisions of the second half of the book. In conjunction with chapter 26, Jer 36 creates a frame around chapters 27–35, a diverse collection that dares to speak of hope after the announcement of dismantling in Jer 1–25. And with the support of chapter 45, it forms bookends that produce literary coherence for the Baruch Narrative.

Exegetical Analysis

The Stage Is Set for the Showdown (36:1-8)

Although Jer 36 may provide valuable insight into scroll production and events in the life of the prophet, its primary purpose is theological and not biographical. The chapter tells the gripping story of the word of the Lord, its dismissal by Jehoiakim, and its ultimate victory. Jeremiah 36:1-8 sets the tone for the story. The word of the Lord comes to Jeremiah during "the fourth year of Jehoiakim," a time of enormous turmoil and political uncertainty. Nebuchadrezzar has just defeated Neco of Egypt and become king of Babylon. His emergence as a world leader holds portentous implications for Judah, for soon the monarch from the east will invade and pillage the land. The "enemy from the north" is poised to descend upon Jerusalem and dash all hope for security and independence.

To heighten the tension, there are conflicts within. Jeremiah and the leadership of Judah are still at odds. For some time, large cross sections of the nation have branded Jeremiah a traitor deserving of death (26:8-9). In a further attempt to bar him from public speech, religious authorities now ban him from the temple. With these events in view, Yahweh instructs Jeremiah to write on a scroll the oracles he has received since the time of Josiah. There is still a slim chance that when the people of Judah hear the threats in the scroll, they will repent and escape divine judgment (36:3, 7). The "word of the LORD" is the last great hope for restoration and forgiveness. Consequently, Jeremiah commissions Baruch to record the prophecies on a scroll and proclaim them on a solemn day of fasting in the temple.

A Powerful King Versus a "Weak" Scroll (36:9-26)

In the ninth month of the fifth year of King Jehoiakim's reign, about a year later, during a solemn assembly, Baruch reads the scroll before the people of Judah as they gather for worship (36:9-10). The reading of the word is a dangerous and compelling act. It subverts, unsettles, and triggers a flurry of activity that culminates in a confrontation with the king. First, Micaiah overhears the words of the scroll and scurries out of the chamber of Gemariah for the palace. He enters the secretary's office and relates to the officials gathered there all that he has heard. The princes then dispatch the court officer Jehudi to find Baruch and bring him to the chamber (36:14). With scroll in hand, Baruch acquiesces and reads the scroll privately before the temple personnel and government officials. Upon hearing it, they turn to one another in fear. All agree: the scroll demands the attention of the king. Indeed, the king must hear. However, before he does, more facts are needed. Recognizing Baruch's ancillary role, the officials demand to know the author of the scroll (36:17). When Baruch discloses that he had written at Jeremiah's dictation, the princes encourage him and the prophet to go into hiding.

The motives and loyalties of the officials are far from clear, at least at this point in the story. Are they sympathetic to Jeremiah and Baruch or to their king? Is their response of "fear" due to reverence or alarm? When they encourage the prophet and his scribe to hide, do they act in self-interest or out of genuine concern for them? What compels them to notify Jehoiakim of the reading of the scroll? The answers to these questions are difficult to determine because the text is concerned primarily with action rather than motive. Moreover, the story is about the "scroll" and its enormous capacity to reorder reality and defy conventional power structures. The potent word, not the princes, generates the events that culminate in the king's court. It is noteworthy, however, that several officials mentioned in Jer 36:10–19, 25 are members of a family that on an earlier occasion had brought a scroll before another Judean king (2 Kgs 22–23). In 622, Shaphan, the grandfather of Micaiah and father of Gemariah, took the "book of the law" discovered during the renovation of the temple to King

Josiah. Now Gemariah, the son of Shaphan, finds himself before Jehoiakim, Josiah's son, urging the king not to destroy a scroll. Echoes from the past clearly inform the ethos of this text. The interpretive community of Jeremiah has a high opinion of this particular family.

When word reaches the king, Jehoiakim dispatches Jehudi to Elishama's chamber (36:20-26). Jehudi retrieves the scroll and recites it before the king who is residing in the winter quarters of the palace. One cannot study this vignette in its Hebrew original without being struck by its many wordplays. As Jehudi "reads" *(qr³)* the scroll, Jehoiakim takes a "scribal knife," which is ordinarily used to cut papyrus in the preparation of scrolls, and methodically "cuts" *(qr^c)* it up and burns it (36:23). The two Hebrew words, to "read" and to "cut," are spelled differently but sound the same. At such a brazen act, the narrator must speak: "neither the king, nor any of his servants who heard all these words, was *alarmed [phd]*, nor did they *tear [qr^c]* their garments" (36:24, emphasis mine). Unlike the princes who had turned "to one another in *alarm*" *(phd;* 36:16), Jehoiakim and his men "[do] not *fear*" *(phd;* 36:24 emphasis mine). Moreover, unlike his father Josiah who "*tore [qr^c]* his garments" when hearing the words of the book of the law (2 Kgs 22:11), Jehoiakim does not "*tear [qr^c]* his garments (emphasis mine)." Instead, he "*tears*" or "*cuts*" *[qr^c]* the scroll. Even after the urging of several advisers, the king is adamant: the scroll must go! Not only the scroll, but Jeremiah and Baruch must also depart from the king's presence. All three— Jeremiah, Baruch, and the scroll—are far too dangerous and pose too great a threat to royal authority. Jehoiakim, therefore, sends his hirelings to arrest the troublemakers, but Yahweh intervenes and frustrates their efforts (36:26).

The King's Victory Frustrated (36:27-32)

The victory of Jehoiakim is short-lived. Though the burning of the scroll represents a frightening show of political muscle, it does nothing to deter Yahweh from acting against the king and the city. After the king's theatrics, Yahweh instructs Jeremiah to produce a second scroll that is to comprise the contents of the first as well as additional words. Included in the scroll is a condemnation of Jehoiakim. The king's abhorrence for the word of God through Jeremiah results in judgment on the king as well as the nation. Jehoiakim will come to a dishonorable end without an heir on the throne of David (cf. 2 Kgs 24:6; 2 Chr 36:5-8), and the people of Judah will suffer inescapable harm (36:31). The implications are clear: the destiny of the nation is now sealed. The initial invitation to "hear" and "turn" and so avoid disaster is rejected. Jehoiakim's recalcitrant response to God's message sets in motion an avalanche of devastating consequences for the Judean people, as will be fully evident in the following chapters (Jer 37–45).

Theological and Ethical Analysis

The entire chapter culminates in a conflict between a king and a scroll. That the two eventually face off in a confrontation is the aim of the story all along. But the encounter hardly seems fair. A king and a meager scroll? At Jehoiakim's disposal is the power of the throne and armies of the kingdom. He wields unlimited political clout and a staunch determination to silence all opposing voices. Also in his grasp are a knife and a fireplace that he uses to destroy scrolls. Clearly, the king is in charge, or is he? What looks like an effortless victory takes a strange turn. In a grand reversal, a powerless piece of papyrus defeats the king and his entourage. Though the scroll goes up in flames, a second stands in its place with new force and range. And if necessary, God can generate as many scrolls as it takes to subdue insolent kings (Brueggemann 1998, 352-53). The word of God, and the dangerous presence behind the scroll, therefore, triumphs over raw human power. All forms of authority, including that of kings, must now take a backseat. Chapter 36 thus makes a faith-filled claim that the word will accomplish all that God intends (cf. Isa 55:10-13), and that God, not human cunning or royal power, is in charge of the destinies of nations.

When Jeremiah's oracles are committed to writing, a transformation occurs, which involves far more than a change in methods of communication. Scroll production in Jer 36 represents an early stage in the development of the scriptures. Although commentators disagree over the nature and content of the scroll, most agree that the account helps us understand the origins of the canonical book, even if by anecdote. Written prophecy also takes on a life of its own. Unlike people, scrolls have few physical constraints. They can be read where prophets are banned, and they are capable of influencing communities far beyond the lifetime of any one person. Furthermore, the written word displaces the prophet as a primary source of authority in the community. Jeremiah withdraws while the scroll breaks in to counter and critique. Earlier in the book, officials cite a written oracle of Micah to judge and ultimately support the legitimacy of Jeremiah's spoken words (26:16-18). A scroll authorizes the destruction of the nation and its king (36:27-31; cf. 25:13-14) as well as its new beginnings after the devastation of exile (30:2). It even predicts and symbolizes the fall of Babylon (51:59-63). The scroll wields the power to judge every social institution and theological claim. Indeed, no ideology or power structure is exempt from its scrutiny. Last, the written word fills the gap created by the toppling of Judah's world. When other tangible signs of God's presence have fallen, including king and palace, priest and temple, land, and even prophet, the scroll survives and testifies to newness in broken lives and communities. "The Temple may be destroyed; the texts which it housed sing in the winds that scatter them" (Steiner 1985, 21). Jeremiah asserts that the written word—the prophetic scroll—is a living, enduring, and trustworthy testimony of God. This word, and the God whose identity it renders, will not be silent. The word of God stands forever (Isa 40:8*b*).

THE BARUCH NARRATIVE (JEREMIAH 37–44)

Commentators generally refer to the next major division of the book as the "Baruch Narrative" (Jer 37–44). That Baruch, Jeremiah's scribe, actually penned any of this prose work is purely speculative. The narrative's bookends, Jer 36 and 45, create the impression that the intermediate chapters constitute the scroll that Baruch wrote at Jeremiah's dictation (36:4, 32; 45:1). This claim, however, has little historical force since the production of the

Baruch's scroll in the "fourth year of King Jehoiakim" (605) predates the events narrated in chapters 37–44 by at least seventeen years (45:1). The anachronism reveals a variety of theological and literary interests, including the role of scribal circles in the preservation of written prophecy. Thus, the question of authorship here is as elusive as it is for the rest of the book.

With the exception of its literary borders, Jer 36 and 45, most episodes in the chapters 37–44 unfold in chronological order covering the siege of Jerusalem to the emigration of a group of Judeans to Egypt after the murder of Gedaliah. Jeremiah 37:1–38:28 narrates the plight of Jeremiah and King Zedekiah during the last days of Jerusalem. As the city comes under attack, a desperate king appeals to Jeremiah for guidance but tragically cannot muster the faith to accept it. Independent of the king, state officials seize and arrest Jeremiah because of his subversive rhetoric. Jeremiah 39:1–40:6 relates the story of the fall of Jerusalem, Jeremiah's oracles of deliverance for Ebed-melech, and the prophet's favorable treatment by the Babylonian military. In Jer 40:7–41:18 Judeans kill Judeans. After a momentary lull under Gedaliah, Ishmael assassinates the Babylonian appointee. The brutality catapults the country into a fierce civil war. Now there are coups and conspiracies, as well as a conspicuous absence of God and God's word. That is, this section mentions neither God nor Jeremiah. In the next two chapters, patriots of Johanan head off to Egypt against the counsel of Jeremiah (42:1–43:13). Such a deliberate rejection of God's word and the audacity to force the prophet to go with them leave little doubt of their guilt. In a fashion similar to speeches in Deuteronomy– 2 Kings, Jer 44:1-14 is an address that recalls the many failures of the nation. Yahweh has given numerous opportunities to "turn" from wickedness, but the people consistently refuse to do so. The chapter construes the entire history of the people of God as one of idolatry and wanton disobedience, leading to the dire events that befell Judah and Jerusalem. The final scene in chapter 44 depicts an idolatrous community paying homage to "the queen of heaven." Nothing more could condemn to death the Diaspora in Egypt.

COMMENTARY

The Baruch Narrative does more than preserve circumstantial details of the final years of the kingdom of Judah or render a biographical account of the harsh conditions that Jeremiah endured during these treacherous times. It represents the culmination and fulfillment of the written oracles of Jeremiah, especially those located in Jer 1–25. Predictions of "plucking up and pulling down, destroying and overthrowing" are now in progress. The text recounts the dismantling of Judah's world. A country falls. Its fortified palaces crumble. Its symbols disappoint. Its kings perish. Its understandings of reality break down. The whole matrix of assumptions and social structures tied to the nation collapse. Regardless of dissenting assertions and outright denials, the narrative corroborates the truth of Jeremiah's message (e.g., 37:19). As fulfilled prophecy, it demonstrates that the end of the kingdom of Judah does not lie outside the realm of God's control. God is still at work ordering human affairs, in, through, and in spite of the unthinkable events.

The Baruch Narrative not only speaks of God's acts of judgment but also of God's acts of salvation. As darkness descends upon the nation, shafts of light and hope appear. The hope that Jeremiah maintains, however, is far different from that entertained by Zedekiah and the military. The Jerusalem establishment remains optimistic that the nation will survive the Babylonian threat intact to enjoy an uninterrupted future in the land. (The sudden death of Gedaliah shatters that confidence one for all.) By contrast, Jeremiah asserts that the king and the capital city will survive only if the nation surrenders its old modes of reality, and specifically that it relinquishes control and submits to Babylon. When the leadership of the nation rejects this challenge, Jeremiah insists that hope for the future of God's people lies with the exiles residing in Babylon, not with those who remain in the land or migrate south to Egypt (40:7–44:30).

This text also conveys a sense of hope in the survival of Jeremiah and Baruch, who, like Joshua and Caleb of old, represent a new beginning for a beleaguered community. Ebed-melech, the Ethiopian official, rescues Jeremiah from the pit. Nebuzaradan releases Jeremiah from his chains and offers him the choice to reside in Babylon or in Judah. At the end of the story, God gives Baruch his life "as a prize of war" (45:5), and Jeremiah ultimately withstands the harsh and unjustified treatment of his countrymen. These few signs of salvation are indications of life beyond the plucking up and pulling down. Neither mega-events of geopolitics nor the self-serving and vindictive actions of kings and princes can ultimately squelch God's purposes.

These claims are intended to help the exiles in Babylon make sense of the tremendous upheaval in their lives. Their new situation required the *re-valuation of everything*. The Baruch Narrative is in part a response to this situation. While it does not provide a full charter for the new Israel, the narrative defends God's justice, argues for Judah's responsibility in the events, and asserts that the end of the nation is not the end of the line for people of God. The tragedy of 587 is a chrysalis: the community must hereafter abandon its defining characteristics for a new identity yet to be revealed.

JEREMIAH IMPRISONED AND RELEASED
(JEREMIAH 37:1–38:28)

Literary Analysis

Chapters 37–38 comprise the initial episode of the Baruch Narrative. The two chapters relate events that take place during the final months of Judah, immediately before Nebuchadrezzar captures Jerusalem. The setting is fraught with great uncertainty. On one hand, the nation enjoys a brief respite from the Babylonian offensive. The approach of the Egyptian military (in the summer of 588) creates a strange calm before the storm. Jeremiah moves among the people without restraints, and the king and state officials entertain hopes for peace in the land. On the other hand, fear dominates each scene. What will come next? Will the Egyptian military stave off the Babylonian armies? Paralyzed by his own failure of nerve, Zedekiah watches anxiously as the kingdom slips through his fingers. Jeremiah himself will soon face a new level of opposition from the Judean authorities. During this tense and unpredictable time, the prophet and king find their destinies curiously intertwined. A weak and vacillating Zedekiah repeatedly implores Jeremiah for counsel and divine intercession, and an embattled prophet begs the king for mercy and protection. The main protagonists in the conflict, the real power brokers, are apparently state officials who lash out against Jeremiah in an attempt to silence him. Their efforts ultimately fail because of the intervention of Ebed-melech, an Ethiopian court official, who appears out of nowhere to rescue Jeremiah. While still under house arrest, Jeremiah reiterates the word of the Lord: surrender to the Babylonians and live. Zedekiah refuses to heed, even though the demand for submission is offered with assurances of well-being. This is no surprise. From the outset the narrator prepares us that neither king nor his "servants nor the people of the land listened to the words of the LORD that he spoke through the prophet Jeremiah" (37:2). The balance of the story merely bears out that defiant position.

Following an editorial transition (37:1-2), the material in these chapters divides into several sections: an appeal of Zedekiah to Jeremiah and the prophetic reply (37:3-10); the seizure and imprisonment of Jeremiah (37:11-16); a second appeal of Zedekiah to Jeremiah and the prophetic reply (37:17-21); the seizure and imprisonment of Jeremiah (38:1-6); Ebed-melech's heroic rescue of Jeremiah (38:7-13); and a third appeal of Zedekiah to Jeremiah and the prophetic reply (38:14-28). Chapters 37 and 38 are curiously similar. Each chapter has scenes in which Zedekiah consults with Jeremiah regarding the word of the Lord and in which state officials arrest the prophet on suspicion of pro-Babylonian activities. In each chapter, moreover, Jeremiah delivers oracles that herald the certain victory of Babylon and demand unconditional surrender to Babylon before state officials throw the prophet into a cistern. These and other parallels indicate that the chapters may be different accounts of the same events, not unlike the temple sermons in Jer 7 and 26. Notwithstanding the growth and development of these passages, the chapters appear as a unified story, which employs redundancy to create an acute sense of danger. The multiple rejections of God's word and repeated attacks on Jeremiah's life drive home the dour reality that the nation has reached a point of no return.

Exegetical Analysis

A Last-Minute Plea (37:1-10)

The opening words of chapter 37 reveal that something is terribly wrong (37:1-2). First, they move rapidly past the reign of Jehoiakim, whose contempt for Yahweh triggered alarming events, and the three-month reign of Jehoiachin, to Zedekiah, whom Nebuchadrezzar appointed king of Judah. Judah is no longer able to choose its own kings! Next, they report that this puppet ruler is no better than Jehoiakim. Neither he nor his cabinet "listened to the words of the LORD that he spoke through the prophet Jeremiah" (37:2). The familiar verb "listen" conveys the sense of being totally answerable and intensely loyal to another no matter the cost. It involves relinquishing the illusion of self-sufficiency for trusting obedience. By "not listening," Zedekiah refuses to give up his own agendas and submit to God.

Despite this blanket dismissal, Zedekiah approaches Jeremiah for help. When the heat is on, Zedekiah, like the pharaoh in the book of Exodus, asks for prayer (see Exod 8:8; 9:27-28 though a different Hebrew word is used). "Please pray for us to the LORD our God" (37:3). Zedekiah apparently thinks he can still broker a deal to save Jerusalem and himself. There is some basis for his optimism. As we have seen, pleas for help reverse bad fortune (Gen 25:21), turn back armies (2 Kgs 19:1-13) and even impinge on God's resolve to destroy (Exod 32:11-14). Additionally, the Egyptian advance toward Jerusalem and the subsequent withdrawal of Babylonian troops spurred hopes for a lasting peace (Jer 37:5). However, Zedekiah runs into a roadblock when Jeremiah, the truth-teller, the troublemaker, the spokesperson for Yahweh, shatters his wishful thinking. According to the word of the Lord, Babylon represents a stark reality that will simply not go away. To suppose that all will go well for Judah and Zedekiah is a terrible miscalculation. That is the message that the envoys must take back to the king. Regardless of encouraging political-military reports, the fall of Jerusalem is certain. No deals can be brokered.

Jeremiah Accused of Treason (37:11-16)

During this quiet period, Jeremiah leaves Jerusalem for the land of Benjamin where he plans to attend to family matters, perhaps involving the acquisition of land from his cousin Hanamel (cf. 32:6-15). When Jeremiah approaches the Benjamin Gate, Irijah the officer of the guard seizes the prophet and takes him into custody. The sentinel announces the charge, "You are [defecting] to the Chaldeans" (37:13). Jeremiah categorically denies the allegation, but as has been the case with others, Irijah "would not listen to him." The sentry brings Jeremiah before state officials in Jerusalem who beat him and throw him into a cistern. Certain of his guilt, they want him dead.

The assault on Jeremiah's life is no reckless undertaking by vigilantes, but a calculated response of the state to alleged sedition. The Jerusalem establishment considers Jeremiah a Babylonian sympathizer, a subversive who has aided and abetted the enemy. At such a volatile time, the guardians of the state can no longer tolerate his "unpatriotic activities." His relentless attacks on their vested interests must end. Decisive action must be taken against him. Interestingly, no one entertains the possibility that Jeremiah's harrowing words may in fact be true, except an ambivalent king and exilic readers who must deal with the reality of a fallen world.

A Clandestine Meeting (37:17-21)

The relationship between Jeremiah and Zedekiah again takes center stage. Tossed and torn by events over which he has little control, the king *needs* a good word, and so he brings Jeremiah from the pit to the palace for a clandestine meeting. Zedekiah apparently realizes that despite Jeremiah's imprisonment, the word of God is not shackled. In desperation, Zedekiah begs the prophet, "Is there any word from the LORD?" Like despondent Esau who entreats his father, "Is there yet a blessing for me?"

(Gen 27:38), Zedekiah yearns for a favorable oracle. Again, he does so in vain. Jeremiah replies cynically, "There is! . . . You shall be handed over to the king of Babylon" (37:17). The prophet does not flinch. Vintage Jeremiah! Yet, the prophet uses the occasion to plead for relief from confinement in the dungeons. In his own defense, he maintains that he has done harm to no one, and, in contrast to other prophets ("your prophets"), has spoken truthfully about the Babylonian incursion (see Deut 18:22). Surprisingly, Zedekiah "listens" to Jeremiah's protest and gives orders to move him to a less objectionable prison. In an unexpected act of kindness, Zedekiah sees to it that Jeremiah receives daily food rations "from the bakers' street" during the siege of the city.

Surrender to Babylon and Live (38:1-6)

While confined in the court of the guard, Jeremiah is back at it, hammering away at the same message: Babylon's victory is as sure as Jerusalem's defeat. Judah's only hope for survival is to surrender to the Babylonians and abandon Jerusalem for the land of their captors. In yielding control of their lives and letting go of their dreams and ambitions, the people of Judah will live. In relinquishing confidence in the old world and its support systems, the people will discover newness. When the government officials "hear" Jeremiah's disconcerting though familiar words, they act in haste to arrest and sentence him. The prophet is undermining the war effort and deserves to die (38:4; cf. 26:8). The judgment against Jeremiah is harsh and unambiguous. The officials are absolutely convinced that Jeremiah is the worst sort of public offender, one who endangers the welfare of the state during a time of extreme vulnerability. Although sympathetic to Jeremiah, Zedekiah can no longer protect him. He is "powerless" against the princes. Clearly, the king has lost control of the kingdom, if it were ever in his grasp. Rivaling factions in the government present a clear and present danger both to the Babylonian pawn and the prophet of Yahweh. Now nothing can prevent the princes from throwing Jeremiah into a muddy cistern to die.

Ebed-melech Comes to Jeremiah's Aid (38:7-13)

Enter Ebed-melech, an Ethiopian court official, whose name means "servant of the king." His abrupt and unexpected appearance creates a measure of opacity and indeterminacy. Who is this non-Israelite in the king's service and whom does he really serve? From what standpoint are we to view his action in the story? Does the narrator intend us to see God's providential hand in his courageous acts? That is, is God working behind the scenes in and through Ebed-melech, or is the situation that the text presents to us entirely ordinary? Does the kind treatment of Jeremiah by an outsider serve as a foil to the ruthless actions of Judean officials (cf. Exod 18:10-12; 2 Sam 11:6-13; Luke 10:25-37)? The scene's reticence is evocative and suggests that the storyteller has more than historical interests in mind.

When Ebed-melech "hears" of Jeremiah's plight, he rushes to his defense. The African court official leaves the palace for the Benjamin Gate where "the king happened to be sitting." The city gate is customarily the place where kings or community elders settle legal matters (see, e.g., Ruth 4:1, 11; 2 Sam 15:2; Isa 29:21; Amos 5:10, 12, 15). At this city tribunal, Ebed-melech protests that a serious injustice has been committed. Before the king, and perhaps in the presence of Jeremiah's assailants (note the demonstrative pronoun "these" men in 38:9), he contends that the princes have acted wickedly when throwing Jeremiah into the cistern to die (38:9). Whether his dispute is ethical or legal in nature is unclear. Perhaps the distinction itself is a foreign one. In any case, the appeal is certainly courageous and humanitarian. Ebed-melech risks the king's wrath and the princes' ill will by speaking out for the welfare of the prophet. Zedekiah responds favorably to Ebed-melech's plea. Although he had cowered before the royal officials during Jeremiah's sentencing, the king now publicly authorizes his rescue, which Ebed-melech carries out with extraordinary care. As at other times in the book, a few faithful individuals come to Jeremiah's aid and thwart the evil intent of others. The faith of a few keeps the message and messenger alive. It is not difficult to hear echoes of God's assurance to Jeremiah given in the call narrative, "Do not be afraid of them, for I am with you to deliver you" (1:8).

Another Attempt to Straitjacket Jeremiah (38:14-28)

While Jeremiah is still under house arrest, Zedekiah once more demands a private consultation. This will be their final meeting before the city falls into the hands of the Babylonians (Jer 39). The king summons the prophet to an entrance of the temple where he subtly asks for divine guidance. By this point, Jeremiah realizes that the encounter may place his life at great risk. First of all, the interaction is clearly between unequal parties. Jeremiah is a prisoner while the king wields the power of life and death. Furthermore, Zedekiah is a fickle player. There is no way of knowing what he will do. In previous encounters, Jeremiah has found himself on both ends of the king's unpredictable rulings. In addition, the prophetic response to the request will certainly disappoint Zedekiah since Jeremiah cannot give blanket guarantees that all will be well.

Zedekiah tries to assuage Jeremiah's concerns by taking an oath in Yahweh's name that he will neither put him to death nor deliver him into the hands of his enemies. With these assurances Jeremiah repeats his counsel: surrender to Babylon and live, otherwise the city and its king will face irreversible repercussions. Jeremiah again places before the king the way of life and the way of death (cf. Jer 21:8-10; Deut 11:26; 30:15, 19). Remarkably, there is still time to choose. Even after all that has been said and done, Zedekiah can still save the city and himself. The choice, however, is demanding, especially for a flawed king who confesses to Jeremiah, "I am afraid of the Judeans who have deserted to the Chaldeans, for I might be handed over to them and they would abuse me" (38:19). That is Zedekiah's decision. Even so, Jeremiah does not write off the king entirely, but offers him, albeit with a proviso, what he so desperately craves: safety and protection. If Zedekiah trusts and obeys the Lord, it shall go well with him and his life shall be spared (38:20). God's mercy is available to the very end. However, judgment also looms large and the cost of disobedience is huge. If he does not surrender, both he and the royal family will face disaster. Zedekiah comes out of the meeting no less conflicted (38:24-28). Still paralyzed by his fear and self-interest, he swears Jeremiah to secrecy. Under penalty of death, the prophet must reveal nothing of their exchange to the royal officials.

What a strange and unpredictable character is Zedekiah. He has neither the evil resolve of the royal officials nor the courage of Ebed-melech. He is not as sinister as Jehoiakim or as principled as Josiah. Zedekiah is betwixt and between worlds, capable of both cowardice and acts of honor. In literary terms, Zedekiah is a "round" character; that is, he is lifelike and multidimensional. At one moment he is prepared to deliver Jeremiah from death and in the next is powerless to prevent attempts on the prophet's life. He is willing to seek out Jeremiah for the word of the Lord but unwilling to obey it. The king seems poised to submit to the prophet's demanding message, but is ultimately incapable of doing so. In the final analysis, Zedekiah lacks the moral courage or political prowess to deliver Judah during its darkest hour. The last king of Judah proves to be a tragic figure: cautious, inept, and compromised. His ambivalence is the ultimate complicity. Nonetheless, the text refuses to demonize him and make him into a scapegoat for all the nation's ills.

Theological and Ethical Analysis

As part of the Baruch Narrative, chapters 37–38 reflect a very distinctive view of life. Judah's circumstances occur because of God's sovereign plan *and* particular human choices. This dual affirmation may appear incongruous but the text refuses to privilege one over the other. It will not pigeonhole God into clear-cut, unambiguous and logical categories. Human history is an amalgam of human and divine workings. On the one hand, the narrative supposes that nothing occurs outside the span of God's will. Babylon and the havoc it brings upon Judah are part of the divine plan, which involves the destruction of nations and kingdoms (cf. 1:10). From the start of the book, Jeremiah anticipates a northern foe that will disrupt and dismantle the Judean nation and its entrenched world. Subsequent texts identify the unnamed enemy as Babylon. Now the upheaval begins, not by accident but by design. No matter how much Zedekiah and other members of the Jerusalem establishment would wish it otherwise, the Babylonian incursion is part of God's sovereign purposes. That the king of Babylon will enter and conquer the city is a reality with which Judah must come to grips. The die is cast, God's judgment is firm, and Judah cannot circumvent the divine will (see, e.g., 37:6-10, 17; 38:1-3). For the exilic audience, such affirmations underscore the divine role in the national tragedy. The losses are not the product of mere geopolitical forces or the impotency of Israel's God; they are rooted in God's long-term intention for the world. Consequently, the exiles must submit to God's will, abandon their hopes for the restoration of the old order, and look for the gift of life in new arenas.

At the same time that the text heralds the power and purposes of God, it leaves little room for dogged determinism. The narrative takes great pains to affirm the openness of God to human options. History is not a closed system in which divinity precludes human choices. The unfolding events in the life of the community are not the consequence of divine whims imposed upon a feeble people. As Clements states, people are "real participants in human history and . . . help to create this history for good or ill" (1988, 223). Even in its final moments, when all seems set in stone, the text imagines that it is not too late for Judah to act. To the very end, it is possible to stem the tide of divine judgment. Life and death remain in the grasp of Judah, or at least its leadership. Human options are real and efficacious.

Human freedom holds enormous repercussions. The text makes it clear that Judah has squandered its many opportunities and is accountable to God for its actions. Jeremiah invites the people to "listen" *(šema')*, but without success. Neither Zedekiah "nor his servants nor the people of the land listened to the words of the LORD" (37:2). When arresting Jeremiah, Irijah will "not listen" to the prophet's defense (37:14). Zedekiah refuses to "listen" to Jeremiah's challenge to surrender to Babylon. Regardless of assurances of safety, the king still fears for his life and will not "[listen to] the voice of the LORD" (38:20). When officials seize Jeremiah and subject him to beatings and abuse, they act with ill intent and so condemn themselves. With each bad decision the nation digs a deeper hole for itself. Highlighting Judah's missed opportunities, an African outsider (Ebed-melech) acts with great courage to save Jeremiah. Judah's poor choices, its determination not to listen, as well as the contrasting deeds of Ebed-melech provide further proof of the nation's culpability. The text is unyielding that Judah must accept a large measure of responsibility for its present circumstances.

Regardless of bad choices already made, the prophetic option of obeying Yahweh and submitting to Babylonian rule still pertains to the listening community residing in Babylon, whose gatherings developed into the first Jewish synagogues. The word rejected by the first generation still applies to the next. The exiles could either submit to the rule of their host community and survive or rebel against Babylonian rule and face severe consequences (cf. 29:1-9). To a large extent the future of the exiles in Babylon also lies in their own hands.

The material in Jer 37–38 also focuses on Jeremiah's suffering. The story of the prophet's cruel treatment at the hands of state officials is part of a rich tradition in the Bible that reminds us that the faithful at times endure great hardship for no fault of their own. We witness such suffering in the murder of Abel (Gen 4) and the contempt of Hagar (Gen 16), in the slavery of the Hebrew people and the laments of the Psalter, in the innocence of Job and the mission of the Servant of the Lord (Isa 52:13–53:12), and most poignantly for Christians in the death of Jesus of Nazareth. Jeremiah clearly stands among this cloud of witnesses. Commentators often describe his story as a passion narrative or a *"via dolorosa."* He is falsely accused, scorned, beaten, imprisoned, ignored, and eventually taken against his will to Egypt. All the while, his physical abuse and mental anguish grow out of undying faithfulness to God. That is to say, Jeremiah suffers because of his call and commitment to the Lord.

The prophet's hardships, however, involve more than innocent suffering or suffering for God's sake. In the suffering of Jeremiah we see the suffering and rejection of God. Von Rad suggests that "here a human being has in a unique fashion borne a part in the divine suffering" (1965, 208). Once again the text depicts Jeremiah as a larger-than-life figure who reveals that God is involved in human suffering in ways that are far more complex than merely punitive.

One final theological observation is worth noting. The story of Jeremiah's deliverance has much in common with dozens of laments and thanksgiving songs in the Psalter. Indeed, the Jeremiah vignette could serve as literary background to these psalms. There are several explanations for the good fit. The most obvious has to do with shared images. References to the "cistern" or "pit" are well-known in the Psalms where the term typically represents trouble and distress. "I am counted among those who go down to the *pit*; I am like those who have no help" (Ps 88:4). "To you, O LORD, I call; my rock, do not refuse to hear me, for if you are silent to me, I shall be like those who go down to the *pit*" (Ps 28:1). Second, the story in Jeremiah and the complaint (and thanksgiving) psalms reflect a world in which the faithful lack insulation from adversaries and where life is unstable and fraught with enormous danger. The petitioner "languishes near death" in a pit because of the "fury and lies of his enemies." "Ruthless men rise against him" and "batter their victim"; dread enemies "scheme and ambush the blameless." Like Jeremiah, the individuals who uttered such words live in a hostile world, vulnerable and at risk to forces beyond their control. Finally, the unpretentious narrative of Jeremiah's rescue reflects archetypal plot motifs of deliverance. Indeed, the story is a microcosm of Israel's story of salvation that the Psalms so often celebrate: when facing insurmountable obstacles, God comes to the aid of people in need. After "sink[ing] in the deep mire where there is no foothold" (Ps 69:2), help unexpectedly arrives. "From the . . . *pit*, out of the miry bog and set . . . upon a rock," Yahweh rescues the supplicant. "O LORD, you brought up my soul from Sheol, restored me to life from among those gone down to the *pit*" (Ps 30:2). The convergence of story in Jeremiah and liturgy in the Psalms creates a rich and fascinating interplay that elicits further reflection.

THE FALL OF JERUSALEM (JEREMIAH 39:1–40:6)

Literary Analysis

The prose account of the fall of Jerusalem and its repercussions for Zedekiah, Jeremiah, and Ebed-melech constitutes the next major section of the Baruch Narrative. Now that Zedekiah and the royal officials have wasted their final chance to avoid disaster (37:1–38:28), the dreaded devastation begins. Babylonian forces enter the city, demolish its structures, and capture the king. The occupation of the city ends a long-standing way of life, especially for the powerful establishment and privileged citizenry. Shortly after the description of city's defeat, the text moves almost effortlessly to overtures of salvation. Speaking on behalf of the king of Babylon, Nebuzaradan, the captain of the guard, makes provisions for Jeremiah. The prophet is entrusted to the safekeeping of Gedaliah, the newly appointed governor of the towns of Judah. And, Yahweh instructs Jeremiah to assure Ebed-melech that he too will survive the invasion. The Ethiopian court official's courage will not be overlooked. Thus, even as the long-predicted disaster materializes, the story cannot resist speaking of hope. In one breath, it tells the brutal truth about losses that defy ordinary categories while planting the seeds of hope for a faithful few.

The material in this section breaks down into four parts: the fall of Jerusalem and the capture of its king (39:1-10), the benevolent treatment of Jeremiah by the Babylonians after the sack of the city (39:11-14), God's promise to save Ebed-melech (39:15-18), and Jeremiah's eventual release by the Babylonians (40:1-6).

Exegetical Analysis

The Fall of Jerusalem (39:1-10)

Jeremiah 39:1-10 contains only minor variations of the same narrative in Jer 52:4-16 and 2 Kgs 25:1-12. The text is a report of the fall of Jerusalem in the year 587. The narrator relates events in a rather detached and dispassionate manner. One finds little commentary or motive. Nor does the narrator allow dialogue or direct divine intervention. The story proceeds by geopolitical logic. Following a lengthy siege, Babylonian troops breach the walls of Jerusalem. To display their spoils and authority over the city, chief officials take seats in the "middle gate." Identifying the commanders by name only underscores their control. Jerusalem is theirs. The old regime can do little except take flight. Zedekiah attempts to escape by night toward the Jordan Valley in the direction of Jericho (39:4). The Babylonian army pursues, captures the king, and takes him to Nebuchadrezzar's headquarters in northern Syria where Zedekiah witnesses the execution of his sons and nobles. Afterward, his captors torment him. Blinded and in chains, the Judean king is taken to Babylon. Even though earlier prophecies had warned of Zedekiah's fate, the text refuses to implicate Yahweh in the brutality of king's captors. Zedekiah's own insubordination to Babylon has brought about his horrible demise.

After disposing of the Davidic ruler, the Babylonians are ready to raze the city. They target the royal palace, burn houses, and level the city walls. Interestingly, Jer 39:8 does not mention the destruction of the house of the Lord (cf. 52:13). It may be that the intent of the invasion as described here is primarily the overthrow of the Davidic house. Nebuzaradan then deports both Judean defectors and loyalists to Babylon. Not all, however, are carried away. The Babylonian commander leaves some of the poor in the land of Judah to care for "vineyards and fields." Although the act apparently is done for economic expediency, the benevolence shown is noteworthy. Whereas the Jerusalem regime had trampled on the poor and exploited their subjects (see, e.g., 34:8-22), Nebuzaradan, a Babylonian military official, relieves the plight of those "who owned nothing." He gives them land and thus a position of honor. The fall of the state involves massive social transformation: the powerful and privileged leave the city with nothing, as the poor and needy receive their land as spoil. Evidently, the presence of foreigners on Judean soil is a sign of the end of one way of life, not the end of life itself.

Jeremiah's Release from Prison (39:11–40:6)

The next three scenes (39:11-14, 15-18; 40:1-6) are problematic because they are disjointed and out of chronological order. We have two complementary versions of Jeremiah's release from prison after the defeat of Jerusalem (39:11-14 and 40:1-6). Located between them is a promise of salvation for Ebed-melech that Jeremiah delivers before the city falls and while he is still confined in the court of the guard (39:15-18). Various attempts have been made to harmonize the three texts. Some read the oracle pertaining to Ebed-melech with the earlier account of the court official's valiant rescue of Jeremiah (38:7-13) or as an addendum to chapter 38. Connecting the texts in this way creates some semblance of thematic and chronological coherence. Commentators often interpret the two stories of Jeremiah's release as distinct events. The first, it is argued, occurred immediately after Jerusalem falls, when Nebuzaradan released Jeremiah from the court of the guard at the command of Nebuchadrezzar. Subsequently, the Babylonians mistakenly seized Jeremiah and transported him to Ramah with the rest of the Judean deportees heading toward Babylon. When the error is discovered, Nebuzaradan once again sets Jeremiah free. Historical interests govern these interpretations, as does a concern to organize the disjunctions and contradictions. However, as is often the case in the book, linear categories of time are not of foremost importance, even in historicized accounts. Moreover, while tidying up the "mess" may make the text more readable by modern standards, it may also distort its own inner logic. The text's lack of coherence may present a ready opportunity to recognize its own focal concerns and theological interests. At the least, the text's disjointed character reflects the collapse of known categories (Brueggemann 2002b, 340-50).

Instead of elaborating upon the fall of the city and the capture of its king, the narrator presents three vignettes of hope. In the first, Nebuzaradan releases Jeremiah from confinement and deals with him humanely (39:11-14). The captain of the Babylonian guard entrusts Jeremiah to Gedaliah and allows the prophet to stay in the land with his people. As is the case with the poor (39:10), the Babylonian occupation of Judah actually improves Jeremiah's plight. In the second vignette, God assures Ebed-melech of asylum even as the divine work of dismantling takes place

(39:15-18). Because the Ethiopian court official has trusted in God, he will survive the devastation of Jerusalem. With words similar to those of the call narrative (1:8; see also 1:19), God promises Ebed-melech, "*I will save you . . .* and you shall not be handed over to those whom you dread" (39:17, emphasis mine).

The third vignette embellishes the story of Jeremiah's release (40:1-6). After Nebuzaradan frees Jeremiah from confinement in Ramah, the Babylonian commander unexpectedly declares that the fall of the city is nothing less than the fulfillment of the divine message. Yahweh had threatened "this place" (see, e.g., 7:7, 20; 16:9; 19:3) with disaster and now has brought it about (40:2). While Nebuzaradan's words sound like a taunt or propaganda, they more likely serve to vindicate the truthfulness of Jeremiah's message (see Deut 18:22). The foreign military official perceives what the leaders and people of Judah have missed from the start: Jeremiah is a true prophet. Then Nebuzaradan gives Jeremiah the option to go to Babylon or stay in the land of Judah. In either case, Nebuzaradan assures Jeremiah of safe passage. The prophet decides to stay in Judah, even though on many occasions he has written off this community as the object of God's wrath (see, e.g., Jer 24). On this occasion, however, Jeremiah casts his lot with Gedeliah and the poor who remain in the land.

Theological and Ethical Analysis

After thirty-eight chapters leading up to the fall of the city, the narrative depicts the sack of Jerusalem in rather anticlimatic terms (39:1-10). From the outset, the book has prepared the reader for massive events that would shake heaven and earth. It employs metaphor, cosmic imagery, prose commentary, poetic utterance, symbolic acts, foreshadowing, and hyperbole all to speak of something that defies ordinary speech. However, when the disaster finally befalls the city and its king, the text turns to ordinary, dispassionate discourse. Rather than referring to the Babylonian invasion as the fulfillment of prophecy or even as divine retribution, the narrative resorts to "historical" testimony. That is, it anchors the unspeakable in the particulars of physicality. Such a move is not a concession that theological reflection must take a backseat to raw geopolitics. On the contrary, the text simply views the memory of 587 as too pivotal to be divorced from real situations in life. In this way, God's rule is not removed from history but is hidden within it.

Once testimony is established, the text takes a sudden turn. It departs from the story of the siege of Jerusalem and Zedekiah's "last stand" for hopeful, even saving, allusions. In the shadow of the collapse of one world, a motley group of "outsiders" begins to shape a new world. First, the poor in the land, who have long been the target of abuse, are afforded a fresh beginning (38:10). Then Jeremiah, who has been maligned, beaten, and ignored, is released and offered land on which to settle. Finally, Ebed-melech, an African official, is praised for his trust in Yahweh and is promised safety during the siege of Jerusalem. The new order will no longer push aside the needy. Those who had been marginalized in the old Jerusalem will enjoy a special place in the new city.

The Babylonian military officer Nebuzaradan is the most important character in this episode. He gives land to the poor, releases Jeremiah twice from bondage, testifies to the truthfulness of the prophet's message, and shows Jeremiah gracious hospitality. Patrick D. Miller describes him as "one of the righteous Gentiles, who . . . deals humanely with Jeremiah, instigates a plan for the recovery of the people in their own land, and sees through to the heart of the matter in a way that none around him seem capable of" (2001, 860). In some sense, these accolades are offensive. To lavish praise upon one who has taken part in the destruction of Jerusalem is clearly disturbing. And yet, the biblical text does exactly that. It insists that insiders do not have a hold on God and that God's work defies coherent systems. Outsiders can become insiders by the force of their actions, social systems can be inverted and religious certainties subverted. We have already observed such transformations in the story of Ebed-melech. However, the African court official is only one of a long procession of women and men in the scriptures that testifies to "scandalous" inversions. Others include Tamar the Canaanite, Jethro the priest of Midian, Rahab the harlot, Ruth the Moabite, Uriah the Hittite, Jonah's "parishioners" from Nineveh, Mary of

Magdala, the Syro-Phoenician woman, the Good Samaritan, the Roman centurion, and a host of unnamed "sinners." Their disconcerting stories are reminders that God's love embraces all people, that faith-claims, no matter how fervently held, must be tempered with humility, and that God will not be confined to or controlled by one's petty assumptions. For the listening community of exiles in Babylon, the story of Nebuzaradan presents another challenge to rethink old certitudes and be open to God's new work in a distant land.

THE ABSENCE OF GOD (JEREMIAH 40:7–41:18)

The fall of Jerusalem resulted in the deportation of its citizens (39:1–40:6; see also 29:1-2; 2 Kgs 24:14-16). However, not everyone is forced into exile. Gedaliah remains in Judah as governor, a few poor people are left behind to look after the land, several Judean military officers and their troops escape to the countryside, and a number of refugees flee to neighboring states. The remaining chapters of the Baruch Narrative focus on these survivors. Under the auspices of a provisional government, a remnant attempts to create some semblance of order in Judah, now a province of the Babylonian Empire (chs. 40–41). When that experiment fails, a patriot named Johanan leads a contingent to Egypt in fear of reprisals (42–44). The stories of fierce warfare between rivaling factions and the rash emigration to Egypt provide a striking account of the post–587 Judean society and its attempts to reestablish itself as a viable community. The narratives also corroborate the claim of Jeremiah that the future of the people of God does not rest with those who reside in Judah or settle in Egypt but rather with the exiles in Babylon.

Literary Analysis

Jeremiah 40:7–41:18 is an account of the Gedaliah government after the fall of Jerusalem. While we are introduced to Gedaliah in the preceding section, he emerges here as a central character. Various citizens of Judah gather round the newly appointed governor in search of well-being and sanctuary. And Gedaliah offers his countrymen such assurances for their loyalty to Babylon (40:7-12). Then several Judean nationalists warn Gedaliah of a plot on his life, which he dismisses as dubious (40:13-16; cf. 43:1-7). The warnings, unfortunately, are well founded. Ishmael, a commander of guerrilla forces that had opposed the Babylonians, murders Gedaliah and those with him at Mizpah (41:1-3). The zealot continues his killing spree by massacring seventy innocent pilgrims on their way to the temple site in Jerusalem (41:4-11). When word reaches Johanan, he pursues Ishmael, catches up with him at Gibeon, and frees the hostages (41:12-18). In fear of Babylonian retaliation, both Ishmael and Johanan flee: Ishmael escapes to Ammon and Johanan and his forces go to Geruth Chimham near Bethlehem, where they prepare to leave for Egypt. These tragic events dash any hope for uninterrupted continuity in the land. The prospect for restoration in the wake of 587 is only briefly entertained before ending abruptly with the death of Gedaliah.

Interestingly, the narrator tells the story of the rise and fall of Gedaliah without reference to the prophet. We last hear of Jeremiah when he decides to go to Mizpah to live with other survivors (40:5-6). He reappears when Johanan asks for counsel before going to Egypt (42:1–44:13). In the interim, during the brief administration of Gedaliah and Ishmael's revolt against Babylonian rule, Jeremiah is missing. Until recently, historical categories have governed most explanations of this lacuna. Jeremiah is silent, the argument goes, because he was either absent or not involved. Such reasoning is problematic for at least two reasons. First, Jeremiah was in all likelihood present at Mizpah with the governor. The text is clear that he had been placed under the custodianship of Gedaliah by Nebuzaradan (40:1-6). Second, and more important, the historical argument assumes that the narrative is primarily a descriptive account of what happened. It is possible, however, that the absence of Jeremiah has less to do with objective representation than poetic performance, less with history than literature. If so, the missing prophet may function artistically as a meaningful part of the story. His silence, and the silence of God, speaks with eloquence and power.

Exegetical Analysis

Gedaliah's Provisional Government (40:7-12)

When the news of Gedaliah's leadership reaches those who had been in hiding since Babylon's victory, Judeans return home and rally around him. The first to arrive at Mizpah, the provincial capital, are resistance leaders who likely fought in the war and subsequently retreated to the Judean hills. For assurances of welfare and amnesty, Gedaliah demands loyalty to Babylonian rule. The commanders and their soldiers must stay in the land, submit to the Babylonians, and "it shall go well" with them. Like Joseph's kind treatment of his brothers (Gen 50:19-21), Gedaliah encourages the Judean nationalists and provides for their needs. This is no time for reprisals. There has already been enough suffering for a lifetime. Now is the time for rebuilding and restoration, for breaking vicious cycles of violence. Soon Judean refugees from Moab, Ammon, Edom, and elsewhere join the commanders and their units. The returnees are united in the land under the care of Gedaliah. The governor responds to their needs by inviting all to partake in a bountiful harvest of wine and summer fruits.

This portrait of abundance has an idyllic quality. We encounter here a world of peace and prosperity, homecoming and restoration, the dawning of a new age. Gedaliah is a heroic figure, a benevolent leader, who accomplishes what Judah's last kings could not. This Babylonian appointee cares for the vulnerable in the land, even "the poorest of the land" (40:7). He attracts Judean survivors from various places where they had been scattered (40:12). When the refugees return, Gedaliah calms their fears, provides for their needs, and serves as their advocate before the Babylonians. He wins the hearts of the survivors and creates a sense of optimism for the future of the community in Judah. Here is one who at last complies with Jeremiah's instructions and submits to Babylonian rule. His speech to the gathering of the remnant echoes Jeremiah's "program" for a sustained life in the land. One could make the case that Gedaliah's gracious policies render Jeremiah's prophetic speech unnecessary. What else could Jeremiah say? The governor's program of hope and restoration embodies Jeremiah's vision for the future. It looks as though that promise is close at hand, when a disturbing conversation takes place.

A Conspiracy Brewing Against Gedaliah (40:13-16)

Johanan and other leading military figures approach Gedaliah with news that his life is in grave danger. Baalis king of Ammon has conspired to kill him, and Ishmael, one of their compatriots, is about to execute the plan. The syntax of the interrogative, "Are you [not] aware," suggests that the governor should know about the conspiracy. This is a time of intense political rivalries. There are enemies nearby and faraway. Gedaliah must surely be privy to these dangers. However, he is not, and so dismisses the warning as groundless. Even after a clandestine meeting in which Johanan volunteers to take matters into his own hands, he refuses to act (40:16). Gedaliah will have no part in a preemptive strike, and so forbids Johanan from slaying Ishmael.

As in previous dialogues, the narrator focuses on the actions of the characters and offers little information on motive or attitude. The portrait of Johanan, however, is an exception to the rule. We are told that he acts out of concern for the surviving Judeans who have gathered around Gedaliah. Johanan believes that the governor's death would result in the end of the remnant of Judah. Therefore, he steps in to prevent it. The reasons underlying Gedaliah's actions are far more obscure. In the previous scene, he appears as a statesman who is courageous and wise, but now he refuses to accept the intelligence report of his advisers. Does the storyteller admire him for not taking part in a preemptive strike or represent him as inept? Is Gedaliah's refusal to resort to violence paradigmatic or problematic? Will he soon be a fallen hero or fool? Because of the dearth of moral commentary and the reticence of the narrator to render a theological evaluation, it is difficult to answer these questions. It follows that some see in Gedaliah "a magnanimous disposition . . . unable to believe evil of one whom he knew personally . . . " (Thompson 1980, 657) while others consider him a flawed and imperceptive leader (Miller 2001, 858). Either way, by the end of the episode it is apparent to all that Johanan's counsel is astute and his concerns are well founded. Gedaliah's refusal to listen costs him his life and the remnant of Judah their future in the land.

The Assassination of Gedaliah (41:1-3)

The story of the assassination of Gedaliah is powerfully understated. The narrator relates the action succinctly without dialogue or embellishment. Ishmael, the subject of the previous conversation, shows up at Mizpah with ten men. The reference to his royal ancestry (41:1) and to Gedaliah's Babylonian loyalties (41:2) suggests from the start that the meeting is laden with political and ideological anxiety. Perhaps Ishmael harbors aspirations for the throne. If so, Gedaliah, a "Babylonian pawn," is the only thing that stands in his way. Even with these signs of trouble and Johanan's previous warning, the parties sit down together. The meal they share represents a gracious act of hospitality. At such settings, it is customary for the host to protect his guests and for guests to bear gifts for their host. We see this kind of gracious exchange between Abraham and the three visitors at Mamre (Gen 18:1-15) and between the widow of Zarephath and Elijah (1 Kgs 17:8-24; cf. Luke 24:13-35). Hospitality is supposed to overcome hostility and bear the seeds of goodwill. However, not in this case! Under the guise of covenant friendship and the banner of patriotism, Ishmael and his cohorts betray their unsuspecting host. During the meal, they rise up and strike down Gedaliah. To complete their coup, Ishmael murders all the Jews with Gedaliah at Mizpah as well as the Babylonian soldiers stationed at the garrison.

The Massacre of the Innocent (41:4-10)

The massacre does not end with the death of Gedaliah and those with him at Mizpah. Ishmael now eyes eighty pilgrims from the northern cities of Shechem, Shiloh, and Samaria who arrive at Mizpah en route to Jerusalem. With beards shaved, cloths torn, and bodies gashed as a sign of mourning, presumably over the tragic events of 587, they bear gifts to present to God at the temple.

Apparently, some form of worship continues at the temple site after the fall of the city. Ishmael intercepts the pilgrims, feigns solidarity, persuades them to meet Gedaliah, and then carries on his killing rampage in the middle of the city. He spares only ten men who had hidden food in the fields (41:8). After desecrating a cistern built by King Asa with the corpses of the seventy, murderous Ishmael takes off with hostages in hand.

Johanan and his brigade hear of the bloodbath and set out in pursuit. They eventually overtake Ishmael near the great waters in Gibeon, six miles northwest of Jerusalem (41:11-18). The pool of Gibeon had been the site of an earlier civil war between Israel and Judah (2 Sam 2:12-17). Now, some four hundred years later, it is the field of Ishmael's last stand. But Ishmael does not even show up. Beset by Johanan's forces, he and his cadre abandon their hostages and flee for their lives to the Ammonites. After that, Johanan gathers the captives and departs for Egypt. He is determined to go there for fear of Babylonian retaliation. Before leading the remnant south, Johanan stops at Geruth Chimham near Bethlehem where Jeremiah reenters the picture (42:1-6).

Theological and Ethical Analysis

Jeremiah 40:7–41:18 is the most grisly section of the book. It is saturated with violence, brutality, and duplicity. The death of Gedaliah and his company as well as the mass murder of the seventy pilgrims flood the streets of Mizpah with innocent blood. All are victims of cunning and cruelty. Whether fueled by patriotic fervor or sheer madness, the murderous acts are indefensible. One can hardly read of the carnage without shock and disappointment. To make matters worse, the killers escape unpunished. Clearly, the text presents to us a world in total disarray (cf. 4:23-27). As the story of the Judean remnant winds down, communal life falls into a downward moral and religious spiral that reaches its lowest point. The social order is broken down, all forms of civility disappear, evildoers run rampant, and innocent people are butchered.

The events surrounding the death of Gedaliah are not only dream-shattering, but also theologically embarrassing. The savage acts fly in the face of principal tenets of the book, which are that life makes moral sense, that actions have consequences, and that the universe is morally coherent. For these reasons, the destruction of Judah posed few ethical conundrums. Judah's incorrigible faithlessness, as demonstrated in its abject rejection of the word and person of Jeremiah, gave rise to its present predicament. In traditional terms, the nation's woes were divine punishment for sin. God is not mocked. People reap what they sow. The meaningless slaughter of Gedaliah and the seventy worshipers, however, clearly challenges such assumptions. Again, here is a leader who finally obeys Yahweh's word, and yet dies without cause. It makes no sense. It ruptures neat and symmetrical worlds. The story of Josiah's sudden death in 2 Kings reads as a stunning narrative analogy. It also defies moral logic and exposes holes in the conventional understandings of suffering.

By bearing witness to human brutality and gratuitous suffering, the Gedaliah fiasco refutes the theodicy argument in the book. We have already seen how the suffering of a few faithful individuals undermines Jeremiah's theology of retribution. Now the murder of Gedaliah and the seventy worshipers demolishes it. The unabashed violence shows that old moral certainties cannot account for the full gamut of human experience. Sometimes the faithful do suffer and sometimes perpetrators of evil get away with their deeds. By facing the moral chaos head-on, the narrative of loss shows remarkable courage. By refusing to resort to easy answers, the story honors ethical ambiguity and human suffering. Slain Gedaliah and the massacred worshipers, alongside a hostage prophet and a reeling scribe, subvert congruent readings of life. This counter-theodicy concedes, perhaps even asserts, that the world is indeed a fissured and broken place. In a haunting manner, this text mirrors the world in which we live, a world that seems at times to be morally irrational and expressly evil. Ishmael's coup and slaughter of the innocent shatter illusions of certitude.

This courageous text not only graphically depicts a chaotic world but it does so without reference to God. This is the only major literary unit in the book in which God is absent. Why is God missing from this tragic chapter of post-war Judah? Why is

God silent? Although the story provides no direct explanation, it nonetheless resonates with interpretive possibilities. Only two will be noted here.

In the first place, God is missing from the dreadful scene because God does not belong there. God does not figure in the bloodbath of Ishmael. God has no part in the treachery, betrayal, or brutal fanaticism of the Judean nationalists. The militants may think God does, they may even act in God's name. But God does not show up, and certainly does not sanction their brutality, whether in the guise of patriotism or religion. Thus, there is no divine voice or presence, no divine intrusion or prophetic witness. In a daring literary move, the narrator distances God from the politics of violence.

Admittedly, the book is replete with the rhetoric of violence, indeed with theopolitical violence; it resounds with the conviction that Yahweh is destroying Judah and its capital city. Jeremiah asserts that Babylon is the divine instrument charged with executing the dangerous dismantling. Nonetheless, when the armies actually arrive, the narrator becomes far more reticent to use God-language (see 39:1-14 and 52:4-30). Rather than seizing the moment to corroborate the prophetic message, the narrator merely presents an "objective" account of the events, with little or no theological commentary. As in the Gedaliah fiasco, the story-teller relates the fall of Jerusalem without reference to God. Consequently, Yahweh is neither implicated nor exonerated: God is just missing and thus extricated from the terrible events.

Besides distancing God from the massacre, the silence of God *speaks* on behalf of the victims. It allows their voices to be heard. It preserves their story and their memory. Any utterance would trivialize their deaths. Any textual explanation would mute their cries. Divine silence is therefore essential. In Chaim Potok's *The Chosen*, Reb Sauders speaks of the force of silence: "You can hear the pain of the world in silence." Kathleen M. O'Connor explores the "missing voice" of God in Lamentations, a book that is traditionally associated with Jeremiah:

> God's frightening silence . . . prevents us from sliding prematurely over suffering toward happy endings. It gives the book daring

power because it honors human speech. God's absence forces us to attend to voices of grief and despair, and it can reflect . . . our own experiences of a silent God . . . . If God spoke, God's words would diminish the voices of pain, wash over them, and crowd them out. Even one word from God would take up too much space in the book. (O'Connor 2002, 86)

Similarly, in Jer 40:7–41:18 the testimony of a slain leader and seventy murdered worshipers lingers and haunts. Their cries must be heard before the unfolding saga can resume. Their cries must be heard before life can go on. No wonder Elie Wiesel remained silent for so many years after the darkness of Auschwitz. Words, although essential for testimony, would only diminish the unspeakable horror of the camps. And no wonder Christians see the silence of God in the death of Jesus Christ (see, e.g., Matt 27:45-46). Perhaps Christians would do well to linger there, that dreadful Friday and long Saturday, attentive to the pain of the world and the anguish of God, before moving on to Easter morning.

FLIGHT TO EGYPT (JEREMIAH 42:1–44:30)

Literary Analysis

Jeremiah 42:1–44:30 covers two biographical accounts of the Judean community in the post-Gedaliah era. The first involves Jeremiah's dealings with the Johanan group in the land of Judah (42:1–43:7). This small remnant seeks counsel from Jeremiah as to whether it should stay in Judah or head south to Egypt (42:1-6). The prophet directs the beleaguered group to remain in the land (42:7-17). Egypt, despite all its power and prestige, will not provide sanctuary from harm. Migrating there, Jeremiah declares, will only occasion further suffering (42:18-22). By the end of the episode, it becomes clear that the Johanan contingent is determined to go to Egypt, regardless of Yahweh's word through Jeremiah (43:1-7). And so, the company leaves the land of Judah to reside in Tahpanhes.

In the second scene, Jeremiah continues his harangue, but now against the Jewish Diaspora in Egypt (43:8–44:30). Through a symbolic action and an accompanying oracle, Jeremiah announces that Egypt will not provide sanctuary from King Nebuchadnezzar (43:8-13). The Babylonian ruler will eventually invade Egypt, set his throne in Tahpanhes, and ravage that country as well. The Diaspora's quest for security is useless. At this point, a prose sermon is introduced (44:1-14). As customary, the prose homily plays a pivotal role in the literary organization of the story and provides important clues for understanding it. The sermon makes three summative claims (cf. 25:1-14): (1) Yahweh has sent "his servants the prophets" to beckon Israel to turn from its wrongdoing, (2) Israel has adamantly rejected their message, and (3) as a result has suffered the consequences of its recalcitrance. Taken together, these claims affirm that the fall of Judah and its capital city did not occur outside the scope of God's sovereign plan. The desolation of Jerusalem and Judah was a direct upshot of the people's idolatry and rejection of the word of God. This sort of reasoning, of course, is nothing new.

What is new about the prose sermon is its function in the present literary setting. As the Baruch Narrative draws to a close, the homily places old words in new contexts. As Deuteronomy reiterates the "speeches of Moses" in fresh ways for communities removed in time and place from the earliest events (e.g., Deut 5:1-5), Jer 44:1-14 makes the past present for a new generation. It *reinterprets* the demands of the covenant for those no longer living in the land and it *re-presents* Jerusalem's fall so as to warn a subsequent people that they too are in jeopardy. The fall of Jerusalem is, therefore, no longer merely a historical datum. Now it is didactic and paradigmatic: the earlier disaster is a frightening prospect of what lies ahead should the Egyptian community not renounce its faithless ways. Whether the implied audience actually witnessed the sack of Jerusalem, as the text suggests, is incidental. The prose sermon intends to overcome temporal and spatial limitations, and place the listening congregation *there*—"you yourselves have seen all the disaster that I have brought on Jerusalem" (44:2)—so it can "participate" in the defining moment of the nation. The "Israel in Egypt" is invited to rearrange its present life so that it can craft a different future.

The response of the people of Judah in Egypt is no better than that of earlier communities (44:15-19). The Judean refugees are completely unfazed by Jeremiah's warning (44:11). As a matter of fact, they are determined "not . . . to listen" (44:16). Even more, they turn Jeremiah's words upside down by claiming that their hardship is recompence for forsaking the queen of heaven, not Yahweh! Upon hearing these words, Jeremiah launches a counterattack (44:20-23). The people's adversity is a direct consequence of their infidelity to Yahweh. It is because they "burned offerings, . . . sinned against the LORD, and did not obey the voice of the LORD or walk in his law and in his statutes" (44:23). Hence, the Judeans in Egypt must brace themselves for further affliction (44:24-30).

Links to the past are present throughout Jer 42–44 (Seitz 1989b, 3-27). Like the ancient people of God (e.g., Num 21:7), the Judeans plead for intercession (Jer 42:1-6). Jeremiah, in the Mosaic tradition, intercedes on their behalf (42:1-6; cf. Num 11:2; 14:19; 21:7) and offers divine guidance (Jer 42:7-17; cf. Exod 19:3–23:33). Similar to the epic literature of Exodus and Numbers, the narrative in Jer 42–44 is oriented around "obeying" and "not obeying" Yahweh's instruction. Both ancient and contemporary communities swear to obey (42:5-6; cf. Exod 24:3, 7) only to renege on their promise. Both yearn for Egypt (e.g., Exod 16:3; 17:3; Num 11:4-6; 14:1-4; Jer 43:1-7) even though it represents the antithesis of Yahweh's will. And both break the central commandment, "you shall have no other gods before me" (Exod 20:3), and so jeopardize their status as the people of God (Exod 32:1-35 and Jer 44:1-30). Consequently, the first Moses as well as "the prophet like Moses" (Jeremiah) declare that the disobedient generation will not enter the promised land but will die in the wilderness/in Egypt (Num 32:13 and Jer 42:13-22; 44:24-30).

Exegetical Analysis

Jeremiah Reappears (42:1-6)

At the conclusion of the previous episode, Johanan's group is intent on fleeing to Egypt for fear of Babylonian reprisals for Gedaliah's death. Even though Johanan had nothing to do with the governor's death and had even attempted to thwart Ishmael's uprising, he still feels it expedient to leave Judah for safe haven in Egypt. Before departing, the Judean patriot and those with him seek divine guidance from Jeremiah, who reenters the picture. Where has the prophet been since the Babylonian commander Nebuzaradan placed him in the custody of Gedaliah at Mizpah? Had Ishmael taken Jeremiah captive along with others residing in Mizpah (41:10)? If so, was he one of the hostages freed by Johanan? The narrator is content to bring Jeremiah back in view without answering any of these queries. He merely resurfaces, and when he does, he is the center of attention.

The scene into which Jeremiah steps is no ordinary event. The narrator organizes it as a pivotal moment in the life of Israel. The entire nation, as it were, the leaders and "all the people from the least to the greatest," assembles around Jeremiah in hopes that he will intercede on its behalf (42:2). Once again, people approach Jeremiah to inquire of the Lord; and again Jeremiah agrees to pray, despite the divine prohibition against intercession (see e.g., 37:3; 38:14-23; cf. 7:16; 11:14; 15:1). But, on this occasion, he emerges as a larger-than-life figure on whom the nation relies for its very breath. Here Jeremiah turns into a full bloom Mosaic intermediary. (Later Jewish literature embellishes this portrait of the prophet as intercessor, see 2 Macc 15:12-16.) As one who stands between heaven and earth, Israel and God, a chaotic past and a precarious future, everything rides on whether this Mosaic figure will hear the cry of the people. When he does, the petitioners take a solemn oath of obedience akin to those made by Israel during covenant ceremonies at crucial times in history (e.g., Exod 24:3, 7; Josh 24:16-18, 21-22, 24; cf. Ezra 10:1-5). Hyperbole and echoes from the past transform this ordinary situation into an event of monumental scope.

Yet, the "Israel" that we encounter here is only a shadow of the past. Having faced years of scarcity and loss, the people are barely a "remnant." Clinging to life by a thread, they are survivors in every sense of the word. War, starvation, deportations, and mass murder have left them fearful and few in number. Painfully they confess before Jeremiah: "there are only a few of us left out of many" (42:2). God's promise of numerous descendants is no longer their reality (Gen 15:1-6; 22:17-18; see also Exod 1:7); nevertheless the memory of the "many" still haunts. Caught in a whirlwind of events over which they have had little control, the disoriented and dislocated people beg God for help (42:2); they call on God to show them where to go and what to do (42:3) and then resolve, by a sacred vow, to obey whatever God should say (42:5). Johanan and the people grasp that their future hinges on wholehearted obedience to God (42:6). Though vulnerable and at risk, perhaps *because* they are vulnerable and at risk, they acknowledge their utter dependence upon God and ask God for help.

While this display of devotion is a stunning testimony of faith, the people's eventual dismissal of Jeremiah's oracular speech diminishes its force. One might even wonder whether the petition is a charade and another disingenuous attempt to coerce God into sanctioning their agenda (see 41:17). It is also possible that the storyteller intends to use the incident as a literary foil, for in the end the people's oath of obedience broadcasts their guilt and Yahweh's right to bring judgment (42:5-6). Furthermore, the reference in verses 2 and 3 (emphasis mine) to "the LORD *your* God" may hint at something amiss, perhaps that dealing with Yahweh is Jeremiah's specialty, not theirs (Holladay 1989, 298-99). Then again, the second-person pronouns may reflect nothing more than proper decorum for approaching a person of honor or the people's acute sense of disentitlement from the covenant promises of God. In any case, there is nothing in the opening scene itself to indicate that the people's petition is anything but sincere. Their cry for God's help is earnest and even paradigmatic. It is a plea that grows out of an experience of deep disruption and in response implores God to pay attention and act. In this way, the narrator depicts a community that is neither inherently evil nor doomed from the start. On the contrary, the Judean remnant has noble intentions but, as we shall see, little nerve to follow through.

Remain in the Land (42:7-17)

After pleading their case before Jeremiah, the people wait. Jeremiah too must wait. Like those he represents, the prophet is absolutely dependent on the coming of God's word. He is not free to speak on his own initiative. After ten days, the divine reply arrives and Jeremiah assembles the community to hear it. Yahweh offers the people a "choice," which is really a call to obedience. Johanan and those with him may remain in the land and enjoy God's blessing and protection or they may go to Egypt where hardship and disaster will engulf them. Two clearly defined paths are available: one leads to mercy and life, the other to judgment and death; one is God's will, the other a brazen act of autonomy. The Hebrew particle "if" regulates both options. The conditional formulation indicates that all rides on the survivors' response to Yahweh's word. Now that God's will is known, it is incumbent upon the people to embrace it. As W. Brueggemann has noted: "The rhetoric of this speech, in the long tradition of Moses, Joshua, and Samuel, is a pattern of blessings and curses which is determined completely by covenant obedience or disobedience" (1998, 389).

This all *seems* so simple. The Johanan group need only stay put for Yahweh to build them up and not pull them down, to plant them and not uproot them (42:10; cf. 1:10). If the Judeans remain in the land, Yahweh promises to protect and be present, to save and rescue. In addition, Yahweh's sorrow over past disasters (42:10) coupled with the assurance of mercy (42:12) opens the door wide for the possibility of hope. How could anyone not walk through! Yet there are "demonic forces" to reckon with: the king of Babylon still lurks in the shadows and the people are beside themselves with fear. To calm their fears, Jeremiah delivers an oracle of salvation in which God promises to deliver them (42:11). Salvation oracles are assurances to fearful people facing perilous times that God hears their prayer and will act on their behalf. Embedded in the prophetic utterance is thus a subtext of fear, a fear that paralyzes, distorts, disables.

Egypt *appears* to be a way out. Given the survivors' harsh economic conditions and political uncertainties, it makes perfect sense to view Egypt as a sanctuary. The people are certain that in Egypt they will "not see war, or hear the sound of the trumpet, or be hungry for bread" (42:14). Its political muscle, they imagine, will provide refuge from an angry overlord in pursuit. Its abundance will stave off hunger. Its stability will restore equilibrium. Ally Egypt looks like the answer to all their fears and troubles. So, like the wilderness generation of old, the people yearn for its shelter. The prophet warns that such a reading is terribly misguided. Egypt is no panacea. In fact, going there would only compound their troubles. The sword that they fear would overtake them; the famine they dread would pursue them; and they would die there "by the sword, by famine, and by pestilence" (42:16, 17). Egypt may look like a refuge, but it is really a place of no return.

It turns out that Jeremiah's clear-cut alternatives are not nearly as simple and straightforward as they appear. Remaining in the land requires enormous courage. To settle in Judah, the remnant must face their fears head-on, submit to a threatening suzerain, and abandon the securities of Egypt. The fate of Gedaliah, who stayed in the land compliant with Jeremiah's instruction, only makes the prospect of settling in Judah all the more frightening. The people could point to the Gedaliah tragedy as a reason to disregard Jeremiah's prophetic counsel. From their standpoint, the prophet's oracle was dangerous, even bordering on suicidal (see 43:1-3). From the narrator's point of view, nothing could be further from the truth. Despite its perils, staying in Judah is the only road to hope. Such a conviction may call into question geopolitical logic; it may defiantly subvert surface readings of security. However, it is not unprecedented. In calling for great faith, Jeremiah merely follows suit here. Faced with Assyrian aggression more than a hundred years earlier, Isaiah gave similar counsel. He challenged the people of Judah to relinquish their dependence on conventional forms of security and rely on God (Isa 31:1). When addressing the worshiping community the psalmist put it this way: "Do not put your trust in princes, in mortals, in whom there is no help. Happy are those whose help is the God of Jacob, whose hope is in the LORD their God" (Ps 146:3, 5).

Egypt Is a Dead End (42:18-22)

Jeremiah 42:18-22 records the final words of Jeremiah in the land of Judah. Like Moses, Joshua, and Samuel (Deut 31:24-29;

Josh 24:19-25; 1 Sam 8:10-18), the prophet concludes his address by anticipating the future as if it were a present reality. According to him, the people will ignore the word of the Lord and go to Egypt where they will suffer the covenant curses (42:18, 21; cf. Deut 28). Yet, he repeats the divine admonition, "Do not go to Egypt" (42:19), no longer as an "if-then" clause, which has governed his oracle response thus far, but as declarative speech. Fleeing to Egypt is therefore not a political misdemeanor but a grave offense against Yahweh. Next, the prophet affirms that he has fulfilled his obligation of warning the people of the consequences of their actions (42:19-20; cf. 1 Sam 12:1-6). Hereafter he bears no responsibility for the people's ill-fated future. They have heard and so responsibility now lies on their shoulders. Then Jeremiah reminds the Judeans of their incriminating oath to abide by Yahweh's instruction no matter what the cost (42:20). Their own words testify against them in no uncertain terms. Finally, he reiterates the grim consequences of their decision to disregard Yahweh's word, this time as though the jury were already in with a damning verdict (42:22).

To summarize, Jeremiah's address to the people highlights the magnitude of the people's decision. Going to Egypt would be an irrevocable mistake that would cost them everything. They would forfeit their stake in the land of Judah and die without survivors (cf. 44:28). Hereafter, the only ones left to realize the promised future in the land (Jer 32) are the Judean exiles in Babylon.

"Hell No! To Egypt We Go" (43:1-7)

The narrator wastes no time relating the reaction to Jeremiah's oracle. As soon as Jeremiah concludes, Azariah, Johanan, and "all the other insolent men" dismiss his words as a "lie," the term that Jeremiah typically uses for his "false" opponents (e.g., 20:6; 23:14; 27:10, 14). To substantiate their claim, the Judean leaders insist that Baruch has inspired the prophet's directive not to flee to Egypt. The scribe, they maintain, has incited Jeremiah against them so that the Babylonians may kill or deport them to Babylon. Their accusation is certainly odd. Baruch has been a relatively minor character who does little independent of Jeremiah. At the request of Jeremiah, Baruch participates in a business transaction involving the purchase of land in Anathoth (Jer 32). At Jeremiah's dictation, Baruch records the words on a scroll, which he then reads in the house of the Lord and before an assembly of royal officials (Jer 36; 45:1). Only when Baruch seeks reassurance from Jeremiah does he act on his own (45:1-5). In literary terms, Baruch is a relatively flat character: he has little depth, complexity, or autonomy. To transform Baruch into Jeremiah's co-conspirator, perhaps even the covert source behind Jeremiah's words, is grasping at straws; backed into a corner, it is a desperate attempt on the part of Azariah, Johanan, and the other leaders to justify their own agenda. Worse, their strategy is a terrible miscalculation, for when they reject Jeremiah's words and head off to Egypt, they reject God's message and God's messenger. Twice the narrator declares that the people have disobeyed the voice of the Lord (43:4, 7). There is no masking the narrator's point of view, no reticence about theological evaluation. The Baruch defense is a ruse that implicates them. The abduction of Jeremiah and Baruch only compounds their guilt.

How do courageous "freedom fighters," who beg Jeremiah to intercede for them, turn into staunch opponents? While intense geopolitical rivalries are certainly at work, the narrative is not interested in these forces per se. It plays down pro-Egyptian versus pro-Babylonian politics, even though they are bubbling beneath the surface of the text. Instead, the story collapses a whole complex of factors into one all-embracing theological contention: the Judeans remaining in the land refuse to "listen" to Yahweh, though Yahweh has repeatedly whispered in their ears. Those who sought the will of God decide to reject it. In doing so, they become "insolent," a term often used to describe people who set themselves above and against the ways of God and God's people (Pss 86:14; 119:21; 119:51; 119:78; Prov 21:24). Humility thus turns into bravado, insecurity to certitude, and openness to stubborn rebellion. As far as the canonical witness is concerned, disregard for God's word and brazen autonomy lead to the metamorphosis of Jeremiah's audience.

Egypt Is No Panacea (43:8-13)

The setting shifts to Tahpanhes, a city in the eastern Delta where the Judeans had come to settle. The prophet is to convey Yahweh's word through a symbolic action and an accompanying interpretation. While Jeremiah has communicated the word of Yahweh through dramatic presentation in the land of Judah, this is the first and only time he does so in Egypt. He takes large stones in his hands and buries them "[under a] clay pavement" (the meaning of the Hebrew is uncertain) in front of the royal palace. The stones symbolize the foundation of the king of Babylon's throne. On the platform that was once representative of Pharaoh's rule, King Nebuchadrezzar will set his throne (43:10). As Yahweh's servant, the Babylonian ruler will enter Egypt and devastate the land, just as he entered and laid waste to Judah. By divine authority, he will bring judgment on Egypt from which no one will escape (43:11; cf. 15:2). The terse language itself suggests a decisive attack that leaves Egypt totally disabled.

Jeremiah declares that the enemy will specifically target the center of Egypt's religious world (43:12-13). Nebuchadrezzar will burn the temples of Egypt and carry off its gods to Babylon. As one picks lice off their clothes, he will plunder the country's shrines with little opposition (Thompson 1980, 671). The conquering king will destroy the obelisks or sacred pillars in the temple of the sun-god Re (i.e., "Beth-shemesh" which is literally "the house of the sun"), a likely reference to Heliopolis, a city ten kilometers northeast of Cairo. The point of the narrative is direct: there is no skirting the will of God. Egypt will not provide sanctuary from Yahweh's judgment. The immense Egyptian empire is no less under the sovereign rule of Yahweh than is Judah's. Egypt's gods are no match for Yahweh. Yahweh reigns over all!

A Recital of Jerusalem's Fate as a Warning to the Egyptian Diaspora (44:1-14)

Jeremiah's final discourse to the Jewish Diaspora in Egypt is set out in Jer 44:1-14. The prose speech does not merely continue the diatribe against those who recently fled to Tahpanhes (43:8-

13) but addresses the Judeans living in Egypt, "at Migdol, at Tahpanhes, at Memphis, and in the land of Pathros" (44:1). That is, it envisions a considerable time lapse; the Jewish emigrants have now settled in several communities in Egypt, during which Jeremiah delivers an oracle of judgment. The indictment concerns the idolatrous activities of these scattered residents (44:1-10) as well as their very presence in Egypt (44:11-14).

First, Jeremiah maintains that the events of 587 provide a searing image of the consequences of idolatry (44:2-3). The memory of a fallen city is a poignant lesson that abandoning Yahweh is no minor infraction. The essence of the covenant relationship, especially from a Deuteronomic perspective, is love and devotion to God. To desecrate this core by serving foreign deities is the worst sort of violation of the sacred order (see also Deut 13:1-18; 17:2-7). Second, Jeremiah declares that Yahweh has sent prophets imploring the people of Judah to turn from false worship (44:4-6). Their refusal to heed the warnings of the prophets resulted in the gravest of consequences. Jeremiah's argument is critical: God cares deeply about the character of worship. The remnant in Egypt dare not follow the example of their kin without considering the cost of such action. Third, a string of damning rhetorical questions intensifies the prophetic charge (44:7-9). The refugees in Egypt must directly consider their own deeds. "Why are *you* doing such great harm to yourselves . . . Why do *you* provoke me to anger with the works of *your* hands . . . Will *you* be cut off and become an object of cursing . . . Have *you* forgotten the crimes of your ancestors . . . ?" Thus, Jeremiah uses historical precedent, prophetic witness, and disputation to expose the people's apostasy and to justify divine judgment looming on the horizon. The Judeans in Egypt are on the brink of perishing; they have lost their senses and forgotten their story; they have embraced alien narratives, surrendered their chance to return home, and are thus on the verge of losing God (44:11-14).

A Pledge of Allegiance to the Queen of Heaven (44:15-19)

While we have come to expect callous disdain for Jeremiah's words, nothing could quite prepare us for the refugees' response.

Their reaction borders on the bizarre and embodies the most brazen contempt for the message of Jeremiah in the book. Like the defiant who assemble to build the Tower of Babel (Gen 11:1-9), the scattered Judeans in Egypt speak with one voice. The adjective "all" (*qôl*) is repeated three times to emphasize collective action, collective responsibility, and collective blame. "*All* the men . . . and *all* the women, a great assembly, [and] *all* the people living in Lower and Upper Egypt answered Jeremiah . . . 'we are not going to listen to you'" (44:15-16) (see Rudolph 1947, 224-25). Without a trace of remorse or ambivalence, the people refuse to "listen." Moreover, they vow to continue making offerings to the queen of heaven. Devotion to the "queen of heaven" likely alludes to a popular form of an Ishtar-Isis cult. Jeremiah has already brought an indictment against the people of Jerusalem and surrounding villages for worshiping the goddess (7:16-20); now the refugees' own words implicate them in apostasy. Even worse, the men and women in Egypt are bent on defending their position. When they venerated the goddess, they insist, everything worked out fine for them; they and their ancestors enjoyed peace and prosperity (44:17). When they stopped making sacrifices to this god— perhaps an oblique allusion to the Josiah's reform in 622 when the Judean king attempted to centralize Yahwistic worship in Jerusalem and halt the worship of rival gods—their lives fell apart. Such an argument turns Jeremiah's theology on its head. The queen of heaven, they assert, not Yahweh, rewards faithfulness and punishes disloyalty. Ishtar, not Yahweh, possesses the power of life and death. This perverse application of Jeremiah's words reveals the depth of their idolatrous thinking. This is what to expect when Israel returns to Egypt! The reader, however, should be on guard that this anti-Egyptian rhetoric indirectly champions the cause of the Babylonian exiles, the target audience of the text.

Jeremiah's Counterattack (44:20-30)

Jeremiah mounts an aggressive counterattack. The people's interpretation of life is altogether unfounded. Their hard times have nothing to do with the queen of heaven, but are the direct outcome of flagrant disobedience and infidelity to Yahweh. To be sure, Yahweh "remembered" the idolatrous rites performed in the streets of Jerusalem (44:21) and found them repugnant. The use of the Hebrew term "remember" *(zkr)* does not mean that God forgets and then suddenly recalls. To remember is to be acutely attentive and intensely involved. When the children of Israel were slaves in Egypt, God "remembered" his covenant and rescued them from their oppressors (Exod 2:24; 6:5). In that case remembering led directly to God's gracious acts of salvation. Now God's remembering gives rise to retribution. Yahweh holds the Judean community in Egypt accountable for its worship of false gods. Disregarding the demands of the Torah, especially the prohibition against the worship of other gods, will bring about the penalties for breach of covenant, "desolation, waste, and a curse" (44:22). The Jewish Diaspora must be answerable to no one but Yahweh.

Jeremiah's dispute turns into a full-fledged judgment oracle (44:24-30). With a heavy dose of sarcasm, Jeremiah prods his listeners to keep up their offerings and libations to the queen of heaven. Then they will get exactly what they deserve: an identity apart from Yahweh. The Judeans living in Egypt will no longer utter Yahweh's name, which is no small matter. To inaugurate the covenant relationship with the Israelites, God revealed God's name to Moses (Exod 3:1-22). God's self-disclosure made possible Israel's story. The absence of the divine name is tantamount to an abrogation of the covenant relationship. Without Yahweh's name on its lips, the community forfeits its core identity as God's people. The allusion to God's name, once revealed in Egypt and now rescinded in Egypt, takes the community full circle.

Next Jeremiah warns that Yahweh is "watching over them for harm and not for good" (44:27). The language of "watching" appears first in the call narrative of Jeremiah where it illustrates the divine resolve to shape Judah's future (1:11-12). While divine "watching" sometimes leads to salvation and hope, that is, to "building and planting" (31:28), this is clearly not the case here. God's scrutiny at this moment brings about chastisement. Though the Judeans in Egypt are no longer attentive to Yahweh, Yahweh is still watching them, intent on carrying out the divine purposes in history.

As a sure indication of coming judgment, Jeremiah declares that the great Pharaoh Hophra (Apries) will be handed over to his enemies (44:29-30). The reference to Hophra's death as a "sign" (ʾôt) makes contact with another text set in Egypt. In the call narrative of Moses, God quells the fears of Moses with a "sign" (ʾôt), apparently that one day Israel would worship God on Mount Sinai (Exod 3:12). While this earlier "sign" signaled the shattering of Egypt's kingdom of violence as a prelude to Israel's freedom, the divine "sign" given to the Egyptian community in Jer 44:29 confirms Jeremiah's announcement of Israel's sentence of death. The signs serve different purposes, but both demonstrate God's victory over mighty Egypt and God's resolve to accomplish what God has promised (44:29).

The promise of a sign corroborating the prophet's message does little to squelch conflicting truth claims among the people. This is not surprising given the multiple accounts of reality saturating the book. From the start, we have witnessed a cacophony of competing voices including prophets, priests, kings, foreign dignitaries, enraged citizens, and political officials. The text is flooded with mutually exclusive constructions of the future, with party politics, and with rival factions vying for preeminence in the post–587 world. Now we encounter, although certainly not for the first time, opposing God claims: Yahweh versus the queen of heaven! Who is in control and whose assertions about reality are true? In addition, how is one to interpret the persistent waves of devastation? These are pressing questions, especially for those caught in the maelstrom of loss. Amidst their freighted world, Jeremiah makes a dogged and unapologetic claim: as in Elijah's face-off with the prophets of Baal (1 Kgs 18:1-16), the prophet declares that *Yahweh is God and Lord of history!* Jeremiah leaves no room for compromise. "The rootage of the claim goes back behind Jeremiah and the prophetic traditions to the earliest recitals of Israel, to Moses, and to some fundamental decisions about covenant at Sinai" (Brueggemann 1998, 412). Jeremiah holds nothing back when he contests the deep-seated convictions of the Egyptian community. For what is at stake is nothing less than the future of the Judeo-Christian tradition(s) and the face of God.

Theological and Ethical Analysis

The two major sections of this unit, Jer 42:1–43:7 and Jer 43:8–44:30, transport the reader from the land of Judah, where Jeremiah and the people are at loggerheads over the Egyptian issue, to the Delta region of Egypt where the dispute is already settled. Although the two accounts reflect different geographical settings, they belong together theologically. Three key elements unify the literature as a whole: (1) the Egypt motif, (2) the word of God and its rejection, and (3) the inversion of the Exodus experience.

First, the community's decision to flee to Egypt and eventually to settle there gives Jer 42:1–44:30 its distinctive character. Apart from the Exodus narrative and its prelude (Gen 37–50), this is the only story in the Bible in which the people of God take up residence in Egypt. Consequently, Egypt comes to frame Israel's history. It begins there and it ends there. Egypt is also the place where Jeremiah is taken hostage and presumably dies. However, Egypt is more than a physical setting in which the characters move and the action takes place. Egypt is so palpably present that it defines the story.

The geographic shift from the land of Judah to the land of Egypt is thick with theological meaning. Egypt functions throughout the story as a robust metaphor; it represents worldly power and a conventional accounting of reality. Egypt symbolizes raw human strength and inexhaustible resources. It is the place of political autonomy and economic opulence. While other nations rise and fall, it exudes enormous staying power. No wonder the Judeans flee the wrath of the king of Babylon by heading south. Only Egypt can rival Babylon's massive resources. Many, therefore, seek the shade of Egypt's shadow (see Isa 30:1-2). Driven by defiance and despair, suffering amnesia and loss of nerve, they scurry to Egypt for safety. Tired of the warring and waiting for a new life, to Egypt they go. But the people of God should know better, for Egypt has almost always spelled trouble. The grand empire only *appears* to be a refuge from the storms; it is actually a *deception*, its comforts are an illusion. Egypt's soldiers, chariots, and horses, though patently seductive, cannot save.

For the reader, the mere mention of Egypt evokes memories of slavery and oppression. "The Israelites groaned under their [bondage]" (Exod 2:23). To remember Israel's story is to call to mind that Egypt is a place of tears and death. It is a place where taskmasters exploit and brutalize. It values production over people and muscle over mercy. Egypt symbolizes the antithesis of all that is good and meaningful in Israelite society. Although its power holds extraordinary sway, it is in the end a place of no return. To journey there for safety is a costly miscalculation, for then Egypt comes to frame the story of this people. At its extremities, at inception and final act, one uncovers an oppressive regime and a desperate Israel.

Even so, Egypt is still not outside the reach of Yahweh's rule. As Israel once discovered, Yahweh can turn Egypt's power hierarchy on its head; the God of Hebrew slaves is able to shatter Pharaoh's imposing regime. Like the Philistine's fallen god Dagon (1 Sam 4:1–7:1), the gods of Egypt are no challenge to Yahweh. Yahweh is a God to be reckoned with. Now Jeremiah makes a similar assertion: Egypt's enormous power structures are subject to divine sovereignty. Egypt's impressive deities and military might are no match for Yahweh; they can neither frustrate the purposes of God nor provide sanctuary from peril. King Nebuchadrezzar of Babylon, Yahweh's provisional servant, will render formidable Egypt powerless. Even mighty Egypt is incapable of negating the intentions of the living God.

That Jeremiah should end his career in Egypt is replete with interpretive possibilities as well. One could hardly imagine a bleaker, albeit fitting, end to a tormented life. We have come to expect prophetic conflict and disappointment at every turn. From start to finish, Jeremiah has faced opposition and rejection. His involvement with God and with God's people has cost him everything. The warnings of hostility and opposition have fleshed out (1:17-19), even if the divine promise of deliverance and protection has not, at least not as one might suppose (1:8, 19). Jeremiah has at best survived the onslaught of his opponents and withstood the abuse of his tormenters. However, he has never escaped insult and ridicule, nor enjoyed a place of power or even equilibrium. Like the God of Israel, Jeremiah has endured the pain of rejection and borne the sorrow of scorn and reproach. Painful beyond words is his collusion with God. Now in this last act, the Egyptian community disregards his counsel, writes him off as a charlatan, and forces him to go to Egypt against his own principles. This portrait of the prophet is a painful reminder of the cost of discipleship (Dietrich Bonhoeffer). It is also a sure testimony that words and witness outlive the nightmare of abuse.

When the Egyptian contingent takes Jeremiah (and Baruch) captive to Egypt, they undermine their own plans of muting and skirting the voice of God. For now Jeremiah can carry on haunting and hounding, confronting and confounding. His captivity thus unwittingly makes possible the sojourn of God to this land of death and alienation. Yahweh follows the people to Egypt and is not about to cave in to their prodigal stance. Yahweh too is resilient and determined to bring his people to repentance.

Second, the literary unit revolves around the theme of "obeying" or "not obeying" the word of God. Obedience to God is one of the book's prominent themes and it is no surprise that it continues to play out as the prophetic drama draws to a close. This motif emerges when Johanan and the people with him swear to "obey the voice of the LORD" (42:6). After Jeremiah receives an oracle demanding that they remain in the land, the people dismiss it as an outright lie and resolve to "not obey the voice of the LORD" (43:4, 7). The prose sermon (44:1-14) expands this theme: the contemporary community is as unwilling to "obey" the word of the Lord as earlier generations (44:5). In this manner, the prose homily construes Judah's entire history as one of rebellion. The word "obey" occurs fourteen times in these few chapters. Perhaps even more telling is the fact that the term appears nine times with a negation, "not obey." The call to obedience and the people's propensity toward disobedience give the narrative its peculiar shape. All along, however, the story is not merely a tale of past mistakes but a somber warning to subsequent communities of faith: unfaithfulness will issue in grave consequences; obedience to God's word is the cornerstone of community life.

The third thread that holds the unit together is the inversion of the exodus story. As Judah's world falls apart and the community comes face-to-face with death, echoes of its birth story resound.

Death's musings evoke memories of birth. Beginnings and endings converge in biting irony as the survivors of Judah, against the counsel of Jeremiah, take flight to Egypt. While Jer 42–44 deals with events that transpire after the destruction of Jerusalem, symbolic overtures permeate the narrative. That is to say, the story of the people's journey to Egypt is not only descriptive but symbolic as well. It represents the community's emigration as an outrageous act of defiance that nullifies the great exodus of Israel out of Egypt. Israel has gone full swing. In returning to the place of bondage, the people of God have dealt a deathblow to the story of salvation. Brueggemann notes in this regard: "The scenario of rescue that began with Moses in this pitiful moment ends in exhaustion, failure, defeat, and despair" (1998, 399). The womb of Israel's birth (Egypt) now becomes the abode of death.

HOPE FOR A FEW (JEREMIAH 45)

Literary Analysis

The Baruch Narrative ends where it began, with a reference to the scroll written at the dictation of Jeremiah in the fourth year of King Jehoiakim (605). In this way, Jer 36 and 45 frame the story. Like the prologue and epilogue of Job, these two chapters form an envelope that holds in place the intervening material. Unlike the framework of Job, the bookends of the Baruch Narrative do not create coherence with conventional categories of conflict and resolution or exposition and denouement. Nor do they unify with chronological arrangements, as evident by the fact that the events narrated in chapters 37–44 take place *after* the scroll production in 605, the fourth year of Jehoiakim. In view of this chronological discrepancy, some regard Jer 45:1-5 as a "misplaced," "unconnected," or "misdated" addendum. However, disinterest in historical categories is not at all surprising. As elsewhere in the book, the conclusion of the Baruch Narrative merely rejects ordinary time for "scroll-time."

Expressed another way, the framework of the Baruch Narrative is anchored in a special transforming moment rather than in events arranged in sequence. Consequently, time stands still in the "fourth year of Jehoiakim's reign" as "scroll-time" unifies the events of the intervening chapters 37–44. The scroll or word of Yahweh surrounds and organizes the chaos of cowardly leaders, mass murderers, shattered dreams, a tormented prophet and scribe, and a fatal descent to Egypt. It exposes the lie of "the emperor's new clothes" and pronounces God's judgment on Judah's kings. It undermines royal power and buoys the faith of the faithful. The scroll is Yahweh's trump card that puts every-thing in perspective. Its bracketing presence is far from accidental (See also Second Isaiah's attention to the word of God in Isa 40:5, 8 and Isa 55:10-11).

Exegetical Analysis

A Final Word for Baruch (45:1-5)

An individual oracle of comfort (45:1-5) brings to a close the so-called Baruch Narrative. As we have seen, the prophecy deliv-ered to Baruch by Jeremiah is dated in the "fourth year of King Jehoiakim," a time fraught with enormous significance. Like the year 587, the year 605 is theologically and politically charged. This is when Baruch writes on a scroll Jeremiah's prophecies read before Jehoiakim (45:1); that is, when prophetic power takes on royal power and prevails. This date marks the start of the dread-filled regime of King Nebuchadrezzar of Babylon and the end of Judah's independence (25:1). The "fourth year of King Jehoiakim" sets in motion a series of events that would shake heaven and earth and transform Judah's character forever. This moment signifies the onslaught of exile and powerlessness, as well as fear, panic, and death.

At zero hour, Jeremiah recalls a complaint of his faithful friend and scribe. Baruch complains that he is distressed, worn out, and can find no respite from his condition. In the vein of other laments in the Bible, the language is vague, lacking a particular social loca-tion or occasion. We do not know whether Baruch's cry of distress arose out of a personal predicament or one related to his scribal vocation. However, since he never appears apart from Jeremiah and the prophetic mission, one might surmise that his involvement in God's work is the source of his suffering. For this reason, he cries out and accuses God of adding sorrow to his pain (cf. 15:10). Baruch expects some consolation for his efforts (45:5). Perhaps in the best of worlds, Baruch would receive divine vindication after faithfully serving God and God's messenger. However, given the gravity of the times, when Yahweh is breaking down what has been built and plucking up what has been planted, conventional modes of orientation are no longer operative. Thus, Baruch's request is not granted. Instead, Jeremiah scolds his friend and demands that he not seek "great things" for himself. It is interesting that the divine rebuke bears a striking resemblance to God's rejoinder to Jeremiah's own complaints (see 12:1-6 and 15:15:21). This is no time for a reprieve from adversity, even for the faithful. When disaster befalls "all flesh" suffering is unavoidable (45:5).

At this point, the divine response through Jeremiah takes a more positive turn. Despite the perilous times, Baruch will receive his "life as a prize of war" (45:5). This individual salvation oracle is modest at best; nonetheless, it represents a pledge of a future. Springing up from the wreckage of a fallen world (45:4) are signs of survival and subdued optimism. As Marion Ann Taylor has argued, "for the reader of chapter 45, the comprehensive promises of future hope and salvation . . . echo but faintly. . . . At the same time, however, the echoes of the salvation oracle given to Ebed-melech, the Ethiopian, resound (cf. 39:17-18)" (1987, 93). Baruch and Ebed-melech, both of whom escape with their lives, represent the faithful few whose presence provides "a telling foil to the flagrantly disobedient multitudes who will necessarily come under judgment" (Taylor 1987, 93).

Theological and Ethical Analysis

Chapter 45 is one of three conclusions to the second half of Jeremiah and the book as a whole (along with the Oracles Against the Nations in chapters 46–51 and the historical appendix in Jer 52). Each ending anticipates better times for the suffering people of God. In chapter 45 God offers Baruch a word of hope: the scribe and confidant of Jeremiah will survive the treacherous times

of breaking down and plucking up. As one flees a burning building or a battle gone amuck, Baruch will escape with his life.
Nothing more, nothing less! Although "there is not yet energy for
rebuilding or planting . . . [and] little space for dancing or laugh-
ing" (O'Connor 2001, 522), one hears a whisper of hope which
leaves its signature on the book.

Ironically, the theological import of this reticent overture of
hope to Baruch could not be more significant, for it unmasks the
illusion of power and hints at God's place among the broken of
the world. The text suggests that hope exists on the margins and
not at the center. It is not found in triumphant nationalism or military might; that is, in the garb of winners. Nor is it held captive
to conventional modes of reward for faithful living. Instead, hope
emerges among the vulnerable and wounded. It is born in those
who are no longer privileged in the old ways and who no longer
benefit from the insulation of a safe and reliable world. Although
Baruch (and those he represents) will not receive the "great
things" that he so much desires, he will at least survive. And the
promise of survival, during times of massive loss, is nothing to
scoff at!

ORACLES AGAINST THE NATIONS
(JEREMIAH 46–51)

Literary Analysis

The final section of the book of Jeremiah (Jer 46–51) is composed of nine oracles (counting Kedar and Hazor as one) against
foreign nations and peoples. With the exception of a few interspersed words of salvation, the speeches bring indictments for
harsh brutality and obscene arrogance. Below is a list of the
Oracles against the Nations in the order in which they appear in
the Hebrew text.

Concerning Egypt	Jer 46:2-28
Concerning Philistia	Jer 47:1-7
Concerning Moab	Jer 48:1-47

Concerning Ammon	Jer 49:1-6
Concerning Edom	Jer 49:7-22
Concerning Damascus	Jer 49:23-27
Concerning Kedar and Hazor	Jer 49:28-33
Concerning Elam	Jer 49:34-39
Concerning Babylon	Jer 50:1–51:64

Each prophecy differs in form, substance, and length. While most are formulations of judgment, some taunt foes, others lament painful times, and still others exult in the demise of enemy peoples as well as in the dawning of an age of justice and divine retribution. All bring to light the meaning of Jeremiah's assertion in the previous passage that God is plucking up "the whole [earth]" (the Hebrew word ʾereṣ can be translated "earth" or "land") and "bring[ing] disaster upon all flesh" (45:4, 5). Now the portrait of Yahweh's massive assault takes definitive shape. As for length, the shortest oracle concerns the kingdom of Aram-Damascus, and the longest, comprising 104 verses and nearly half of the collection, is a diatribe against Babylon (Jer 50–51). With regard to organization, prophecies denouncing two of Israel's perennial foes function as bookends to the collection (chapters 46 and 50–51). The first speech assails longtime nemesis Egypt, Israel's first oppressor, while the final one exacts punishment upon Judah's most recent captor Babylon. With a few exceptions, the intervening prophecies address nations with whom the people of Judah and Israel have had a long history of animus. That Yahweh should judge and ultimately defeat their enemies can only signal hope and salvation for them.

The sheer volume of the oracle against Babylon affords it cumulative status: it is the main act in the reenactment of God's reign on earth. The first eight oracles serve as an opening to Yahweh's center stage performance against Judah's archenemy. The overthrow of Babylon represents the climax and culmination of God's judgment against the nations. By concluding the Oracles Against the Nations with the defeat of brazen Babylon, the nation that holds the keys to the future of an oppressed and demoralized community of exiles, the text both celebrates Yahweh's sovereignty and opens the door to an epoch of hope for the refugees residing there. Through written utterance and liturgical reenactment, the oracle against Babylon in Jer 50–51 creates a matrix through which suffering exiles are able to see through their shattered world to new social realities. Although their world has spiraled out of control, the text is adamant that God is still in control.

It is noteworthy that the portrayal of Babylon in Jer 50–51 is altogether different from elsewhere in the book. Before reaching the collection, Babylon is depicted as God's instrument of retribution, the nation commissioned and empowered to punish Judah and its neighbors (see, e.g., Jer 27–28). Babylon's king is "the servant" of Yahweh (25:9; 27:6; 43:10) who cannot be opposed. Noncompliance to his decrees amounts to insubordination to Yahweh. Babylon is also the distant place where the people of Judah must live out their time of exile. To go elsewhere or to stay in the land of Judah is to rebel against God's will. Actually, it is difficult to find a negative word against Babylon prior to Jer 50–51 (see though 25:12; 27:7). This constructive assessment of Babylon changes drastically in the Oracles Against the Nations. Now Babylon is the archenemy of God. Its monstrous deeds have left their mark on the world. Consequently, Yahweh must take drastic measures. To expedite justice and liberate Judah (50:8-10), Yahweh must dispose of proud Babylon and its belligerent ruler once and for all.

Historical and symbolic language run together in the oracle against Babylon. On the one hand, the text refers to a real historical entity, a nation born out of the maelstrom of Assyria's weakness in the seventh century. Certain historical realities thus inform the oracle, such as Babylon's political domination in the Near East from the late-seventh century to the mid-sixth century, the presence of Jewish refugees in Babylon and their eventual return to Jerusalem, as well as the eventual overthrow of Babylon by Persia in the year 539. On the other hand, the text is far more elemental and visceral than literal; symbolic interests in many ways eclipse historical constraints. The figure of Babylon functions as a metaphor, which represents human insolence and power gone berserk. Though once an obedient vassal of Yahweh, Babylon now encroaches upon divine boundaries and thus endangers the world (cf. Gen 11:1-9). For the sake of the suffering exiles and the order of creation, God musters all God's resources to wage warfare. Babylon *must* be defeated. The battle between God and Babylon is therefore nothing less than a battle between good and evil. And justice ultimately prevails.

The prophecy against Babylon is a composite containing a number of poems and prose additions that reflect an extended process of composition. Although commentators are nowhere near a consensus, six scenes reenacting the fall of Babylon can be delineated (cf. Bellis 1995):

> The Intertwining Destinies of Babylon and Judah: 50:1-20
> The True Colors of Babylon Revealed: 50:21-32
> The Utter Desolation of Babylon: 50:33-40
> The Re-identification of the Foe from the North: 50:41-46
> God's Power and Resolve to Punish Babylon: 51:1-33
> The True King Revealed: 51:34-58

Each of these units could be easily subdivided. Framing the six major scenes is a superscription that introduces the whole prophecy as the word of Yahweh through Jeremiah (50:1) and a concluding narrative about the preservation of Jeremiah's utterances against Babylon in written form (51:59-64).

The placement of the Oracles Against the Nations as a collection is fraught with interpretive import. The Oracles against the Nations appear at the end of the book (and in their present order) *only in the Hebrew text* (MT). The Septuagint (LXX) places the collection after Jeremiah's indictment against Babylon and other nations in chapter 25: "I will bring upon that land all the words that I have uttered against it, everything written in this book, which *Jeremiah prophesied against all the nations*" (25:13, emphasis mine). The final words of this verse then introduce the oracles. The vision of Yahweh's cup of wrath poured out on the nations (25:15-38) then concludes the collection. By associating the Oracles Against the Nations with the cup of poison and by including Jeremiah and the towns of Judah on the list of nations that must drink from it (25:18), the LXX ends the first half of the book with universal judgment. The LXX thus amplifies the nature and extent of God's judgment and marginalizes any hope for Judah's asylum. No one will escape destruction, not even God's people. The placement of the collection in the MT serves a different purpose. The order of the oracles and their penultimate position in the book convey a keen sense of optimism for the people of God. Even though they have encountered violence, hardship, and exile, the Oracles Against the Nations envisage the demise of the very power(s) responsible for their condition. In their present position in the MT, the prophet's last words display God's stunning victory over the powers of evil, including and especially Babylonian hegemony. The anthology opens the door to happier times for those banished to faraway places. In this way, the composers bring closure with overtures of renewal and rebuilding. And the book's overall framework follows the prophetic pattern of judgment and salvation, plucking up and planting.

Exegetical Analysis

An Oracle Against Egypt (46:1-28)

After a messenger formula introduces the entire collection (46:1), the first of the Oracles Against the Nations targets Egypt, the once perilous place of slavery and the new home for the Judean remnant fleeing the wrath of Babylon. This oracle separates into three distinct poems (46:2-12, 13-24, 25-28). The first two broadcast bad news for Egypt: the armies of Egypt will fall into the hands of their enemies. The last announces the positive repercussions of this collapse for the people of Judah. Introducing each vignette is a prose reference to Babylon and Nebuchadrezzar (46:2, 13, 25-26). The editorial headings historicize the poems. They place Egypt and Babylon on the battleground engaged in fierce conflict. War imagery, therefore, pervades all three scenes. But these poems are not reports of warfare; they are "acts of imagination" by which a powerless people can harness the massive memory of the Egyptian Empire. By re-enacting Egypt's rout, a captive and vulnerable community envisions an alternative world which Yahweh manages with justice.

The first scene of this drama is set "in the fourth year of Jehoiakim son of Josiah of Judah" (605) when Babylon and its military leader Nebuchadrezzar defeated the Egyptian armies by the Euphrates at Carchemish (46:2-12). As we have seen, this particular date holds enormous significance. In the year 605, Babylon erupted as the dominant power in Syria-Palestine and prince Nebuchadrezzar ascended to the throne. In light of these developments, the year 605 is thick with metaphorical meanings. It reappears at crucial junctures in the book to convey danger and unrest (25:1; 36:1; 45:1; cf. 26:1; 27:1). The "fourth year of Jehoiakim" signals a great unraveling of long-standing certainties and a turning point in life; it marks the end of one world and the start of a new one. No less significant than the year 587, the geopolitical events of 605 bring to an end Judah's hope for independence. Indeed, the historical distance between 605 and 587 collapses into a singular moment of terror and judgment. In the present context, the year 605 symbolizes that time is running out for Egypt. When the armies of Babylon prevail at Carchemish, they deal a death-blow to Egypt's territorial ambitions to "cover the earth" (46:7-8). Egypt's quest for world domination ends abruptly on the killing fields by the river Euphrates.

At this freighted place and time, Yahweh calls on military troops to prepare for battle. "[Get ready] . . . advance . . . harness the horses; mount the steeds . . . take your stations, . . . whet your lances, [prepare] your [armor]" (46:3-4). The staccato-like force of the commands reveals military readiness and resolve. Whether Yahweh addresses the armies of Babylon or Egypt is unclear. But the parallel call for war preparations in 46:9 suggests that the divine warrior is directing the Egyptian military machine. If so, the intent is to dishonor and destroy since from the very outset the Egyptian army is helpless before the enemy (46:5-6). The assault leaves the lines demoralized and in total disarray. Warriors stumble and break ranks; the swift retreat in panic with nowhere to run. The offensive strikes such fear into the hearts of the Egyptian infantry that it can see only "terror [on every side]," a phrase that elsewhere denotes divine judgment (46:5; see also 6:24-25; 20:3, 10).

The poet interrupts the retreat to mock Egypt's haughty position (46:7-8). In light of its present plight, Egypt's vast power and center-stage prestige look silly. Its imperialistic ventures fade into obscurity. Though Egypt once boasted, "Let me rise [like the Nile], let me cover the earth, let me destroy cities and their inhabitants" (46:8*b*), the pompous nation now runs scared. Back at the front lines, Yahweh musters Egyptian warriors and ancillary forces for further engagement (46:9-12). But again their efforts are in vain. Egypt's defeat is inevitable because this is no ordinary battle and the enemy is no ordinary foe. Unwittingly, Egypt is engaged in warfare with Yahweh on Yahweh's day and therefore the outcome for Egypt can only be disastrous. On this day, the Lord God of hosts exacts retribution and gains vindication from his foes (46:10). Often related to oracles against foreign nations (see Isa 13:6, 9; Ezek 30:2, 3; Obad 1:15, 16; cf. Amos 5:18), the day of Yahweh is Yahweh's time of reckoning; it is the occasion when Yahweh intervenes in world affairs to punish evildoers, right the wrongs of people, save the righteous, and establish justice on earth. On this day, Egypt's fate is certain. Three vivid portraits depict its horrible end: (1) like a wild beast consuming its prey, a bloodthirsty sword will devour its victim; (2) the wounded and dead of the war effort will become Yahweh's sacrificial meal (cf. Zeph 1:7); and (3) virgin daughter Egypt is too ill for the medicinal oils from the trees of Gilead. Without healing or help, Egypt's funeral speech is certain: "The nations have heard of your shame, and the earth is full of your cry; for warrior has stumbled against warrior; both have fallen together" (46:12).

The second scene in the drama involves further engagement in warfare (46:13-24). A hauntingly vague reference to Nebuchadrezzar and Babylon sets the stage (46:13). The prose allusion mentions the invading enemy and moves the conflict from Carchemish to the land of Egypt (46:2). Then the prophet summons strategic cities in Egypt to prepare for battle. The call to arms no longer contemplates a frontal attack; battle orders are just defensive. Troops are to take their stations and brace themselves for the devouring sword (46:14). As before, though, preparations are futile and the outcome is certain. This theo-military assault turns Egypt's symbolic and social worlds on its head. An anonymous voice, perhaps that of Yahweh, derides Egypt's wretched condition. "Why has Apis fled? Why did your bull not stand?" (46:15). As Yahweh once leveled the Philistine god Dagon (cf. 1 Sam 5), so Yahweh thrusts the mighty bull-god Apis down to the ground. Egypt's gods are no competition for the living God; nor are Egypt's mercenary forces. Once the backbone of its military machine, they now desert and head home in disgrace. Even Pharaoh (Hophra?), king of the Egyptian empire, is really nothing more than an inept leader, whom the poet renames "braggart who missed his chance" (46:17). In stark contrast to this pageant of folly and debacle of a king stands the true "king" whose name is Yahweh of hosts (46:18; cf. Isa 6:1, 5). Yahweh acts decisively to bring an invader against Egypt whose assault is so devastating that "sheltered daughter Egypt" must pack the bags for exile.

To the delight of downtrodden Jews in Babylon, routed gods, stumbling warriors, baffled kings, and banished people all expose the vulnerability of the great empire. The text intends to amuse as much as mock. By the force of this defiant script, the powerless are empowered and the well-established power arrangements of Egypt are reduced to naught. Yahweh is acknowledged as the principal player in life's drama, the God who acts in, through, and behind the scenes to create a just and moral world.

The parody on Egypt blossoms in a rich display of metaphors (46:20-24). Egypt is a "beautiful heifer" beset and driven mad by a "gadfly" from the north. Its soldiers are like "fatted calves" that flee before their time for slaughter. Like a snake Egypt slithers away to evade "enemies march[ing] in force . . . with axes" to fell the forest. Due to their sheer numbers, these foes destroy impenetrable defenses: "they are more numerous than locusts; they [cannot be counted]." The massive invasion from the north, the portentous symbol of peril and crumbling worlds, results in Egypt's humiliation and defeat. Rhetoric once used against Judah and Israel is re-directed against Egypt. Interestingly, the poet does not identify the invader here, nor does he need to since the real agent of devastation all along is Yahweh. Yahweh conducts the dread military exercise against Egypt, which makes the outcome certain.

Resembling its earlier counterparts (46:2, 13), the prose comment sets up the next scene with an allusion to warfare between Egypt and Nebuchadrezzar of Babylon (46:25-26): Yahweh intends to deliver Egypt over to "King Nebuchadrezzar of Babylon and his officers." This prose statement is distinctive in several respects. First, it mitigates the divine judgment against Egypt by promising future restoration. Though Yahweh delivers Egypt into the power of the Babylonian ruler, Egypt will recover from the ravages of war and eventually thrive again. Second, the prose opening not only launches the next scene but comments on the previous one, echoing, clarifying, and elaborating existing motifs. Whereas the preceding poem speaks of Egypt's demise with engaging ambiguity, the prose explanation is far more direct: it simply asserts that disaster is coming upon Egypt. Yahweh is acting against Egypt's gods and institutions. The sixfold preposition "upon" (or "[against]") reveals intense antagonism for Egypt's entire social and symbolic systems (46:25). Besides Amon, the chief deity of Thebes, Yahweh will punish "Pharaoh, and Egypt and her gods and her kings . . . Pharaoh and those who trust in him." This clumsy and repetitive construction speaks of sweeping judgment. Finally, the prose statement introduces a tale of two countries, Egypt and Judah, "lands with a strange history of intersections and parallels" (46:25-29). Both nations endure enormous upheaval before God commutes their death sentence and reverses their fortunes. Both suffer the pangs of Babylonian domination and subsequent exile. Yet, the tale of these two cities could not be more different. Whereas Egypt is the target of wrath, Judah is the recipient of enduring love. Egypt must brace itself for disaster, but Judah can look forward to salvation (46:27-28; see also 30:10-11). God quiets servant Jacob's debilitating fear with words of assurance and hope. Yahweh promises to rescue from afar and protect Judah from its captors. And Judah can be confident of returning from its captivity in peace and serenity. Although God's people are not let off scot-free, their future is indeed bright in light of God's deep concern and intent on bringing judgment against the regimes that have oppressed them.

An Oracle Against Philistia (47:1-7)

Israel's fierce rival Philistia is the brunt of the second of Yahweh's oracles against the nations. The Philistines were an Aegean people who settled on the coastal plain along the Mediterranean in the late-thirteenth and early-twelfth century. According to biblical accounts, their interactions with the people of Israel were vexing almost from the outset and their presence in the land created a state of emergency (Judg 13–16). The crisis surfaced in several venues. It was played out in the theatre of war as well as at sacred shrines (1 Sam 4:1–7:1). The Philistine threat was so intense that Israel found it necessary to consolidate its loose tribal confederation into a more centralized government. This move involved compromising venerable covenantal and theocratic structures for monarchic arrangements, sending shockwaves through the nation. Only after years of warfare did the people of Israel finally subdue the Philistines and win control of the land (2 Sam 5:17-25; 8:1; 21:15-22). Hostilities, however, continued until the fall of Jerusalem. This antipathy is evident in the books of 1 Kings and 2 Chronicles (e.g., 1 Kgs 15:27; 16:15; 2 Chr 26:6-7; 28:18) and in prophetic sayings against foreign nations, which list Philistia among the peoples against whom Yahweh will bring judgment (Isa 14:29-32; Ezek 25:15-17; Amos 1:6-8; Zeph 2:4-7). Isaiah, Ezekiel, Amos, and Zephaniah condemn the Philistines for acts of vengeance and inhumanity, for boasting in the suffering of an enemy nation, and for infidelity to God. Jeremiah apparently announces coming disaster without reference to particular crimes.

Three features distinguish this prophecy concerning the Philistines. First, the heading associates the oracle with an attack on Gaza by Pharaoh from the south (47:1), although the remainder of the oracle suggests an assault from the north. Though discrepancies clearly exist, the text imagines dread forces from the north (Babylon) *and* the south (Egypt) blitzing the Philistines and swallowing up the once fierce nation. Israel's rival does not have a chance against these two superpowers, and all the more so since Yahweh is in collusion with them. Second, Jeremiah appears as one whose predictions concerning the Philistines come true. He receives the word of the Lord "before Pharaoh attacked Gaza" (47:1), yet soon after his prophecy (47:2-4), the events occur (47:5-7). In this way, the passage presents Jeremiah as a true prophet, that is, as one whose oracles come true (Deut 18:22). Third, this brief poem is bursting with sibilants in the Hebrew text—*sh, s, ts*. The first three verses alone contain nine. The number of sibilants totals twenty-five. The literary effect of this surplus is cumulative. The "hissing" of the "sh," "s," and "ts" shames and derides as much as the indictment itself. Thus, through form as well as content, the poetry achieves its purpose.

To describe the coming incursion (47:2-4), the poet exploits an array of metaphors that denote danger and disorder. He warns of torrential waters flooding land, city, and inhabitants and leaving the Philistines wailing (47:2). In the ancient world, the resurgent waters of the sea symbolize disruptive and life-threatening forces. In creation accounts, for instance, primeval waters threaten the order of creation. This is clearly the case in the Babylonian epic *Enuma Elish*, where the goddess Tiamat represents the oceanic chaos subdued by the head god, Marduk. In the priestly creation in Genesis, the "[watery deep]" ("*tehôm*," which may be etymologically related to "*tiamat*") represents primordial chaos tamed by Yahweh (see, e.g., Gen 1:2; cf. Pss 42:7; 104:6). As primeval history unfolds, humankind revolts against Yahweh and Yahweh turns the ordered universe back to chaos in the form of an undifferentiated mass of water: the deluge destroys all life except for that preserved on the ark (Gen 6–9; see esp. Gen 7:11; 8:2). Thus, the image of raging waters symbolizes the ever-present possibility of the collapse of the very structure of life (e.g., Ps 46). When the prophet speaks of waters rising out of the north, he envisions dread forces creating havoc in the land of the Philistines. The northern waters would inundate the land and reduce the Philistines to nothing (47:2). The connection to the north, another symbol of impending doom, intensifies the force of the metaphor exponentially. Next, the poet shifts from treacherous waters to galloping stallions and the rumbling of enemy chariots (47:3). Invading troops enter the land and instill such fear that parents, in their search for safety, abandon their children. The poet's final metaphor is the impending "day" (47:4; cf. 46:10). The mere mention of the "day of Yahweh" makes plain what the previous images had only implied: the destroyer of Philistia, and the coastal countries of Tyre and Sidon, is Yahweh.

While Yahweh is the speaker of 47:2-4, anonymous voices, perhaps including the victims of the assault themselves, speak in 47:5-7. One cries out that the predicted invasion has in fact taken place (47:5). Another appeals for calm and pleads for mercy. "Ah, sword of [Yahweh]! How long until you are quiet? Put yourself into your scabbard, rest and be still!" (47:6). In this liturgical drama, the tellers are not oblivious to the enemy's grief and sorrow (cf. 48:3-6). Another voice, however, will not entertain the enemies' petition for a reprieve. Yahweh's program and purposes are irreversible (47:7). As is the case for the people of Judah, they can plead with Yahweh but not pigeonhole Yahweh, who is under no obligation to respond.

An Oracle Against Moab (48:1-47)

The prophet turns his attention next to Moab, another long-standing foe of Israel and Judah. Moab was a nation across the Jordan and to the southeast of Judah. For most of its history, it shared borders with Ammon to the north and Edom to the south. According to the Bible, the interactions of Moab with Israel were hostile from the time of the exodus to the fall of Jerusalem, and perhaps even into the early second temple era (see Ezra 9:1; Neh 13:1, 23). When the Israelites were in the Transjordan en route to Canaan, Moab joined forces with its ally Midian to prevent the Israelites from entering its land. The king of Moab, Balak son of Zippor, sent the prophet Balaam to curse the Israelites in order to "defeat them and drive them from the land" (Num 22:6). Although Balak's efforts fail the Israelites end up yoked to the Baal of Peor, a deity associated with the place, in violation of its covenant relationship with Yahweh (Num 25). Deep-seated hostilities between Moab and Israel continued well into the time of the monarchy (1 Sam 12:9; 14:47; 2 Sam 8:2). The Moabites were sometimes victors in battle and other times vassals to Israel, but they were almost always a thorn in Israel's flesh. They posed a nearby military threat and a constant religious and social danger to the people of Israel and Judah (see, e.g., Num 25; Judg 10:6; 1 Kgs 11:7, 33; Neh 13:23). As late as the reign of Jehoiakim, bands of Moabites joined Babylonians, Syrians, and Ammonites to raid Judah (2 Kgs 24:2). Although contacts were occasionally amicable (see 1 Sam 22:3-4; Jer 27:1-11), Moab for the most part was Israel's bitter enemy. According to oracles against the nations in Jeremiah, Isaiah, Ezekiel, Amos, and Zephaniah, Moab's defeat and punishment was an important component of Yahweh's reign and Israel's salvation. In the postexilic period, however, the Moabite Ruth became a stunning example of an outsider converting to Judaism: the novella named for its heroine illustrates that even the worst of enemies can find favor with God (see Jonah's use of the Assyrians to demonstrate a similar point). Longtime rivals can sit down together at the table of God's covenant love.

Jeremiah 48 is the most extensive treatment of Moab in the prophetic books. Its repetitive and jumbled character, as well as its links to other texts in the Bible, suggests that the chapter is the product of a complex history involving many writers over considerable time (cf., e.g., vv. 43-44 and Isa 24:17-18 and vv. 29-39 with sections in Isa 15–16). Its extensive sections of poetry interspersed with short prose pieces support this conclusion. Moreover, a perusal of commentaries reveals serious problems in delimiting literary units. The complex and incoherent makeup of the chapter frustrates efforts to discern literary boundaries. Attempts to isolate early materials from later materials are just as problematic.

Jeremiah 48 reads as a cacophony: a torrent of voices spoken over considerable time that perceives the fall of Moab to be a demonstration of Yahweh's sovereignty. This cacophony reenacts the shattering of the "horn" or power of Moab as a theological datum: Yahweh overthrows arrogant Moab and so holds another wayward nation accountable for its deeds. It also represents a bold subversion of social conventions as apparent in the inordinate degree of sorrow for the fall of Moab, who is not only enemy but also distant kin (Gen 19:30-38). Next to announcements of judgment, the lament is the dominant genre of the chapter.

At the start, Yahweh announces that cities and fortresses in Moab have fallen (48:1-3a). An unnamed voice interrupts to spread the news: "Desolation and great destruction! Moab is destroyed!" (48:3b-4a). The devastation causes grief and anguish. The threefold use of the Hebrew word "cry" *(zᶜq)*, especially in association with little children, drives home the horrible effects of war (48:3-5). Amid the destruction another yells, "Flee! Save yourselves" (48:6). As the community of worshipers reenacts Moab's defeat, it listens in on the bitter weeping of the victims.

From the weeping of children the poet turns to crime and punishment. Moab is not innocent and its destruction is not without cause (48:7-9). God holds the nation responsible for its reliance on military prowess (reading with the LXX; Heb. reads "in your works") and financial systems. "You trusted in your strongholds and your treasures" (48:7). While these structures created a façade of stability in the past, they are now exposed as a root cause of Moab's demise. Due to its "false trust," the "destroyer" will pillage every village, and Chemosh, Moab's god, with priests and attendants will go into exile. The nation's loss will be total given that the destroyer's salt makes the land uninhabitable (cf. Judg 9:45).

A zealous voice from the sideline breaks in to pronounce a curse on one, perhaps the "destroyer of Moab," who is "slack in doing the work of [Yahweh]; and . . . who keeps back the sword from bloodshed" (48:10). Another uses the metaphor of winemaking to describe Moab's complacency, false sense of security, and future ills (48:11-13). Like an aged and undisturbed wine (cf. Zeph 1:12), Moab's aroma has been "unspoiled" and its flavor rich. Moab has lived at peace from its youth without adversity or exile. Yet this will soon change when Yahweh sends "decanters to decant him, and empty his vessels, and break his jars in pieces" (48:12); that is to say, when Yahweh's troublers arrive they will disrupt Moab's tranquil world and unmask its trusted systems. At that time, Moab will be ashamed of its god Chemosh, perhaps for not being able to save the nation from harm.

Contempt of Moab's power and arrogance gains momentum in Jer 48:14-27. A participant in the drama disputes the claim of the powerful in Moab that they are "heroes and mighty warriors" (48:14). Such boasting reflects an earlier time when Moab's fortunes were bright and its world was intact. At present the assertion is a glaring misreading of reality. The poet sees through this illusion and reveals the unimaginable to the well-positioned in Moabite society: the "destroyer of Moab" (mentioned in verses 15 and 18), and far more seriously, "the King, whose name is the LORD of hosts" (48:15) is about to cast down mighty Moab from its pedestal. The first will be last as Yahweh brings down the powerful from their thrones. This inversion of social and geo-political categories of privilege recurs throughout the poem:

"The choicest of his young men have gone down to slaughter."
   (v. 15)
"How the mighty scepter is broken,
   the glorious staff!" (v. 17)
"Come down from glory
   and sit on the parched ground,
   enthroned daughter of Dibon." (v. 18)
"Moab is put to shame, for it is broken down." (v. 20)

Boasting of power and position is ludicrous given Moab's present conditions. Far more appropriate is language of mourning. And indeed while the text confronts Moab's pride and insolence it also laments the nation's war-torn plight.

"The calamity of Moab is near at hand,
   and his doom approaches swiftly." (v. 16)
"Mourn over him, all you his neighbors,
   and all who know his name." (v. 17)
"Moab is put to shame . . .
   Wail and cry." (v. 20)

COMMENTARY

Harsh prose speakers interrupt the call to lamentation (48:21-28). Unsympathetic to Moab's troubles, they attack and deride. With declarative force, one lists the cities in Moab that have come under divine judgment. Indeed, judgment is so invasive that it has penetrated "all the towns of the land of Moab, far and near" (48:24). Yahweh's devastating assault has brought Moab to its knees and crushed its power ("horn" and "arm"). Then an even more abrasive participant jumps to demand that Moab drink from Yahweh's cup of wrath (48:26; cf. 25:15-29). "Make him drunk, because he magnified himself against [Yahweh]; let Moab wallow in his vomit" (48:26). Hence, the proud will get what they deserve; those who once demeaned Israel shall themselves become the brunt of jokes and derision.

After this prose interjection, the lament-taunt resumes (48:28-33). The fusion of vengeance and sorrow conveys a sense of ambivalence over Moab's predicament. On one hand, the community (note the pronoun "we" in 48:29) revels in the enemy's humiliation. Considering Moab's arrogance and disdain for Yahweh, it should meet defeat (48:28). It only makes sense! With six synonyms for pride, most derived from the same Hebrew root and sounding alike, a poet ridicules Moab's inflated view of itself. Moab is presumptuous and proud, arrogant and boastful, conceited and insolent (48:29). Even Yahweh mocks, "I myself know his insolence . . . his boasts are false, his deeds are false" (48:30). Moab's egotistical display of power and autonomy impresses no one, least of all Yahweh who dismisses it as deluded. Despite this battery of insults, the God of Israel takes no pleasure in the pain and defeat of Moab. The listening community may derive some satisfaction in the fall of its enemy, but Yahweh weeps over suffering Moab (48:31-33; cf. Isa 16:8-11), as Yahweh wept over suffering Judah (e.g., Jer 8:22-9:1; cf. 31:15). Devastation and sorrow in Moab, the cessation of joy and celebration, move Yahweh to tears: "I wail for Moab; I cry out . . . I mourn . . . I weep." Although Yahweh humbles the proud, Yahweh still mourns the loss.

This sorrowful mood sets the tone for the next section (48:34-39; cf. Isa 15:2-6). The scene is one of drought, devastation, and death. There is palpable disease everywhere and all mourn the end of life as it was known. Joining Yahweh's lamentation are Moab's war-torn cities. Their cries resound far and wide. Even the waters of Nimrim are dried up; they have no more tears to shed. Signs and sounds of grief define the once proud country: shaved heads, cut beards, gashed hands, and the garb of sackcloth. Housetops and streets echo with eerie wailing. The teller is unapologetic about Yahweh's involvement. The end of Moab is Yahweh's doing. Yahweh has "broken Moab like a vessel that no one wants. . . . How it is broken! How they wail! How Moab has turned his back in shame!" (48:38-39). Even so, Yahweh joins the chorus of mourners in Moab. God's heart "moans" for the fallen country like a flute playing the funeral dirge.

A series of divine oracles end the diatribe (48:40-47). The messenger speech, "says [Yahweh]" (using the two most common formulas), occurs four times. The final voice of the chapter is, not surprisingly, that of Yahweh, the One in whose hands rests the fate of Moab. As before, Yahweh speaks of the advent of enemy forces commissioned to attack and destroy. The foe will approach like a vulture (or eagle) swooping down on its prey (48:40). Its advance on Moab will be swift and powerful (see Deut 28:49; Hab 1:8; Ezek 17:3). The outcome of the assault is laid out in three brief scenes (48:41-43, 44, 45-46). The first unfolds with military logic:

> Fallen cities;
> Seized strongholds;
> Terrified warriors;
> The death of the nation!

The fall of Moab's bastions of power leads to its demise. Its collapse is a direct consequence of hubris (48:42; see also 48:26). The country's defeat, thus, is no mere geopolitic datum. It is a sure sign of Yahweh's victory, a victory that brings an end to Moab's pretensions of greatness. The next silhouette elaborates the wreckage (48:44; see also Isa 24:18). Everyone flees the terror only to fall into a pit; and all who climb out of the pit are caught in a trap (cf. Amos 5:19). With nowhere to hide, judgment on Moab is inescapable. The third scene telescopes the fall of one of Moab's principal cities. Once a city of prominence, Heshbon now lies in ruins. As the city goes up in flames, the teller remembers King Sihon of the Amorites who ruled from Heshbon and who forbade Israel from entering its land on its journey to Canaan (Num 21:21-35). Again, stories from the beginning and the end converge in a strange sort of way. A lamentation marks the death of the country: "Woe to you, O Moab! The people of Chemosh have perished, for your sons have been taken captive, and your daughters into captivity" (48:46). Without children Moab's fate appears to be sealed. Yet unexpectedly, a word of hope paves the way for the survival of Moab (48:47). Yahweh promises to restore its fortunes in the distant future. In this way, the final note of the cacophony whispers softly that mercy awaits Israel's longtime foe (see also, e.g., 46:26; 49:6, 39).

An Oracle Against Ammon (49:1-6)

Chapter 49 consists of a series of oracles concerning Ammon (49:1-6), Edom (49:7-22), Damascus (49:23-27), Kedar and Hazor (49:28-33), and Elam (49:34-39). Little holds these texts together aside from their denunciatory tone. One encounters a variety of forms, circumstances, and judgments against these nations. Most of the oracles are relatively brief and straightforward, the condemnation of Edom being an exception to the rule. The complex prophecy against Edom consumes over a third of the chapter. To our knowledge, only four of the six nations were enemies of Judah and Israel. Kedar and Hazor were Arabian tribes of the eastern desert with whom the people of Judah had little contact. It is possible that the nations are mentioned here because they were victims of Babylonian imperialism. It is certain that they set the stage for a massive literary assault on Babylon in the following chapters.

The first oracle centers on Ammon, another rival ethnic group according to Gen 19:30-38. The Ammonites lived east of the Jordan to the north of Moab. With borders far more fluid than those of Moab or Edom, Ammon emerged around its capital Rabbah and the valley of the river Jabbok. As far as can be determined, contact between Israel and Ammon was frequently hostile (e.g., Deut 23:3). Biblical stories recall Ammon repeatedly harassing their distant kin Israel. Ammon joined anti-Israelite coalitions (Judg 3:12-14), subjugated Israel (Judg 10:6-18), engaged in frequent military skirmishes (e.g., 1 Sam 11:1-11), and brutalized pregnant women to enlarge its own borders (Amos 1:13-15). During the time of Jeremiah, Ammon conspired with Ishmael in the coup of Gedaliah (Jer 40:13-14) and provided asylum for his assassins (Jer 41:15). Although the Ammonites joined Judah in a stance against Babylonian domination in 594 (Jer 27) and later offered Jews a refuge from the Babylonian army after the fall of Jerusalem (Jer 40:11), their involvement in the collapse of the government of Gedaliah fueled old hostilities.

The prophecy against Ammon breaks down into three brief parts (49:1-2, 3-5, 6). In the first, Yahweh accuses Ammon of confiscating land that belonged to Israel. With incriminatory questions, Yahweh lays bare Ammon's illicit annexation of land (49:1). Yahweh asks if Israel has no sons or heirs. The rhetorical question demands a negative response: Israel indeed has descendants and therefore enjoys legitimate land claims, which the Ammonites have not honored. When Ammon and its patron god Milcom dispossessed the people of Gad, they acted in flagrant disregard for family inheritance rights. Ammon's military aggression proceeds as if the children of Israel were dead. Israel's divine warrior and arbiter will not tolerate Milcom's unauthorized seizure of Gad, and so will respond by invading Rabbah and destroying its villages. At the end of the day, Israel will repossess its land and dispossess the dispossessor (49:2). And Yahweh will triumph over competing forces.

Next, Yahweh's decisive action brings Ammon to grief (49:3-5). The poet summons Heshbon and the daughters of Rabbah to lament the desolation of its country and the defeat of its god. Yahweh will ban Milcom with his priests and attendants from its own borders. Yet Ammon, like Moab, still boasts of its trusted resources. So cocky is the nation that it scoffs, "Who will attack me?" Ammon's aggrandizement, however, does not impress Yahweh, who penetrates its seemingly impenetrable defenses and crushes the state. Even so, in the last scene, Yahweh promises to one day "restore the fortunes of the Ammonites" (49:6).

An Oracle Against Edom (49:7-22)

Israel's vengeful "brother" Esau/Edom is next in line for divine critique (see also Gen 25:29-34; Deut 23:7-8). Dealings between these two eponymous brothers and their offspring were rarely amicable (see Num 20:14-21; 1 Sam 14:47; 1 Kgs 11:14-17). But after 587 they deteriorated to an all-time low. According to the Bible, the Edomites abetted the Babylonian destruction of Jerusalem and taunted their suffering brethren (Ps 137:7; Lam 4:21-23; Ezek 25:12-14). When Edom confiscated southern parts of Judean territory, it galvanized kinship enmities (Ezek 35:1-15; 36:5; Obad 11-14). Interestingly, the oracle against Edom does not directly refer to this cruelty toward Judah; the only transgression specifically mentioned is pride (49:16).

The oracle against Edom uses a barrage of images, rhetorical questions, biblical echoes and citations, and wordplays to depict approaching devastation (49:7-22). Yahweh inquires whether wisdom has disappeared from Teman, an area in southern Edom traditionally known for its sages (49:7; e.g., Job 2:11). The question itself is alarming. If the people of Edom possessed wisdom and counsel, they would surely understand the gravity of the times and would flee for cover (Jer 49:8). To draw attention to Moab's exigent situation, the poet contrasts Yahweh with grape-gatherers and thieves. The comparison is also disconcerting. Whereas thieves steal only what they want and grape harvesters leave some of the gleanings for the poor, Yahweh's punishment of Esau is thorough. Edom will be stripped naked (cf. Jer 13:22; Isa 47:3) and its progeny destroyed until no one remains (49:9-10). A prose teller escalates the impassioned tone with the cup imagery (49:12; see also 25:15-29). If the innocent from the nations must drink the cup of suffering, how much more shall guilty Edom? Disaster shall overtake all flesh and no one will escape, especially not Edom. Yahweh pinpoints fortified Bozrah as the epicenter of the devastation (49:13). A play on the words *bāṣrâ* (Bozrah in 49:13), *bōṣrîm* ("grape-gathers" in 49:9) and *bāzûy* ("despised" in

49:15) in conjunction with the divine oath to punish Edom's capital city accentuates the nation's terrible fate.

The "I" of the next section is no longer Yahweh, but an unnamed speaker who hears a "report from [Yahweh]" (49:14-15; cf. Obad 1-4). A messenger rallies the nations to take action against Edom, a country that inspires terror but is soon to become the "least among the nations." Yet again, pride and military prowess deceive a nation into believing it is invincible. Edom's high ground and impregnable positions, however, are no contest for the forces to come. Yahweh will topple Edom from its "nest as high as the eagle's" and reduce the proud nation to nothing (49:16).

Several figures convey the totality and intensity of the destruction (49:17-22). First, the teller recalls the fate of Sodom and Gomorrah in order to imagine Edom's total desolation (49:18). Second, Yahweh appears as a ravenous lion from the thickets of the Jordan (49:19-20). In deadly pursuit, the ferocious attacker will drive Edom from its land and drag away "the little ones of the flock." Third, so thunderous is the sound of Edom's fall from the heights that it echoes throughout the world (49:21). The text uses cosmic language to speak of the collapse of the nation. Fourth, like a vulture spreading its wings over its victim, an unnamed invader will swoop down on Bozrah and terrify Edom's mighty warriors. Interrogative clauses heralding God's incomparable power and tenacious determination to act against Edom strengthen the power of these allusions. "For who is like me? Who can summon me? Who is the shepherd who can stand before me?" (49:19). To each rhetorical question the reader must reply, "No one!"

Unlike Egypt, Moab, and Ammon, there is no promise of restoration for Edom. Yet, nestled in the grim imagery of this oracle is a brief verse that appears to challenge the picture of wholesale destruction. Yahweh promises to protect the orphans and widows of war-torn Edom (49:11). Despite the force of the divine offensive, God still acts with tenderness toward the vulnerable and needy. Yahweh the warrior is still "father of orphans and protector of widows" (Ps 68:5). The excess of violence does not entirely obscure hope for the hopeless, even among Israel's foes.

An Oracle Against Damascus (49:23-27)

The announcement of judgment against Damascus, another traditional nemesis of Israel, is brief and conventional. It includes neither a setting nor a description of guilt. The prophecy merely reports the angst of Hamath and Arpad, two smaller city-states in the central and northern region of Syria, at the news of impending doom. In addition, the poem anticipates the defeat of the great city of Damascus. These three Syrian states were at odds with Israel during the ninth and eighth centuries, although Damascus was by far the most menacing foe. Damascus and its neighboring kingdoms eventually fell to the Assyrian Empire toward the end of the eighth century; nonetheless, the writer of 2 Kings recounts bands of Arameans harassing Judah well into the reign of King Nebuchadrezzar of Babylon (2 Kgs 24:1-2).

The brief poem relates that bad news has finally reached the north. To this point, words of divine judgment have centered primarily on countries in the south and east of the Jordan. Now Syrian cities hear the dreadful reports, presumably of a world under Babylonian siege. The news strikes terror into the hearts of the people of Hamath and Arpad. The hearers "melt in fear" and are "troubled like the sea" (49:23). Damascus too is alarmed, especially upon hearing that it is the object of the aggression. The famous city becomes feeble and panic-stricken. Like "a woman in labor," Damascus is seized by pain. Like its neighbors, it will fall to enemy forces. Its soldiers shall be destroyed, its walls shall be set ablaze, and its strongholds shall be devoured (cf. Amos 1:5). Damascus must brace itself for defeat; it is Syria's turn to face the demolition of its once secure world.

An Oracle Against Kedar and Hazor (49:28-33)

The next oracle concerns the people of Kedar and Hazor, tribes located in the Arabian Peninsula east of Palestine. Although we know virtually nothing about Hazor—which is not to be confused with the ancient city referred to in Josh 11:1-13—Kedar is mentioned several times in the Bible. We first meet Kedar as one of Ishmael's sons (Gen 25:13). Isaiah prophesies that Kedar's warriors would fall in battle within a year of his oracle (Isa 21:16-17). Yet, Kedar is included among the faraway nations that would one day come to Zion (Isa 60:7). The psalmist laments that he must live "among the tents of Kedar," presumably during the Diaspora (Ps 120:5); Ezekiel speaks of the princes of Kedar as "dealers in lambs, rams, and goats" (Ezek 27:21). Jeremiah alludes to Kedar to the east and Cyrus to the west as distant boundary markers (Jer 2:10). We can surmise from the oracle itself that Kedar was likely a nomadic or seminomadic tribe (49:29) and Hazor a sedentary village without walls (49:31-32). Unlike other nations alluded to thus far in the Oracles Against the Nations, Israel and Judah apparently had little contact or ill will toward Kedar and Hazor. Nonetheless, these two peoples would find themselves in the fierce crossfire of the military enterprise of Babylon under Nebuchadrezzar (49:28, 30). Like other nations, they too would suffer great loss because of this aggressor on the prowl.

The announcement of invasion falls into two distinct units, with both introduced by identical imperatives—"rise up, advance"—followed by a description of the consequences of the assault (49:28b-29 and 49:31-33). The first authorizes the destroyer to attack Kedar, "the people of the east," even as the second urges the foe to strike down "a nation at ease, that lives secure." Between these battle calls is a summons to flee for safety (49:31), even if attempts to escape are futile. Whereas most poems are reticent to identify the attacker, this one provides names: "Nebuchadrezzar of Babylon has made a plan . . . and formed a purpose" (49:30). The king of Babylon is determined to invade and disassemble the people of Kedar and Hazor. For other nations invasion has meant the loss of strongholds, city walls, fortresses, and other facets of settled, urban life; for the Arabian tribes of the East, Babylon's attack ends their nomadic, desert lifestyle: the seizure of tents and flocks, curtains and goods, camels and herds. All are taken as the spoils of war. Even though Kedar and Hazor exist outside the mainstream urban culture of Syria-Palestine, they still cannot elude the grasp of Babylon. Even remote communities in the desert without "gates or bars" (49:31) are not safe. None can escape the disaster coming upon all flesh (45:5).

An Oracle Against Elam (49:34-39)

The next oracle of the collection is directed against Elam, a country several hundred miles east of Babylon with whom Judah and Israel had minimal contact. Its inclusion in the Oracles Against the Nations may serve to represent the furthest imaginable place on the eastern edge of the geographical horizon. The lack of geopolitical specificity (except for the heading in 49:34) and the predominance of symbolic rhetoric support this contention. The writer may know little about this remote nation. The scarcity of references to Elam in the Bible supports this premise. The Table of Nations lists Elam as a descendant of Shem, in all probability because of its location in Mesopotamia (Gen 10:22; 1 Chr 1:17). Isaiah refers to Elam as one of the places where Israelites were dispersed and whence they would return (Isa 11:11). An enigmatic text speaks of Elam's hordes, victims of the sword, surrounding their graves (Ezek 32:24-25). The book of Daniel problemmatically refers to Susa as the royal city "in the province of Elam" (Dan 8:2).

The oracle against Elam is harsh, uncompromising, and replete with military-symbolic language. Dominating the text are declarative statements lacking condition or rationale. Yahweh merely speaks in the first person with determination and devastating force. The series of unilateral assertions amount to a divine assault against the "bow of Elam, the mainstay of their might" (49:35). Yahweh marshals the "four winds from the four quarters of heaven" and threatens to "scatter," "terrify," "bring disaster," "send the sword," "set [up]" his throne, and "destroy their king and officials" (49:36-38). The blow subdues the nation of warriors and renders Elam defenseless. Ultimately, however, Yahweh promises to "restore the fortunes of Elam" (49:39). Hence, the text confesses that divine judgment and grace have no limits. God's sovereignty extends to the uttermost parts of the world.

The Intertwining Destinies of Babylon and Judah (50:1-20)

We now arrive at the text's main performance: Yahweh's decisive defeat of Judah's archenemy Babylon. The drama unfolds in

six consecutive scenes. The first opens with a stunning announcement of Babylon's fall (50:2). All must hear the news: mighty
Babylon and its gods have gone down in defeat. Destruction is so
certain that the poet presents it as already accomplished. A nation
from the north, perhaps referring to Persia, has come up against
Babylon (50:3). Babylon, the once fierce northern foe, is no match
for its new counterpart. This single "nation from the north" soon
blossoms into a "company of great nations from the land of the
north" (50:9). When this company aligns itself against Babylon
and flings arrows into its heart, the outcome is certain: the aboli-
tion of the empire.

Several themes and images depict the nation's ruin. Babylon will
be uninhabitable (50:3) and plundered by the enemy (50:10).
Though gleeful "[as calves frisking on the grass] and [as neighing]
stallions" (50:11), mother Babylon will be shamed and disgraced.
The great empire will be reduced to "the [least] of the nations"
(50:12). To orchestrate the attack, Yahweh issues orders for all
out war: the army is to take its position around Babylon and
"spare no arrows" (50:14). To encourage the troops, Yahweh
reports that the campaign will be swift and trouble-free: Babylon
will surrender before the battle breaks out and its bastions will
tumble to the ground (50:15). When the city is taken, the army is
to cut off the food supply so that Babylon's captives can return
home (50:16; see also 50:8). The military action is in the service
of divine vengeance for Babylon's great wrongdoing. At the same
time, it facilitates the homecoming and restoration of captive
peoples.

The first scene can hardly speak of Babylon without reference
to Israel-Judah, for the empire's downfall holds enormous promise for the exiles (50:4-8, 17-20). When their captors go down
in battle, the people of Israel and Judah are able to turn their
minds back to Zion and return to their homeland with tears of joy
(50:4-5). Though they had once broken covenant with Yahweh,
now they will enter "an everlasting covenant that will never be
forgotten" (50:5). At the prospect of this renewed relationship,
the memory of past failures all but disappears. Yahweh
empathizes with the suffering exiles. They are "lost sheep" whose

shepherds/kings have led them astray. Defenseless and unguarded, they have been ravaged by enemies who glibly claim to be punishing them for their sins (50:6-7). However, Yahweh views their plight as undeserved and unprovoked (50:17-20). Israel is little more than a helpless lamb hunted and devoured by ravenous lions. How could it have defended itself against fierce Assyria and Babylon? But Israel's defender will take action; Yahweh will punish Babylon, just as Yahweh punished Assyria. Then the true shepherd/king will lead the scattered sheep to good pastures and provide for them on Mount Carmel and in Bashan. And God's flock will finally be safe. To dispel any lingering guilt, God categorically pardons the surviving remnant (50:20).

The True Colors of Babylon Revealed (50:21-32)

In the second scene, the cosmic battle intensifies around Yahweh's intent to punish Babylon (50:21-32). Yahweh gives a series of instructions regarding the assault (50:26-27, 29-30). The first commands the agent of destruction, perhaps still the enemy from the north, to attack and "utterly destroy" "Merathaim" and "Pekod," which means in Hebrew "Double Rebellion" and "Punishment" respectively (50:21). The play on two regions in Babylon, Marratu in the south and Puqudu to the east, highlights Babylon's wrongdoing and its looming fate. To "utterly destroy" or "to devote to destruction" (50:21, 26; 51:3) is a technical designation for placing everything captured in battle under the ban. By divine command, nothing can be spared without incurring divine wrath (see, e.g., 1 Sam 15). The attackers of Babylon, therefore, must show no mercy. To accomplish this goal Yahweh instructs the army to surround the city and take dead aim at the heart of the empire: its boundless agricultural resources and mighty warriors. Food supplies are to be cut off and Babylon's "bulls" are to be slaughtered (50:27). The "bulls" of Babylon likely refers to the virile men of war who defend the kingdom. Divisions of archers must be summoned to prevent anyone from escaping. Indeed, Yahweh has opened the "arsenal" and brought "out the weapons of his wrath, for [Yahweh], the God of hosts, has a task to do in the land of the Chaldeans" (50:25). The full-blown siege is a sure sign that "their day, the time of their punishment" has come (50:27). Nothing will foil this moment of divine retribution.

The appalling character of the empire sharpens in this act. Babylon is no longer a nation that has merely "sinned against God" (50:14) but is at this point the "hammer of the whole earth" (50:23), "a horror among the nations" (50:23), a country that has "challenged" (50:24) and "arrogantly defied the LORD" (50:29); indeed Babylon is the "arrogant one," the epitome of insolence (50:31-32). The true colors of Babylon now appear. Such pride and aggression incite Yahweh to address the nation directly. "I am against you . . ." (50:31; see also 51:25). If there were any doubts as to the appropriateness of divine judgment, they are now gone. Babylon's affront to God must be avenged. "Alas for them, their day has come, the time of their punishment!" (50:27*b*). If there were any qualms about Yahweh's intentions, they also are now dispelled. Yahweh declares war.

The Utter Desolation of Babylon (50:33-40)

The third scene of the divine drama opens with a robust word of encouragement for Israel-Judah. The poet again peppers the massive condemnation of Babylon with hopeful overtures for the Jewish exiles. Consistent with the first two scenes, Yahweh acknowledges that the people of God have suffered unduly under a cruel regime. Their oppressors have callously detained them without hope for freedom (50:33). In the face of glaring injustice and human suffering, Yahweh will not stand by idle. The strong "Redeemer" of Israel will champion their cause and so bring "rest to the earth" and "unrest" to repressive Babylon. In the end, Yahweh will deliver the oppressed and humiliate the oppressor. Although confident Babylon could hardly imagine itself going down in defeat, its captives and their God have little problem envisioning the downfall of the empire. A day of reckoning will come upon the proud nation. Indeed, every facet of the savage empire will come under the power of the sword (50:35-38): its citizens, leaders, troops, weaponry, economy, ecosystems, and religion. The devouring sword, perhaps from Yahweh's own arsenal, will spare nothing. It shall destabilize Babylon's secure universe and reduce it to shambles. The proverbial fate of Sodom and Gomorrah reinforces the vision of wholesale destruction (50:40; Gen 19).

Literary innuendos from the exodus story structure the Jewish experience in Babylon. Comparable to Israel's suffering in Egypt, the people of God find themselves "oppressed" in Babylon (50:33; cf. Neh 9:27). Their captors, like the Pharaoh of old, "[hold] them" and "refuse to let them go" (50:33; Exod 7:14-24; 9:2, 17, 35). Yahweh comes to Israel-Judah's aid as their powerful "Redeemer" (50:34), a title referring to a relative's obligation to protect an injured family member from ill treatment. In acting as Israel's kinsman-redeemer, Yahweh identifies with and pleads for a displaced and marginalized people. The idea of redemption *(gā ʾal)* of course plays a central role in the exodus story. With an "outstretched arm," God "redeems" enslaved Israel from Egyptian domination (Exod 6:6; 15:13).

The litany of the sword erupts with echoes from the exodus tradition (50:35-38). Whereas God sent plagues against the Pharaoh to liberate an oppressed Hebrew people, so God mobilizes the sword against Babylon for the release of the Judean captives (Bellis 1995, 89-90). The allusions to "sages" (50:35; cf. Exod 7:11), "horses" and "chariots" (50:37; cf. Exod 14:9, 23; 15:19), and "foreign troops" (50:37), which has the same Hebrew consonants as the word "swarms" (of flies) in Exod 8:17, recall aspects of the Israelite-Egypt confrontation. The reference to "drought against her waters" (50:38) brings to mind Yahweh turning the "sea into dry land" (Exod 14:21-22). All this amounts to coded language for the rout of Babylon and the liberation of Israel. By using a hidden script of resistance as a vital part of the community's worship, powerless exiles mock and defy a savage captor.

The Re-identification of the Foe from the North (50:41-46)

The fourth scene consists of two quotations of prophetic sayings found elsewhere in the book. Verses 41-43 reiterate almost verbatim Jer 6:22-24 and verses 44-46 are very similar to Jer 49:19-21. The vignette, however, does not intend merely to replicate earlier materials. It re-performs earlier texts in a different literary setting for an altogether different purpose. Whereas the earlier passages refer to the demise of Judah and Edom respectively, the tables now turn and Babylon, once the agent of destruction, becomes the object of wrath.

In 50:41-43 the foe from the north again comes into view. This perilous presence has generated a sense of alarm throughout Jeremiah. Its sporadic "apparitions" induce dread. Its identity is always shadowy, although whenever invoked, Babylon lurks close by. Even so, the enemy from the north is the divine instrument whose purpose is to invade, destroy, and dismantle. Its terrifying forces were once directed against unfaithful "daughter Zion" (6:23) but now change course and head toward rebellious "daughter Babylon" (50:42). As a result, the destroyer from the north no longer strikes terror into the hearts of the people of Judah (6:24-25) but rather into the heart of the "king of Babylon" whose hands fall helpless (50:43). The biblical citation thus inverts the fortunes of Judah and Babylon. Israel, the insider turned outsider, once again enjoys insider status, while Babylon, the outsider turned insider, tumbles from its privileged position.

The second quotation in the scene transforms a text directed to Edom into oracle of doom for Babylon (50:44-46). Lion Yahweh springs forth from the thicket of the Jordan to lunge at Babylon and drive it out of its land. Babylon's defeat and subjugation are as sure as Edom's. The poet then asks three rhetorical questions to press home Yahweh's determination to judge and Yahweh's ability to follow through: "For who is like me? Who can summon me? Who is the shepherd who can stand before me?" Each question demands from the listening community a resounding, "No one!" Yahweh is incomparable and Yahweh's plans are inexorable. Mighty Babylon dwarfs before Yahweh. And its fall will be another sign of Yahweh's vigilance in the world.

God's Power and Resolve to Punish Babylon (51:1-33)

The divine resolution to castigate Babylon takes further shape in Jer 51:1-33, a scene made up of a number of smaller parts (e.g., 51:1-5, 6-10, 11, 12-14, 15-19, 20-23, 24, 25-26, 27-33).

Harvesting motifs frame the scene (in 51:2 and 51:33), which is otherwise controlled by cosmic war imagery. From the start, metaphors merge to paint a picture of thorough destruction. Yahweh stirs up a destroying wind and sends winnowers that leave the land bare (51:1-2). Military rule demands that warriors show no mercy to the enemy (51:3-4). Babylon is "a golden cup" of wine that shatters into pieces (51:7-8*a*; cf. 25:15-38). The image of an irreparable cup shifts seamlessly to that of incurable illness. Babylon has contracted a terrible disease for which there is no cure. Despite all efforts, she is beyond help. The exiles can only mourn her condition. She is winnowed, fallen, decimated, shattered to pieces, terminally ill, and without hope.

Piercing through these dark clouds are rays of hope for the Jewish exiles. Once again the concerns of suffering refugees in Babylon are not far from the surface when imagining the fall of Babylon (51:5-6). The collapse of the empire is evidence that Israel has not been "[widowed]" (51:5). Yahweh, Israel's husband, remains faithful to his consort and ready to mend their troubled marriage (cf. 2:1-4:4). Babylon's demise also presents an opportunity for the exiles to return home (51:6, 9). On their way back to Zion, the captive people celebrate their vindication wrought by Yahweh.

In the remainder of the scene we encounter a concentrate of combat images (51:11-33). Yahweh is determined to crush Babylon and therefore gives orders to prepare for battle (51:11-14). Babylon's enemy must sharpen the arrows, lift up the shields, and raise the standard. To execute the assault, the military must strengthen the guard, post the sentries, and take up its position. Yahweh then addresses Babylon, the target of the offensive. Though rich in power and resources, its end is in sight. "Troops like a swarm of locust" will descend upon the land and "raise a shout of victory." Only briefly does a prose text interrupt the symbolic imagery to identify the players: "the kings of the Medes" will destroy Babylon as a reprisal for the temple (51:11). This historicized note strengthens the claim that Babylon's defeat is certain. Also fortifying the contention is a hymn exalting the living God, whose power and wisdom make foreign deities look foolish (51:15-19). The present context urges us to read this doublet (cf.

10:12-16) with reference to Babylon. As such, it confesses that the gods of Babylon are powerless to act during their nation's time of need. They are no match for Yahweh, "the portion of Jacob," who wields the power to defeat Babylon and free hostage Israel.

The cosmic battle escalates as Yahweh commissions one to wreck havoc with the "war club" or "hammer" (51:20-23). The ninefold use of the construction "and with you I [shall] shatter" pulsates with "a staccato rhythm of destruction" (O'Connor 2001, 525). The demolition is massive and methodical. It targets nations and kingdoms, military forces and civilian populations, economic interests and political systems. Nothing is spared. Yahweh, who speaks in the first person, carries out the frontal attack with full power and chilling precision. To bring Yahweh's judgment into greater focus, the poet draws on language from the exodus story (see, e.g., the direct object "the horse and its rider" and "the chariot and the charioteer" in 51:21; cf. Exod 15:1, 21). As the Divine Warrior defeated Pharaoh at the sea, so Yahweh subdues every power hostile to divine rule.

Intriguingly, the poet leaves open-ended the identity of the one wielding the "war club" as well as the victim of the attack (51:20-23). Pronouns appear without explicit referents. Specifically, the "you" lacks an antecedent. Thus, it is impossible to determine whether Babylon is Yahweh's war club or the object of its punishment. The over-all theme of chapters 50–51 lends support to the latter view, that Babylon is the one being shattered. If so, Yahweh commands a new destroyer with a war club in hand—perhaps a veiled reference to the Persian king Cyrus—to decimate the old power broker Babylon. However, this is by no means certain in light of the subsequent poem in which Yahweh takes Babylon to task for mistreating Zion and destroying the whole earth (51:24-26), a possible reference to Babylon's role as war club "smash[ing] nations and . . . kingdoms." Furthermore, Babylon is identified elsewhere as "the hammer of the whole earth" (50:23) and in a more general way as Yahweh's instrument of judgment. For these and other reasons, commentators sometimes understand the "you" in "you are my war club" (51:20) as a reference to Babylon. In any case, the intentional lack of clarity heightens the poem's mythic character. It refuses to pin down and flatten; it is by design porous and cryptic.

Since the "destroying mountain" has devastated the whole earth (51:24-26), Yahweh deploys the nations against Babylon (51:27-33). They have been the brunt of Babylon's abuse, and it stands to reason that they must witness and participate in the liturgical drama of Babylon's defeat. (Though Judah has suffered sorely at the hand of Babylon, Yahweh does not summon the citizens of Jerusalem to battle, perhaps so as not to encourage military engagement or political unrest. Yahweh directly repays Babylon for the wrong it has inflicted on Zion.) With discipline and alacrity, Yahweh mobilizes the multitude. A series of commands initiates the military campaign: "Raise a standard . . . blow the trumpet . . . summon Ararat, Minni, and Ashkenaz," three peoples from northern Mesopotamia, "appoint a marshal . . . bring up [the cavalry] . . . prepare the nations for war against her" (51:27-28). The stage is now set for the drama's dénouement. Every nation, as it were, takes its shot at Babylon for the damage it has done. Yahweh not only authorizes the engagement, but leads the way. The outcome is catastrophic for Babylon. At the approach of Yahweh and the nations, the "land trembles and writhes," its warriors falter and surrender, its buildings burn, and its defenses fail. Conveniently, widespread panic does not prevent couriers from reaching the king of Babylon with the news: your "city is taken from end to end" (51:31; cf. Job 1:13-19). The text envisions more than a national military disaster involving the loss of land and power. At the approach of the Divine Warrior-King, Babylon totters on extinction. "Yet a little while and the time of her harvest will come" (51:33). For the exiles listening, this enactment of divine vengeance on evildoer Babylon flags Yahweh's just kingship in the world. Yahweh reigns!

The True King Revealed (51:34-58)

To open the final scene the suffering inhabitants of Jerusalem get their chance to speak (51:34-35). They have been silent observers, but now express their emotional tirade against Nebuchadrezzar. In the first person, the exiles dare speak of unspeakable acts committed against them. However, instead of registering a long list of offenses, they resort to symbols and metaphors, perhaps because the crimes are too painful to chronicle. Like a primordial sea monster, the Babylonian ruler has devoured and crushed them. He has swallowed them alive, filled his belly with their delicacies, and spewed them out. Such heinous deeds cry out for justice and Yahweh, alert to their plea, takes up their cause and plans a course of action (51:36-37). For the sake of the suffering refugees, Yahweh pledges to "dry up her sea" and transform Babylon into a "heap of ruins, a den of jackals" (51:36-37). Yahweh turns the once lush and well-watered country into an uninhabitable place of horror and hissing. The land is so parched that ravenous lions lap up Yahweh's poisonous brew (cf. 25:15-27) and "sleep a perpetual sleep" (51:39). When sedated, they are presented as sacrificial slaughter (51:38-40), thus making the inversion complete: Israel's defender has turned terrifying lions into lambs on the altar.

With Babylon's fate certain, the funeral begins (51:41; cf. 25:26; 50:23). Unlike a typical dirge, this one celebrates rather than mourns. The end of Babylon's domination means hope for the world. How can anyone be sad? The poet returns to the image of the "sea" to depict the fall of Babylon (51:42; cf. 51:36). This time the "sea" no longer alludes to Babylon's depleted water sources but to the terrifying forces of primordial chaos and divine judgment (see, e.g., Pss 46:2-3; 65:7; 93:3-4; cf. Rev 21:1 where the "sea is forever gone" in the poet's vision of the new heaven and earth). The tumultuous "sea" inundates Babylon and reduces it to chaos. When the waters recede the land becomes a wasteland, "a land of drought and a desert, a land in which no one lives, and through which no mortal passes" (51:43). And Babylon's patron Bel must "[spew out] what he has swallowed" (51:44), a reference to the Judean victims eaten alive by the sea monster (51:34). Now disgorged from its jaws, God's people are free to go home (51:45-46). Indeed, they must flee in order to save themselves from the disaster about to befall the city.

Images of judgment continue to amass in 51:47-58. The planet rejoices at the certainty of Babylon's punishment. The heavens and earth shout for joy and all that is in them breathe a sigh of relief at the prospect of the empire's defeat (51:47-48). God's punitive action, however, does not serve some exacting moral order, which demands the triumph of good over evil. The text does not trade in such certainties. The reign of Babylon must end for the sake of "the slain of Israel [and] the slain of all the earth" (51:49). To preserve their memory Babylon must go down in defeat. Also, Babylon must fall for the future of the "survivors of the sword" (51:50). When Babylon is overthrown the exiles are able to return home (51:50-51). In preparation for their exodus, they are to remember the Lord and the holy city Jerusalem. Such memories trigger sadness. The psalmist understood this well when lamenting, "By the rivers of Babylon—there we sat down and there we wept when we remembered Zion" (Ps 137:1). Likewise, the exiles here express sorrow at the thought of the desecration of the temple. Yet, at this crucial moment, when memory is rekindled and pain is embraced, the healing work of the wounded begins.

In response to their lament (51:51), Yahweh reassures the refugees that mighty Babylon will come crashing down from its heights (51:52-58; see also Gen 11:1-9). Military imagery resumes as the poet speaks of Babylon's ruin. At the instigation of Yahweh, destroyers come and lay Babylon to waste. The terms "destroy" or "destroyer(s)" occur four times in this final section (51:48, 53, 55, 56). Warriors are taken, weapons are shattered, city walls are leveled, and high gates are burned; all is reduced to rubble. Out of the ruin, the true King, "whose name is [Yahweh] of hosts" (51:57) emerges as victor. The tyrannical regime of Babylon whose raw power once appeared invincible is over, at least in this liturgical enactment. Soon it would actually end. When it did, the Jewish exiles in Babylon would know that it was neither a geopolitical fluke nor the upshot of the military-political genius of Cyrus, king of Persia. The fall of Babylon was nothing less than the work of the true King whose "right hand and his holy arm have gotten him victory" (Ps 98:1).

Four Bold Acts Testifying to Babylon's Downfall (51:59-64)

The Oracles Against the Nations conclude with a brief narrative relating the interaction of Jeremiah and the chief quartermaster

Seraiah, brother of Baruch (51:59-64). Jeremiah prepares a scroll of the prophecies of disaster against Babylon and entrusts it to Seraiah. Upon arriving in Babylon, Seraiah is to read the scroll and remind God to fulfill the oracles against "this place" (cf. 7:20; 16:9; 19:3). After prayer and public recitation, Seraiah is then to tie a stone to the scroll and throw it into the middle of the Euphrates, symbolizing the drowning of Babylon. As Brueggemann notes, this is not magic but "a political act of a special, lyrical kind" (1998, 487). Tossing the scroll into the Euphrates is a daring act of resistance. Seraiah's symbolic action is liturgical theater, a re-visioning of reality. By engaging in theater, the exiles re-image the world and its power structures through the eyes of faith.

These final instructions have a strangely familiar ring: the transformation of spoken prophecy into written form, the public reading of the scroll, prayer, and symbolic action or liturgical performance have all enjoyed a central place in the book and, according to Jeremiah, are to play a vital role in the formation of a new community. To bring "the words of Jeremiah" to an end, these four bold acts herald Yahweh's ultimate triumph over Babylon (51:64; cf. 1:1). The fall of Babylon is documented in "scripture," read in public, recited in prayer, and performed in theater.

Theological and Ethical Analysis

The Oracles Against the Nations present some of the most serious theological and ethical problems in the book of Jeremiah. Their language of violence is disturbing. Their displays of divine vengeance and their fascination with war imagery are troubling. Moreover, the Oracles Against the Nations treat issues and address countries that often seem irrelevant to the twenty-first century. For these and a host of other reasons, a great many interpreters dismiss these chapters in Jeremiah outright or merely read them as cultural artifacts of ancient Israel. Those who risk grappling with the meaning of these sacred texts for faith communities today find themselves addressing a number a difficult questions. Do the Oracles Against the Nations condone the use of violence? Do they justify revenge as a response to ill treatment? Do they militate against inter-religious or international dialogue? Is the image of God as warrior constructive in today's culture of violence? The background and social location of these oracles in the life of ancient Israel *(Sitz im Leben)* as well as their function in the book *(Sitz im Buch)* help clarify, and even resolve, some of these theological and ethical dilemmas.

With respect to the *Sitz im Leben,* it is important to recognize that oracles against foreign nations are not unique to Jeremiah. They appear in Amos 1–2, Isa 13–23, Ezek 25–32, and to a certain extent in Joel 3. Though this genre is well attested, we still know relatively little about its development and function in the life of ancient Israel. It is unlikely that prophets uttered these diatribes on the battlefields despite their entrenched war imagery. Far more likely, the utterances against foreign nations emanate from Israel's public worship. The worshiping community would publicly re-enact God's involvement in history, God's victory over oppressive regimes, and God's reign on earth. Through ridicule, revel, and affirmation, the worshiping congregation would envision God subverting and disassembling pretentious world powers as a way to carry out divine justice and sovereignty. Along these lines, Brueggemann suggests that the oracles may have "emerged in the midst of liturgic celebrations of the sovereignty of Yahweh, and served to voice the claim that God's sovereign rule extended not simply over Israel but over all peoples" (1998, 418). Several royal psalms and hymns provide a literary analogy (e.g., Pss 2, 18, 68, 95–97, 99; see also Pss 83, 94). They also celebrate in liturgy Yahweh's victory over world-destroying nations, as well as over chaotic natural forces.

If the Oracles Against the Nations in Jeremiah belong to the *world of worship and not warfare,* their weapons are rhetoric and imagination, not military hardware. They represent the liturgical literature of refugees who find themselves on the margins of society without power, temple, land, or hope. These survivors bear the fresh wounds and psychological scars of invasion and dislocation, abuse and disappointment. Their symbolic and cultural worlds have been shattered. They have lived under an oppressive regime in Babylon where they have been haunted by questions regarding God's power and justice. In this situation of subjugation, the only power they wield is the power of theater, which re-imagines and reframes social reality. Through the theater of worship the exiles dare to make a number of startling assertions. They declare

> that the Lord reigns and is involved in the world;
> that God's purposes are realized in and through the contingencies of history;
> that the plight of suffering people is not beyond the scope of God's power and concern;
> that God neither forgets nor ignores those whose lives are full of pain and brokenness;
> that God acts on behalf of those who cannot defend themselves;
> that unjust and oppressive power structures will not endure;
> that raw power is not ultimate reality;
> that acts of callous disregard for life do not impugn divine justice;
> that God holds all people responsible for their actions regardless of military muscle and religious claim; and
> that God's salvation extends beyond the borders of any one people.

While such pronouncements are clothed in strange and unfamiliar garb, they nevertheless resound within the context of worship, the matrix through which the faithful claim to see the world clearly. Nonetheless, John J. Collins's warning should still be noted: "the line between actually killing and verbal, symbolic, or imaginary violence is thin and permeable" (2003, 4). He is also correct that in certain instances language of violence gives "hope to the oppressed" (2003, 18), which is likely the case here.

The liturgical character of the Oracles Against the Nations in the life of ancient Israel gives us insight into the character of worship in ancient Judaism. It also holds importance for contemporary understandings of worship, especially for communities of faith that are located on the fringes of society. Worship involves not only praise and adoration but also bold, social defiance. It refuses to accept abusive power structures as normative. It says "no" to distorted cultural assumptions and idolatrous systems.

The act of worship is "revisionist" in that it sees through sinful political arrangements and risks writing new social and symbolic scripts based on standards of justice and compassion. Regardless of what anyone might say, including the Nebuchadrezzars of the world, it insists that powerhouses like Babylon do not last. Worship, moreover, empowers broken people with the will to survive and the courage to resist. It is the medium through which they can call into question, subvert, and defy seemingly hopeless worlds as well as cruel and relentless oppressors. It ennobles the faithful to protest and dissent, ridicule and revel, and imagine a counterworld order. Such worship, as the exiles in Babylon well knew, is anything but innocuous: it is rather a dangerous weapon of hope that refuses to knuckle under to political aggression and military hardware. The Oracles Against the Nations, thus, have less to do with violence and war than hope and the promise of justice for the underdog.

In their present literary context in Jeremiah *(Sitz im Buch)*, the Oracles Against the Nations achieve three important goals. First, they conclude the book with the triumphant note that Yahweh reigns. The collection of utterances testifies that Yahweh will bring the wayward and arrogant nations to their knees. To this end, the One who wages a dreaded assault on Judah conducts a full-fledged cosmic war against every force that opposes divine rule. Yahweh threatens to topple all governments that resort to politics of force and self-assertion. As warrior-king, Yahweh is intent on destabilizing raw military-political power and creating in its place a just moral order.

The establishment of divine justice demands above all else the defeat of the brazen Babylonian Empire. While Yahweh had authorized Babylon's world domination, which is indeed a disconcerting assertion, Babylon's military action far exceeded the divine mandate. Babylon's pride and imperial ambitions surpassed all bounds. Therefore, Yahweh takes decisive action to tame and ultimately bring down a rebellious vassal. In so doing, the text declares that Yahweh rules all nations, even the most menacing. Yahweh, not Nebuchadnezzar, is the true king. King Yahweh (46:18, 51:57) will ultimately squash every self-inflated state.

Second, when the text announces that Yahweh intends to judge the nations and defeat mighty Babylon, it paves the way for a new epoch of salvation for Judah. Divine judgment provides the conditions necessary for the restoration of those banished to distant lands. Large sections of Jer 50–51 make it clear that Babylon's downfall represents God's redemptive activity on behalf of Judah/Israel (e.g., 50:4-7, 17-20, 28-30, 33-34). Despite a past wracked with pain, God has neither forsaken Israel and Judah nor forgotten their plight (51:5). Yahweh will plead their case and take vengeance for them (see 50:34, 51:36). When Babylon falls, Judah will return home (50:8-10, 17-19), enjoy divine forgiveness (50:20), and enter an everlasting covenantal relationship (50:4-5). The text is emphatic: the people of Judah should not fear, for God still deeply cares about them and will act on their behalf (Calvin 1989, 572-73). All told, God's judgment against repressive Babylon inaugurates an epoch of *shalom* for the oppressed.

Third, in addition to encouraging the people of God, the Oracles Against the Nations serve the broad purposes of theodicy. That is, this final collection in Jeremiah defends God against accusations of injustice. Why should God call Judah to account when nations that are far worse escape without a scratch? How can Babylon, the perpetrator of injustice, brutality, and rebellion, elude divine retribution (see also Hab 1:2-17)? Such ethical madness makes a mockery of the character of God. The Oracles against the Nations answer accusations of mismanagement, callous indifference, and divine impotence. They announce that God not only stands in judgment against Judah but all who set themselves above and against God's purposes. God holds all peoples accountable for their actions, though divine judgment begins with the household of God.

THE FINAL WORD (JEREMIAH 52)

Literary Analysis

One encounters a number of "endings" when reading the book of Jeremiah: to name a few, chapters 25, 45, 46–51, and 52 all convey a sense of finality. Chapter 25 brings resolution to the first part of the book by summarizing twenty-three years of Jeremiah's prophetic preaching, that is, the central themes in chapters 1–24 concerning Judah and Jerusalem. That Judah and Jerusalem are first in line to drink from the cup of wrath draws attention to the message of judgment that infuses the entire first half of the book. Chapter 45 ends the Baruch Narrative by hinting at a hopeful future for a faithful few beyond the breaking down and plucking up. God's promise of safe passage for Baruch, and the survivors he presumably represents, whispers "there's hope" despite the wreckage. The Oracles Against the Nations herald a similar message. When chapters 46–51 announce God's judgment upon the nations, especially upon arrogant Babylon, they pave the way for the building and planting of the Judean exiles. It is worth noting that a scroll of prophetic oracles plays a key role in each of the endings (25:13; 45:1; 51:59-64).

Chapter 52 has the very last word. This so-called "historical appendix" does not appear in its present location by accident. It is the book's intended ending. First, it provides a temporal frame for prophecies that elsewhere are not overly concerned about time sequences. With chapter 52 in place, the reader spans the full breadth of Judah's final days, from 627 to 560. Beginning with the thirteenth year of Josiah (1:1) the book traverses through time and space to the royal court of King Evil-merodach of Babylon where King Jehoiachin of Judah enjoys an honored place. In this way, the prologue (chapter 1) and epilogue (chapter 52) create an overarching chronology. Second, the unadorned rendering of Judah's final years in chapter 52 telescopes events that play a prominent role in the prophecies of Jeremiah throughout the book. From the start, Jeremiah anticipates the death of Judah's political and religious world. The divine work of judgment targets land and city, temple and worship, king and palace. The loss of these arrangements so defies human management that the text must use metaphorical language: cosmic war, northern enemies, creation coming unglued, the shaking of heaven and earth, a cup of wrathful poison. Now in chapter 52 these key themes, though still fraught with disabling anxiety, materialize in geopolitical terms:

the armies of Babylon destroy, maim, and torture; they systemati-
cally execute members of the royal family and officials of Judah;
they burn the temple and royal palace; and over a course of fifteen
years they carry off into exile 4,600 Judean citizens. The dead and
departed now testify to what was once ethereal and symbolic. And
the veracity of Jeremiah's words comes to light for all to see. What
Jeremiah had long envisaged now takes on physicality. Finally, like
other endings in the second part of the book, the depiction of
destruction contains seeds of hope (see below). Although a culture
has died and a world has collapsed, the kind treatment of King
Jehoiachin of Judah suggests the survival of Judah. Thus, the final
words of the book bring to mind the promissory motif of building
and planting (1:10).

Exegetical Analysis

The End (52:1-34)

Jeremiah 52:1-34 is very similar to 2 Kgs 24:18–25:30 except
that the former excludes any mention of Gedaliah's short-lived
government and includes a reference to three deportations to
Babylon in 597, 587, and 582. Introducing the account of the fall
of Jerusalem is a formulaic statement of culpability. Attention first
centers on Zedekiah, the indecisive king who reigned eleven
difficult years in Jerusalem. According to the conventional royal
formula, Zedekiah did "evil in the sight of [Yahweh], just as
Jehoiakim had done" (52:2). This pronouncement of unqualified
rejection knows nothing of Zedekiah's tortured ambivalence.
None of the earlier complexities of King Zedekiah matters any-
more. At the end of the day he is written off as a wicked king who
defied the king of Babylon against the council of Jeremiah and
who therefore must pay the piper (52:3). Jerusalem and Judah also
bear responsibility for the devastating events. They have so angered
Yahweh that Yahweh has "expelled them from his presence"
(52:3). As the book draws to a close, it is apparent that theological concerns are still very much on the mind of the composers.
What is about to be described in the starkest geopolitical terms is
no indication of divine indifference; nor is it merely a neutral

report of events that transpired in the sixth century. The dismantling of the state is the work of Yahweh who holds Jerusalem and
Judah accountable for their actions.

The text dates and describes the account of the destruction of
Jerusalem with military discipline (52:3*b*-16). For eighteen
months, from January 587 to July/August 586 (though these dates
are disputed), the city suffers the unbearable strain of Babylonian
aggression. In a series of calculated moves King Nebuchadrezzar
drives Jerusalem to ruin. His armies advance toward the city and
surround it. They build siege ramps, cut off food supplies, and
eventually break through the city walls. The Babylonians capture
Zedekiah, who apparently tries to escape with others by night,
and take him to Riblah for sentencing. There the Judean king
must witness the execution of his sons and officers until
Nebuchadrezzar tortures and banishes him to Babylon. Soon
afterward, Nebuzaradan enters Jerusalem to finish the job (52:12-
16). He burns the city, including the temple and royal palace, tears
down the walls, and carries cross-sections of the citizens of
Jerusalem into exile. The captain of the guard only leaves behind
the poorest people to tend the land.

The looting of the temple occupies center stage of the military
occupation (52:17-23). Now that the city is under Babylonian
control, the army turns its undivided attention to the temple treasures. What it does not destroy it confiscates and carries off to
Babylon. The account of the booty reads like a police inventory of
stolen property: "the pots, the shovels, the snuffers, the basins, the
ladles, and all the vessels of bronze used in the temple service . . .
the small bowls also, the firepans, the basins, the pots, the lamp-
stands, the ladles, and the bowls for libation, both those of gold
and those of silver" (52:18-19). Supposedly, one could make the
case that when the Babylonians sack the temple they do nothing
that exceeds conventional standards of warfare. The booty is
theirs for the taking and they merely help themselves. However,
from the perspective of the implied reader, foreigners have desecrated the house of God and reduced its sacred contents to mere
goods. Besides plundering the temple's valuables, Judah's enemies
have humiliated the Lord of the temple. If their goal was to shame

and demean the God of Israel, for a moment—for a long and lingering moment—the Babylonians appear to have succeeded. As Brueggemann observes, "this is indeed the Good Friday of the temple" (1998, 491). The cold-blooded execution of Judah's religious and political leaders together with sixty men discovered outside the city only makes the day darker and less manageable (51:24-27; cf. 41:4-8).

Jeremiah 52:28-30 summarizes the damage of exile. "In the seventh year" of Nebuchadrezzar's reign, that is in the year 598, 3,023 persons went into exile; "in the eighteenth-year" (587), 832 persons were taken away and "in the twenty-third year" (582), 745 others were deported for a total of 4,600 persons. The number of exiles is smaller than that reported in 2 Kgs 24:13-17, the latter likely including women and children. Regardless of the numbers, the symbolic effects of exile were still disproportionate to the actual losses. Even though the losses were not massive, exile became a "meaning making" event that changed everything. Exile was the great divide. For the surviving Jews, and even for those who never experienced exile firsthand, it became as definitive as the exodus. Exile meant the end of the state, its policies, institutions, and intellectual traditions, and at the same time, the inception of something strangely new.

The closing vignette takes place sometime later in the court of King Evil-merodach (52:31-34). In the year 560 the Babylonian monarch releases Jehoiachin from prison and affords him a place of honor at the royal court for as long as the Judean king lives. The reference to the kind treatment of Jehoiachin, literally the lifting of his head, is the same expression used in the Joseph novella to describe Pharaoh's treatment of the chief baker. The Pharaoh graciously frees the baker from prison, that is, lifts up his head (Gen 40:18-23). This final scene in Jeremiah seems to indicate a measure of hope for a brighter future, especially for those held captive in Babylon.

Although Jer 52 is a later addition to Jeremiah, it is no mere afterthought. The concluding chapter of Jeremiah resonates with the dominant themes of the book: "to pluck up and to pull down, to destroy and to overthrow" and the embryonic element of hope, "to build and to plant." The drama of the dismantled nation ends in a decisive battle. In fulfillment of God's word through Jeremiah, Babylon trounces on Judah and Jerusalem. The city falls, the temple is destroyed, the Davidic king is deposed, and the land is largely deserted. The stronghold of the old configurations of reality tumbles. What remains is an unstable and terrifying world, a place of violence and travail, of loss and despair.

Theological and Ethical Analysis

Following the report of the defeat of Judah is a rather strange text that is difficult to pin down. Jeremiah 52:31-34 speaks of the kind treatment of the deposed Jehoiachin in Babylon. King Evil-merodach of Babylon shows favor to the Judean king and releases him from prison; he is brought to the palace where he is given a position above the other vassal kings who are with him in Babylon. He receives from the Babylonian king a "regular daily allowance," a daily portion "as long as he lived" (52:34). These verses, which are essentially a repetition of 2 Kgs 25:27-30, seem to hold out faint hope that all is not permanently lost. Von Rad saw in the pardon of Jehoiachin a cryptic indication that the line of David had "not yet come to an irrevocable end" (1953, 91). H. W. Wolff understood the release and kind treatment of Jehoiachin as implying that God was "still acting for his people" (1975, 99). Robert P. Carroll suggested that to read "the story of Jehoiachin's release from prison is to glimpse briefly a sunny upland seldom seen in the book of Jeremiah. It is a shaft of sunlight on a darkling plain and it lifts the heart of the reader after a long day's journey through the valley of the shadow" (1989, 113). The final words of the book leave open-ended the future of a people who had undergone unspeakable hardship and whose demise seemed certain. Indeed, for the contemporaries of Jehoiachin, the king's good fortune in Babylon apparently inspired hope for the restoration of Judah.

By concluding the book with words of hope, albeit cryptic and ill-defined, the interpretive community of Jeremiah follows a well-established prophetic pattern: regardless of the severity of the message of judgment, words of salvation and renewal, divine love and comfort bring closure to the corpus (Clements 1996, 191-202). We see this pattern in the book of Amos, which ends with a message of coming salvation and homecoming after terrifying words that the end has come (Amos 9:11-15). Zechariah concludes with a description of God's final victory and the gathering of every nation in Jerusalem to worship Yahweh as King (Zech 14:1-21). The prophecies of Malachi close with the promise that the prophet Elijah will come and turn the hearts of the parents to their children and the hearts of the children to their parents (Mal 4:1-6). The final poems in the book of Micah present extraordinary imagery of forgiveness and reconciliation (Mic 7:18-20). Habakkuk makes a stunning confession of faith in the saving God, despite lingering questions about God's character (Hab 3:17-19). The last chapter of Zephaniah envisions a God who dances with joy and renews Israel in love, a God who consoles those devastated by divine judgment (Zeph 3:14-20). Both Isaiah and Ezekiel conform to the judgment-salvation structure, even though recent studies have highlighted the complexity of these books. And Jeremiah, rather than being a "hopeless hodgepodge," follows the pattern of the prophetic canon. The three endings of the book— God's promise to Baruch in chapter 45, the Oracles Against the Nations in chapters 46–51, and the reference to the kind treatment of Jehoiachin in chapter 52—together with an overall architecture organized around God's work of "plucking up and pulling down" and "building and planting," all point to the judgment-salvation schema.

Bringing Jeremiah to a close with the prospect of restoration has far-reaching literary, pastoral, and theological implications. First, from a literary perspective, the emphasis on salvation after judgment creates a measure of order out of the book's jumbled and chaotic world. From the outset we have encountered a literary text that has little linear logic, chronological coherence, or formal structure. By modern standards, one could argue that Jeremiah is hardly readable. But the pattern of "plucking up and pulling down" and "building and planting" does produce literary coherence. That this coherence is superimposed by a later interpretive community does nothing to impugn its character. That it does not fully contain the book's rich labyrinth of expressions does nothing to undermine its contribution. Bringing order out of chaos is a monumental literary achievement (Stulman 1998, 185-88).

Second, the concluding message of hope plays a pastoral role in the life of the community. It recognizes that without hope survival is hardly possible. The hope of salvation buoys a community of refugees who can barely endure the weight of their suffering. In their fractured world, and in ours as well, such hope asserts that enormous loss does not nullify God's love. This message of hope may be the most urgent one of our time. With economic systems faltering, and cynicism permeating political and religious institutions, with the increasing threat of environmental disaster as well as nuclear and biological fallout, with palpable despair all around, the world is in desperate need of hope. Jeremiah is a stunning text that champions the love and faithfulness of God amidst cosmic crumbling.

Third, Jeremiah's message of hope is not only literary and pastoral but theological as well. It refuses to let divine judgment have the final say. It asserts that hope ultimately triumphs over all, that God's love covers a multitude of sins, and that the most enduring facet of God's character is compassion. While this message does not invalidate earlier oracles of judgment against perpetrators of injustice, it does serve as an interpretive guide for reading the book. Subsequently, the working out of God's justice in judgment cannot be construed apart from God's gracious intervention in history. Hence, Jeremiah joins a chorus that proclaims "hope of coming salvation in relation to all of the forewarnings of doom which individual prophets made" (Clements 1996, 196).

SELECT BIBLIOGRAPHY

WORKS CITED IN THE TEXT

Barton, John. 1999. "Jeremiah in the Apocrypha and Pseudepigrapha," in *Troubling Jeremiah*, ed. A. R. Diamond, K. M. O'Connor, and L. Stulman, pp. 306-17. Sheffield: Sheffield Academic.

Bellis, Alice Ogden. 1995. *The Structure and Composition of Jeremiah 50:2–51:58*. Lewiston, Queenston, Lampeter: Mellen Biblical.

Berridge, John M. 1970. *Prophet, People, and the Word of Yahweh: An Examination of the Form and Content in the Proclamation of the Prophet Jeremiah*. Zurich: EVZ Verlag.

Biddle, M. E. 1996. *Polyphony and Symphony in Prophetic Literature: Rereading Jeremiah 7–20*. Studies in Old Testament Interpretation, 2. Macon: Mercer University Press.

Brueggemann, Walter. 1986. *Hopeful Imagination: Prophetic Voices in Exile*. Philadelphia: Fortress.

———. 1997. *Theology of the Old Testament: Testimony, Dispute, Advocacy*. Minneapolis: Fortress.

———. 2002a. *Ichabod Towards Home: The Journey of God's Glory*. Grand Rapids: Eerdmans.

———. 2002b. "Meditation Upon the Abyss: The Book of Jeremiah." *Word & World* 4/22:340-50.

Campbell, E. F. 1992. "Relishing the Bible as Literature and History." *Christian Century* 109:812-15.

Carroll, Robert P. 1989. *Jeremiah*. Old Testament Guides. Sheffield: JSOT.

Childs, B. S. 1959. "The Enemy from the North and the Chaos Tradition." *JBL* 78:187-98.

———. 1979. *Introduction to the Old Testament as Scripture*. Philadelphia: Fortress.

Clements, Ronald E. 1996. *Old Testament Prophecy: From Oracles to Canon*. Louisville: Westminster John Knox.

Collins, John J. 2003. "The Zeal of Phinehas: The Bible and the Legitimation of Violence." *JBL* 122:3-21.

Diamond, A. R. 1987. *The Confessions of Jeremiah in Context: Scenes of Prophetic Drama*. JSOTSS 45. Sheffield: JSOT.

Diamond, A. R. Pete, Kathleen M. O'Connor, and Louis Stulman. 1999. *Troubling Jeremiah*. JSOTSS 260. Sheffield: Sheffield Academic.

Fretheim, T. E. 1984. *The Suffering of God: An Old Testament Perspective*. Overtures to Biblical Theology. Philadelphia: Fortress.

———. 1994. "The Book of Genesis." *NIB*, vol. 1, 321-673. Nashville: Abingdon.

Gutiérrez, Gustavo. 1997. *On Job: God Talk and the Suffering of the Innocent*. Maryknoll, N.Y.: Orbis.

Habel, Norman. 1965. "The Form and Significance of the Call Narratives." *ZAW* 77:297-323.

Heschel, Abraham. 2001. *The Prophets*. New York: HarperCollins.

Hill, John. 1999. *Friend or Foe? The Figure of Babylon in the Book of Jeremiah MT*. Leiden, Boston, Köln: Brill.

Holladay, William L. 1972. "The Covenant with the Patriarchs Overturned: Jeremiah's Intention in 'Terror on Every Side' (Jer 20:1-6)." *JBL* 91:305-20.

———. 1976. *The Architecture of Jeremiah 1–20*. Lewisburg: Bucknell University.

Hyatt, J. Philip. 1951. *The Deuteronomic Edition of Jeremiah*. Vanderbilt Studies in the Humanities 1:71-95.

Kremers, H. 1953. "Leidensgemeinschaft mit Gott im Alten Testament: Eine Untersuchung der 'biographischen' Berichte im Jeremiabuch." *Evangelische Theologie* 13:122-40.

Levine, Baruch A. 1970. "On the Presence of the Lord in Biblical Religion," in *Religions in Antiquity: Essays in Memory of Erwin Ramsdell Goodenough*. Studies in the History of Religions, Supplements to Numen 14, ed. J. Neusner, pp. 71-87. Leiden: Brill.

Lindblom, Johannes. 1962. *Prophecy in Ancient Israel*. Philadelphia: Fortress.

Mowinckel, Sigmund. 1914. *Zur Komposition des Buches Jeremia*. Kristiania: Jacob Dybwad.

Muller, Wayne. 1999. *Sabbath: Restoring the Sacred Rhythm of Rest*. New York, Toronto, London, Sydney, Auckland: Bantam Books.

Nasuti, H. P. 1987. "A Prophet to the Nations: Diachronic and Synchronic Readings of Jeremiah 1." *Hebrew Annual Review* 10:249-66.

Neusner, Jacob. 1997. *The Way of Torah: An Introduction to Judaism.* 6th ed. Belmont: Wadsworth.

Nicholson, E. W. 1970. *Preaching to the Exiles: A Study of the Prose Tradition in the Book of Jeremiah.* New York: Schocken.

Nouwen, Henri J. M. 1972. *With Open Hands.* Notre Dame: Ave Maria.

———. 1975. *Reaching Out.* New York: Doubleday.

———. 1977. *The Living Reminder: Service and Prayer in Memory of Jesus Christ.* San Francisco: Harper & Row.

O'Connor, Kathleen M. 1988. *The Confessions of Jeremiah: Their Interpretation and Role in Chapters 1–25.* SBLDS 94. Atlanta: Scholars.

———. 1998. "The Tears of God and Divine Character in Jeremiah 2–9," in *God in the Fray: A Tribute to Walter Brueggemann,* ed. Tod Linafelt and Timothy K. Beal, pp. 172-85. Minneapolis: Fortress.

———. 2002. *Lamentations and the Tears of the World.* Maryknoll: Orbis.

Osswald, Eva. 1962. *Falsche Prophetie im Alten Testament.* Tübingen: J. C. B. Mohr.

Overholt, Thomas W. 1970. *The Threat of Falsehood: A Study in the Theology of the Book of Jeremiah.* London: SCM.

Potok, Chaim. 1967. *The Chosen.* New York: Fawcett Crest.

Prestowitz, Clyde. 2003. *Rogue Nation: American Unilateralism and the Failure of Good Intentions.* New York: Basic.

Reventlow, H. Graf. 1966. *Liturgie und prophetisches Ich bei Jeremia.* Gütersloh: Gütersloher.

Rudolph, W. 1947. *Jeremia.* Handbuch zum Alten Testament 12. Tübingen: J. C. B. Mohr.

Seitz, C. R. 1989a. "The Prophet Moses and the Canonical Shape of Jeremiah." *ZAW* 101:3-27.

———. 1989b. "Theology in Conflict: Reactions to the Exile in the Book of Jeremiah." *BZAW* 176. Berlin: de Gruyter.

Skinner, J. 1922. *Prophecy and Religion: Studies in the Life of Jeremiah.* London: Cambridge University Press.

Smith, M. S. 1990. *The Laments of Jeremiah and Their Contexts: A Literary and Redactional Study of Jeremiah 11–20. SBLMS* 42. Atlanta: Scholars.

Steiner, George. 1985. "Our Homeland, the Text." *Selmagundi* 66: 4-25.

Stulman, Louis. 1984. "Some Theological and Lexical Differences Between the Old Greek and the MT of the Jeremiah Prose Discourses." *Hebrew Studies* 25:18-23.

————. 1986. *The Prose Sermons of the Book of Jeremiah*. SBLDS 83. Atlanta: Scholars.

————. 1998. *Order Amid Chaos: Jeremiah as Symbolic Tapestry*. Sheffield: Sheffield Academic Press.

Taylor, M. A. 1987. "Jeremiah 45: The Problem of Placement." *JSOT* 37:79-98.

Tov, Emanuel. 1972. "L'incidence de la critique textuelle sur la critique littéraire dans la livre de Jérémie." *RB* 79:189-99.

von Rad, Gerhard. 1953. *Studies in Deuteronomy*. Studies in Biblical Theology 9. Chicago: Henry Regnery.

————. 1965. *Old Testament Theology*. Vol. 2. Translated by D. M. G. Stalker. New York: Harper & Row.

————. 1983. "The Confessions of Jeremiah," in *Theodicy in the Old Testament*, ed. James L. Crenshaw, pp. 88-99. Philadelphia: Fortress.

Welten, Peter. 1977. "Leiden und Leidenserfahrung im Buch Jeremia." *ZThK* 74:123-50.

Westermann, C. 1991. *Prophetic Oracles of Salvation in the Old Testament*. Louisville: Westminster John Knox.

Wiesel, Elie. 1960. *Night*. New York: Bantam.

————. 1981. *Five Biblical Portraits*. Notre Dame: University of Notre Dame Press.

Wilson, Robert R. 1999. "Poetry and Prose in the Book of Jeremiah," in *Ki Baruch Hu: Ancient Near Eastern Studies in Honor of Baruch A. Levine*, ed. Robert Chazan, William W. Hallo, and Lawrence H. Schiffman, pp. 413-27. Winona Lake, Ind.: Eisenbrauns.

Wolff, H. W. 1975. "The Kerygma of the Deuteronomic Historical Work." Translated by F. C. Prussner in *The Vitality of Old Testament Traditions*, ed. W. Brueggemann and H. W. Wolff, pp. 83-100. Atlanta: John Knox.

COMMENTARIES ON JEREMIAH

Boadt, Lawrence. 1982a. *Jeremiah 1–25*. OTM 9. Wilmington: Michael Glazier.

————. 1982b. *Jeremiah 26–52, Habakkuk, Zephaniah, Nahum*. OTM 10. Wilmington: Michael Glazier.—An eminently readable and theologically rich treatment of Jeremiah.

Bracke, John M. 2000. *Jeremiah 1–29*. Louisville: Westminster John Knox Press.

————. 2000. *Jeremiah 30–52 and Lamentations*. Louisville:

Westminster John Knox Press.—This very helpful two-volume commentary is part of a series geared to Christian laity.

Bright, J. 1965. *Jeremiah: A New Translation with Introduction and Commentary*. AB 21, Garden City, N.Y.: Doubleday.—Bright's classic introduction to the book is still one of the finest in the field.

Brueggemann, Walter. 1998. *A Commentary on Jeremiah: Exile and Homecoming*. Grand Rapids: Eerdmans.—An evocative and eloquent commentary that pays particular attention to the aesthetic and theological character of the book of Jeremiah in its present form.

Calvin, John. 1989. *A Commentary on Jeremiah*. Vol. 4. Edinburgh: The Banner of Truth and Trust.

Carroll, Robert P. 1986. *The Book of Jeremiah*. OTL. Philadelphia: Westminster.—Unfortunately no longer in print, this fine work has generated more criticism and praise than any other in the twentieth century. It sees much of the book of Jeremiah as a product of later editors.

Clements, Ronald E. 1988. *Jeremiah*. Interpretation. Atlanta: John Knox.—Written especially for pastors and teachers, this outstanding commentary examines the literary and theological coherence of larger units of Jeremiah.

Craigie, Peter C., Page Kelley, Joel F. Drinkard Jr. 1991. *Jeremiah 1–25*. WBC 26. Dallas: Word Books.—In addition to offering detailed bibliography, this commentary, written from an evangelical perspective, carefully considers the form and detail of the text.

Fretheim, T. E. 2002. *Jeremiah*. Macon: Smyth & Helwys.—This commentary offers a comprehensive exposition of all facets of the book. Its treatment of Jeremiah's confessions and suffering is groundbreaking.

Habel, Norman C. 1968. *Jeremiah, Lamentations*. Concordia Commentary. St. Louis: Concordia.

Holladay, William L. 1986. *Jeremiah 1: A Commentary on the Book of the Prophet Jeremiah, Chapters 1–25*. Hermeneia. Philadelphia: Fortress.

———. 1989. *Jeremiah 2: A Commentary on the Book of the Prophet Jeremiah, Chapters 26–52*. Hermeneia. Minneapolis: Fortress.—This historically oriented two-volume commentary provides a wealth of philological and exegetical knowledge.

Jones, Douglas R. 1992. *Jeremiah*. NCB. Grand Rapids, Mich.: Eerdmans.—A reliable exegetical analysis of the book.

Keown, G., P. Scalise, T. Smothers. 1995. *Jeremiah 26–52*. WBC 27. Dallas: Word.—The second volume of an evangelical treatment of the book which includes a marvelous bibliography and fine treatment of individual passages.

Lundbom, Jack R. 1999. *Jeremiah 1–20*. AB 21A. N.Y.: Doubleday.— The first volume of a rhetorical critical treatment of Jeremiah.

Martins, E. A. 1986. *Jeremiah*. Scottdale: Herald Press.—A Mennonite reading of Jeremiah which is especially attentive to matters of peace and justice.

McKane, W. 1986. *A Critical and Exegetical Commentary on Jeremiah*. 2 vols. ICC. Edinburgh: T.&T. Clark.—An erudite philological analysis of Jeremiah.

Miller, Patrick D. 2001. *The Book of Jeremiah*. NIB 6, pp. 555-926. Nashville: Abingdon.—A lucid analysis of Jeremiah that is replete with theological and exegetical insights.

O'Connor, Kathleen. 2001. "Jeremiah," in *The Oxford Bible Commentary*, ed. John Barton and John Muddiman, pp. 487-528. Oxford, N.Y.: Oxford University Press.—A brief though important literary and theological reading of Jeremiah, especially attentive to the final form of the text.

Thompson, J. A. 1980. *The Book of Jeremiah*. NICOT. Grand Rapids: Eerdmans.—This evangelical commentary provides a detailed introduction to the book and an extensive treatment of every passage.